DATE DUE

GAYLORD			PRINTED IN U.S.A.

HOMELAND SECURITY

HOMELAND SECURITY

PROTECTING AMERICA'S TARGETS

VOLUME I: BORDERS AND POINTS OF ENTRY

Edited by James J.F. Forest

PRAEGER SECURITY INTERNATIONAL
Westport, Connecticut • London

Library of Congress Cataloging-in-Publication Data

Homeland security : protecting America's targets / edited by James J. F. Forest.
       v. cm.
    Includes bibliographical references and index.
    Contents: v. 1. Borders and points of entry—v. 2. Public spaces and social institutions—v. 3. Critical infrastructure
    ISBN 0–275–98768–X (set : alk. paper)—ISBN 0–275–98769–8 (vol. 1 : alk. paper)—ISBN 0–275–98770–1 (vol. 2 : alk. paper)— ISBN 0–275–98771–X (vol. 3 : alk. paper)
    1. Civil defense—United States. 2. Terrorism—United States—Prevention.
UA927.H658 2006
    363.325′1560973—dc22   2006010948

British Library Cataloguing in Publication Data is available.

Library of Congress Catalog Card Number: 2006010948
ISBN: 0–275–98768–X (set)
      0–275–98769–8 (vol. 1)
      0–275–98770–1 (vol. 2)
      0–275–98771–X (vol. 3)

First published in 2006

Praeger Security International, 88 Post Road West, Westport, CT 06881
An imprint of Greenwood Publishing Group, Inc.
www.praeger.com

Printed in the United States of America

The paper used in this book complies with the Permanent Paper Standard issued by the National Information Standards Organization (Z39.48–1984).

10 9 8 7 6 5 4 3 2 1

CONTENTS

EDITOR'S NOTE

America is a target; the homeland is under threat. While Americans have been targets of terrorist attacks for quite some time, September 11, 2001, awoke the nation to the reality that we are vulnerable in our homes, in our places of work and worship, and in our public transportation system. And yet, we must continue to function as best we can as the world's most vibrant economic and political community. The current threat environment requires greater engagement with the public, as the necessary eyes and ears of the nation's homeland security infrastructure. However, to be effective the public must be equipped with the knowledge of where and why specific locations and activities may be a terrorist target, what is being done to protect those targets, and how individuals can help.

The chapters of *Homeland Security: Protecting America's Targets* revolve around a core of central questions. Are we safer today than we were pre-9/11? What steps have been taken to protect ourselves? What are the threats we face, and what new threats have developed since 9/11? Are we staying one step ahead of those who wish to do us harm? In 2002, more than 400 million people, 122 million cars, 11 million trucks, 2.4 million freight cars and 8 million containers entered the United States. Over 59,596 vessels entered the United States at its 301 ports of entry. Clearly, the amount of activity this represents will require a long-term commitment to innovation, organizational learning, and public vigilance to complement an already overstretched network of government agencies and security professionals.

Contributors to the volumes have been drawn from the nation's security, academic, and intelligence communities, and they address specific issues of security, threat, and prevention. While civil liberties and privacy are a key dimension to the homeland security debate, several recent publications on this topic have emerged which need not be duplicated in this effort. For the same reason, preparedness and response are a small part of the discussion, but individual chapters are not devoted to such issues. For analysis and recommendations regarding such issues, please see an earlier three-volume set, *Community Preparedness and Response to*

Terrorism (edited by James Johnson, Gerald Ledlow, and Mark Cwiek), published by Praeger in 2005. Rather, the overall emphasis of these volumes is on the big picture—building the nation's intellectual capacity for prevention and deterrence by examining America's vulnerabilities in critical areas such as aviation, public transportation, borders, critical infrastructure, ports and maritime commerce, and water and food supplies.

The chapters are organized in three volumes. Chapters in the first volume cover borders and points of entry, including coastal ports and issues of maritime security. Some authors address what the United States. has done since 9/11 or what it should be doing, while other authors expand our discussion of homeland security beyond mere lines drawn on a map, emphasizing the need for greater international cooperation. The second volume provides a variety of insights on the protection of public spaces and social institutions. While these are sometimes referred to as "soft targets," the reality is that virtually all potential terrorist targets—except, perhaps, military bases and a relatively small handful of buildings with fortified security barriers and armed personnel—could also be included under the same category. Thus, we have limited the discussions in this volume to issues which would be most salient to communities, large and small, throughout the United States. Contributors to the third volume focus on securing elements of the nation's critical infrastructure, exploring what federal, state, and local authorities can do to ensure that our water, food, and energy supplies; transportation systems; and financial and technical infrastructure are protected against a terrorist attack.

In all three volumes, authors were asked to focus on what has been done in recent years to increase security, but also to alert us to persisting vulnerabilities. However, while a critical analysis of vulnerabilities is needed, authors have been encouraged to avoid "fueling the fear"—that is, giving an already troubled nation new reasons to "duct tape themselves inside their homes." Instead, an underlying mission of this publication is to educate the general public on what each of us can do to reduce the vulnerabilities we share as a nation.

This project complements an earlier three-volume set, *The Making of a Terrorist: Recruitment, Training and Root Causes,* released in November 2005, and it will be followed next year by a third and final project, *Countering Terrorism in the 21st Century: Strategies, Tactics, and Lessons Learned.* Together, these multivolume publications address the primary topics of the national security debate in the post-9/11 policy environment and will be valuable to educators, leaders in the public and private sectors, and the general public for many years to come.

In sum, the chapters of *Homeland Security: Protecting America's Targets* illuminate critical areas of vulnerability to terrorist attack in the United

States, and in doing so, inform our understanding of the overarching national security challenges we face today. As a whole, the volumes reveal the need for increased vigilance and public-private cooperation throughout the country, and they underscore the importance of the daily decisions made by every policy maker and individual citizen.

PREFACE

The chapters of this volume of *Homeland Security* highlight recent efforts to improve the nation's border and port security. Each author was asked to simplify as much as possible the complexities of policy and practice, while highlighting both pre- and post-9/11 security challenges. After a brief introductory chapter, the volume is organized into two sections: border security and maritime/port security. Some chapters focus on what has been accomplished within the United States to better secure our borders and ports, while others bring a more international flavor to our understanding of homeland security. As a collection, the chapters advance our understanding of key national security challenges, as well as raise important questions and issues for further research.

PART I: BORDER SECURITY

The first section of the volume begins with a chapter by Dr. Joseph Vorbach III, a commander in the U.S. Coast Guard and an associate professor of International Relations at the U.S. Coast Guard Academy, in which he explores the challenges of securing the substantial land border between the United States and Mexico. Vorbach points to the massive flows of goods and people that cross the border, in contrast with finite resources to filter and inspect them. His analysis provides a framework for thinking about our nation's response to the homeland security threat and offers several recommendations for improving border security on the southern border—such as increased funding and surveillance, new investments in technology innovations, and a great commitment to facilitating cross-national cooperation. As he acknowledges at the close of his chapter, no border will ever be perfectly secure, but there are a number of ways in which the U.S. border with Mexico can become more secure.

Professor Stuart Farson of Simon Fraser University presents a similar analytical framework in the next chapter with his discussion on the (much longer) border between the United States and Canada. He notes that the response of the U.S. government to the attacks of September 11, 2001, has strongly influenced how Canadians and Americans now view their common borders, moving from being an essentially linear concept to one that is now multifaceted and multidimensional. Further, he argues, there are indications that values are diverging between the two nations, reflected in part by the fact that the Canadian government has responded in significant but different ways to the threat perceived by the U.S. government. And yet, the United States is much more reliant for its own domestic security on its friends and neighbors than perhaps it ever was. Thus, Farson recommends a greater level of attention to managing the relationship between the two countries.

On a similar note, the next chapter—by Dr. Christopher Rudolph, an assistant professor at American University—also emphasizes multinational cooperation. Prior to 9/11, he notes, scholarly discussions on border security focused on the need for a multilateral regime that would help facilitate the movement of people across borders in order to achieve economic gains. However, since 9/11 three different perspectives have emerged about the appropriate way to manage border security. Americans have put forward the notion of a "security perimeter," Canadians have referred to the establishment of a "zone of confidence," and the Mexicans have suggested that only a comprehensive approach is acceptable. His analysis suggests that including Canadian and Mexican officials in U.S. threat assessment discussions and providing access to antiterrorist intelligence would make an important contribution to achieving the common goal of advancing cross-border flows of people and goods. However, Rudolph notes, while a formal agreement to resolve these differences of opinion would be useful, a formal comprehensive North American regime is unlikely; thus, it is perhaps more reasonable to expect improved "harmonization" among NAFTA countries regarding information infrastructure and sharing.

A different perspective on multinational cooperation is provided by Dr. Farid Kahhat, a professor at the Catholic University in Lima, Peru. Since the 1990s, he notes, increasing trade cooperation and economic interdependence have significantly enhanced the level of cross-national cooperation throughout North and South America. His chapter explores the theoretical and practical dimensions of Latin America's role in the global fight against terrorism and suggests some areas in which these efforts can be strengthened. Specifically, his discussion moves beyond border security issues and addresses some of the underlying regional dimensions to collaborating on a comprehensive security strategy.

Continuing with the theme of international cooperation, Dr. Justin Kastner (assistant professor at Kansas State University) and Dr. Jason Ackleson (assistant professor at New Mexico State University) focus on the intersection of border security and international trade, particularly in agricultural products. Globalization presents many challenges for the U.S. government as it seeks to ensure its national security, they argue.

One challenge arises because the pursuit of free trade may compromise America's ability to secure its domestic security; on the other hand, a different challenge arises when demands for security threaten the essential cross-border flows needed for U.S. economic growth. Food security exemplifies these contrasting challenges; cross-border trade flows help ensure food security, but cross-border flows also potentially represent a security threat to America's food supply and agricultural base. These security tensions often manifest themselves at the U.S. border; it is at America's land frontiers and other ports of entry that the U.S. government attempts to screen the vast flows of incoming goods and individuals. The authors conclude that hedging against conventional, nonterrorist threats can have positive consequences for counterterrorism and food security policy, and they offer several recommendations for security policies along both the U.S.-Mexico and U.S. Canada borders.

The next chapter, by West Point professor and legal expert Margaret Stock, explores the complicated relationship between immigration and national security. She argues that an effective national security-oriented U.S. immigration policy must focus on letting in the right people. Immigrants are a key asset in fighting the global war on terrorism and maintaining U.S. military dominance. They are also key to the U.S. maintaining its economic dominance, which is necessary to support our military power. Yet, the United States has no national security strategy for immigration. Immigration policy must be an explicit part of our homeland security strategies, she argues, not an afterthought. In essence, a key aspect of our nation's future security will be a comprehensive immigration policy that allows us to distinguish between legitimate immigrants and the small number of people who intend to do us harm.

Immigration policy is also the focus of the next chapter, by Dr. Jason Ackleson, who provides an analysis of the new "smart border" security environment of the post-9/11 era. The term "smart border" refers to bilateral accords signed by the Bush administration, Canada, and Mexico, which involve limited cooperation on a number of policy issues related to border control—including inspections, preclearances of goods and people, database coordination, and biometric identifiers. The smart border plan has emerged as the preferred policy solution to the difficult problem of screening for terrorist incursions into the United States while maintaining flows of goods and individuals, key drivers of globalization. After describing the international political context of border security and U.S.-Mexico bilateral relations in the post-9/11 period, Ackleson's chapter then turns to major policy options that seek to facilitate the movement of goods, services, and people into the United States—including workers—while also providing adequate security for its international borders. Special emphasis is placed on efforts to enact some kind of migration reform in the United States. The chapter concludes by offering several policy recommendations to help deal with the question of undocumented migration and border security in the post-9/11 era.

A different perspective on migration reform is offered by Dr. Matthew Kenney, an assistant professor at Austin Peay State University, in his chapter on international human trafficking. Human trafficking poses moral and practical challenges to U.S. security interests at home and abroad. Contemporary human trafficking is slavery, and it exhibits features that are every bit as brutal and terrorizing as the worst forms of slavery from past eras. Meanwhile, vulnerabilities along the U.S.-Mexico borders have created attractive business opportunities for profit-seeking traffickers and coyotes—guides hired by Mexicans seeking to enter the United States illegally. Kenney's analysis reveals the need for greater funding to support programs and activities that address the problem of human trafficking, as well as the need for an extensive effort to educate the public about human trafficking networks and how to combat them.

According to University of San Diego professor David Shirk, market-driven criminal activities (much like those described by Kenney in his chapter) formed a considerable amount of the security challenges along the U.S.-Mexico border before 9/11. However, unlike the long-standing challenges rooted in basic economic forces of supply and demand, the new national security challenges confronted in the post-9/11 context are the result of the deliberate intent to cause harm. His chapter explores how this new context has impacted U.S. and Mexican law enforcement and security relations and how new policy directions may offer a framework to develop mutually beneficial practices and approaches to shared challenges. As the U.S. and Mexican federal governments move toward implementing the laws and administrative structures for dealing with law enforcement and security challenges, the 22-point Smart Border Agreement provides a helpful bilateral framework for addressing these priorities and for building strong U.S.-Mexican ties in the aftermath of recent tensions over immigration and Iraq. However, the United States needs to take care to ensure that the Department of Homeland Security cooperates effectively with other federal, state, and local agencies sharing jurisdiction in this area. At the same time, in order to ensure that Mexico can operate as an effective partner in this agreement, the United States will need to help its neighbor develop its security capabilities. Over the long term, he argues, the harmonization of North American security standards would be mutually beneficial to all three countries and would constitute a positive step toward the creation of a stronger economic and security community in North America.

Daniella Bove-LaMonica, a former diplomatic fellow at the U.S. Consulate General in Monterrey, Mexico, follows this discussion with a chapter on improving the security of our nation's visa processing system. Despite alleged accusations of harsher policies due to the new security environment, she notes, nearly three-fourths of all applicants for a U.S. visa in 2004 were successful. This final chapter of the section on border security examines the visa application process and demonstrates how, even four years after 9/11, the consular arena is still extremely vulnerable despite new security policies. New laws, harsher punishments for immigration violators, additional personnel, and smarter technology—none of these strategies will greatly improve our national defenses if the core of the visa adjudication process—particularly, the training of the individuals in whose judgment we trust—is not examined more closely.

PART II: MARITIME AND PORT SECURITY

The second section of the volume explores the challenges of protecting America from threats to its ports and coastlines. The first chapter of this section is provided by two retired Coast Guard officers, Joe DiRenzo (currently the Anti-Terrorism Coordinator for the Coast Guard's Atlantic Area) and Chris Doane (Chief of Response and Port Security for the Coast Guard's Atlantic Area). They remind us that the United States remains a maritime nation—over 90 percent of the raw materials, parts, and products imported and exported by this nation still move by ship. Clearly, the security of our maritime transportation system and maritime borders are critical to this nation's economic health and security. The authors examine America's Maritime Homeland Security campaign in three phases: (1) historical efforts before 9/11, (2) current efforts following 9/11 and (3) future challenges in view of the asymmetric threat to the maritime domain. The first part of this discussion reviews how the United States has sought to secure its maritime domain in the past. This is followed by an exploration of how the United States has responded nationally and as a member of the global maritime community that has come to the realization that terrorism knows no boundary, no respect for human life, and poses a threat to all nations, the world's maritime transportation system, and the world's economic health. Finally, the chapter concludes with a look at what more needs to be done in terms of leveraging technology, employing limited assets, and adjusting cultural views to address the terrorist threat in the maritime.

The next chapter of this section highlights the importance of international cooperation and is authored by Tracey Gray (a program analyst in the Office of the Assistant Secretary of Defense for Homeland Defense and a primary author of the *National Strategy for Maritime Security*) and Frank L. Jones (Principal Director for Strategy, Plans, and Resources in the Office of the Assistant Secretary of Defense for Homeland Defense and co-chair of the interagency working group that wrote the *National Strategy for Maritime Security*). They argue that because the maritime domain is an immense and largely unsecured medium for a number of threats, the United States should seek to increase maritime security by strengthening regional cooperative security efforts and enabling other nations by sharing expertise, information, and technology. Finding common ground and mutual strategic interests allows for synergy greater than any one nation can achieve. The transnational terrorist threat in the maritime domain is a global menace, and it demands a global response.

In the next chapter, Lieutenant Colonel Jerry Kidrick examines the unique challenges of border and port security in Alaska. Securing a part of the United States that is geographically separated from the continental 48 states, and yet encompasses 586,400 square miles and has a massive coastline, clearly warrants considerable resources and effort. Further, Alaska offers a number of locations which can be considered potential terrorist targets. To illustrate this, Kidrick provides an analysis of the security challenges around the Port of Valdez and terminus of the Alaska Oil Pipeline, which is what can be called a "target-rich environment." The oil from the Alaska Oil Pipeline accounts for roughly 20 percent of U.S. oil production annually, and one-tenth of all the oil Americans use daily passes through this pipeline and port. From general aviation airplanes (carrying passengers on sightseeing flights) to cruise ships and recreational boats, there are several potential means by which a terrorist could transport explosives or other weapons to the port and cause considerable damage. Improving security at this key component in the nation's critical infrastructure, he argues, will require new federal regulations, enforcement, and funding to pay for security equipment and training.

Finally, Priya Dixit (a terrorism researcher at American University) concludes the volume with a chapter on the maritime security challenges of the Pacific coast. After reviewing a brief history of maritime security efforts in this region, the chapter provides a brief analysis of trade- and tourism-related activities in three major ports of the U.S. Pacific coast: Seattle, Los Angeles, and Long Beach. With regard to each of these ports, case studies of trade and tourism illustrate their importance to the socioeconomic health of the United States. The chapter then describes some of the major initiatives that have been operationalized to ensure port security in the post-9/11 era. The final section looks at the unique challenges faced by U.S. Pacific maritime security in terms of new security threats, such as bioterror and geographical challenges, and offers some recommendations for improving maritime security.

CONCLUSION

Together, these chapters address an impressive breadth of issues related to securing our nation's borders and ports. However, there are obviously other avenues to explore beyond what is covered in this volume. Thus, this collection will hopefully also stimulate readers to pursue further research on their own, in order to expand our collective understanding of border and port security, as well as potentially influence policy making at the federal, state, and local levels. In a country as vast as the United States, the challenges of homeland security require a broad, collaborative effort between government agencies at all levels, private corporations, community groups, and the general public.

ACKNOWLEDGMENTS

The views expressed herein are those of the author and do not purport to reflect the position of the United States Military Academy, the Department of the Army, or the Department of Defense.

ACKNOWLEDGMENTS

For their continued support, I extend my sincere gratitude foremost to the faculty and staff of the Combating Terrorism Center (CTC) at West Point (Joe, Kip, Jarret, Brian, Lianne, Thalia, Bill, Clint, and Rick), from whom I continue to learn much every day. Special thanks are owed to General (R) Wayne Downing, Chair of the CTC, for his inspiration and leadership. And my faculty colleagues throughout West Point—and particularly the leadership of the Department of Social Sciences, Colonel Mike Meese and Colonel Cindy Jebb—have been a constant source of support and encouragement, and I offer them my sincere gratitude. And on behalf of everyone at the CTC, it is my honor to acknowledge and thank Mr. Vincent Viola and Mr. Ross Perot, without whose generous support of our research and educational programs, none of this would be possible.

The academic contribution to improving homeland security is clearly an important one, and to this end each of the chapters in these three volumes is the product of thoughtful research and analysis. I offer my sincere thanks to the authors for their hard work and commitment to excellence, particularly given the relatively short time frame in which they were asked to produce their chapters. The analysis and suggestions they have provided in these pages will undoubtedly inform discussions and debate in a variety of policy making and academic environments for the foreseeable future.

This project is the second installment of an ambitious trilogy, which began with *The Making of a Terrorist* (released by Praeger in 2005) and will conclude with *Countering Terrorism in the 21st Century* (to be released in 2007). I would like to thank Hilary Claggett at Praeger Security International for her vision and encouragement of this effort. She and her staff continue to be remarkable collaborators in this venture.

Finally, and most importantly, I extend my sincere gratitude to my family—Alicia and Chloe, as well as our parents, our siblings, and extended family members—without whom the term "homeland" would certainly have a different, more hollow meaning. It is my sincere hope that the research and recommendations contained in these volumes will help improve the security of all families throughout this great nation.

James J.F. Forest

CHAPTER 1

PROTECTING AMERICA'S BORDERS AND POINTS OF ENTRY: AN INTRODUCTION

James J.F. Forest

In a barren stretch of desert along the U.S.-Mexico border, a member of the Border Patrol is driving his sport utility vehicle, armed with night-vision goggles and satellite global positioning devices, while helicopters with powerful spotlights hover overhead. Motion sensors are buried in the ground beneath them, and high-resolution infrared cameras mounted on poles help monitor the area. Every day of the year, these and other border security instruments help authorities nab over 3,000 people illegally entering the United States across the southern border. Yet, despite the unprecedented investment in technology and manpower, illegal immigrants are still coming in waves, and their numbers are increasing. U.S. officials made over one million arrests along this border in 2004, a 24 percent increase over the year before.[1]

With some 95,000 miles of coastline, 26,000 miles of navigable inland rivers and waterways, and 6,500 miles of land borders, access into America is almost limitless.[2] Every year, roughly 120 million people travel into or out of the United States.[3] Major points of entry for international travelers and goods include hundreds of international airports, 360 ports, over 3,700 marine terminals, and recreational marinas beyond count. The 4,500-mile border between the United States and Canada was wide open, virtually unguarded on September 11, 2001 (9/11); the 9,000-plus strong U.S. Border Patrol had only 334 agents along the Canadian border, which is twice as long as the U.S.-Mexico border.[4] Each year, hundreds of millions of cars, trucks and people cross the border into the United States.

Obviously, our nation's ability to know exactly who these people are—and more importantly, what their intentions are while in the United States—is limited by the enormous scale of cross-border traffic. In addition, the United States faces a tough challenge of increasing illegal immigration, some of it across the northern border, but most of it across the southern border. In Arizona alone, nearly 600,000 people were arrested trying to cross the border in 2004.[5] Today, the United States captures many more illegal immigrants than we can send home—especially non-Mexicans. In 2004, the United States identified 160,000 non-Mexican illegal immigrants who crossed the southwest border, only 30,000 of whom were successfully captured, processed, and returned to their country of origin.[6] In a July 2005 hearing before the House Appropriations Subcommittee on Homeland Security, Border Patrol Chief David Aguilar said his agency has apprehended 919,000 illegal immigrants in the first six months of the year—119,000 of them were classified as "other than Mexicans."[7]

According to a recent study by the National Academy of Sciences, our borders and airports were designed to facilitate travel and trade, not enforce security. The hallmarks of this system are its openness, accessibility, ubiquity, efficiency, diversity, and competitiveness.[8] As most observers agree, U.S. border security and port security were not considered high priorities by Congress or the White House prior to 9/11. The primary agencies responsible for security—the Customs Service, the Coast Guard, and the Immigration and Naturalization Service—faced severe funding shortfalls for operations and overdue capitalization projects, and their efforts were not integrated by any common strategy, doctrine or information networks.[9] The ever-increasing volume of international trade through our borders and ports, a product of globalization, has led to further challenges for these already overstretched agencies.

As described throughout this volume, the attacks of 9/11 brought new attention to these security challenges and produced a political will to address them with resources, strategies, and a new commitment to multinational cooperation. The 9/11 Commission report clearly increased the nation's political will to address its "permeable borders and immigration controls," by pointing out that the hijackers:

- included known al Qaeda operatives who could have been watchlisted;
- presented passports manipulated in a fraudulent manner;
- presented passports with suspicious indicators of extremism;
- made detectable false statements on visa applications;
- made false statements to border officials to gain entry into the United States; and
- violated immigration laws while in the United States.[10]

Since 2001, the federal government has increased funding for border security by 60 percent and hired more than 1,900 new Border Patrol agents.[11] New technologies like unmanned aircraft, ground sensors, and infrared cameras have been deployed. Stemming the flow of illegal immigration has been the centerpiece of these efforts. Since 2001, several million illegal immigrants have been apprehended and expelled from the United States—including nearly 300,000 with criminal records.[12] And on October 18, 2005, President Bush signed the *Homeland Security Appropriations Act*, which provides more than $2.3 billion for the Border Patrol—with funding for 1,000 new agents, $139 million to improve technology and intelligence capabilities, $82 million to improve and expand Border Patrol stations, and $70 million to install and improve fencing, lighting, vehicle barriers, and roads—and another $3.7 billion is provided for Immigration and Customs Enforcement to hire new agents and expand programs to identify, apprehend, and expel illegal immigrants.[13]

With this overview as our intellectual point of departure, the chapters of this volume explore various dimensions of border and port security, with particular focus on efforts at the national, state and local levels to address pre-9/11 vulnerabilities. In order to frame our understanding of the threat as we know it today, this introductory chapter will review a number of recent events and news reports related to border and port security. Also, as discussed in this and other chapters of the volume, it is important to recognize the critical dimension of international cooperation in securing our borders and ports.

RECENT EVENTS

Throughout the last several years, a steady parade of high-profile events and new reports have kept a spotlight on the nation's border security challenges. Alarming headlines like "Border Still Easily Crossed" and "Illegal Workers' Arrests Point to Holes in Security"[14] have led to a widespread belief that the nation's border security is in a state of crisis. To those on the front lines of this border security challenge, crisis may indeed be an apt description.

In August 2005, New Mexico Governor Bill Richardson declared a state of emergency in four counties (Dona Ana, Luna, Grant, and Hidalgo) along the Mexican border that he said have been "devastated" by crimes such as the smuggling of drugs and illegal immigrants.[15] This region "is inadequately funded or safeguarded to protect the lives and property of New Mexican citizens," he said. "Recent developments have convinced me this action is necessary—including violence directed at law enforcement, damage to property and livestock, increased evidence of drug smuggling, and an increase in the number of undocumented immigrants."[16] The following week, Arizona Governor Janet Napolitano declared a state of emergency along her state's border with Mexico.[17] In both states, these declarations allowed for the release of emergency funding from state and federal sources that can be used to hire additional law enforcement officers, repair border fences, and address other needs. A month later, as part of a new project called Operation Safe Border, New Mexico State Police officers were being sent from all over the state to the border for five-day rotations to look for smugglers of drugs and humans as well as responding to other immigration-related crimes such as property damage.[18]

A report published October 31, 2005, revealed that assaults against U.S. Border Patrol agents nearly doubled along the Mexican border over the previous year, as patrols cracking down on drug trafficking and migrant smuggling encountered increasing resistance—including the use of rocks, Molotov cocktails, and gunfire. At least 687 assaults against agents were reported during between September 30, 2004, and September 30, 2005, up from the previous year's total of 354 and the highest since the agency began tracking assaults across the Southwest border in the late 1990s. Most assaults occurred near urban smuggling havens such as Nogales, Arizona, and Tijuana, Mexico, but cross-border skirmishes took place from remote California deserts to the banks of the Rio Grande in Texas. In Tucson and San Diego, the most violent sectors, agents reported being shot at 43 times—up from 18 the previous year. Officials attribute the increased number of assaults to rising frustration among drug and immigrant traffickers, who have seen traditional smuggling routes blocked by the border buildup.[19]

Meanwhile, since cell phones don't work in remote areas of New Mexico, and there is little ranchers can do to contact authorities if they see illegal activity along the border, state and federal officials began giving two-way, police-style radios to border residents.[20] In Arizona, lawmakers proposed building a climb-proof fence along the state's 341-mile border with Mexico, but the potential costs of doing so (a similar fence erected by federal officials near San Diego cost about $1.7 million per mile) did not engender much enthusiasm.[21] Meanwhile, illegal immigrants threw rocks at a Border Patrol helicopter in August 2005, forcing the pilot to make an emergency landing when one of the rocks damaged the rotor.[22] Later that month the Border Patrol purchased an unmanned aerial vehicle—a Predator B plane—to patrol the Arizona-Mexico border, the busiest corridor for illegal immigration into the United States.[23]

Recognizing the seriousness of the situation, Arizona Governor Napolitano and her Mexican counterpart, Sonora Governor Eduardo Bours, announced a plan to coordinate new "surprise" checkpoints at highway exits that lead in and out of the border city of San Luis Rio Colorado as well as along the route that connects Baja California with the interior of Mexico.[24] Through this and other forms of cross-border cooperation, both countries have begun to increase the resources devoted to stemming the tide of illegal immigration and drug smuggling, as well as combating the violence associated with these activities. For example, on October 13, 2005, U.S. Attorney General Alberto Gonzales met with his Mexican counterpart, Daniel Cabeza de Vaca, in Laredo, Texas to iron out the details of a plan to combat border violence in the area by using personnel from the Bureau of Alcohol, Tobacco, Firearms and Explosives, U.S. Marshals Service, FBI, and Drug Enforcement Administration.[25] The violence throughout this region has reached a crisis level. Just across the border from Laredo, escalating violence in Nuevo Laredo, Mexico—largely driven by drug cartel turf wars—led the United States to temporarily close its consulate, something the United States usually does only in countries where civil war, terrorism, or some other form of violence threatens the safety of its embassy employees or American travelers to the region.[26] The fact that this consulate is just across the border from the United States should alarm policy makers in Texas and on Capitol Hill.

In San Diego, a half-mile-wide canyon known as "Smuggler's Gulch" lies between Otay Mesa—California's largest commercial land border port—and the Pacific Ocean, and (as the nickname suggests) has provided a popular route for smugglers. In 2005, Border Patrol officials lobbied for funding to complete a partially-erected fence, create a 175-foot earthen berm, level off several of the mesas, and backfill Smuggler's Gulch in an effort to slow the steady stream of illegal immigrants trying to navigate through that area.[27] In September, Department of Homeland Security (DHS) Secretary Michael Chertoff announced that he would expedite the completion of a new 14-mile Border Infrastructure System (BIS) near San Diego, which would improve border security by including multiple physical layers of security: building access roads to enable Border Patrol to speed response efforts; installing stadium style lighting to deter border crossers; and installing surveillance cameras to monitor incursion.[28]

Perhaps the most dramatic example in recent years (or at least, the most dramatic media coverage) of the nation's concern over border security has involved the so-called Minutemen, a group of citizens who have volunteered to camp in remote areas of Arizona and New Mexico, armed with communications equipment and weapons, in an effort to help slow the tide of border crossings in these areas.[29] "The borders are absolutely wide open, and we're under invasion from drug dealers, criminals and people from all around the world," says Chris Simcox, president of the Minuteman Civil Defense Corps, based in Tombstone, Arizona. "Our Department of Homeland Security is absolutely impotent."[30] The group prohibits its members from making contact with immigrants, and instead focuses on patrolling and reporting to the authorities anything out of the ordinary—including a suspicious bag tossed across the border by a moving van, which often contains marijuana or other contraband which someone on the U.S. side of the border will try to collect. Members must pass a background check, conducted with a $50 application fee, and can carry weapons for self-defense in states where the practice is permitted by law, such as Texas. At an August 2005 training session in Houston, Texas, Simcox compared the organization's border surveillance efforts to that of a neighborhood watch: "We sit in lawn chairs and we observe. And when we spot illegal activity, we report that to the proper authorities . . . .We do nothing but act as eyes and support for law enforcement and Border Patrol."[31]

While some observers have raised concerns over potential civil rights abuses and vigilantism (the ACLU and others are closely monitoring their activities), the Minutemen appear to be having some positive impact. According to the U.S. Border Patrol, in April 2005 the undocumented immigrant traffic in Arizona dropped by half in places where the Minutemen were stationed. Results like these have not gone unnoticed. In August, several Texas Congressmen began circulating a proposal to approve "deputized civilians" as an auxiliary to the U.S. Border Patrol. The proposed "Border Protection Corps" would consist of volunteers who go through a background check and receive training, and would then accompany Border Patrol officers as they search for illegal aliens and drug activity.[32] In California, nearly 800 volunteers signed up for "Friends of the Border Patrol Border Watch," a private group founded by San Bernardino County resident Andy Ramirez, in which members camp in tents along the California-Mexico border and report illegal immigrant crossings to the authorities.[33] At least 40 other groups have been established nationwide, in states like Utah, Minnesota, and Maine. These groups have no direct affiliation with the Minuteman project, but share a high level of dissatisfaction with the government's efforts to combat illegal immigration, and a common goal of doing what they can to help secure over 6,000 miles of southern and northern U.S. borders.[34]

In October 2005, the Minutemen expanded their presence to seven states along the 4,000-mile northern U.S. border with Canada, where a lack of fences and patrols has created alarm for many observers. In places like Lynden, Washington, the two countries are separated only by a 3-foot wide drainage ditch that runs between two parallel dirt roads. Here, it would take a person less than 30 seconds to cross the border into the United States unchallenged and unmonitored.[35] The U.S.-Canadian border has received additional attention at the national level in recent months. The *Homeland Security Appropriations Act of 2005* includes $18.3 million to establish a Northern Border Security Wing based in Great Falls, Montana. Run by the U.S. Immigration and Customs Enforcement, this effort will include the purchase of several aircraft, including a Black Hawk helicopter, to provide aerial surveillance along the northern border.

Concerns about the security of the U.S.-Canadian border gained attention even before 9/11, when on December 14, 1999, a man with explosives was caught trying to enter Washington State from Canada. In what has become known as the millennium terrorist plot, Ahmed Ressam—an Algerian native who had settled in Montreal—had developed a plan to bomb the Los Angeles International Airport on New Year's Eve. As he crossed the border at Port Angeles, Washington, U.S. customs officers noticed that he appeared nervous and approached Ressam, whereupon he panicked and attempted to flee. After eventually confessing and agreeing to cooperate with the authorities in other terrorism investigations, Ressam was sentenced to 22 years in prison on July 27, 2004.

Obviously, our response to the terrorist threat must involve a high level of cooperation with Canada. Indeed, according to the Canadian Security Intelligence Service (CSIS), counterpart of the CIA, at least 50 terrorist organizations have some presence in our neighbor to the north. These groups are actively raising money, procuring weapons, "manipulating immigrant communities," and facilitating travel to and from the United States and other countries.[36] In addition to al Qaeda, those groups include Islamic Jihad, Hezbollah and other Shiite groups, Hamas, the Palestinian Force 17, Egyptian Al Jihad, and various other Sunni groups from across the Middle East. The Irish Republican Army, Tamil Tigers, Kurdistan Workers Party (PKK), and major Sikh terrorist groups also have supporters in Canada. The terrorist threat to Canadians is also very real. Osama bin Laden named Canada one of five so-called Christian nations that should be targeted for acts of terror. (The others, reaffirmed in 2004 by his al Qaeda network, were the United States, Britain, Spain, and Australia.)[37] Criminal networks have also exploited the relatively unguarded U.S.-Canada border, largely to smuggle drugs and other contraband. In July 2005, Canadian border guards discovered a 360-foot drug smuggling tunnel beneath the border and arrested five people on marijuana trafficking charges. The elaborate tunnel, equipped with lights and ventilation, ran from a hut on the Canadian side to the living room of a home on the U.S. side, 300 feet from the border. According to investigators, what tipped off the guards were the loads of dirt coming out of the boarded-up hut and the loads of construction materials going in—a prime example of how local authorities are required to do so much more than monitor border crossing checkpoints.[38]

Of course, it should also be remembered that some of those who have entered the country illegally have done so through border checkpoints, using falsified passports and other documents. Experts in passport fraud say that significantly more passports are fraudulently obtained every year, in part because it is so easy to buy the documents needed to get a passport. A few hundred or a few thousand dollars can buy a birth certificate in most cities. In 2004, according to the Government Accountability

Office (GAO), the State Department issued 8.8 million passports from 7,000 locations. During that same year, the State Department's Bureau of Diplomatic Security arrested 500 people for passport fraud. The fact that it is possible for criminals and individuals on the terrorist watch list to obtain a U.S. passport has prompted a nationwide debate over how to create "fraud-proof" passports using new technology like biometric identifiers—iris scans or fingerprints—embedded in computer chips within the passport.[39]

The presence of illegal immigrants of any kind becomes more worrisome when they are discovered to have access to sensitive sites within the nation's critical infrastructure. In 2005, U.S. Immigration and Customs Enforcement (ICE) special agents arrested several illegal aliens performing contract work at nuclear plants and other nuclear-related facilities around the country.[40] That same year, several high profile investigations raised concern among Department of Defense leaders about military base vulnerabilities. For example, in April 2005, over half of the workforce of a contractor in San Diego that paints ships for the U.S. Navy were found to be in the country illegally.[41] They had been granted security badges to enter a Naval base that is home to more than 50 ships and thousands of sailors. In October, two Indonesians and a Senegalese were arrested at Fort Bragg, the home of U.S. Army Special Forces, for being in the U.S. illegally.[42] That same month, seven illegal aliens were arrested at the U.S. Air Force Base in Mountain Home, Idaho. The men (who had crossed the borders from Canada and Mexico) were working for a construction company that built housing on the air base.[43] And on October 18, the ICE announced the arrests of 36 foreign nationals who were illegally working for a Durham, North Carolina contractor that provides work to the Department of Defense, NASA, and the Department of Energy. Those arrested were from Congo, the Gambia, Ghana, Guatemala, Indonesia, Israel, Kenya, Mexico, Pakistan, and Togo. Several of them had used invalid, altered, or falsified documents to illegally obtain employment.[44]

On October 28, 2005, ICE announced the arrests of dozens of illegal aliens who were performing contract work at the U.S. Naval Air Station Joint Reserve Base-New Orleans in Belle Chasse, Louisiana; the White Sands Missile Range in Las Cruces, New Mexico; the U.S. Army's Fort Irwin Training Center in San Bernardino, California; and the U.S. Marine Corps Logistics Base in Barstow, California. As John P. Clark, Acting Assistant Secretary for U.S. Immigration and Customs Enforcement noted, "Unauthorized workers who gain access to sensitive U.S. military installations through fraudulent documents or other methods pose serious homeland security threats. Not only are their identities in question, but they are also vulnerable to potential exploitation by terrorists and other criminal organizations given their illegal immigration status in this country. Removing these individuals from sensitive worksites is a priority for ICE and the Department of Homeland Security."[45]

Earlier in the year—on August 1, 2005—Secretary of Homeland Security Michael Chertoff and Marcy Forman, Director of Investigations for U.S. Immigration and Customs Enforcement, announced the arrest of 582 street gang members and associates during a two-week, nationwide enforcement action under the auspices of "Operation Community Shield," ICE's ongoing national antigang initiative. According to Chertoff. "[O]ur threat assessments indicate that many gang members come to this country from overseas, or from other parts of the North and South American continent, which means that they are subject to our immigration laws and that when they violate those laws, we can take action against them. We are deeply committed to enforcing these immigration laws and restoring integrity to our immigration system."[46]

Identifying illegal immigrants in the U.S. requires broad collaboration between local, state, and federal authorities, but assistance is also needed from the general public and private sector. For example, the importance of homeland security collaboration between the private sector and federal authorities was highlighted by a recent case in the Houston, Texas area. In July 2005, a United Parcel Service (UPS) clerk in Mont Belvieu, Texas, became suspicious of a customer who paid $80 to ship a package of "clothing" overnight to an address in South Carolina. The customer, wearing an earpiece connected to a cell phone, appeared to be receiving instructions about the package from the device. This package was shipped, and then the same customer appeared the next day with a similar package that he again said was clothing. Upon inspection of this package, three small boxes filled with stacks of $100 bills wrapped in carbon paper were found. A specially trained police dog was brought to the UPS office to sniff the money. According to authorities, the dog "went crazy," indicating the cash might have been in contact with drugs or explosives. The ensuing investigation resulted in the apprehension of two immigrants from India who were found in possession of firearms and living in the U.S. without legal documentation.[47] Clearly, an alert shipping clerk could mean the difference between the success or failure of a criminal or terror plot, whether or not it involves illegal immigrants.

Other recent efforts to combat illegal immigration include high-tech tracking mechanisms. For example, on December 29, 2004, the U.S. Visitor and Immigrant Status Indicator Technology (US VISIT) program was fully implemented at the nation's 50 busiest land border ports of entry, in addition to 115 airports and 15 seaports. The US VISIT program, which was mandated for all U.S. land ports of entry by January 1, 2006, applies to all visitors who apply for entry with a nonimmigrant visa, including those using a Border Crossing Card to travel beyond the border zone or for more than 30 days, or under the Visa Waiver Program. As part of the process, Customs and Border Protection officers collect digital, inkless finger scans and take a digital photo of the visitor.[48] In addition, new repositories of digitally recorded biometric data are allowing Border Patrol agents to check the fingerprints of every illegal immigrant detained near the border. Using this technology, officers have identified 437 people wanted, previously charged or convicted of homicide; 579 who had sexual assault records; and more than 18,000 others with records involving robberies, drugs, kidnappings, or assaults.[49]

The science of biometrics relies on unique human characteristics—including fingerprints, facial dimensions, or the rings and furrows in the colored tissue of the eye—that can verify a person's identity. The high cost of this technology comes from the extensive computer networks that must be built to tie together the data and make it accessible to U.S. officials around the world.[50] In October 2005, DHS officials announced plans to require visitors entering the country to submit all their fingerprints into the US VISIT biometric system.[51] Meanwhile, travelers from one of the 27 countries participating in the Visa Waiver Program (VWP) are required to carry passports with digital photographs. These countries are: Andorra, Australia, Austria, Belgium, Brunei, Denmark, Finland, France, Germany, Iceland, Ireland, Italy, Japan, Liechtenstein, Luxembourg, Monaco, the Netherlands, New Zealand, Norway, Portugal, San Marino, Singapore, Slovenia, Spain, Sweden, Switzerland, and the United Kingdom.[52]

In another technology-related example, the Department of Homeland Security (DHS) has installed radio frequency technology at posts along the borders with Canada and Mexico to track foreigners driving in and out of the United States.[53] After a foreigner entering the United States has passed a thorough security check once, he or she will be given a document containing a wireless digital signal chip. This document will need to be renewed every six months. The document must be placed on the dashboard of a car so that a person's personal information can be read as he or she approaches a border crossing. If a person's identifying data produce no red flags, he or she will get just a cursory check at the border rather than lengthy questioning. The mandatory program will apply, however, to all foreigners with U.S. visas—including those from the 27 countries (see above) whose citizens don't need visas for short U.S. visits—who cross into the United States at those points. These wireless chips for vehicles became mandatory at designated border crossings in Canada and Mexico on August 4, 2005.[54]

Meanwhile, in recognition that true border security requires a multinational effort, a group of Canadian business leaders have lent their time and effort to evaluating U.S.-Canadian border security and suggesting ways to improve it. The Coalition for Secure and Trade-Efficient Borders was formed by over 55 Canadian business associations and individual

companies to help the federal government successfully deal with U.S. border and security issues.[55] Steered by the Canadian Manufacturers and
Exporters, the Canadian Chamber of Commerce, and the Canadian Federation of Independent Business, the group's goal is to recommend measures to facilitate the passage of low-risk goods across Canada's borders;
to recommend ways to strengthen Canadian security, immigration, and
border management; and to increase cooperation between Canada and
the United States to prevent the entry of terrorists and illegal goods into
each country. In July 2005, the Coalition issued its fourth report on the efficiency of the Canada-U.S. border since 9/11, calling for the integration,
cross accreditation and designation of Canadian and U.S. Customs agencies and officers, and the establishment of shared facilities located on
either side of the border. Like most other business groups that depend
on U.S. trade, the coalition is urging governments to expedite infrastructure enhancements at border crossings—specifically at Detroit-Windsor,
which experts say is the international gateway most in need of a new
crossing.[56]

In the realm of maritime and port security, which has also received a
great deal of media attention in recent years, a recent report by the
Department of Homeland Security's inspector general found deficiencies
in an inspection system used by the Customs and Border Protection
Bureau (CBP).[57] Called the Automated Targeting System, it is used by
CBP inspectors at domestic and foreign ports to help identify high-risk
cargo containers for inspection. About nine million containers arrive
annually at U.S. seaports, making it impossible to physically inspect each
of them without hampering the flow of commerce. The report made several recommendations, all of which CBP agreed need to be addressed.[58]
Meanwhile, in August 2005, a freighter named *Jana* raised alarms when
it motored past a checkpoint in Lake Erie but failed to radio a standard
message to traffic control on the river. Two countries, seven federal and
local agencies, the U.S. Department of Homeland Security, and at least
one dog reacted to the event.[59]

Over the next 16 hours, the mystery freighter—sailing under an Anti-
guan flag, with a Russian and Lithuanian crew and an American pilot at
the wheel—raised a spectrum of possible worries. As described elsewhere
in this volume, the Great Lakes and rivers that comprise the nation's
northern commercial shipping lanes are tied together through an extensive network of check-in points—physical markers like lighthouses or
concrete structures where ships are required to call in their location and
destination to Canadian or U.S. marine officials. When the *Jana* neared
another checkpoint, this one on the Detroit River, both U.S. and Canadian
officials were monitoring the ship. Only this time, the ship identified
itself. As the *Jana* entered U.S. waters, it was escorted by the Coast Guard
to a dock in Detroit. The *Jana* was then boarded by U.S. Homeland

Security agents, Customs and Border Protection officials, and a border patrol dog trained to sniff out drugs and people.[60]

This event illustrates the important role of the U.S. Coast Guard in protecting the nation's ports, ships, and commuter ferries from a terrorist attack. New maritime safety and security teams—called Sea Marshals— are highly trained to respond to a situation at a moment's notice.[61] On some missions, they board cruise ships to observe passengers, along with their luggage and cargo coming onboard. Coast Guard enforcement officers also screen crew members on board foreign vessels coming into port. They check their passports to see if they might be on a terrorist watch list and do interviews asking them about their last ports of call. In addition to its expanded antiterrorism mission, the Coast Guard is still fulfilling its traditional duties such as ensuring safe coastal navigation and search and rescue missions.[62]

However, as several media services have reported over the past few years, the Coast Guard's ships, planes, and helicopters are breaking down at record rates, which may threaten the service's ability to carry out its post-9/11 mission of protecting ports and waterways against terrorism.[63] Key members of Congress, maritime security experts, and a former top Homeland Security Department official have all indicated that the fleet is failing and that plans to replace the Coast Guard's 88 aging cutters and 186 aircraft over the next 20 years should be accelerated. Some ships are more than 50 years old, well beyond the recommended age for replacement.[64] Further, on 9/11 the entire U.S. Coast Guard was a smaller force than the New York City Police Department, significantly hampering our nation's ability to secure our ports. As U.S. Coast Guard veterans Joe DiRenzo and Chris Doane observe in their chapter of this volume, "securing a target-rich maritime domain, highly sensitive to disruption, and open to a wide range of potential methods of exploitation and attack by a covert enemy is like looking for a needle in a stack of needles."[65] It has only been in the past few years that we have seen a substantial commitment by our nation's leaders to address these challenges.

CONCLUSION

These and other recent events in the areas of border and port security illustrate the complex nature of the challenges faced by the public and private sector leaders responsible for improving homeland security. Despite these challenges, or perhaps because of them, criticism of our national insecurity has become all too commonplace. Hundreds of editorials, articles, and books published since 9/11 have helped bring the level of debate over homeland security to a fever pitch. For example, a Council on Foreign Relations (CFR) task force report published in 2002, *America: Still Unprepared, Still In Danger*, suggested that "America remains

dangerously unprepared to prevent and respond to a catastrophic terrorist attack on U.S. soil. In all likelihood, the next attack will result in even
greater casualties and widespread disruption to American lives and the
economy."[66] The report called attention to the fact that local and state
police officials need access to the terrorist watch lists which the U.S.
Department of State provides to immigration and consular officials, and
argued that "domestic security measures must be pursued within an
international context."[67] Further, the report focused on the homeland
security vulnerabilities that exist at the nation's ports of entry:

> While 50,000 federal screeners are being hired at the nation's airports to check
> passengers, only the tiniest percentage of containers, ships, trucks, and trains
> that enter the United States each day are subject to examination—and a
> weapon of mass destruction could well be hidden among this cargo. Should
> the maritime or surface elements of America's global transportation system
> be used as a weapon delivery device, the response right now would almost
> certainly be to shut the system down at an enormous cost to the economies
> of the United States and its trade partners.[68]

As described elsewhere in these volumes, much has been accomplished in
the areas of aviation and port security since the CFR report was issued.
However, there are still many challenges to address in reducing America's
vulnerability to foreign threats—challenges which remain the subject of
considerable public discourse.

From one perspective, the United States is being invaded by an unstop-
pable swarm of criminals, terrorists, illegal aliens, disease-laden animals,
and pests—all threatening to destroy our economic stability, our health,
our social fabric, and our way of life. From another perspective, our
nation is part of a globally interdependent system, where all civilized
nation-states are challenged by nonstate actors and criminal networks
seeking to achieve a variety of goals and objectives (from establishing a
caliphate to increasing their profit from the international trafficking of
arms and drugs). From yet another perspective, the very idea of homeland security is laughable in a country as vast and open as the United
States, and thus our efforts to do so are largely a waste of massive public
and private resources that could be better spent on other problems, like
Social Security, education, health and welfare, etc. Whatever an individual's perspective toward it, homeland security has taken center stage in
public debates throughout the nation, and will likely remain there for
many years to come.

In dramatic fashion, the attacks of 9/11 awakened the United States to
the fact that not only do certain foreign individuals have considerable animosity toward the United States, they are willing and able to act on this
hatred in ways that few of us could have foreseen. In response, a flurry
of strategies have been formulated, investigations have been launched
(like the 9/11 Commission), and new organizations have been established

to examine and—we hope—mitigate U.S. vulnerabilities to another attack of this kind. A key centerpiece of these efforts has been the need to improve security at America's borders and ports of entry—the subject of this volume.

At the end of the day, the academics, pundits, policy makers and practitioners all seem to agree that yes, America is indeed vulnerable to various dangers beyond our shores. Further, despite our military, economic and technological advances, this vulnerability is a permanent part of our world. Our challenge, then, is to minimize our nation's vulnerability to external threats as best we can, through vigilance, international cooperation, and coordination at the federal, state, and local level. The general public also has an important role to play in minimizing border and port security vulnerabilities, particularly by serving as the eyes and ears of the Border Patrol, the Coast Guard, the Transportation Security Agency, and other relevant organizations. Vigilance—and more importantly, *informed vigilance*—can make a real difference, but in order for the average citizen to be truly useful, we must broaden and deepen our understanding of border and port security throughout the nation. This is the primary goal to which the remaining chapters of this volume now contribute.

ACKNOWLEDGMENTS

The views expressed herein are those of the author and do not purport to reflect the position of the United States Military Academy, the Department of the Army, or the Department of Defense.

NOTES

1. "An Often-Crossed Line in the Sand," *Washington Post*, March 6, 2005, http://www.washingtonpost.com/wp-dyn/articles/A12368-2005Mar6.html.

2. Frank Hoffman, "Border Security: Closing the Ingenuity Gap," in *Homeland Security and Terrorism*, ed. Russell Howard, James Forest, and Joanne Moore (New York: McGraw-Hill, 2005).

3. "Leadership and Comprehensive Plan Needed to Protect against Importation of Infectious Diseases and Bioterrorism Agents at U.S. Ports of Entry," National Academies, Press Release, September 1, 2005,: http://www4.nationalacademies.org/news.nsf/isbn/030909951X?OpenDocument.

4. Frank Hoffman, "Border Security: Closing the Ingenuity Gap," in *Homeland Security and Terrorism*, ed. Russell Howard, James Forest, and Joanne Moore (New York: McGraw-Hill, 2005).

5. John Ritter, "'Minuteman' Effort Moves Northwest: Volunteer Observers Keep a Watchful Eye on Washington State's U.S.-Canadian Border," *USA Today*, October 25, 2005, p. 3A.

6. White House, "President Bush Signs Homeland Security Appropriations Act," Fact Sheet issued October 18, 2005, http://www.whitehouse.gov/news/releases/2005/10/20051018-3.html.

7. "Illegal Entry by Non-Mexicans Rises," *Christian Science Monitor,* July 26, 2005, http://www.csmonitor.com/2005/0726/p01s01-usfp.html .

8. These characteristics were drawn from a major study by the National Academy of Sciences, *Making the Nation Safer: The Role of Science and Technology in Countering Terrorism*, Washington, DC: National Research Council, Oct. 2002, p. 212-213. Cited in Hoffman, 2005.

9. Frank Hoffman, "Border Security: Closing the Ingenuity Gap."

10. National Commission on Terrorist Attacks Upon the United States, *Report of the National Commission on Terrorist Attacks Upon the United States* (the 9/11 Commission Report).Washington: Government Printing Office, 2004, http://www.gpoaccess.gov/911. Executive Summary, p. 13

11. White House, "President Bush Signs Homeland Security Appropriations Act."

12. White House, "President Bush Signs Homeland Security Appropriations Act."

13. White House, "President Bush Signs Homeland Security Appropriations Act."

14. "Border Still Easily Crossed," *Washington Post,* March 7, 2005; "Language Instructors Arrested at Fort Bragg; 3 Charged with Immigration Violations," *Associated Press,* October 5, 2005; "Illegal Workers' Arrests Point to Holes in Security," *Chicago Tribune,* July 4, 2005; "Navy Contract Workers Found to be Illegal Immigrants," *Associated Press,* April 14, 2005.

15. "Border Emergency Declared in New Mexico," CNN, August 13, 2005, http://www.cnn.com/2005/US/08/12/newmexico/index.html.

16. Ibid.

17. "Arizona Joins New Mexico's Efforts at the Border," *Albuquerque (NM) Tribune,* August 16, 2005, http://www.abqtrib.com/albq/nw_local/article/0,2564,ALBQ_19858_4006214,00.html.

18. "Operation Safe Border: State Police get Involved," *Santa Fe (NM) New Mexican,* September 11, 2005, http://www.freenewmexican.com/news/32348.html.

19. "Violent Border Clashes Surging,"*Los Angeles Times,* October 31, 2005, http://ccs.berkeley.edu/~border/list_articles/OPT_Oct31_ViolentBorderClashes.html (accessed March 14, 2006).

20. "Border Residents Use Radios to Fight Illegal Immigration," *Associated Press,* August 1, 2005, http://www.woai.com/news/local/story.aspx?content_id=6CD95762-E029-4E94-9D73-78C9EE77AD05

21. "Arizona Lawmaker Proposes Fence Along Border," *Arizona Daily Sun,* August 17, 2005, http://www.azdailysun.com/non_sec/nav_includes/story.cfm?storyID=113823 (accessed November 5, 2005).

22. "Rocks Thrown at Border Patrol Chopper," *Associated Press,* August 25, 2005, http://www.breitbart.com/news/2005/08/25/D8C71P6O.html.

23. "Border Patrol Buys Unmanned Plane to Watch Mexican Border," *Associated Press,* August 31, 2005, http://www.thedesertsun.com/apps/pbcs.dll/article?AID=/20050831/NEWS10/508310330/1024.

24. "Mexico Casts Crime Net on Border," *Yuma (AZ) Sun,* August 23, 2005, http://sun.yumasun.com/artman/publish/articles/story_18654.php.

25. "Federal Task Force to Combat Border Violence," *Associated Press,* October 13, 2005, http://www.newschannel5.tv/News/Other/2838/Federal-task-force-to-combat-border-violence (accessed October 30, 2005).

26. "Gang War Shuts Down U.S. Consulate," *WorldNetDaily,* July 30, 2005, http://worldnetdaily.com/news/article.asp?ARTICLE_ID=45526.

27. "U.S. Calls Entry Point in San Diego a Possible Security Risk," *Washington Post,* March 10, 2005, http://www.washingtonpost.com/wp-dyn/articles/A21825-2005Mar9.html.

28. "San Diego Border Infrastructure System Cleared for Expedited Completion," Department of Homeland Security, Press Release, September 14, 2005, http://www.dhs.gov/dhspublic/display?content=4814. See also, "Long Term Measures To Protect Environment, Border Infrastructure System," http://www.dhs.gov/dhspublic/interapp/editorial/editorial_0722.xml.

29. Minuteman Civil Defense Corps,: http://www.minutemanhq.com.

30. John Ritter, "'Minuteman' Effort Moves Northwest: Volunteer Observers Keep a Watchful Eye on Washington State's U.S.-Canadian Border," *USA Today,* October 25, 2005, p. 3A.

31. "Minuteman Group Holds Training Session in Houston," *Associated Press,* August 15, 2005, http://www.heralddemocrat.com/articles/2005/08/15/texas_news /iq_1923519.txt (accessed October 12, 2005).

32. "Border Patrol 'Civilian Auxiliary' Proposed," *WOAI (TX) TV,* August 11, 2005, http://www.woai.com/news/local/story.aspx?content_id=5563B550-5B97-4ABC-8E00-687ABE7BBD0A

33. "Border Operation in Works," *San Bernardino (CA) County Sun,* July 18, 2005, http://www.sbsun.com/Stories/0,1413,208~12588~2970886,00.html (accessed November 5, 2005).

34. "Fighting Immigration Far From the Mexican Border," *Associated Press,* July 18, 2005, http://www.saukvalley.com/news/295758935438439.bsp (accessed October 25, 2005).

35. John Ritter, "'Minuteman' Effort Moves Northwest: Volunteer Observers Keep a Watchful Eye on Washington State's U.S.-Canadian Border," *USA Today,* October 25, 2005, p. 3A.

36. "Terror Groups Believed to Be in Canada," *Associated Press,* July 4, 2005, http://sfgate.com/cgi-bin/article.cgi?f=/n/a/2005/07/04/international/i092329D03.DTL

37. Ibid.

38. "Drug-Smuggling Tunnel Shut Down," *The Associated Press,* July 22, 2005, http://www.washingtonpost.com/wp-dyn/content/article/2005/07/21/AR2005072101049.html (accessed October 25, 2005). Also, see the U.S. Attorney's statement at http://www.usdoj.gov/usao/waw/press_room/2005/jul/raj.htm (accessed November 7, 2005).

39. "U.S. Tries to Stamp 'Secure' on Passports," *Christian Science Monitor,* June 30, 2005, http://www.csmonitor.com/2005/0630/p03s01-uspo.html

40. "Immigration Agents Arrest Illegal Aliens at Nuclear Plant," Immigration and Customs Enforcement, Press Release, September 15, 2005, http://www.ice.gov/graphics/news/newsreleases/articles/050915blair_2.htm

41. "Navy Contract Workers Found to be Illegal Immigrants," *Associated Press,* April 14, 2005.

42. "Language Instructors Arrested at Fort Bragg; 3 Charged with Immigration Violations," *Associated Press,* October 5, 2005.

43. "Illegal Workers Arrested at Defense Contracting Company," U.S. Immigration and Customs Enforcement Agency, Press Release, October 18, 2005, http://www.ice.gov/graphics/news/newsreleases/articles/051018durham.htm.

44. Ibid.

45. "Immigration Officials Arrest Illegal Workers at Department of Defense Facilities," Immigration and Customs Enforcement Agency, Press Release, October 28, 2005, http://www.ice.gov/graphics/news/newsreleases/articles/051028washington_2.htm

46. "Operation Community Shield Yields 582 Arrests," Department of Homeland Security, Press Release, August 1, 2005, http://www.dhs.gov/dhspublic/interapp/press_release/press_release_0712.xml.

47. "Officials Investigating Why $29,000 was Hidden in Package," *Houston (TX) Chronicle,* July 25, 2005, http://www.chron.com/cs/CDA/rssstory.mpl/metropolitan/3281940 (accessed October 12, 2005).

48. "US VISIT Begins Deployment of Biometric Entry Procedures to Additional Land Border Ports of Entry with Canada and Mexico," Department of Homeland Security, Press Release, September 26, 2005, http://www.dhs.gov/dhspublic/display?content=4858.

49. "High-Tech Efforts to Track Border Crossings,"*New York Times,* August 7, 2005, http://www.nytimes.com/2005/08/10/politics/10biometrics.html.

50. Ibid.

51. "Department of Homeland Security to Expand Biometric Visitor Tracking System," *GovExec News Service,* October 25, 2005, http://www.govexec.com/story_page.cfm?articleid=32658&dcn=to daysnews.

52. "Majority of Visa Waiver Program Countries to Meet Digital Photo Deadline," Department of Homeland Security, Press Release, October 26, 2005, http://www.dhs.gov/dhspublic/display?content=4907. Passport guidelines for compliance are also online at http://www.dhs.gov/dhspublic/interapp/content_multi_image/co ntent_multi_image_0021.xml (accessed October 30, 2005).

53. "DHS to Launch Radio Frequency Systems at Border Crossings," *Associated Press,* July 28, 2005, http://informationweek.com/story/showArticle.jhtml?articleID=166403260 (accessed October 12, 2005). Also, information about US-VISIT is available online at http://www.dhs.gov/dhspublic/display?theme=91.

54. Ibid.

55. "Canadian Business Coalition Makes Border Recommendations," *Today* (Canada), July 26, 2005, http://www.todaystrucking.com/displayarticle.cfm?ID=4221 (accessed November 5, 2005). Also, see the Canadian Manufacturers

and Exporters Web site (http://www.cme-mec.ca), the Canadian Chamber of Commerce Web site (http://www.chamber.ca), and the Canadian Federation of Independent Business Web site (http://www.cfib.ca).

56. Ibid.

57. "Federal Cargo Inspection System Found Wanting," *GovExec News Service,* August 5, 2005, http://www.govexec.com/dailyfed/0805/080505c1.htm. The inspector general's summary report is available online at http://www.dhs.gov/interweb/assetlibrary/OIG_05-26_Jun05.pdf

58. Ibid.

59. "Security Reacts After Freighter Skips Check-in," *Detroit (MI) Free Press,* August 6, 2005, http://www.freep.com/news/metro/ship6e_20050806.htm (accessed November 5, 2005).

60. Ibid.

61. "U.S. Coast Guard is Expanding Operations in Ports and Waterways," *Voice of America,* September 7, 2005, http://www.voanews.com/english/2005-09-07-voa37.cfm

62. Ibid.

63. "Coast Guard Plagued by Breakdowns," *USA Today,* July 6, 2005, http://www.usatoday.com/news/nation/2005-07-05-coast-guard_x.htm

64. Ibid.

65. Please see the chapter 12 of this volume by Joe DiRenzo and Chris Doane.

66. Gary Hart and Warren B. Rudman, *America: Still Unprepared, Still in Danger.* Council on Foreign Relations Task Force Report (2002), p. 9. Available online at http://www.cfr.org/content/publications/attachments/Homeland_Security_TF.pdf.

67. Ibid.

68. Ibid.

PART I

BORDER SECURITY

CHAPTER 2

SECURING THE U.S. BORDER WITH MEXICO

Joseph E. Vorbach III

The United States faces a massive challenge in its effort to achieve security along its substantial land border with Mexico. This analysis presents the threat, provides a framework for thinking about the U.S. response to it, and makes several recommendations for improving border security on the southwest border. Though the security challenge is enormous and an ultimate solution likely elusive, there are actions that can be taken on the strategic and tactical level, some of which amount to persistence on initiatives already undertaken, that can positively affect security along the shared border with Mexico.

THE CHALLENGE ON THE U.S. BORDER WITH MEXICO

The United States shares with Mexico a nearly 2,000-mile land border. The 294 million American citizens who live north of that border benefit from an economy that produces a per capita gross domestic product (GDP) of $36,006 whereas the 102 million Mexicans living to the south subsist in an economy that generates a per capita GDP of $6,320.[1] This economic asymmetry provides the beginning of an explanation for the long-standing legal and illegal efforts of Mexican citizens to migrate to the United States. Of the estimated 33 million foreign-born persons in the United States as of 2004, 10.3 million are believed to be illegal migrants.[2] Of those, 5.9 million (57 percent of the total) are undocumented Mexican migrants.

Illegal immigrants attempting to enter the United States by crossing the land border might attempt to do so either by defeating enforcement efforts at a port of entry (by hiding or successfully presenting false immigration paperwork) or by eluding the United States Border Patrol between the ports of entry, often with the assistance of human traffickers referred to as coyotes. Achieving illegal entry via the first approach is worth the risk given the sea of private and commercial activity along the border into which one can become lost. Commercial activity along the border, always significant, has become even more robust since the conclusion of the North American Free Trade Agreement (NAFTA).[3]

A few of the known statistics about the flow of people and goods accumulated by the federal government shed light on the challenge of scrutinizing all that crosses the border. In 2004, over 91 million personal vehicles with nearly 191 million passengers crossed into the United States at the 25 ports of entry in Arizona, California, New Mexico, and Texas.[4] In addition, 4.5 million trucks, nearly 5.2 million empty and loaded shipping containers, 269,027 buses with nearly 4 million passengers, and 48,910,252 pedestrians crossed the border that year.[5] At the world's largest land border crossing, the San Ysidro, California port of entry (south of San Diego) alone, an average of 53,000 cars a day cross the border, along with an average of 26,000 pedestrians and 300 to 350 buses. Between 80 and 200 human smuggling cases are uncovered at San Ysidro each day.[6]

This port of entry data stands apart from estimates of the number of illegal immigrants who pass undetected across the border each year by various means. Since 1997, the United States Border Patrol has been apprehending from between 900,000 and 1,600,000 deportable aliens along the southwest border annually.[7] If Border Patrol estimates of 75 percent operational effectiveness are employed, this means that between 300,000 and 600,000 illegal migrants are entering the country successfully each year.[8]

In the years since the terrorist attacks on the United States of September 11, 2001, the prospect that a foreign terrorist would enter illegally across the southwest border, possibly with a weapon of mass destruction, has received significant attention. Although the vast majority of persons apprehended are Mexicans seeking economic opportunity, there is concern about the growing number of illegal migrants crossing the southwest border who are "other than Mexican" (OTMs). In July 2005, the Chief of the Border Patrol David Aguilar testified before the House Appropriations Subcommittee on Homeland Security that OTM apprehensions on the southwest border were occurring in fiscal year 2005 at a rate that was 131 percent of the previous record of 75,371 set during the previous fiscal year.[9] Mr. Aguilar noted that 644 of those apprehended in the 2004 reporting year came from "countries of concern."[10] An Associated Press report of July 2005 explored the activities of several smuggling networks involved in the movement of OTM illegal migrants across the southwest border. The story included reference to a Lebanese café owner in Tijuana, Mexico suspected of having smuggled about 200 fellow

Lebanese into the United States, including some Hezbollah sympathizers, before his arrest by Mexican authorities in December 2002.[11]

Finally, no assessment of the security of the U.S. border with Mexico is complete without a consideration of the threat posed by the smuggling of illicit narcotics into the United States. from Mexico. Going back at least as far as President Nixon's first use of the term "war on drugs," drug smuggling has been the primary security challenge at the Southwest border. That challenge continues largely unabated today and has been made more complex by the rise to prominence of Mexican drug cartels in the hemisphere as well as the possibility of linkages between drug smuggling revenues and terrorist activities.[12] In the summer of 2005, a Congressional Research Service report noted that, "Despite increased eradication of drug crops and interdiction efforts under Plan Colombia, U.S. government agencies responsible for tracking drug trends report that the availability, price, and purity of cocaine and heroin in the United States have remained stable."[13] At the same time, U. S. government officials were acknowledging publicly that Mexican drug traffickers are now the dominant actors (surpassing Colombians) in the control of illicit drugs sold on the streets of the United States. The U. S. Drug Enforcement Administration noted that 92 percent of the cocaine sold in the United States in 2004 came through the U.S.-Mexico border (most of it Colombian grown) as compared to 77 percent in 2003.[14] In addition, the 3,600 pounds of crystal methamphetamines seized along the southwest border represents a 74 percent increase over the 2001 figure.[15] Due to stricter controls on precursor ingredients in the United States and Canada, primarily on over-the-counter pseudoephedrine, it is believed that approximately half of the methamphetamine in the United States is manufactured in Mexico and smuggled in.[16]

The economic asymmetry between the two countries combines with the incentive to engage in illegal activity, the massive volumes of legal trade that must be processed, and the realities of climate and terrain to create a monumental border control challenge for the United States. As might be imagined, a wide array of programs and approaches are in place and are expanding in an effort to achieve greater success. The next section of this chapter situates the U.S. effort in a theoretical context that facilitates understanding of the multiple aspects of the border control challenge and ensures a more organized presentation of the manner in which control and security are being pursued.

THINKING ABOUT BORDER SECURITY CHALLENGES

Questions about how best to secure the physical borders of any nation-state must be preceded by questions about the nature of the threat. When the threat is the army of another nation, certain military responses are likely to be prescribed. However, when the threat is a more amorphous nonstate structure (a drug cartel or terrorist organization)that is harder to physically locate and that can operate without the restrictions that normally confine the activities of a nation-state, the exact best response is much harder to develop. For some time, beginning well before the events of September 11, 2001, and even before the end of the Cold War, the challenge of defining national security has occupied scholars and practitioners, and it is instructive to review some of that literature in advance of a consideration of the best ways to secure the U.S. border with Mexico.

In 1983, Richard Ullman posited that, "defining national security merely (or even primarily) in military terms conveys a profoundly false image of reality."[17] Ullman was, at the point when Cold War tensions between the United States and the U.S.S.R. had been raised to new peaks in the first Reagan administration, drawing attention to the possibility that a narrow definition of security might cause states to ignore nontraditional threats. He proposed a new definition of security that would consider a threat to be any:

> Action or sequence of events that (1) threatens drastically and over a relatively brief span of time to degrade the quality of life for the inhabitants of a state, or (2) threatens significantly to narrow the range of policy choices available to the government or a state or to private, nongovernmental entities (persons, groups, corporations) within the state.[18]

Ullman's definition speaks, for example, to the economic security issues raised when the United States closed its borders after September 11, 2001.

The dramatic changes in the international system that ensued with the end of the Cold War prompted further lively debate among scholars[19] and practitioners[20] about the changing security environment. These exchanges, in some cases, pitted traditionalists who sought to delimit the scope[21] of that which would be considered a threat to security against those favoring a broader construction.[22] Today, the security studies debate spans a spectrum that includes a growing literature in global and human security.[23] Harvard professor Joseph Nye has theorized very usefully over the past four decades about the role and impact of actors other than states in the international system. In a more recent work on the phenomenon of "soft power" in international politics, he uses the model of a three-layer chessboard to hypothesize about different kinds of interactions between units, primarily nation-states, in the international system. A game played on three planes simultaneously is an apt model for describing the multiple social, cultural, economic, and security interactions that make up the U.S./Mexico border relationship.

THE UNITED STATES, MEXICO AND THREE-LAYER CHESS

Nye's suggestion that "the agenda of world politics has become like a three-dimensional chess game in which one can only win by playing vertically as well as horizontally"[24] suggests a useful model for an analysis of the U.S./Mexico border relationship. Envisioning international relations as taking place on a three-layer chessboard suggests distinctions between different types of interactions that take place in the system. Nye employs the model specifically in an effort to understand better when a nation is more likely to be effective using its soft power,[25] and it is a useful tool for highlighting the persistence of new complexities in state-to-state interactions.

On the top of Nye's board, where "classic interstate military issues" are considered, there are great asymmetries and often equally large sensitivities in the U.S./Mexico border relationship because of historical enmities that have endured for more than 150 years. More specifically, U.S. counterdrug and antimigrant smuggling efforts can take on the appearance of militarized border control operations and aggravate Mexican sensitivities about the history of the border. The most tangible outcome of this sensitivity is enduring Mexican Army suspicion of U.S. intentions and a reluctance to engage directly in military-to-military contacts with U.S. land forces.

The middle board of Nye's game is reserved for "interstate economic issues."[26] In the U.S./Mexico context, compelling trade issues exist alongside the historical matters of the first plane, and private sector actors play more important roles. The increases in the rate and magnitude of trade since the passage of NAFTA have made the border security challenges greater and the bilateral relationship more complex. Separating good from bad at the border has become a substantially greater challenge for U.S. Border Control authorities since trade volumes began increasing in the mid-1990s.

The bottom of Nye's hypothetical chess game is the plane on which transnational issues, including terrorism and international crime, operate. The manner in which governments, unilaterally or together, choose to respond to the issues that emerge on the third plane, is informed by first and second plane variables. The military power on the first plane, if leaders choose to exercise it, must function with, and usually in support of, state, local and federal law enforcement in a much more ambiguous environment.

On each layer of the chessboard, Mexico and the United States have unilateral options and they may consider bilateral cooperation as a third possibility. Because the security threats posed by terrorists, drug organizations, human smugglers, and others can be said to exist on Nye's third plane, the question confronted in the analysis that follows is how actions taken by the United States on the first and second planes, including bilateral engagement with Mexico, can enhance border security on the third plane. In simple terms, U.S. approaches on the first plane are federal law enforcement efforts and military support to those efforts. U.S. approaches on the second plane involve outreach initiatives to private sector actors that offer the prospect of expedited trade flows across the border in exchange for private-sector-funded security initiatives that make supply chains more transparent and secure. Engaging on the upper two layers of the board to confront the challenges posed on the third is, in Nye's terms, "playing vertically as well as horizontally."[27]

FIRST LAYER APPROACHES—LAW ENFORCEMENT AND DEFENSE DEPARTMENT SUPPORT

Customs and Border Protection

Port of Entry

The creation of the Department of Homeland Security in 2003 included a major reorganization of the federal approach to border control. Below an Undersecretary for Border and Transportation Security, Customs and Border Protection became the single unified agency for border security, consolidating customs, immigration, and animal and plant control functions that had resided in disparate branches of the federal government bureaucracy. More importantly, the primacy of the counterterror mission for Customs and Border Protection (CBP) field operations and Border Patrol personnel was enshrined in the strategic documents of the new organization.

An overarching component of CBP's strategic approach is to increase security using overlapping layers of initiatives and technologies. For example, with respect to the estimated 9 million shipping containers that enter the United States by truck, rail and ship each year, CBP efforts include partnering with 35 port of origin countries through the Container Security Initiative to identify suspect shipments earlier, ideally before they leave on ship for the United States. An electronic screening of shipping data using an automated targeting system is employed to detect anomalies and ensure the optimal deployment of inspection assets for containers arriving at U.S. ports. The data needed to conduct this screening is acquired in sufficient time because of the enforcement, since February 2003, of a 24-hour rule that requires the submission of manifest data 24 hours before a container is loaded aboard a ship in a foreign port.

Notwithstanding efforts to enhance security before problems present themselves at the physical border, there are 19,000 CBP officers at 55 ports of entry and over 11,000 Border Patrol agents patrolling the land borders of the United States. At the ports of entry, layering and filtering continues for both commercial and private border crossers. Initiatives related to commercial crossings will be discussed in the next section, but here it can be noted that incentives have been created for Mexican citizens to pass through the port of entry more expeditiously if they submit to a more rigorous prescreening via enrollment in the Secure Electronic Network for Travelers Rapid Inspection (SENTRI).[28] The objective of SENTRI is to process prescreened vehicles and persons more rapidly in order that scarce resources can be applied to the sea of unknown persons and vehicles arriving each day, especially when intelligence indicates a specific threat. During the period from October 1, 2003 through September 30, 2004, Customs and Border Protection processed more than 262 million non-U.S. citizens at the ports of entry, identifying in the process nearly 650,000 who were inadmissible under U.S. law.[29] That number included 399 persons who were "apprehended for terrorism or national security concerns," nearly 20,000 criminal aliens, and 566 stowaways.[30] These data make clear the enormity of the screening challenge that exists at the ports of entry and the potential for employing technologies to improve the filtering and thus the targeting of enforcement resources.

Still, there is criticism of the mechanism by which most Mexican (and Canadian) citizens gain entry. An estimated 7 million Mexicans have been issued border crossing cards with biometric components that allow entry for up to 30 days for shopping, tourism, business, and family reasons (not work or study).[31] One recent study has noted that U.S. efforts to implement fully the ambitious US-VISIT[32] is severely hampered by the fact that Mexicans and Canadians are not processed in the system and those visitors represent the vast majority of crossers at the land ports of entry.[33] Further, analysts point out that persons who overstay their visas can only be tracked if US-VISIT captures exits as well as entries. At the moment the Department of Homeland Security is only collecting data on the former. While President Bush has pledged his continued commitment to President Fox with respect to an immigration reform package that will regularize the transits of many guest workers, skeptical lawmakers are likely to want a more robust US-VISIT database before they facilitate such an outcome. Time is running out on the Fox presidency in Mexico, though, and the Bush administration remains preoccupied with the war in Iraq, and now, the response to Hurricane Katrina as well.[34]

Weapons of Mass Destruction Detection Capability

Given CBP's principal focus on combating terrorism, enhancing the capacity of officers to detect the presence of weapons of mass destruction has received noteworthy attention, including a $125 million request in the fiscal year 2006 budget to continue the deployment and enhancement of these technologies.[35] Customs and Border Protection possesses the capacity to detect the presence of radiation and then to isolate the specific isotope that has been detected. Approximately 10,400 CBP officers and agents carry personal radiation detectors and over 60 radiation isotope identification detection systems are deployed in the field. Containers aboard trucks crossing the southern border pass through the more than 400 radiation portal monitors now in place at the ports of entry, and targeted vehicles and palletized cargo can be sent through nonintrusive inspection systems that are available on both fixed and mobile platforms.

Border Patrol

While ports of entry are fixed spaces where noncitizens present themselves to federal officials, the Border Patrol operates in a less predictable environment, where smugglers intent on profiting from the desperation of illegal migrants play a game of cat and mouse in an environment where weather, geography, and legal issues relating to land rights combine to challenge federal agents. There are places along the southwest border where it appears that something close to 100 percent physical control of the border has been achieved. An example is a nine-mile stretch of land in the Border Patrol's San Diego sector where the boundary is constituted of a primary fence at the actual border; a 120-foot-wide band of land in U.S. territory that is lighted and patrolled by agents day and night on an all-weather road; a second fence; and, increasingly, infrared camera surveillance. To the west of that area as one approaches the Pacific Ocean, a deep gulch and some environmental legal impediments currently prevent the Border Patrol in San Diego from realizing its vision of 100 percent operational control of the border all the way to the Ocean. To the east of the well-controlled nine-mile stretch, the fencing ends when the 3,500 foot Otay Mountain begins. Viewed from a helicopter flying east along the border, the mountain is the first obvious impediment to any goal of achieving uninterrupted physical control of the border from California to Texas. As one continues east, other challenges present themselves—private lands, tribal lands, and unforgiving desert. Even back along the nine-mile stretch that enjoys lighting and double fencing[36] in San Diego County, the most brazen smugglers still take on the Border Patrol in well-timed forays using hastily constructed ladders, sometimes creating diversions by shooting ball bearings launched from wrist rockets at the Border Patrol.

The success of the physical border control efforts put in place in San Diego, modeled on a similar effort in El Paso known as "Operation Hold-the-Line," has had the effect over the past several years of pushing would-be smugglers and the migrants resigned to their guidance further to the east in California and beyond into Arizona and New Mexico. There have been at least three noteworthy effects of the border control success in California. The first is that property values in southern San Diego County have increased noticeably in recent years, so much so, and somewhat ironically, that younger agents in the Border Patrol find it difficult to afford housing on their salaries. Even though some illegal migration persists, the perception of a border area out of control has been significantly reduced and homeowners and businesspersons have taken note. The second effect is that migrants have been forced to take more physically taxing routes through the desert to arrive at and successfully cross the border. This has resulted in a significant increase in dehydration and exposure deaths among border crossers.[37] Finally, the migrant smugglers have pursued corridors leading into Arizona and New Mexico, and there has been in those states a concomitant rise in illegal smuggling activity.

The increase in illegal activity in Arizona and New Mexico has had dramatic effects in those states and on the national debate in the United States regarding homeland security costs and the relative wisdom of various immigration reform proposals under discussion since the beginning of the Bush and Fox presidencies. The most recent developments were the nearly concurrent declarations of states of emergency on the border by Governor Napolitano of Arizona and Governor Richardson of New Mexico, both seeking more resources from the federal government to deal with a range of problems created by the greater presence of illegal migrants and both seeking better coordination between federal agents and their state law enforcement personnel dealing with the illegal migrant problem. Earlier this year, much attention was focused on Arizona citizens who had organized themselves as so-called Minutemen to patrol a border they did not feel was being adequately controlled by the federal government.

These challenges highlight the fact that border control has to be conceptualized systemically in a manner that anticipates well the inevitable action/reaction processes that will occur. Two examples are illustrative. First, the movement of illegal migration into Arizona and New Mexico might have been better anticipated, as it has necessitated the reallocation of Border Patrol resources. In San Diego, patrol agents and aviation assets have been assigned temporarily to the Tuscon sector in Arizona. Those temporary reassignments, combined with difficulty in hiring agents for the San Diego sector caused by cost-of-living issues, have resulted in a depleted force in the San Diego area where fewer agents must attempt to man the border around the clock. These kinds of overall manning challenges undoubtedly exist throughout the Border Patrol system. Second, illegal migrant apprehensions typically mean the need for detention facilities and, in the case of those migrant smugglers against whom a strong legal case can be made, there must be sufficient capacity in the U.S. Attorney's office to accept and prosecute migrant smuggling cases.

The most alarming challenge raised by insufficient detention space is the release with a "Notice to Appear" of migrants "other than Mexican" who cannot simply be returned to Mexico and must be processed for deportation. The Department of Homeland Security's Bureau of

Immigration and Customs Enforcement estimates that there are 465,000 undocumented immigrants in the United States who have received final court orders but have failed to appear.[38] Many analysts fear that this reality is bound to be exploited by terrorists. The Director of Central Intelligence and other government officials testifying before Congress on February 16, 2005, spoke of the possibility that al Qaeda would seek to infiltrate the United States by crossing undetected over the southern land border from Mexico.[39] Eugene Davis, a retired former Deputy Chief of the Border Patrol sector in Blaine, Washington said, "I absolutely believe that the next attack will come from somebody who has come across the border illegally."[40]

The Role of the U.S. Military on the Southern Border

The possible involvement of the Department of Defense forces, primarily in support of civil authorities, is the other first-layer means for the United States to deal with third-layer challenges. The roots of Defense Department activity along the southwest border in recent history can be traced most immediately to the drug war in the late 1980s. With the *Defense Authorization Act of 1989,* Congress made the Defense Department the lead agency for detection and monitoring of aerial and maritime trafficking of illicit drugs, a step which led to the creation of Joint Task Forces in Key West, Alameda and Fort Bliss, Texas.[41] The Texas-based task force, known until recently as JTF-6, "was established to serve as the planning and coordinating operational headquarters to support local, state, and federal law enforcement agencies within the southwest border region to counter the flow of illegal drugs into the United States" and has conducted 5,800 missions in that effort since its inception.[42] In the particular case of JTF-6, the intent of Congress was operationalized in the form of military deployments along the southwest border to provide a variety of military capabilities that supported the counterdrug mission.

In the aftermath of the terrorist attacks of September 11, 2001, the creation of the United States Northern Command (NORTHCOM) signaled a more focused approach to homeland defense and the manner in which the U.S. Defense Department would provide support to law enforcement and other civil authorities pursuing homeland security objectives, including but not limited to the enduring counterdrug mission. Given Mexico's historic discomfort regarding the role of the U.S. military along its northern border, the challenge for NORTHCOM as a new U.S. combatant command is to contribute to U.S. border security without inflaming political passions in Mexico that would cause reactions that run contrary to that effort.

From Mexico's perspective, a new U.S. combatant command in the U.S. joint force architecture charged with defense of the U.S. homeland presents new challenges to the prospects for potentially constructive cooperation. The first and perhaps least surprising, is the fact that NORTHCOM's area of responsibility (AOR) includes Mexico, and Mexico rejects the notion that it would reside in a U.S. military command's AOR.[43] The second is that NORTHCOM recently subsumed under its control and expanded the mission of the military unit that since 1988 has been charged with Department of Defense support to civil authorities engaged in counterdrug efforts along the U.S.-Mexico border. Joint Task Force-North (formerly JTF-6) has a mandate to provide defense support to civil authorities to deter and defend against all illicit transnational threats along both land borders.[44] Reflecting the expansion of its mandate beyond the southwest border, one of the unit's first deployments under its new title was for "Operation Winter Freeze" along the New Hampshire/Vermont/New York borders with Canada.[45]

On the southwest border, a key role for JTF-North in recent months has been to support the U.S. Border Patrol with border testing of Army twin-engine Hunter aerial drones as a possible deterrent to illegal immigration. Tests of the Hunter, exercising the cameras and radar in the drone, follow on earlier exercises that employed a Hermes 450 drone in a manner that is said to have aided in 780 apprehensions of illegal migrants, 11 drug detections, and the seizure of more than 500 pounds of marijuana.[46] An important albeit less glamorous component of U.S. military support to federal law enforcement at the border has been the large number of National Guard and Reserve personnel who have contributed their labor to the construction of the secondary fencing and all-weather road along the border between San Diego and Tijuana.

One analyst of the challenge faced by NORTHCOM given Mexican Army reluctance to engage with it has observed that, "NORTHCOM has got to understand the situation, roll with the punches and work through the Joint Staff."[47] Those charged with advancing theater security cooperation at NORTHCOM describe their approach as "working through proxies"[48] like the Joint Staff and the military services and note that they are "learning forward as much as possible"[49] with respect to the development of positive relationships with Mexican military counterparts. Lieutenant General Walter Sharp, the Joint Staff's Director of Strategic Plans and Policy did meet recently with the Mexican Secretary of National Defense General Gerardo Clemente Ricardo Vega Garcia, an officer whose responsibilities are equivalent to those held by seven different senior officials in the U.S. defense structure (one of the reasons for NORTHCOM's difficulty establishing direct networks).[50] Joint staff officers traveled to Mexico City in January 2005 for meetings with the Secretary of National Defense, and a few months later the Mexican Secretary of the Navy was hosted in Washington, two developments that led a senior military official to remark that bilateral military relations were "good and trending toward improving."[51]

Some of the most promising activity in the realm of military-to-military engagement between the two countries has been taking place for some time in the maritime arena. In terms of the U.S./Mexico relationship in the maritime arena, it does not suffer from the same structural challenges that NORTHCOM faces along the land border. Further, bilateral cooperation is slightly more advanced between the neighboring maritime forces than it is for the various land-based counterparts. These facts may combine to make naval cooperation the wedge for broader improvement in military-to-military interaction between the United States and Mexico at some point in the future.

Whereas the Secretary of National Defense in Mexico has a spectrum of responsibilities that are shared in the United States by seven different senior defense personnel, the Chief of Naval Operations (CNO) in the United States has a direct counterpart. In recent years, the U.S. CNO Admiral Vernon Clark has developed a "strong personal relationship" with the Chief of Staff of the Mexican Navy, Vice Admiral Alberto Castro Rosas—in fact, the fruits of the relationship in terms of counterdrug cooperation were so significant in Clark's eyes that he awarded Vice Admiral Castro Rosas the Legion of Merit in a Washington, D.C. ceremony on October 26, 2004.[52] A number of other noteworthy recent developments in the relationship include:

- Establishment of a Mexican Foreign Liaison Officer position for a Mexican Navy officer at U.S. Fleet Forces Command in Norfolk, Virginia.
- Mexico agreeing to join in full membership the U.S. CNO-sponsored Inter-American Naval Conference.
- Security assistance in the form of maintenance as well as pilot and maintenance training provided by the U.S. Navy to the Mexican Navy to support their effort to make operational several E2C aircraft acquired from Israel.
- Joint coordination of the delivery of Tsunami relief supplies to Asia using both U.S. and Mexican ships. This effort involved Mexican naval ship port calls in Hawaii and Guam.[53]

The combination of Mexican sensitivity to the establishment of NORTH-COM, the developments described above, and the recent appointment of a naval officer as the second commander of NORTHCOM raises interesting questions about where future bilateral maritime cooperation is headed. Admiral Timothy Keating's appointment as the NORTHCOM Commander is, at least in part, an acknowledgment that the maritime component of NORTHCOM's responsibilities received relatively less attention during the command's first two years in existence. At the same time, given relatively positive signs emerging from the recent bilateral engagement between the U.S. and Mexican Navies, a naval officer in command of NORTHCOM may facilitate further positive momentum. Commenting on the prospect of establishing a "Maritime NORAD,"[54] Admiral Keating "cautioned against taking a narrow view that would cast the new [maritime security] initiative as simply a maritime version of the existing bilateral NORAD initiative between the United States and Canada.[55] Keating said, "...we don't want it to be just bilateral—we want the Canadians to help us and we want the Mexicans to help us."[56] Getting to that stage will require the continuation of positive engagements like those fostered by the Navy under Admiral Clark.

Cause for relative optimism on the maritime front is further supported by Mexican Navy/U.S. Coast Guard cooperation in law enforcement operations. The Coast Guard's unique character as a multimission agency with both law enforcement and national defense functions places it in interesting waters in the post-9/11 environment. It has, through its search and rescue and oil spill response functions, developed a reasonably constructive level of engagement with the Mexican Navy over the years, including engagement in counterdrug operations. This cooperation has resulted in successful drug interdiction cases like the recent seizure of two tons of cocaine by the Mexican Navy after receiving a tip from the U.S. Coast Guard. In that case, the U.S. Coast Guard discovered the concealed cocaine and alerted Mexican authorities about the status of the Mexican-flagged vessel.[57] Given the Mexican Navy's caution about stepping out too far in its engagements with U.S. counterparts, planned joint operations are not conducted, but the forces have from time to time engaged in so-called coincidental operations, when vessels from each force are coincidentally in the same operating area at the same time.[58] Perhaps the most promising, even if symbolic, breakthrough regarding NORTHCOM and the military-to-military relationship with Mexico is the invitation extended by Mexico to Admiral Keating, in his capacity as the NORTHCOM Commander, to observe the annual El Grito[59] celebration in Mexico City.

SECOND LAYER APPROACHES—ENGAGING THE PRIVATE SECTOR

A decade before NAFTA, the need for more creative ways to strike a balance between trade and security along the southwest border led to the development of public/private partnership programs that would reward companies engaged in cross-border trade activity for demonstrating the integrity of their supply chain. These developments illustrated both the extent to which increasing volumes were challenging U.S. enforcement capacity and the motivation of the private sector actors to encourage such thinking in government in order to expedite the clearance process at the border.

In 1984, the United States Customs Service introduced the Carrier Initiative Program, an endeavor designed initially to "find an alternative to substantial fines and seizures of conveyances…" in the fight against illicit drug shipments.[60] The program required that air and sea carriers agree to enhance their security at foreign terminals, aboard their aircraft, ships and trucks, and at their facilities in the United States. In exchange, their employees received training from the U.S. Customs Service. Further, in the event that illicit contraband was found aboard one of their vehicles, their compliance with the program was a mitigating factor when fines and other penalties were considered. At present, there are over 3,800 Carrier Initiative Agreements in place.[61] It was expanded in 1989 to give special attention to "super carriers," those deemed by the Service to be particularly threatened by drug traffickers. Customs concluded 27 super carrier agreements.[62]

An example drawn from the Customs relationship with land carriers (truck and rail) provides some evidence of the way in which the Service engaged constructively with the import industry before 9/11 to combat the drug threat. A trade facilitation initiative begun in the late 1980s known as "Line Release" allowed repetitive, high volume shipments to receive expedited treatment at the U.S. land border. In 1995, an offshoot of the Carrier Initiative Program, the Land Border Carrier Initiative Program (LBCIP) was instituted and the service linked the benefit of Line Release with the use of land border carriers who were voluntarily participating in LBCIP. For importers, continued participation in the preferential Line Release opportunity became contingent upon their contracting with one of the 1400[63] trucking firms enrolled in the LBCIP.[64] What was Line Release became known as "Border Release Advanced Screening and Selectivity" (BRASS). The Customs Service's program manager for industry partnerships estimated in 2001, before 9/11, that 60 percent of the trucking firms doing business along the U.S.-Mexico land border are participating in the LBCIP; the other 40 percent cannot haul BRASS cargo.[65] Today, Customs and Border Protection is in the process of converting BRASS participants to the latest evolution—Free and Secure Trade or "FAST."

Some of the creative thinking in the search for a balance between trade facilitation and border control was advanced by the industry. Early in 1996, an initiative proposed to the Customs Service by the business community demonstrated that some in the private sector wanted to be proactive in self-enforcement. The Business Anti-Smuggling Coalition (BASC) was born when the Mattel Corporation came to the Customs Service in search of ways to improve accountability for manufactured goods from the time they left a foreign factory until they arrived at the ordered destination in the United States. The initiative was an indication of the desire of manufacturers to protect their brand names from association with criminal activity, and obviously to do what they could to avoid costly fines and lost income. By the end of 1997, there were 160 companies participating in the BASC program and their participation led to the seizure of 6,000 pounds of cocaine that year.[66] The BASC program was structured to improve security at four key stages: in foreign manufacturing plants, with commercial carriers of goods, with customs brokers, and at warehouses and/or distribution and purchase points. Between October 1995 and October 2000, the Customs Service attributed the seizure of nearly 300,000 pounds of illegal drugs to either "foreign intercepts" or "domestic assists" by industry partners.[67]

The reach of this new thinking began to grow beyond the terrestrial borders of the United States. Relevant intergovernmental and nongovernmental organizations began to embrace the BASC concept and fold it into efforts with the potential for wider impact. Based on an agreement arrived at in 1996 between the International Chamber of Commerce (ICC) and the World Customs Organization (WCO), businesses and customs administrations around the world agreed to pursue greater efficiency in customs processes. A Mattel corporation executive who was part of the initial BASC initiative, and who served as the head of the ICC's Committee on Customs and Trade Regulations, argued in 1997 that partnerships like BASC should be "applied internationally without delay."[68] Progress in that direction was signaled most dramatically on June 23, 2005, when the Director Generals of Customs of the 166 member states of the WCO unanimously adopted the Framework of Standards to Secure and Facilitate Global Trade, an ambitious document that, when implemented, will raise the threshold internationally for those engaged in global trade.[69]

The immediate U.S. reaction to the terrorist attacks of September 11, 2001, was to close the borders for over a week. That was an untenable long-term response and the approach that has unfolded since has sought to provide enhanced security while still allowing the flow of goods and people essential to the health of the U.S. and Mexican economies. On the law enforcement side, this has meant the emergence of counterterrorism efforts that find their roots in the strategies of the Carrier Initiative and BASC programs. Of greatest significance to the U.S.-Mexico border are a range of objectives, organized around the goals of "secure infrastructure," "secure flow of people," and "secure flow of goods" that were enshrined in the March 22, 2002, Smart Border Agreement reached by Presidents Fox and Bush at Monterrey, Mexico. With respect to secure flow of goods, important developments that are direct outgrowths of the BASC and CIP initiatives are the Customs-Trade Partnership Against Terrorism (C-TPAT) and the related implementation of the Free and Secure Trade (FAST) lanes at key border crossings for use by participating companies and their approved carriers. The C-TPAT is a program designed to incentivize private corporations into voluntary security precautions and increased transparency by offering the possibility of more rapid clearance across the border. Once offered, C-TPAT quickly enrolled 60 U.S. companies including General Motors, Ford, Target, Sara Lee, Motorola and DaimlerChrysler.[70] Today it has over 7,000 participants and is the "largest public/private Federal government partnership in U.S. history."[71] In the spring of 2003, one year after the conclusion of the Smart Border Agreement, progress on the implementation of FAST lanes along the southern border was slow and broad implementation was expected to take until August or September of 2003.[72] That timeline appears to have held given that the sixth southern border crossing with a dedicated FAST lane, at Calexico, opened formally in January 2005.[73]

RECOMMENDATIONS AND CONCLUSION

This analysis leads to a variety of recommendations which can be loosely categorized as either strategic or tactical in nature.

Strategic Recommendations

- The Department of Homeland Security must remain committed, in a broad sense that includes the Mexico border, to the resourcing of a layered approach to security that begins as far from the physical border as possible and includes the participation of as many committed partners as can be recruited into it without compromising security. The integrity of filtering systems like SENTRI and C-TPAT must be ensured by staffing levels that make spot checks for compliance possible on a sufficiently regular basis.

- As efforts guided by the commitments of the Security and Prosperity Partnership enshrined at Waco, Texas in the spring of 2005 continue in the months and years ahead, attention and focus on the maintenance of a healthy bilateral relationship with Mexico must remain a prime concern of U.S. officials, even in the face of reorganizations in the Department of Homeland Security that may occur and despite growing pains in that Department and/or in NORTHCOM. Security cooperation that has been achieved, and delicate new possibilities that exist on the horizon, should not be jeopardized by clumsy unilateralism. Even if Mexican contributions to the collective goal of a more secure border endure domestic challenges south of the border, a bilateral agenda can be advanced if the United States is always ready to engage constructively. Actions that confirm Mexico as an equal partner yield dividends. In the wake of the devastation of Hurricane Katrina, the U.S. accepted Mexico's offer of a relief convoy, and the Mexican government deployed 45 vehicles with 2,000 support personnel to San Antonio, marking the first time Mexican military personnel had been on U.S. soil since 1846.[74] This relief effort has important symbolic value that can yield further benefits to the cooperative security relationship in the future.

- A prime responsibility of the new Assistant Secretary of Homeland Security for Strategic Plans should be to assess related border security processes in a holistic way to avoid gaps in the overall approach. The effort should include, for example, reviews of staffing models for the Border Patrol sectors and the ports of entry as well as the control challenges posed by illegal migrants "other than Mexican" once apprehended. Additionally, this review should contemplate the benefits to be realized from a complete implementation of the US-VISIT system, including the entry of data on Mexican and Canadian citizens as well as the collection of exit information not presently being captured. Close care should be taken to anticipate and manage Mexican concerns in this process.

- A priority should be placed on maintaining a strong relationship with the Mexican Navy. Although the Navy and the Army are distinct entities and positive relations with the former will not necessarily yield the same with the latter, there is value in the continued modeling of constructive military-to-military contacts. While Admiral Keating is the NORTHCOM Commander, there may be particular opportunities in this regard.

Tactical Recommendations

- Both Customs and Border Protection at the ports of entry and the Border Patrol need more personnel to do the taxing work of guarding the border. Though this is a matter that has been receiving targeted attention from the Department of Homeland Security, particularly with respect to Border Patrol needs in Arizona, both entities need more personnel in order to fully staff their shifts, even when personnel must be detailed to training.[75] Given the dynamic technological environment, especially with respect to weapons of mass destruction detection equipment, staffing models that accommodate training needs more effectively should be realized.

- Congress should continue to fund CBP requests for the continued deployment of weapons of mass destruction detection equipment. This recommendation should not be interpreted as supportive of a perpetual and unending pursuit of figurative "silver bullets" that can solve forever the border security challenge. At the same time, it is clear that funds are needed to ensure that at least some of the technology is available at all ports of entry. While the commercial port of entry at Otay Mesa, California has a full spectrum of detection capacity, other facilities on both the northern and southern borders are just beginning to receive some of what is available.

- Congress should continue to support the integrated surveillance system known as the America's Shield Initiative in a manner that is fused smartly with Border Patrol staffing decisions in order that an optimal array of people and technology can be established to provide more comprehensive coverage of the Border Patrol areas of responsibility.

- In an April 2004 report entitled "U.S.-Mexico Border Security and the Evolving Security Relationship: Recommendations for Policy Makers," the U.S.-Mexico Bi-National Council advocates cross-border bioterrorist attack simulation exercises, disease surveillance, and the establishment of a joint Mexico-U.S. Incident

Command and Operations Facility.[76] At the moment, prospects for transformation in the relationship that might lead to such developments appear limited. Still, Assistant Secretary of Defense for Homeland Defense Paul McHale said recently, "The message that we have communicated to Mexican military authorities is we are looking for a much closer level of engagement."[77] Given cooperation on search and rescue and oil pollution in the maritime environment, disaster management exercises might be an effective mechanism for easing into something that approximates direct military-to-military contact on the land border. Again, Mexico's support of the Hurricane Katrina relief effort may provide a precedent to build upon, and Secretary McHale has more recently emphasized the importance of cross-border connectivity "…in anticipating how to manage a terrorist attack along the border involving a weapon of mass destruction."[78]

These recommendations speak to a spectrum of challenges and possibilities on the U.S.-Mexico border. They reflect an effort to deal with a reality consisting of massive flows of goods and people and finite resources to filter and inspect them. No border will ever be perfectly secure, but there are a number of ways in which the U.S. border with Mexico can become more secure.

ACKNOWLEDGMENTS

The views expressed herein are those of the author and do not necessarily reflect the position of the Commandant or the Coast Guard. I thank my colleagues in the Humanities Department at the U.S. Coast Guard Academy for the support that made it possible to pursue this project. An important component of the research for this chapter was made possible by funding from the Defense Threat Reduction Agency. I am grateful to the very dedicated men and women of U.S. Customs and Border Protection in San Ysidro and Otay Mesa, California for their time and perspective. I am thankful most especially for the constant loving support of my wife, son, and daughter.

NOTES

1. United Nations, United Nations Development Program, "Human Development Report," http://hdr.undp.org/statistics/data/pdf/hdr04_table_13.pdf (accessed August 30, 2005).

2. Jeffrey S. Passel, "Estimates of the Size and Characteristics of the Undocumented Population," Pew Hispanic Center report, March 21, 2005, 1.

3. Pre-NAFTA exports to the United States grew modestly between 1982 and 1992, rising from $24.1 billion to $46.2 billion. Between 1994 and 2000, they rose from $60.9 billion to $166.4 billion. See Manual Pastor and Carol Wise, "A Long View of Mexico's Political Economy: What's Changed? What are the Challenges?" in *Mexico's Politics and Society in Transition,* ed. Joseph S. Tulchin and Andrew D. Selee (Boulder, CO: Lynne Rienner, 2003), 67.

4. U.S. Department of Transportation, Bureau of Transportation Statistics, *Border Crossing Entry Data*, available from http://www.transtats.bts.gov/Fields.asp?Table_ID=1358 (accessed March 13, 2006).

5. Ibid.

6. Estimate provided to author during August 8, 2005 tour of the San Ysidro port of entry.

7. Department of Homeland Security, Office of Immigration Statistics, "Yearbook of Immigration Statistics 2003—Enforcement," http://uscis.gov/graphics/shared/statistics/yearbook/YrBk03En.htm (accessed September 3, 2005).

8. Estimate provided to author by Border Patrol personnel during August 9, 2005 tour of the U. S. Border Patrol San Diego Sector area of responsibility. The higher of these two figures conforms roughly with the Pew Hispanic Center's estimated flow of 700,000 undocumented migrants per year during the period from 2000_2004. See Passel (note 2), 8.

9. U.S. Congress. House. Committee on Appropriations, Subcommittee on Homeland Security, *Coping with Illegal Immigration on the Southwest Border*, Statement of David Aguilar, Chief, Office of Border Patrol, U. S. Customs and Border Protection, Department of Homeland Security before the Subcommittee on Homeland Security, http://usinfo.state.gov/gi/Archive/2005/Jul/14-680142.html (accessed September 3, 2005).

10. Kris Axtman, "Illegal Entry by Non-Mexicans Rises," *The Christian Science Monitor*, http://www.csmonitor.com/2005/0726/p01s01-usfp.html (accessed July 26, 2005).

11. Pauline Arrillaga and Olga R. Rodriguez, "AP Investigation: Smuggler Pipelines Channel Illegal Immigrants Into U.S. from Nations With Terror Ties," *Associated Press*, July 2, 2005; available from LexisNexis Academic Universe (accessed July 4, 2005).

12. This is a linkage that is much debated. Although it is relatively easy to produce connections between drug trade revenues and the activities of the Revolutionary Armed Forces of Colombia (FARC) or the Taliban in Afghanistan, conclusive evidence that al Qaeda has funded its terrorist actions against the United States using illicit drug trade revenues remains elusive. This issue was reported on in the *Washington Times* in October 2005. See Sharon Behn, "Retired General Says Drug Money Fueling Taliban, Al Qaeda," *Washington Times*, October 1, 2005, A7.

13. Congressional Research Service, Report for Congress, "Plan Colombia: A Progress Report, http://fpc.state.gov/documents/organization/50264.pdf (accessed September 3, 2005), 3.

14. Pablo Bachelet, "Mexico Now Top Supplier of U.S. Drugs," *Miami Herald*, July 31, 2005, 1.

15. Ibid.

16. David J. Jefferson, "America's Most Dangerous Drug," *Newsweek*, August 8, 2005, 47.

17. Richard H. Ullman, "Redefining Security," *International Security* 8, no. 1 (Summer 1983): 129.

18. Ibid., 133.

19. See, inter alia, Netta Crawford, "Once and Future Security Studies," *Security Studies* 1 (Winter 1991); Stephen M. Walt, "The Renaissance of Security Studies," *International Studies Quarterly* 35 (June 1991); Helga Haftendorn, "The Security Puzzle," *International Studies Quarterly* 35 (March 1991); and Joseph S. Nye Jr. and Sean M. Lynn-Jones, "International Security Studies: A Report of a Conference on the State of the Field," *International Security* 12, no. 4 (Spring 1988): 5–27. Peter Andreas and Richard Price write of the "growing gap between traditional security concepts and paradigms and the contemporary practice of security" in Peter Andreas and Richard Price, "From Warfighting to Crime Fighting: Transforming the American National Security State," *International Studies Review* 3 no. 3 (Fall 2001): 31.

20. U.S. General Accounting Office, "Drug Control: Assets DOD Contributes to Reducing the Illegal Drug Supply Have Declined," GAO/NSIAD-00-9, December 21, 1999. This GAO report confronts the dilemma faced by a Defense Department facing a continually widening array of obligations related to nontraditional threats.

21. Lawrence Freedman articulated the concern of traditionalists when he wrote: "Once anything that generates anxiety or threatens the quality of life in some respect becomes labeled a 'security problem' the field risks losing all focus." Lawrence Freedman, "International Security: Changing Targets," *Foreign Policy* (Spring 1998): 53.

22. See, for example, regarding the environment as a security threat, Marc A. Levy, "Is the Environment a National Security Threat?," *International Security* 20 no. 2 (Fall 1995) and Erik K. Stern's chapter, "The Case for Comprehensive Security," in *Contested Grounds: Security and Conflict in the New Environmental Politics*, ed. Daniel H. Deudney and Richard A. Matthew (Albany: State University of New York Press, 1999), 135–142.

23. See, inter alia, Peter J. Katzenstein, *The Culture of National Security: Norms and Identity in World Politics* (New York: Columbia University Press, 1996) and Keith Krause and Michael C. Williams, eds., *Critical Security Studies: Concepts and Cases* (Minneapolis: University of Minnesota Press, 1997).

24. Joseph S. Nye Jr., *Soft Power: The Means to Success in World Politics* (New York: PublicAffairs, 2004), 4.

25. Nye says, "soft power—getting others to want the outcomes you want—co-opts people rather than coerces them." He distinguishes it from the traditional conceptions of power—resources, territory, military strength, etc.—that he and others have referred to as hard power. See Nye (note 24), 4–5.

26. Nye, 4.

27. Ibid.

28. For information about SENTRI, see http://www.cbp.gov/xp/cgov/travel/frequent_traveler/sentri.xml.

29. U.S. Congress. House. Committee on Appropriations, Subcommittee on Homeland Security, Statement of Robert C. Bonner, Commissioner of U.S. Customs and Border Protection before the Subcommittee on Homeland Security, 109th Cong., 1st sess., March 15, 2005.

30. Ibid.

31. Jessica M. Vaughan, "Modernizing America's Welcome Mat: The Implementation of US-VISIT," Center for Immigration Studies, August 2005;available from: http://www.cis.org/articles/2005/back905.html (accessed September 8, 2005).

32. United States-Visitor Immigration Status Indicator Technology.

33. Vaughan.

34. The post-9/11 initiatives discussed above are captured under the umbrella of a 22-point "Smart Border" agreement signed by Presidents Bush and Fox in March of 2002. See "The Monterrey Commitments: Joint Statement by the Presidents of the United States and Mexico," March 22, 2002, http://www.state.gov/p/wha/rls/rm/8948.htm (accessed April 4, 2002). A more recent trilateral initiative being referred to as the "Security and Prosperity Partnership" affirms the "Smart Border" approach that the United States has committed to with both Canada and Mexico and directs regularized ministerial-level meetings and working groups on a host of hemispheric issues including security and trade facilitation. See U.S. Department of State, "North American Prosperity Depends on Security," http://usinfo.state.gov/wh/Archive/2005/Mar/23-128896.html (accessed September 8, 2005).

35. U.S. Congress. House. Statement of Robert C. Bonner.

36. The massive fencing, lighting, and road building project at the San Diego County/Tijuana, Mexico border, still ongoing, was begun on October 1, 1994 and is referred to as Operation Gatekeeper. See Joseph Nevins, *Operation Gatekeeper: The Rise of the "Illegal Alien" and the Making of the U.S.-Mexico Boundary* (New York: Routledge, 2002), 92.

37. This problem has been recognized on both sides of the border. The U.S. Border Patrol in San Diego created the Border Search Trauma and Rescue Team in 1998, and there are now 22 agents in San Diego and 100 nationwide committed to the task of rescuing physically distressed migrants. The Mexican government published *A Guide for Mexican Migrants* in an effort to ensure that migrants being led into difficult areas by inhumane smugglers (known as "coyotes") could increase their chances of survival. The fact that Mexico produced a document that might be seen as encouraging illegal immigration was not well received in many corners of the United States, but the Mexican view was that it had a humanitarian obligation to its citizens who were going to attempt the transit anyway. The guide can be viewed in Spanish and in English at http://www.amren.com/mexguide/mexguide.html.

38. Pauline Arrillaga, "AP Investigation: 'Catch and Release' Policy Frees Illegal Immigrants to Move About U.S.," *Associated Press*; available from LexisNexis Academic Universe (accessed September 8, 2005).

39. Douglas Jehl, "U.S. Aides Cite Worry on Qaeda Infiltration From Mexico," *New York Times*, February 17, 2005.

40. Arrillaga.

41. The Task Force in Key West, originally known as JTF-4, eventually became Joint Interagency Task Force-East (JIATF-East) and is now known as JIATF-South. JTF-5, based in Alameda, California is now known as JIATF-West. JTF-6, based in

Texas, retained that name under different operational commanders until recently.

42. "Joint Interagency Task Force-North History," http://www.jtfn.northcom. mil/subpages/history.html (accessed February 26, 2005).

43. Mark Milardo, Deputy Chief of Theater Security Cooperation, U.S. Northern Command, J-523, telephone interview with author, January 25, 2005.

44. Ibid.

45. Rear Admiral Gene Brooks, U.S. Coast Guard, Deputy Director of Operations, U.S. Northern Command, telephone interview with author, January 31, 2005.

46. Arthur H. Rotstein, "Patrol: New Drones Serving as a Deterrent," *Associated Press State and Local Wire,* December 7, 2004; available from Lexis/Nexis Academic Universe (accessed December 8, 2004).

47. Jay Cope of National Defense University as quoted in Jason Sherman, "U.S., Mexico to Cooperate," *Defense News,* November 8, 2004, 6.

48. Milardo, telephone interview.

49. Brooks, telephone interview.

50. Jason Sherman, "U.S., Mexico to Cooperate," *Defense News,* November 8, 2004, 6.

51. Jason Sherman, "U.S. Proposes Exercises with Mexico Focusing on Homeland Defense," *Inside the Pentagon* 11 (August 2005): 1.

52. Ibid.

53. Lieutenant Commander Mark A. Imblum, Office of International Security Strategy–Western Hemisphere (CNO N5), email communication to author, February 16, 2005.

54. North American Aerospace Defense Command.

55. Aarti Shah, "Admiral: 'Maritime NORAD' Should be Multilateral, Interagency," *Inside the Navy,* February 14, 2005.

56. Ibid.

57. "Drugs Seized," *Liverpool Daily Echo,* October 23, 2004, 6; available from Lexis Nexis.

58. Efforts to quantify the number and frequency of these activities via the Coast Guard's Office of the Assistant Commandant for Operations and the Office of Law Enforcement in the Eleventh Coast Guard District were unsuccessful.

59. Celebration of Mexican Independence each September 16.

60. Department of Homeland Security, U.S. Customs and Border Protection, *Carrier Initiative Program,*http://www.cbp.gov/xp/cgov/border_security/ international_activities/partnerships/cip.xml (accessed March 14, 2006).

61. Ibid.

62. Ibid.

63. Ed Moriarty, Program Manager, Industry Partnership Programs, Anti-Smuggling Division, U.S. Customs Service, telephone interview by author, July 6, 2001.

64. Department of the Treasury, U. S. Customs Service, "Carrier Initiative Fact Sheet," provided to author by Mr. Edward Moriarty by electronic mail on July 6, 2001.

65. Moriarty, telephone interview.

66. Ibid.

67. Department of the Treasury, U. S. Customs Service, PowerPoint slide entitled "Industry Partnership Program," provided to author by Mr. Ed Moriarty by electronic mail on July 6, 2001.

68. Fermin Cuza, "Business and Customs Must Join Forces Against Drug Smuggling," *The International Herald Tribune*, July 16, 1997, http://www.iccwbo.org/home/news_archives/1997/business_and_customs.asp (accessed December 14, 2000).

69. World Customs Organization, *Framework of Standards to Secure and Facilitate Global Trade* (Brussels: World Trade Organization, June 2005, http:/www.wcoomd.org/ie/En/en.html (accessed March 14, 2006).

70. Gary Fields, "Customs Unveils Security Moves," *Wall Street Journal*, April 16, 2002, A4.

71. Department of Homeland Security Fact Sheet, "President Bush Signs Maritime Security Policy National Security/Homeland Security Presidential Directive," 5.

72. Elizabeth Sullivan, C-TPAT Program Manager, U.S. Customs Service Headquarters, telephone interview with author, February 24, 2003. In this conversation, Ms. Sullivan noted that the impending transfer of the Customs Service on March 1, 2003 to the new Department of Homeland Security was impacting the agency's ability to keep all initiatives moving forward at an ideal pace.

73. FAST lanes were opened previously at Laredo, Pharr, Brownsville, and El Paso, Texas and at Otay Mesa, California. "Secretary of Homeland Security Ridge Visits New FAST Lane at Calexico," Department of Homeland Security, Press Release, January 17, 2005, http://www.dhs.gov/interweb/assetlibrary/2004_US-Mex_Book.pdf (accessed February 11, 2005).

74. "Mexican Troops Cross Into U.S. for Hurricane Relief," *CNN*, http://www.cnn.com/2005/US/09/08/katrina.mexico.ap/index.html (accessed September 9, 2005).

75. President Bush's 2007 budget request includes funding for 1,500 new Border Patrol agents, but that figure is below the 2,000 number required by the 2004 *Intelligence Reform Act* and border security legislation passed by the House of Representatives in December 2005. See Patrick Yoest, "Budget '07: Budget Puts Emphasis on Border Security," *CQ-Homeland Security*, February 6, 2006.

76. "U.S.-Mexico Border Security and the Evolving Security Relationship: Recommendations for Policy Makers," Report of the U.S.-Mexico Bi-National Council (Washington: Center for Strategic and International Studies, 2004), 22 and 24.

77. Jason Sherman, "U.S., Mexico to Cooperate," *Defense News*, November 8, 2004, 6.

78. Sherman, "U.S. Proposes Exercises."

CHAPTER 3

FROM "49TH PARALLEL" TO "SECURITY PERIMETER": CHANGING CONCEPTIONS, VALUES AND STRUCTURES ALONG THE U.S.-CANADA BORDER

Stuart Farson

Three arguments are pursued in this chapter. At the central core is one suggesting that the response of the U.S. government to the attacks of September 11, 2001, has strongly influenced how Canadians and Americans now view their common borders. It has moved from being an essentially linear concept to one that is now multifaceted and multidimensional. Second, the response has also had unintended consequences. For Canadians it has meant a closer examination of their values. For the most part these have been found to be diverging—not converging—from those of their neighbors to the south. And third, the Canadian government has responded in significant but different ways to the threat perceived by the U.S. government.

It is not possible here to discuss all of the ways in which our collective notions of the border have changed and why. Instead, this chapter focuses on five main themes: the general nature of borders and their origin; the way in which Canadian-U.S. border arrangements changed during the decade following the end of the Cold War and immediately prior to the terrorist attacks of September 11, 2001; the key characteristics of the new post-9/11 "smart border" environment; the converging and diverging nature of North American values;

and finally, some important differences in approaches to homeland security.

THE ORIGINS AND CHANGING NATURE OF BORDERS

Traditionally, national borders have been reflective of three, frequently interconnecting, histories. Some are the direct product of conquest, resulting either directly from full-scale belligerence or the drive for empire and colonies. A second source of national borders is that derived from the pursuit of trade. In this regard, colonization and belligerence are often themselves associated with the search for raw materials, transportation routes, and the need to protect them. The third origin of borders stems from what one may term ethnicity and shared social and cultural values. Although these have historically been important factors in the causes of conflict, they have again emerged—particularly in the era of decolonization—as contributing factors in so-called movements of national liberation and religious nationalism.

More recently, a focus on borders has emerged for somewhat different reasons. These have *not* focused on national entities, but rather on conglomerations of states with extranational borders. A common starting point has often been the establishment of easier trading arrangements between partner states, with consequently more difficult access to trade for those outside. These have in some instances led to conglomerations of a more political nature, aspiring to have such things as a common legislative body; common legal rules; equal access to all states; and a right of abode in each jurisdiction for citizens of all the national entities, as well as common security and defense policies, and a common currency. In the case of the European Union—which epitomizes this model—the individual partner states have relinquished a certain degree of national sovereignty in order to achieve mutual benefits. However, a primary goal underpinning the formation of the European Union was to ensure that the belligerent history of Europe was not perpetuated. The same rationale has not applied in the case of the North American Free Trade Agreement (NAFTA) or other such conglomerates in the Western Hemisphere, where an absence of historical animosity between neighbors has influenced a unique set of perceptions toward borders and border security.

CHANGES TO U.S.-CANADA BORDER ARRANGEMENTS PRIOR TO SEPTEMBER 11, 2001

In two important respects, Canadians are border people. Though they live in the second largest country in the world, bounded directly only by three oceans and the United States, the vast majority live within 150 kilometers of their southern border. Similarly, each of Canada's major economic and commercial centers lies within close proximity to the United States and its vast marketplace. The trading relationship between the two countries is the largest and most comprehensive in the world.[1] In 2004, bilateral trade ran close to $680 billion. Canada accounts for 23.5 percent of American exports and 17.4 percent of its imports. In return the United States accounts for almost 80 percent of Canada's exports and 66 percent of its imports. For 39 of the 50 states Canada is the number one foreign market for goods exports. It is in the top three of another eight. Significantly, on average some $1.8 billion worth of goods and services cross the border between Canada and the United States every single day.

Second, for more than a generation Canadians have reflected upon the possibility that their country might someday disintegrate into the sum of its parts. The 1960s saw the emergence of the Front de Libération du Québec (FLQ), a relatively small Québec separatist group willing to use political violence to achieve an independent Québec.[2] Initially, it targeted only the more minor symbols of federal power. However, in 1970 it dramatically revamped its strategy by kidnapping both the British Trade Commissioner in Montréal and the Province of Québec's Labour Minister. Though the former was eventually released, the latter was murdered, his dead body being unceremoniously dumped into the trunk of an abandoned car. The federal government responded—some would argue overreacted—to these events by invoking the *War Measures Act*. Though initially drawn up to deal with emergencies during wartime, this legislation also covered so-called apprehended insurrections. It thus permitted an armed military presence in the Province, gave the police extraordinary powers to arrest and detain suspects, and temporarily suspended many civil liberties. Within three years of what has been called the "October Crisis" the FLQ was for all intents and purposes a spent force.[3] Separatists' aspirations, however, did not diminish. Rather they were transferred to the legitimate political arena with the formation of the Parti Québécois (PQ) on the provincial scene and the Bloc Québécois at the national level. Ironically, the latter would become "Her Majesty's Loyal Opposition" in the early 1990s after the Progressive Conservative government of Brian Mulroney (and subsequently Kim Campbell) self-destructed. The PQ has taken full advantage of its times in office by holding two referenda on separation. The most recent, held in 1995, very nearly succeeded. Currently, opinion polls suggest that most Québeckers would support a new relationship with the rest of Canada.[4] Another referendum therefore may well eventuate if and when the PQ are returned to power. The significance of Québec politics to the national agenda means that all future federal actions need to be seen, in part at least, through a Québécois lens. It is significant for Canada-U.S, relations to recall that Québeckers have a long history of not favoring conscription and involvement in foreign wars.

By contrast, Canada's external borders have seldom been given much detailed or continuous thought.[5] Since Confederation in 1867, Canada's borders with the United States have remained peaceful and open to trade. As befits two long-standing allies who have fought two major world wars together, this has allowed both countries to claim with an element of pride that they possess "the longest undefended border in the world."

Recently, however, Canadians have become much more conscious of their international boundaries. This new awareness may be directly related to two things: the attacks against the symbols of American power and prestige perpetrated by a small group of Jihadists that occurred on September 11, 2001, and the subsequent reaction of the U.S. government to those attacks on New York and Washington.

From an outsider's perspective, this response might best be described as the "globalization of the U.S. national security threat," as it captures important dimensions of the response strategy hitherto rarely discussed in any detail. These are essentially twofold. First, there is an element of pressure to comply with American thinking. In this sense other countries are "required" to conform with American policies both by accepting the notion of the threat as defined by the U.S. government and by responding to it along lines largely subscribed by its Administration. Second, following the vulnerability of the U.S. heartland exposed by the 9/11 attacks, there is now an expectation that other states will have to consider how best to ensure U.S. security in their national security planning. In this sense, the United States has partly passed responsibility for its national security outwards—beyond its national borders—to the hands of others.

This globalization of the U.S. national security threat has been felt by states of quite different hues—from newfound friends, to friends of convenience, to traditional allies. However, it has been felt most acutely by states bordering the United States and those wanting to trade with the United States or to transport people to its shores. Clearly, there is no reason to anticipate that such pressures will abate any time in the near future. Numerous spokespersons for the U.S. Administration—from the President on down—have reminded its friends and allies that the so-called "global war on terrorism" will be a very protracted conflict.

This new pressure to conform to a particular view of the world and how to respond to its new and emerging threats has forced Canadians to confront certain difficult questions about their neighbors to the south. They have found in the process that the United States has moved from being "family"—to employ a characterization used by the current U.S. Administration—and enjoying the "special relationship" that such ties naturally entail, to some lesser status. Some in Canada have even called the country a "nuisance neighbor" and a "security threat."[6]

But such rude awakenings may also have had a positive and unintended set of consequences for the Canadian psyche. These may well in years to come be perceived as a "tipping point" both in terms of how Canadians see themselves and their relationship with their American neighbors.[7] Certainly, the old shibboleth of Canadians defining themselves as "not being Americans" will no longer suffice, if it ever did.

Instead, we may find a much more carefully defined notion of what Canadian interests are and how they are best achieved, determining what the real threats to Canada are—whether they are strategic or merely national security problems—and how they are best thwarted by soft or hard power; what Canada is perceived to stand for; and how it should behave abroad.

Since Confederation, relations between the United States and Canada have been peaceful. That the shared border has not been militarized has led both countries to take some pride in having the longest undefended border in the world. This notion of the border was essentially a linear one, albeit one perceived to be unstructured and unproblematic. Reference to it as the "49th parallel"—though obviously abbreviated and inaccurate—captured the essence of this conception.

Following the signing of NAFTA, it was often posited that the U.S.-Canada border would gradually fade away as greater economic integration occurred. Far from "vanishing"—as a book title of the period suggested—the border was in fact brought into sharper focus.[8] The 1990s saw Canada and the United States forge a series of important agreements that focused on a number of outstanding security issues. And, as Christopher Sands has cogently argued, it was this ongoing dialogue that made it possible for both countries to come to a broad-scale consensus agreement on new border arrangements after 9/11.[9]

In 1995, the shared border accord was signed. This concerned measures to improve cooperation between customs and immigration officials in both countries. It did not include specific antiterrorism measures that might have been expected to flow from the 1993 attack on the World Trade Center because it was thought that all involved were either in custody or would soon be apprehended. In February 1997, the United States and Canada agreed to form the Anti-Smuggling Working Group and the Northeast Border Working Group to combat human and contraband smuggling across the border. An integral part of this agreement was the sharing of information and intelligence. In April of the same year, the two governments announced a "new border vision" initiative. This set out to improve coordination between Citizenship and Immigration Canada and the U.S. Immigration and Naturalization Service (INS), as well as the sharing of intelligence on illegal migration. And the Cross-Border Crime Forum was established the following September, with the explicit purpose of encouraging the law enforcement agencies of both countries to work more effectively on such transnational crime issues as cybercrime, missing children, money laundering, smuggling, and telemarketing fraud. The forum was also responsible for two particular initiatives that would be further enhanced after 9/11: the first integrated border enforcement team (IBET) and binational threat assessments. Each of these owed its origins to new U.S. legislation—which in turn was set in train by new worries about illegal immigration into the United States and its perceived connections to recent terrorist incidents.

Though the Mexican border was clearly of much greater concern, Canada was not immune. Testimony of the INS Counterterrorism Coordinator in February 1998 labeled Canada as now being an important "alternative gateway" for illegal immigration. Apparently, in 1996, illegal immigrants from some 118 countries had attempted to enter the United States from Canada.[10]

KEY CHARACTERISTICS OF THE NEW "SMART BORDER" ENVIRONMENT

Prior to 2001, both countries tended to have a shared vision of border priorities—one in which border management should not impede but enhance the single-most important trading relationship in the world. But as we have seen, the agreements of the 1990s suggest that illegal immigration—and the terrorism that it was seen to portend—was having an impact on U.S. priorities. The events of September 11 dramatically emphasized this shift. As Paul Cellucci, the former U.S. Ambassador to Canada, so often reminded audiences, the world had changed dramatically. The new era was one for the United States. and those who wished to do business with her in which "security trumped trade."[11]

On December 12, 2001, the United States and Canada signed the Smart Border Accord, then covering some 30 items (now expanded to 32).[12] Together these clearly attempted to ensure that the primary interests of both parties—trade and security—were assured. It had four key elements: the secure flow of people; the secure flow of goods; secure infrastructure; and the coordination and information sharing in the enforcement of these objectives.

Most items had intelligence or surveillance implications. Over the next few years they would change the once linear border to one that was multidimensional and multifaceted. The border now had to be considered not only in terms of what went visibly through it but in a variety of other ways as well. Prior warning of those coming to the United States by passenger airplane was now required. In addition, efforts were made under this requirement to include passengers on planes that flew over the United States but did not land there. The transfer of data electronically from Canada to the United States via the Internet or other means was also seen to have civil liberty repercussions.[13] The clearest example of this occurred when it was found that the British Columbia government had contracted with an American company to handle its provincial health records, the confidentiality of which had long been a matter of some sensitivity to Canadians. It was believed that under the *USA PATRIOT Act* the U.S. government could force the company to release the records to U.S. investigating agencies. The August 2003 blackout that affected both the northeastern United States and parts of Ontario and Quebec indicated the interconnectivity of the critical infrastructure that traversed the border, particularly those that supplied energy and communications.[14] Similarly, the fact that diseases affecting animals, plants, and humans recogniz no borders was brought home by the 2003 SARS outbreak in British Columbia and Ontario, the outbreak of "mad cow" disease in Alberta, and the advance of both West Nile disease northward and westward and the Mountain Pine Beetle in the opposite direction. The recent discovery of a tunnel underneath the border between British Columbia and Washington State for the specific purpose of transferring illicit drugs focused attention on the subterranean dimension of the border as well.[15] To these must be added a whole variety of tracking systems that further monitor people and goods.

Borders were also extended outwards beyond the shores of North America by a variety of measures. Systems for both preclearing and tracking cargo containers bound for North America were established and developed. So too were systems for preclearing individuals at source to ensure that those traveling to North America had authentic, machine readable documentation (eventually with biometric identifiers). Carriers were made liable for those who tried to enter the United States without such documentation. In addition, both Canada and the United States required other forms of information about those traveling by air to North America so that they could be checked against a variety of watch lists.

Thinking about the border also changed in terms of timing. Instead of conceptualizing it in terms of merely the present, Canada has started to look further towards the future. Global warming means that the Canadian government now has to concern itself more with the condition of the Arctic icecap. The rate at which it is currently melting will likely mean that the Northwest Passage will soon be open to ships traveling from either the eastern seaboard of North America or Europe to Asia for longer periods of time.[16] In addition to taking steps to ensure its sovereignty over its northern borders, Canada has to ensure that the environment is properly protected. Environmental concerns are at issue along the Alaska-Yukon borders, where the U.S. government now appears to ready to drill for oil in wildlife refuges, thus putting in jeopardy not only the Porcupine Caribou herd that routinely cross the border to reach their mating grounds but the local native peoples that rely on these animals for part of their food supply.[17] Another way in which the cross-border environment has potentially been threatened concerns water transfer. While there have long been legal agreements in place to address problems arising over cross-border water flows, the decision of North Dakota's government to release water from the landlocked Devils Lake into the Sheyenne River, and hence to the Red River, has raised particular concerns over increased pollution and the possible introduction of foreign plant life and fish species into the province of Manitoba.

SOME THEORETICAL CONSIDERATIONS

Some commentators have suggested that Canada has two options when responding to U.S. concerns regarding international terrorism in the post-9/11 world. One is a "weak state" approach, where it presumes the threat to be primarily a U.S. matter in which it tries to placate U.S. concerns with a minimum of effort, while at the same time protecting Canadian sovereignty and avoiding North American defense commitments. The other is a "strong state" strategy in which Canada takes—with or without U.S. involvement—three key steps. The first involves adopting a strategy for countering international terrorism based on the perception that its own citizens are threatened. The second concerns maintaining the best possible relationship with the United States. because it is in Canada's national interest to do so. The third centers on the need to ensure that its borders are secure and that its laws relating to them are aggressively enforced.

Such an assessment of the Canadian options lacks both subtlety and nuance. Furthermore, it gives short shrift to the comprehensiveness of the real problems at hand, especially if it is accepted that Canada is one of the few countries that has the luxury of responding in either way. Perhaps this is why Dr. Condoleezza Rice, the former U.S. National Security Advisor and current Secretary of State, is reported to have advised Ambassador Cellucci that she believes America's relationship with Canada to be one of the most complex it has.[18] Recent actions of the Martin government would suggest that this view is also shared north of the border.

THE DIVERGENCE AND CONVERGENCE OF VALUES

Commentators who believe that Canada should adopt a strong state strategy do so, it seems, without either challenging the notion that Canadian interests and values are the same as those of the United States or realizing the potential irony of the strategy incorporating a paternalistic element—particularly in seeing the same threat qualitatively and quantitatively and hence responding in an organizationally similar fashion.

Until recently, it was generally accepted that Canadian values and those of Americans were converging. This perhaps explains the difficulty which Canadians have allegedly had in defining themselves. In his new book

Fire and Ice: The United States, Canada and the Myth of Converging Values, one of Canada's leading pollsters Michael Adams set out to find:

> Why an initially 'conservative' society like Canada has ended up producing an autonomous, inner directed, flexible, tolerant, socially liberal and spiritually eclectic people while an initially 'liberal' society like the United States has ended up producing people who are, relatively speaking, materialistic, outer-directed, intolerant, socially conservative and deferential to traditional institutional authority. Why do these societies seem to prove the law of unintended consequences?[19]

The book thus poses a direct challenge to the converging values thesis. Based on a series of in-depth interview surveys conducted by his company between 1992 and 2002, the author suggests that Canadians and Americans are now clearly diverging across a broad range of values. This is particularly noticeable regarding immigration. And in the most recent survey, which was conducted after 9/11 but before the Iraq invasion, a majority of Canadians (52 percent) wanted to see Canada less like its neighbor. Only 12 percent wanted to see greater convergence.[20] In one respect, however, Canadians have become more like Americans. In another recent survey, this time on behavioral attributes of people in different countries, the perception that Canadians were a deferential lot was delivered a savage blow. Apparently, in this regard they have become similar to Americans in being insistent.[21]

These differences in values are reflected in the way citizens of both countries see the world and in how they believe their respective countries should respond to it. Consider for a moment some of the following issues.

- The Land Mine Treaty
- International Criminal Court
- The Kyoto Accord on global warming
- Human Security
- Ballistic Missile Defense
- The sale of low-cost prescription drugs over the Internet
- Universal health care
- Responsibility to protect
- Multilateralism/unilateralism
- The role of the United Nations
- The role and size of the Security Council
- Safe injection sites and the "war" on illicit drugs
- The Geneva Convention
- The practice of "rendition"
- The use of torture by agents of the state

- Softwood lumber
- Regime change
- Gay rights and same-sex marriage
- Capital punishment
- The right to bare arms, gun control, and homicide rates

All of these constitute issues on which there is a broad divergence of views across the border. Disagreements on these issues are evidenced by public opinion polls, national policies, and in some cases even legal statutes. Clearly, Americans and Canadians do not see eye-to-eye on a number of important issues of global concern.

RELATIONAL *SINE QUA NONS*

For the U.S.-Canada border relationship to be a highly positive one, it will be necessary not only to agree both on those elements that are crucial—the *sine qua nons* if you will—to the relationship, as well as those on which there is room for a difference of views. Arguably, it is in Canada's interest to ensure that at least four things happen on the security side of the ledger. First, the illegal infiltration of goods and people through the Canadian back door into the United States must be prevented. Second, shared critical infrastructure must be adequately protected and made resilient. Third, Canada's intelligence community should as a matter of priority share with its U.S. counterparts—in a timely and full manner— any information that might prevent an attack on the U.S. heartland. And finally, Canada should take the necessary steps to prevent the possible spread of infectious diseases across the border.

Thus, it is essential that the new Border Service Agency, the Royal Canadian Mounted Police (RCMP) and integrated enforcement teams, Canada's intelligence community, and its public health system are all adequately financed with the appropriate resources. It may *not*, however, be in Canada's interest to participate in foreign wars—such as that in Iraq —or to participate in military actions that do not have multilateral support. To do so may not only prove to be counterproductive but may bring Canada into the line of fire unnecessarily.[22] Nor may it be in Canada's interest to beef up its military to help pursue American interests abroad before it has first adequately improved its domestic operational capacity, its capacity to protect its own sovereignty, especially in the Arctic, and its readiness for peacekeeping and disaster-relief missions. As Mark Tamthai has so aptly argued in the case of Thailand, "the enemy of my friend is not necessarily my enemy."[23] Significantly, Canadians in a recent survey strongly agreed with the general tenor of this proposition, wanting to see greater use made of soft power options across the world's trouble spots.[24]

DIFFERENT APPROACHES TO SIMILAR PROBLEMS

There are several important differences in the way Canadians approach the post-9/11 environment. Two, however, perhaps offer more useful insights than others.

Department of Homeland Security (DHS) Versus Public Safety and Emergency Preparedness Canada (PSEPC)

The formation of the Department of Homeland Security in the United States was in direct response to the events of September 11, 2001. It constituted the biggest reorganization of American government since that which took place immediately following the Second World War. The primary concern of the DHS is to thwart terrorist attacks within the continental United States and to ensure that the country is resilient to this type of threat. Though other man-made and natural hazards are considered by the department, the response to the devastation caused by Hurricane Katrina clearly suggests that they are currently of secondary importance. While much has been made of the work of the new U.S. threat assessment centers, these should not be perceived as truly "all-threats"-oriented but rather as centers primarily concerned with bringing together all available intelligence on the terrorist threat for evaluation.

Given such a mandate and the magnitude of the reorganization involved, one might have expected the new organization to have been focused either around an existing organization with intelligence expertise in this field—the Federal Bureau of Investigation, for example—or to have had a new domestic intelligence organization grafted on to it specifically for the new remit. Neither has been the case.

In Canada, the creation of the Ministry of Public Safety and Emergency Preparedness—which also constituted one of the most significant reorganizations of Canadian government in modern times—needs to be seen in a more evolutionary context, one that attempted to fix a number of outstanding problems which had long been identified by both internal and external critics. Hitherto, the Ministry of the Solicitor General, as it was then known, had traditionally been perceived as a junior portfolio within the federal cabinet hierarchy. It was generally perceived as a "bad news" portfolio that few with high political aspirations wanted to—or did—stay in for long. The structure of the ministry was unusual in Canadian government, in having a small departmental staff—primarily concerned with policy and research—with four very powerful agencies over which those in the department itself had little effective control. Consequently, senior bureaucrats also looked on such departmental responsibilities with disfavor.

An earlier attempt at reorganization by the last Progressive Conservative government in the early 1990s was short-lived. Though eminently sensible in bureaucratic terms, it was quickly dispensed with by the new Liberal government because it was perceived to focus on the negative dimensions of immigration. Thus, it was thought to offend a key liberal constituency—newcomers to Canada—and hence its long-standing policy of multiculturalism. The events of September 11, 2001, however, provided an opportunity for the Liberals to revisit the policy and to fix the inherent problems. Not the least of these was finding a better home for the Office of Critical Infrastructure and Emergency Preparedness, which had demonstrated that it was culturally adrift within the Department of National Defense, and amalgamating the various organizations that worked the border into a new Border Services Agency.

The creation of the new portfolio has many things for which to be commended, as does the administration that orchestrated it. Four, however, deserve special mention. First, its minister was also the Deputy Prime Minister. This gave the ministry a significantly different status within Canadian government. Second, she was made both the tzar of intelligence and security. In this regard, her ministerial responsibility extended beyond the ministry to leadership of a special cabinet committee, to its and other secretariats within the Privy Council Office—the key central agency of government—and to intelligence agencies within the Department of National Defence. Third, PSEPC was focused around the two agencies that have most to do with collecting intelligence and analyzing threats to the security of Canada and leading the charge against all forms of terrorism—the Canadian Security Intelligence Service (CSIS) and the RCMP. Finally, there is some reason to believe that the PSEPC's efforts to adopt an all-hazards approach to threat assessments offers more than mere lip service. Nevertheless, it is not yet fully clear whether the current approach, focused as it is around the Integrated Threat Assessment Centre, has limitations. At issue is whether its work encompasses more than mere threats to the security of Canada, i.e., national security threats and those that might be thought to constitute emergencies, to cover those of a more endemic nature.

The Nature of the Terrorist Threat

Canada has responded comprehensively to the security threat the United States perceives to its heartland—and at no small cost, it must be noted! In particular, it has introduced new antiterrorism legislation, beefed up its security and intelligence apparatus, reorganized its governmental structures, and sent its military to Afghanistan. Still more developments are promised.

However, Canada decided not to participate in the American-led invasion of Iraq, ostensibly to "fight terror," much to America's chagrin (if we are to believe Ambassador Cellucci). What does this portend and how might one explain the different response north of the border, especially given that the Canadian government was not very publicly forthcoming about its reasons? At the most obvious level, Canadian public opinion was very much against Canadian participation in the invasion of Iraq.[25] One suspects that most Canadians would have countenanced participation only once an invasion had been sanctioned by the United Nations and bolstered by a resolution. So in this sense the Canadian government might be said to have merely followed the public's lead.

Nevertheless, there may be other explanations. One notion that has been floated is that Canada's intelligence community did not find the American assessment of Iraq's weapons of mass destruction sufficiently compelling.[26] This is not to imply that the Canadian intelligence community had better or different intelligence. It is unlikely that it did. Rather it is to suggest that the evidence provided by its traditional intelligence partners was not of sufficient quantity or quality either to draw the conclusion that the Iraqi government was covertly developing weapons of mass destruction or that the threat from such weapons was of imminent importance requiring an immediate response.

Another concerns the linkage between what was initially called the "war on terrorism" and the broader "war on terror." The first was used initially in the context of Afghanistan. It related solely to the hunting down of those terrorists who were clearly responsible for the attacks of September 11, 2001. By contrast, the term "war on terror" has been used to cover the broader rubric of both the hunt for Bin Laden and the overthrow of Saddam Hussein. This linguistic distinction may not initially appear to be important if you assume the Jihadi movement should be considered as being all of a piece. Looked at in this light—we might call it the "al Qaeda as a network or franchise" thesis—one might well assume that the "war on terror" is reflective of Americans perceiving it as a full-blown "strategic threat" to the United States and its western allies. However, if there is little or no linkage between the various Jihadist movements, one should see the problem as being only a "national security problem" that needs a detailed and sustained response. Thus, to attempt regime change in Iraq before dealing fully with events in Afghanistan and the broader hunt for Bin Laden and his supporters looks strategically like taking one's eyes off the ball and even being counterproductive. Certainly, it would be so if, rather than linkage, there was in fact cleavage within the Jihadi movement. This is in fact the argument that Fawaz Gerges—building on the work of Gilles Kepel—has put forward so compellingly in his recent book, *The Far Enemy: Why Jihad went Global.*[27]

CONCLUSION

Canada and the United States have been the closest of allies and friends for generations. Yet, in little more than a decade, Canadian appreciation of both the United States as a country and particularly its Administration has dramatically eroded.[28] In 1981, when Ronald Reagan was U.S. President, a mere 7 percent of Canadians had an unfavorable impression of the United States. A recent poll put this number at 48 percent. In 2004, only 15 percent of Canadians would have voted to reelect President George W. Bush had they had the opportunity. He is, therefore, the most unpopular U.S. President for Canadians since before Confederation—a time when Americans were actually shooting at their neighbors to the north during the War of 1812.

There is also substantial opposition among Canadians to specific U.S. policies. Three examples are particularly poignant. A poll conducted for the Strategic Counsel of Canada in September 2005 reported that 76 percent of Canadians did not believe their government had sufficiently pressed the U.S. Administration over softwood lumber. Other polling has confirmed that over 80 percent of Canadians supported Prime Minister Chrétien's decision not to participate in the Iraq invasion. And on the question of a ballistic missile defense system for North America, nearly 60 percent of Canadians opposed the idea. Significantly, Canadians also want their government to be more insistent, adopting a firmer stand with the United States. Some 70 percent of Canadians want their government to get along with their neighbors but to hold the line where they disagree. A further 19 percent insist that their government should actively oppose the U.S. government where policies are at odds.

These data should sound a warning bell throughout North America. On the one hand, the United States is much more reliant now for its own domestic security on its friends and neighbors than perhaps it ever was. Knowing that Canada can be trusted to do everything possible to prevent it being a "haven for terrorists" and an entry point for attacks on the United States. will be crucial. Though the current Canadian Government has taken considerable steps to ensure that Canada is not a viable back door for terrorists and other undesirables, such policies cannot and should not be taken for granted. On the other side of the ledger, the *quid pro quo* for Canadians is continued open access to the U.S. market both for its exports and imports. The Smart Border Accord fully embodies and underscores these very principles. What needs attention and requires other forms of dialogue are the numerous other issues that detract from the quintessential components of the relationship. An important principle seems currently to be missing, the fact that close friends should be able to disagree—even strongly at times—and yet be given a full hearing.

NOTES

1. Government of Canada, "The Canada-U.S. Trade and Investment Partnership," http://www.dfait-maeci.gc.ca/can-am/washington/trade_and_investment/trade_partnership-en.asp (accessed March 14, 2006).

2. See Louis Fournier, *F.L.Q.: The Anatomy of an Underground Movement* (Toronto: NC Press Limited, 1984).

3. For the history of the October Crisis, see Ron Haggart and Aubrey E. Golden, *Rumors of War* (Toronto: New Press, 1971).

4. Lysiane Gagnon, "Separatism: Don't Write it Off Yet," *Globe and Mail*, October 3, 2005, A15.

5. That is not to say Canadians do not think about being taken over by the United States. The Centre for Research and Information on Canada has polled questions on independence on several occasions. About two-thirds of Canadians are confident that they will remain independent. Nor does it mean that its external borders have not been of major concern from time to time. In 1969, the supertanker *S.S. Manhattan* successfully navigated the Northwest Passage. While it proved that the Canadian Arctic was commercially feasible as a marine route for transporting oil to east coast refineries, it simultaneously raised sovereignty issues. These were not resolved until 1988 when the two countries agreed that U.S. icebreakers could cross Arctic waters after approval by Canada on a case-by-case basis. In the early 1990s cigarette and gun smuggling through aboriginal reserves that straddled the border between New York State and Ontario was problematic. See John Thompson, "Sin-Tax Failure: The Market in Contraband Tobacco and Public Safety," Mackenzie Institute Occasional Paper (Toronto, 1994).

6. MIT professor Harvey M. Sapolsky began a full-length opinion page article, "A Nuisance Neighbor," *National Post*, July 27, 2005, by suggesting that "Canada (was) a security threat to the United States" and went on to argue that it was on "a Lilliputian quest to bind American power."

7. For a broader discussion of "tipping points," see Malcolm Gladwell, *The Tipping Point: How Little Things Can Make a Big Difference* (Boston: Little Brown, 2002).

8. See Fen-Osler Hampson and Maureen Appel Molot, eds., *Canada Among Nations 2000: Vanishing Borders* (Toronto: Oxford University Press, 2000).

9. Christopher Sands, "Fading Power or Rising Power: 11 September and Lessons from the Section 110 Experience," in *Canada Among Nations: A Fading Power*, ed. Norman Hillmer and Maureen Appel Molot (Toronto: Oxford University Press, 2002), 49-73.

10. Ibid., 58.

11. See especially, Paul Cellucci, *Unquiet Diplomacy* (Toronto: Key Porter Books, 2005), chap. 7.

12. For the details of the Accord, see Government of Canada, "32-Point Action Plan," http://www.dfait.gc.ca/can-am/main/border/32_point_action-en.asp (accessed March 14, 2006).

13. Jim Bronskill, "Cross-Border Data Worries Canadians," *National Post*, June 20, 2005.

14. Clifford Krauss, "Blackout Shows Canada-U.S. Links in Security Vulnerability," *New York Times*, August 26, 2003.

15. Terrie Theodore, "Cross-Border Tunnel Called 'Quite a Venture'," *Toronto Star,* July 22, 2005.

16. Clifford Krauss, Steven Lee Myers, Andrew C. Revkin, and Simon Romero, "As Polar Ice Turns to Water, Dreams of Treasure Abound," *New York Times,* October 10, 2005.

17. Tim Harper, "Diplomat Scoffs at Arctic Oil Spat," *Toronto Star,* November 5, 2005.

18. Cellucci, *Unquiet Diplomacy,* 229-30.

19. Michael Adams, *Fire and Ice: The United States, Canada and the Myth of Converging Values,* (Toronto: Penguin, 2003), 10.

20. Ibid., 3.

21. Bill Taylor, "We Aren't Who We Like to Think We Are," *Toronto Star,* October 8, 2005.

22. In an unusually frank interview, the Director of CSIS, James Judd, expressed concern that Canadians who had traveled to Iraq to oppose the anti-American insurgency would likely someday come home with newly acquired terrorist skills. When asked by reporters whether President Bush might have opened Pandora's box, he replied, "Diplomacy is not my field. Security intelligence is. And from a security intelligence perspective, the conflict in Iraq may be creating longer-term problems, not just for Iraq but for other jurisdictions as well." He also noted that despite the fact that Canada did not join the U.S.-led coalition, CSIS would let the Americans know if any Canadians bent on trouble were headed to Iraq. "To the extent we do know about it, we would want to tell our allies." See Jeff Sallot, "War Could Spawn Terrorists, CSIS Chief Says," *Globe and Mail,* October 21, 2005.

23. Keynote address delivered at "A Global Assessment of Terrorism: Perspectives from Current and Future Leaders on Policy, Doctrine and Operational Implication," University of Central Florida, November 1–3, 2005.

24. Michael Den Tandt, "Canadians Losing Faith in Aid Policy, Poll Shows," *Globe and Mail,* October 11, 2005.

25. Alan Thompson,"Canadians Balk at Iraq War," *Toronto Star,* September 9, 2002.

26. For example, see Stewart Bell, "Foreign Affairs Rejected Report on Iraqi WMDs," *National Post,* May 7, 2003; and Jeff Sallot, "Proposed Iraq Briefing Had Canada Skeptical," *Globe and Mail,* March 12, 2004.

27. Fawaz A. Gerges, *The Far Enemy: Why Jihad Went Global* (Cambridge: Cambridge University Press, 2005). See also Anthony Bubalo and Greg Fealy, "Between the Global and the Local: Islamism, the Middle East, and Indonesia," *The Brookings Institution Analysis Paper* 9 (October 2005) and Gilles Kepel, *The War for Muslim Minds: Islam and the West* (Cambridge: Harvard University Press, 2005).

28. The polling data are drawn from Michael Adams, "Bash Thy Neighbour," *Globe and Mail,* October 19, 2005.

CHAPTER 4

INTERNATIONAL MIGRATION AND HOMELAND SECURITY: COORDINATION AND COLLABORATION IN NORTH AMERICA

Christopher Rudolph

> There is probably no more important tool for preventing attacks on U.S. soil than the nation's immigration system because the current terrorist threat comes almost exclusively from terrorists who arrive from abroad.[1]
> —Steven Camarota, Center for Immigration Studies

> In many ways, the age of unilateralism in border controls may be over.[2]
> —Demetrios G. Papademetriou, Migration Policy Institute

MIGRATION AND HOMELAND SECURITY: THE "NEW" THREAT

The events of September 11, 2001, reintroduced a term to the American lexicon not widely heard since the "red scare" of 1950s McCarthyism: homeland security. Moreover, the fact that the 9/11 terrorists manipulated U.S. immigration laws in order to infiltrate the country and to carry out their attack on U.S. soil made the link between global terrorism and international migration explicitly clear.[3] In terms of the migration-terrorism link, the key questions facing policy makers are, "How did we get so vulnerable?" and "What can we do to protect ourselves from global terrorism?"

Increasingly, policy makers, pundits, and the general public recognize that migration is an international phenomenon, one that both facilitates processes of globalization and interdependence, and is also affected by them.[4] Although immigration and border control have long been central to our notions of sovereignty,[5] dynamics of contemporary international migration suggest that it is difficult, if not impossible, to achieve complete control over flows unilaterally.[6] Prior to 9/11, scholarly discussions regarding the need for a multilateral regime focused on addressing the need to *facilitate* the movement of people across borders in order to achieve economic gains.[7] Although dialogue regarding migration regimes has been most rigorous in the European Union (EU), strong interests exist among North American countries to craft policy in the EU mold. For the United States and Canada, the information technology revolution created significant demand for highly skilled labor, and certain sectors of the economy have shown a "structural embeddedness" of demand for unskilled foreign labor as well.[8] For Mexico (and other developing countries), emigration not only offers a safety valve for unemployment pressures, but also represents a significant source of needed foreign exchange—some $14 billion annually.[9]

With the emergence of the homeland security linkage and the threat of global terrorism, discourse regarding the need for cooperation and coordination has again sustained momentum.[10] Given the clear tension between strong economic interests for policy openness and strong security interests favoring closure, we have seen policy makers increasingly argue that the only solution is to craft "smart borders"—borders that have an unprecedented ability to filter out terrorists, criminals, and other undesirables while enabling cross-border flows to remain relatively unhindered. Tom Ridge, then-Secretary of Homeland Security, made this point clear in a 2002 speech: "We're working with Canada and Mexico to institute smart borders that will keep terrorists out, while letting the flow of commerce in."[11]

Given the traditional view of immigration and border patrol as belonging exclusively in the realm of domestic public policy, such pronouncements represent not only a radical departure from traditional views about immigration, but also call into question the nature of sovereignty and the role of borders in international society. Significant advances in information technology certainly provide us with the tools necessary to facilitate a "smarter" border,[12] but having an increased *ability* to cooperate does not necessarily mean that states *will* cooperate. This chapter thus addresses three primary questions: (1) Where is cooperation and/or coordination likely; (2) what challenges do we face in facilitating such endeavors? and (3) What are the prospects for a regional migration control regime—a North American security perimeter?

This chapter argues that the process of regime formation (or failure to enact a formal regime) in terms of a North American perimeter will involve the interaction of power-based, interest-based, *and* idea-based variables rather than begin dominated by a single causal variable. Mexican president Vicente Fox and his administration have often spoken of a desire for a comprehensive agreement on migration—indeed, Fox has repeatedly said that this was the cornerstone of Mexican foreign policy.[13] For Mexican policy makers the objective was not an incremental or piecemeal approach, but rather (in their words), "the whole enchilada." However, when examining the interaction of the three primary variables identified here, my analysis suggests that such a "grand bargain" seems rather unlikely. Instead, we are more likely to see any regime formation take the form of bilateral rather than multilateral agreements, and these agreements will likely produce increased coordination (shallow integration and retention of policy sovereignty) rather than collaboration (deeper integration, harmonization of immigration, and refugee policy).[14]

International Cooperation in North America

Recognition of regional—if not global—interdependence concerning international migration has pressed policy makers to shift political discourse from one solely rooted in a domestic perspective to one that moves beyond national borders. This does not necessarily mean that policy makers see management issues from a regional interest, but rather, that regional cooperation is necessary in order to achieve national interests. In an address to the Senate Judiciary Committee on March 4, 2003, John Ashcroft explained that "close working relationships with international allies" would allow the United States to "leverage our anti-terrorism efforts throughout the world."[15] Ashcroft's remarks suggest that, for American policy makers, international cooperation is seen as an extension of U.S. interests and strategy. This strategy to "leverage" U.S. efforts through international cooperation has initially taken two primary forms: the Smart Border Declaration with Canada and the U.S.-Mexico Border Partnership Action Plan.

U.S.-Canada Smart Border Action Plan

Bilateral cooperation between the United States and Canada has a long tradition, and has been described as "the most extensive bilateral relationship in the world."[16] In 2003, Tom Ridge explained the desire for intergovernmental cooperation as an issue of common interests. He stated, "By working together we can better reach our common goals of ensuring the security and prosperity of our citizens."[17] Yet, when we examine the parameters of the existing bilateral measures taken concerning migration and border control, it appears that "common interests" have not generated movement toward a formal regime. Rather, the extension of egoistic self-interest (i.e., "leveraging" domestic efforts) is the driving force behind the increased cooperation that we have seen, especially since 9/11.

From the American viewpoint, cooperation with Canada is deemed increasingly important for U.S. security. Concerns about terrorist activity and infiltration from the north rose with the apprehension of Ahmed Ressam in December 1999, and these were later bolstered by a 2003 report which suggested that some 50 terrorist groups were present and active in Canada at that time.[18] Moreover, there is a considerably widespread belief that Canadian immigration and border policies are somewhat lax, especially those concerning refugees and asylum.[19] From the Canadian standpoint, although the 9/11 attacks in the United States increased the salience of counterterrorism as a policy imperative (from the standpoint of self-interest), expressed interests continued to focus on building a more open border. Inability to increase security along the border and allay U.S. concerns would no doubt put this goal in jeopardy. The tremendous backups at key points along the border in the days following 9/11 made this perfectly clear.

With mutual interest in increased cooperation, Canadian Deputy Prime Minister John Manley and (then) Governor Tom Ridge signed the Smart Border Declaration on December 12, 2001. The declaration was accompanied by a 30-point action plan based on four pillars: (1) the secure flow of people, (2) the secure flow of goods, (3) secure infrastructure, and (4) information sharing and coordination in the enforcement of these objectives. Table 4.1 summarizes elements of the 30-point action plan most relevant to pillars 1, 3, and 4 of the Smart Border Declaration. What becomes quickly evident, even with only a cursory examination of the language used within the document, is that the Smart Border Declaration advances integration of border management more so in terms of coordination rather than collaboration. Indeed, according to a 2003 progress report of the action plan, there has been considerable progress made in the area of coordination.

In terms of bilateral cooperation and the creation of "smarter" borders, several examples are particularly noteworthy. The U.S.-Canada NEXUS program represents a model example in terms of migration control. NEXUS is intended to concurrently facilitate migration flows while maintaining protocols to increase security. The program enlists the cooperation of several agencies on both sides of the border, including the U.S. Bureau of Immigration and Customs Enforcement (ICE), the Canadian Customs and Revenue Agency (CCRA), and Citizenship and Immigration Canada (CIC). NEXUS is intended to facilitate the flow of "low risk" travelers who are prescreened and must be approved by officials in both Canada and the United States.[20] The number of designated lanes for NEXUS participants has been continually expanding, beginning with one site in June 2000 (Port Huron-Sarnia) and expanding to 15 by the fall of 2003.[21]

The expansion of the Integrated Border Enforcement Teams (IBETs) also suggests progress in bilateral cooperation in border control between the

Table 4.1   Degree of Harmonization with Selected Elements of the U.S.-Canada Smart Border Action Plan

Area	Description	Coordination or Collaboration?
Biometrics	Establish common standards for biometrics	Coordination
Single Alternative Inspection System	Expedited inspection lanes for frequent travelers	Coordination
Refugee and Asylum Processing	Share information regarding refugee/asylum applicants	Coordination
Refugee and Asylum Policy	Establish "safe third country" policy	Collaboration
Visa Policy Coordination	Increase cooperation in visa processing by sharing intelligence information	Coordination
Air Preclearance	Expand air preclearance procedures	Coordination
Advance Passenger Information	Provide passenger name records for travelers	Coordination
Joint Passenger Analysis Units	Cooperate on identifying potentially high-risk travelers	Coordination
Immigration Officers Overseas	Allow deployment of immigration officers between countries	Coordination
Integrated Border Enforcement Teams	Shared training and increased cooperation among border security and law enforcement agencies	Coordination
Integrated Intelligence	Establish Integrated National Security Enforcement Teams on a case-by-case basis	Coordination
Fingerprint Information Sharing	Implement electronic system for exchange of fingerprint and criminal records information	Coordination

Source: Canadian Embassy (Washington, D.C.), October 3, 2003.

United States and Canada. Initially established in 1996 along the border in the western region of Washington state to combat drug smuggling and illegal immigration, IBETs have now been expanded across the entire U.S.-Canada border. IBETs establish coordination between numerous agencies, including ICE, the Bureau of Customs and Border Protection, the FBI, the Bureau of Alcohol, Tobacco and Firearms, the U.S. Secret Service, the Royal Canadian Mounted Police (RCMP), the CCRA, and numerous local law enforcement agencies on both sides of the border. These are then managed by a Joint Management Team comprised of senior officials drawn from participating agencies that facilitate intelligence sharing and conduct joint operations for border security. Such cooperation, especially in terms of intelligence, increases control capacities for both Canadian and American agencies. Roy Hoffman, head of the ICE office in Blaine, Washington, suggested that, "Sharing information with our Canadian counterparts allowed both sides to better determine where our efforts had to be centered and gave all of us a better chance of success."[22]

Such improvements in bilateral coordination have been touted as evidence that security can be established and smart borders can be created at the same time. In the one-year progress report, John Manley argued that, "The speed with which we have been able to expand programs like NEXUS, FAST and our Integrated Border Enforcement Teams demonstrates our commitment to making the smart border a reality."[23] As shown in Table 4.1, however, the level of integration in terms of the smart border remains relatively shallow, with little effort made to formally link or harmonize policy. That said, there is some progress in terms of collaboration in the areas of visa issuance and refugee/asylum policy. Informal convergence is evident in the area of visa issuance. The United States and Canada now share common visa policies with 175 countries, though they still differ with respects to 18 other countries.[24]

Refugee and asylum policy also reflects increased collaboration, although there seems to be a considerable difference in attitudes between Canadian and American policy makers. At issue is whether or not Canada is "soft" on refugees and asylees, and both the ideational and political obstacles to policy change in this area to conform to American desires for increased security. American policy makers need not rely solely on their own suspicions. Skepticism has also been raised by critics north of the border. For example, a Fraser Institute study suggested that, "Canada's refugee-determination system and migration-control policies are out of step with what appears to be a clear convergence of policies and practices in the developed world."[25] Joe Bissett, former executive director of the Canadian Immigration Service, seconded this opinion: "We have the most generous refugee system in the world. Much too generous."[26]

Although harmonization of asylum policy is listed under the 30-point action plan, a closer look at the issue warrants pessimism as to the probability of increased collaboration. In terms of current policy, several dimensions of the Canadian system make it disproportionately open relative to other advanced industrial states. These include high rates of approvals, a generous social welfare system, infrequent prosecutions, and lax deportation procedures. In 2002, the refugee recognition rate (for in-country determinations) in Canada was nearly double the U.S. rate, while the per capita acceptance rate of refugees from 2000–2002 (in-country Convention refugee recognitions) was four times the American rate.[27]

Moreover, authorities detain few refugees and asylees while their claims are pending adjudication, even though Canadian law permits detention of those applicants who might represent a possible security threat or flight risk.[28] In fact, generally only 5 percent of refugees entering Canada are detained, while the remaining 95 percent are released until their immigration hearing is held.[29] Also, in Canada there are few barriers to claimants working and accessing social entitlement programs while their claims are pending. In contrast, the 1996 *Illegal Immigration Reform and Immigrant Responsibility Act* added to existing restrictions on access to social welfare for applicants while their case is being adjudicated by requiring that employment authorization not be authorized for a period of *at least* six months. Because "first instance" determination of asylum status must be processed within 180 days according to U.S. law, employment opportunities are reserved only for those who warrant an affirmative determination of their case.[30] As well as detaining claimants pending review of their case, the United States also has an "expedited removal" system in place that facilitates detention and removal of individuals apprehended who do not have proper immigration or travel documents. In addition, out-of-status foreigners in the country for more than one year are barred from applying for asylum and are subject to deportation if apprehended.[31]

In contrast to its American usage, the use of the term "expedited" in the Canadian sense has been to "speed positive claims toward recognition."[32] Failure to detain applicants pending what is often a lengthy judicial review process is coupled with a de facto policy of failing to deport those who either fail to appear at their hearing or are denied refugee status. One analyst noted, "Not only does Canada permit anyone who arrives to make an asylum claim, but many of those eventually denied refugee status are never removed from the country. Only about 9,000 people are removed from Canada each year, and of these, approximately two-third[s] are failed asylum seekers."[33] According to the Auditor-General's 2003 report, Canadian authorities have lost track of 36,000 foreigners that were supposed to be deported over the past six years.[34]

Canada's refugee and asylum policies have resulted in trends that are disconcerting to some security-minded American policy makers. Certainly, Canada's stance vis-à-vis asylum and refugees make it a first choice for those seeking protection, as well as for those seeking admission that failed through other channels.[35] Unfortunately, this also creates conditions conducive for the infiltration of foreign terrorists. The Canadian Security Intelligence Service (CSIS) has confirmed the presence of some 50 active terrorist organizations operating in Canada, ranging in scope from the Irish Republican Army to Hezbollah, Hamas, and al Qaeda.[36] Moreover, Hani Al-Sayegh, Gazi Ibrahim Abu Mezer, Nabil Al-Murabh, and Ahmed Ressam (all known terrorists) gained access to Canada by seeking political asylum upon entry.[37] Canadian officials were recently outraged when a report issued by the Federal Research Division of the Library of Congress listed Canada among the nations that are "hospitable to organized crime and terrorism."[38] The authors quoted a senior CSIS official who argued that, "in most cases, [terrorists] appear to use Canadian residence as a safe haven, a means to raise funds, to plan or support overseas activities or as a way to obtain Canadian travel documents which make global travel easier."[39] From a U.S. security point of view, this represents a potential threat to American security as terrorists can exploit Canadian policy and then use their Canadian base as a potential staging ground for terrorist attacks.

In the European Union, policy makers have sought to increase security through integration and policy harmonization, including "fast track" processing to dismiss "patently unfounded" asylum claims and applying "safe third country" and "safe country of origin" principles in asylum processing to reduce the practice of "asylum shopping." Indeed, in the case of Germany, EU harmonization provided a rationale for a significant tightening of asylum policy, one that had been the most liberal in post-WWII Europe and had been protected by the German Basic Law.[40] Applying this strategy in North America has proven to be politically challenging, even given the strong bilateral relationship between Canada and the United States.

Canadian concerns for protecting the human rights of bona fide refugees and asylum seekers fleeing persecution made them weary to apply strict limitations on "safe third country" entrants. For example, a Canadian refugee bill that included a "safe third country" provision was tabled in Parliament in 1987. After heated debate and considerable political opposition, the bill finally was approved in July 1988. However, when the new law came into effect, government officials were unable to establish a list of "safe countries." Moreover, the Cabinet did not consider the United States to be a "safe country" for Salvadorans and Guatemalans that fled Central America in the 1980s. Ultimately, the Minister of Immigration announced that, "at the present time I am prepared to proceed with no country on the safe third country list."[41] New legislation passed after 9/11 has yet to change Canada's concerns about the practice of safe third country principles in asylum processing. The *Immigration and Refugee Protection Act*, passed in November 2001, actually increases restrictions on applying the "safe third country" principle in the practical processing of asylum claims. A report released in December 2003 points out that, "Article 102(2)(a) of the IRPA requires the government to 'consider' whether a 'responsibility-sharing' agreement exists between Canada and the transit country before a refugee claim can be considered 'ineligible' for determination in Canada."[42] In contrast to American legislation passed after 9/11 that stresses security interests (e.g., the *USA PATRIOT Act*, the *Enhanced Border Security and Visa Entry/Exit Reform Act*), the title of the 2001 legislation touts Canada's commitment to refugee protection with no reference to security. Moreover, policy makers have made their discomfort at policy harmonization quite clear. In October 2001, Immigration Minister Elinor Caplan suggested that U.S.-Canada discussions concerning a security perimeter focus on information sharing rather than harmonization: "Let there not be any misunderstanding. Canadian laws will be made right here in the Canadian Parliament."[43]

On the American side, there appears to be less incentive for a bilateral third country agreement with Canada, since the flow of asylum seekers generally flows toward Canada from the United States. Rather, a U.S. State Department official suggested that the "safe third country" agreement is something that "…Canada wants and that we are willing to agree to as a trade-off for other important counter-terrorism measures."[44] Reluctance for deeper integration and harmonization in this area is also evidenced in practice. For example, U.S. treatment of the case of Maher Arar suggests wariness with Canada's commitment to the war on terrorism and may also hint at a reluctance to turn over individuals that appear on U.S. antiterrorist watch lists. U.S. immigration officials at Kennedy Airport detained Arar, a naturalized Canadian citizen born in Syria, on September 26, 2002, when he was suspected of having ties to al Qaeda. Rather than deporting him to Canada, American authorities unilaterally decided to send Arar to Syria, without consulting Canadian authorities.[45] A recent report by the Center for Strategic and International Studies suggests that, "By refusing to send [Arar] to Canada, the U.S. government appears to have believed Canada would let Arar walk free, or at a minimum fail to gain any information from him."[46]

The political inertia involved may explain the lag in implementing the safe third country agreement. The agreement was signed on December 5, 2002, but was not implemented until December 29, 2004. Under the terms of the agreement, refugee claimants are required to submit their claim in the first country they enter—either the United States or Canada.[47] In addition to being limited in scope (including only Canada and the United States), other limitations were included. An exception exists for refugee claimants attempting to enter Canada from the United States if they have family in Canada or if they are an unaccompanied minor. In addition, the agreement applies only to land border crossings. It does not include claims processed at airports or in the country's interior.

The safe third country agreement is a significant development in border management and definitely suggests that increased collaboration between the United States and Canada is possible. However, there are many obstacles facing the creation of a more expansive North American security perimeter regime. For Canadians, immigration and border policy preferences are based on (1) maximizing the economic gains from migration, (2) upholding Canada's liberal humanitarian tradition, including protection for refugees and for those fleeing persecution requiring asylum, (3) facilitating the social integration of new immigrants, and (4) border control as a component of homeland security.[48] Liberal, open policies have strong domestic lobbies in Canada that have been instrumental in shaping both immigration and asylum policies. Moreover, consistent with the liberal state hypothesis forwarded by James Hollifield and other migration scholars,[49] the human rights and immigration law lobbies have successfully institutionalized protections for migrants within the judiciary (as well as the Immigration and Refugee Board) that constrain policy makers from enacting restrictionist policies. A Fraser Institute report argues that "…any effort to harmonize policies with other developed countries to address the challenge of illegal immigration…will evoke strong criticism from refugee advocacy and human rights groups as it has in all other developed countries."[50] Indeed, defense of Canadian liberal identity is also evidenced in its preference for the term "zone of confidence" rather than "security perimeter" when discussing bilateral cooperation.[51] Additionally, protection of Canada's approach to immigration reflects its distinctiveness and sovereignty. John Manley made this expression of a defense of Canadian sovereignty explicit: "Working closely with the United States does not mean turning over to them the key to Canadian sovereignty."[52]

The Americans also have an economic-based interest in relatively liberal border policies. On this point, there is commonality between American and Canadian interests. However, the emphasis the Bush administration has placed on security and the war on terrorism warrant that economic interests cannot be forwarded at the expense of security. It is here that interests diverge. The Americans see coordination as a necessary means to increase security. From the U.S. standpoint, maximizing the capacity to screen entrants is not only a homeland security imperative, but a prerequisite for maintaining a relatively open stance regarding migration— both permanent and temporary. Coordination and collaboration would seem to forward this aim. However, like their Canadian counterparts, U.S. policy makers are also keenly defensive of their sovereignty in the issue of migration, making policy integration politically difficult. Echoing the sentiments of Canadian policy makers, President Bush remarked, "You pass your laws, we'll pass our laws."[53] Christopher Sands of the Center for Strategic and International Studies argues, "It is not at all clear that the United States has abandoned its preference for managing the border unilaterally since September 11. Indeed, in the absence of any clear Canadian initiatives or counterproposals for improving border security and fighting terrorism in North America, the bilateral cooperation since September 11 is impossible to distinguish from a combination of U.S. unilateralism and Canadian acquiescence to the U.S. agenda."[54]

Clearly, when we differentiate between coordination and collaboration, bilateral cooperation between Canada and the United States is centered primarily on the former rather than the latter. The smart border plan artic-ulates several areas to cultivate increased coordination but few regarding policy harmonization or integration—in other words, few constraints are placed on independent policy decision making. Howard Adelman notes that, "Immigration and refugee policy has not been harmonized between Canada and the United States. Nor are there any indications that they will be."[55] The fact that the driving force behind such a regime is one that is more in line with a common aversion (terrorist alien infiltration) than a common interest (preference for a single common outcome), and is influ-enced by ideas regarding the goals and structures of such a regime, all would suggest that deeper integration remains unlikely in the foreseeable future. Yet, we might also note that, given the fact that immigration and border control has long been considered a purely domestic interest, recent developments can be considered a significant step in the direction of deeper collaboration. As practices involving coordination foster the development of new norms, it is possible that concerns about sovereignty and ideas regarding appropriate policy may become less of a barrier to regime formation, at least on a bilateral basis between Canada and the United States.

The U.S.-Mexico Border Partnership Action Plan

The border between the United States and Mexico is an active one. Levels of trade have continued to grow since the creation of the North American Free Trade Agreement (NAFTA), and Mexico is now the second largest trading partner with the United States. Migration flows, both offi-cial and undocumented, have grown as well. The San Ysidro port of entry remains one of the world's busiest land border crossing points in the world, including both transborder workers and tourists. Evidence sug-gests that illegal immigration flows have increased as well. Border Patrol statistics show that the number of illegal immigrants apprehended along the southwest border increased from 979,101 in 1994 (fiscal year) to 1,159,802 in FY 2004.[56] These numbers reached a peak of over 1,600,000 in FY 2000 before the economic downturn in 2001–2002 reduced the economic incentives for migrants. The difficulty of managing an exten-sive land border between two countries with such disproportionate economies and wages has prompted some analysts to suggest that a grow-ing gap exists between control policies and policy effects on migra-tion flows.[57]

The southern border has been a security concern for American policy makers since the President's Commission on Migratory Labor issued a warning in 1951 about an emerging "wetback invasion."[58] This perception of threat has continued since then, evidenced by public statements regarding "regaining control" of our "neglected border" in the 1970s and

1980s and regarding the "alien invasion" in the 1990s. For the most part, however, the nature of the perceived security threat was not linked to a military dimension, but rather to a combination of security's economic and societal dimensions.[59] Concern over securing the southern border has dominated U.S. policy making over the past 30 years, with a disproportionate amount of resources and manpower allocated to achieve this goal.[60] The events of 9/11 have only served to strengthen support for this approach and have increased demands for more rigid controls of migration flows between the United States and Mexico.

The Mexican perspective of the border—and migration in general—sharply contrasts the American view. For Mexicans, migration is a fundamental way of life and is considered a basic human right. This right of free movement is codified in the Mexican constitution, but public opinion shows attitudes toward open migration that don't stop at the nation's borders. A 2002 Zogby poll found that 57 percent of Mexican respondents agreed with the statement, "Mexicans should have the right to enter the United States without U.S. permission."[61] In addition to ideational aspects, material interests also favor open migration policies. For a country that continues a sometimes rocky road to advanced industrialization, international migration offers an important safety valve to stem unemployment pressures in the Mexican economy.[62] Moreover, the increasing volume of currency remittances from emigrants working abroad—now estimated to amount to at least $14 billion annually—offers a significant inflow of foreign exchange necessary to increase the country's balance of payments position. For Mexico, it is estimated that remittances represent the third largest source of hard currency for the economy.[63]

It is little wonder then, that Vicente Fox has consistently placed the issue of international migration at the top of high foreign policy priorities. Indeed, the Mexican government views the issue of migration as at least as important as the issue of trade, and considers both integral facets of any North American integration regime.[64] Among the leaders of North American countries, Fox has been the most forceful in pushing for a deepening of regional integration following the European model.[65] His vision for a deepening of NAFTA integration is based on facilitating the free flow of people, in addition to goods and capital.

Initially, the election of George W. Bush seemed to bode well for a new round of negotiations regarding immigration. During the election, Bush sought to build his foreign policy base on the positive relationship he had established with Fox when he was governor of Texas. Politically, the divisive anti-immigration rhetoric that proved volatile in the United States during the 1990s was quelled by a combination of the economic boom and the highly visible border defenses that had been established at key points along the border.[66] After a February 2001 meeting between Fox and Bush, the U.S-Mexico High Level Working Group on Migration was established and a subsequent meeting between the leaders was held on September 5, 2001 to further this agenda.[67]

The political effects of September 11 clearly affected the momentum of the migration talks and U.S.-Mexican relations more generally. As noted by Peter Andreas, "Fox's border-free vision of North America was one of the first casualties of the devastating terrorist attacks...."[68] Bilateral talks regarding migration were immediately and indefinitely tabled as the United States focused on the issue of homeland security and the emerging war on terrorism. Fox soon complained that the United States had become too focused on the issue of security and that the U.S.-Mexican relationship was suffering because of it.[69] Jorge Castañeda, the Mexican Foreign Minister, suggested that, "In many ways, the region, at least in terms of U.S. attention, has become once again an Atlantis, a lost continent."[70]

From the American perspective, the newly acknowledged link between migration control and terrorism cast the southern border in a new light. What had been largely a political problem prior to 9/11 had now become a key issue for strategic security. A Library of Congress report suggested that, "Because of its close proximity to the United States, its porous borders, its strategically significant oil industry, and a large U.S. commercial and tourism presence, Mexico may serve as a transit or target environment for a foreign terrorist operation."[71] The issue of porous borders is particularly sensitive to U.S. security interests. Traditionally, Mexico has served as a transit point for economic migrants coming from Central and South American countries. This, however, poses a risk that terrorists and their organizations may exploit the same openness. Describing the border situation, Mexican Congressman Emilio Zebadua said, "The Mexican government is either unable or unwilling to really take this southern border as a major priority." He added, "They have pretty much left it as an open border."[72]

Prior to September 11, the U.S. government pressured the Fox Administration to address the security by suggesting that increased security is a necessary condition for talks concerning a bilateral migration accord. The result was the Plan Sur ("South Plan") that was aimed at apprehending and repatriating illegal aliens crossing Mexico's southern border. The events of 9/11 increased U.S. support for the program and prompted material support. The U.S. government supplied boats to the Mexican navy to patrol the southern shore, and also provided needed capital to pay for the repatriation program. In 2002, the program repatriated 120,000 immigrants to their home countries, and another 141,000 were returned in 2003.[73] Though such measures have increased security on the border somewhat, it is far from "secure." A representative of the UNHCR suggested that control remained elusive: "Controlling this border is impossible. And it's not only a question of will. It's a question of geography, corruption, violence, and the well-organized nature of the trafficking."[74]

The issue of government corruption not only plagues security along the southern border, but also in terms of access into Mexico and the United States more generally. Moreover, events immediately following 9/11 suggested that this could contribute to infiltration by terrorists, who would then attempt to cross the border into the United States. In October 2001, an Iraqi-born migrant smuggler confessed to establishing a working relationship with a corrupt Mexican immigration officer in order to smuggle over 1,000 migrants from the Middle East into the United States. A Heritage Foundation report argues, "Despite direct intervention by President Fox to end bribery on the U.S.-Mexican border, customs and immigration services are weak elsewhere and plagued by corruption."[75]

Mexico has long been sensitive to U.S. policy makers referring to illegal immigration as a security threat. Ironically, though, security has paved the way for a renewal of talks on a bilateral accord dealing with migration. Although from a normative standpoint framing migration in a security context is anathema to Mexican sensibilities, it provides a "more politically palatable rationale for Mexico to cooperate on immigration control."[76] The key issue is where the "security" focus is placed. For Mexicans, immigration control is not problematic so long as it is not directed primarily at them but rather, other foreign nationals who may use the country as a transit point to gain entry into the United States. Moreover, using a security rationale has also given Mexican diplomats another tool to use to garner U.S. support for two of its primary foreign policy goals: (1) amnesty for the current population of undocumented workers living in the United States, and (2) a legal alternative to undocumented access to the American economy. Mexican policy makers are careful in how they define the security interests involved.

Interior Minister Santiago Creel remarked, "The Mexican migratory flow represents no risk whatsoever, even less if it is documented."[77] Careful to emphasize that Mexican migrants do not represent a potential terrorist threat, Creel argued that, "Migrant regularization would provide the United States with a greater margin of security than the one it currently has."[78]

American desires to leverage its homeland security program by garnering assistance from its neighbors, combined with the emerging desire of Mexican officials to leverage cooperation in return for renewed talks concerning migration, led to the U.S.-Mexico Smart Border Agreement, announced in March 2002. The agreement put forward a 22-point action plan that outlined the specific areas for increased coordination and harmonization in three categories, including the secure flow of people, goods, and infrastructure.[79] Table 4.2 lists the elements of the 22-point action plan specifically addressed to the issue of bilateral

Table 4.2   Degree of Harmonization with Selected Elements of the U.S.-Mexico Smart Border Action Plan

Area	Description	Coordination or Collaboration?
Precleared Travelers	Expand the use of SENTRI lanes at high-volume ports of entry	Coordination
Advanced Passenger Information	Establish a joint API system for U.S.-Mexico flights	Coordination
FacilitatingTravel Within NAFTA Countries	Explore methods to facilitate the movement of NAFTA travelers	Coordination
Safe Borders	Increase safety along the border for migrants; reduce migrant smuggling	Coordination
Visa Policy	Continue consultations on visa policies and visa screening procedures; share intelligence information	Coordination
Joint Training	Conduct joint training in the areas of investigation and document analysis	Coordination
Compatible Databases	Develop systems for exchanging and sharing intelligence	Coordination
Screening Third-Country Nationals	Enhance cooperative efforts to detect, screen, and deal with potentially dangerous third-country nationals	Coordination

Source: The White House, September 9, 2002.

cooperation in the category of international migration. As is the case with the smart border agreement between the United States and Canada, the action plan is intended to identify areas where increased cooperation can be mutually beneficial and to establish a framework for future development.

When examining the U.S.-Mexico agreement and action plan in detail, two features are readily apparent. First, as is the case with the U.S.-Canada agreement, the emphasis is exclusively on increasing *coordination* rather than *collaboration* or *harmonization*. Second, the verbiage in many of the items in the action plan is vague, especially when compared to the verbiage used in the U.S.-Canada plan.[80] Where the word "harmonization" is used, it refers to the standardization of infrastructure, such as compatible databases, or to synchronizing operations at ports of entry.[81] It makes no attempt to suggest that migration *policies* would be harmonized. Where policy issues are identified, such as visa policy, "harmonization" is intended to refer to establishing "enhanced cooperation" in screening third country nationals by facilitating information sharing. Along many of the areas specified in the agreement, particularly those dealing with migration, participants are bound only to "explore methods" or "continue consultations"—suggesting both an extremely limited degree of integration and a palpable uncertainty about the prospects for such integration in the future. The agreement clearly emphasizes those dimensions of border issues where there is a high degree of common interest, including facilitating trade flows, facilitating the movement of "low risk" travelers, and protecting human rights. In 2003, Tom Ridge and Interior Minister Santiago Creel pointed to several developments as evidence of "tremendous progress" over the previous year, including the expansion of the SENTRI program, the Border Safety Program (to reduce deaths of migrants trying to cross the border), and FAST lanes at ports of entry.[82]

Security issues receive much less emphasis and/or specificity. The limited gains achieved through the U.S.-Mexican accord were highlighted in other statements by Ridge and Creel. In February 2004, Ridge and Creel touted two developments as evidence of progress in bilateral cooperation: (1) a tentative agreement that affirms U.S. policy to deport illegal immigrants to their home regions, not just across the border, and (2) the establishment of a secure telephone line between Ridge and Creel.[83] There has also been progress in terms of the Advanced Passenger Information System, as well as expressed desires to implement the NEXUS program as has been done between the United States and Canada.

Regarding security, the most significant development in terms of the possibility for an integrated U.S.-Mexican approach for migration control is the change in the tenor of the discussions. By reframing their arguments in terms that emphasize security benefits gained through "safe, orderly, and secure" migration, Mexican policy makers have helped to restart discussions that were essentially dead in the water after 9/11. Santiago Creel points out that, "Without a doubt, security is an area that has allowed us to draw closer."[84] Mexican authorities hope that giving security a favorable ear will provide the necessary political leverage to pressure U.S. lawmakers to pass an amnesty bill through Congress and establish a new guest worker program for Mexican laborers. However, it is not likely that we will see this new dialogue or the Smart Border Declaration produce a comprehensive, integrated approach to migration control in the near future, even on a limited bilateral basis. U.S. policy makers face considerable obstacles to fulfilling Mexican desires for such a comprehensive plan, especially the issue of amnesty—a politically unpopular policy for a vast majority of the American public. Instead, the Americans have shown a preference for a much more limited type of cooperation. Roger Noriega, the U.S. Assistant Secretary of State for Western Hemispheric affairs, clarified the U.S. position:

I think (small steps) will allow us to continue to consult with and gauge the interest from our Congress. But decisions on [a comprehensive U.S.-Mexican migration accord] have to come from the very top, and at this point we're not in position to go forward on the bigger agenda, the broader, more comprehensive approach.[85]

Colin Powell, who suggested that a migration accord is "going to take us a lot more time and a lot more effort," echoed this sentiment. He added that immigration involves "extremely complex and difficult issues" that involve a lot of "political interests."[86]

THE ROAD AHEAD

Policy makers in each of the NAFTA member states have expressed a desire for some form of multilateral action concerning migration control. Americans have put forward the notion of a "security perimeter," Canadians have referred to the establishment of a "zone of confidence," and the Mexicans have suggested that only a comprehensive approach is acceptable—"It's the whole enchilada or nothing."[87] The empirical evidence presented here suggests, however, that the unequal distribution of power among NAFTA states, disparate interests, and ideational factors make the establishment of a comprehensive, harmonized regime governing migration and border policy in North America highly unlikely. Peter Andreas suggests that North American adoption of a deeply integrated strategy similar to that used in the EU "would require a level of formal institutionalization and policy harmonization that is difficult to imagine in the present context."[88]

Reflecting disparate interests, policy makers in each state have a different notion of what a "North American security perimeter" would consist of. The Americans stress increasing security through screening, while the Mexicans have always favored an EU-style "open borders" regime. The Canadians fall somewhere in between. Each has an interest in increasing protection against terrorism, but for markedly different reasons. Clearly, given its power and the leadership role it has assumed in the global "war on terrorism," the American government is most acutely threatened by the proliferation of international terrorism and has placed the most emphasis on security regarding migration and border policy. The Canadian and Mexican governments appear more concerned that terrorists targeting the United States may use their countries in transit to their target and that such terrorist actions would deteriorate bilateral relations. This, in turn, would complicate their desire for more open borders. However, neither Canada nor Mexico seems ready (or able, in the Mexican case) to acquiesce to U.S. security interests, nor are their interests necessarily convergent. Moreover, each remains committed to sovereignty over policy decisions, as is the United States.

Power, interest, and ideational variables identified by regime theorists all suggest that a formal comprehensive North American migration regime is unlikely. This is certainly supported by the available empirical evidence of current developments and expressed interests. NAFTA has always forwarded a process of *shallow* rather than *deep* integration, as is the case with the European Union, and has been focused primarily on the issue of trade liberalization. With the exception of the Fox Administration in Mexico, there has been little support for deepening North American integration. Rather, political support has been directed toward expanding the *scope* of existing integration to include countries in Central and South America—the creation of a Free Trade Area of the Americas. Although the post-9/11 security dilemma may have heightened interests for increased integration that would include migration control, there is little to suggest that this "dilemma of common aversion" will result in a comprehensive, formal regime. Instead, the "security perimeter"—at least regarding migration—will likely consist of myriad points of *bilateral* rather than *multilateral* coordination, and will also maintain state sovereignty with regard to migration policy.

Given these political realities, what are the available options? Where do we go from here? At this point it is not at all clear that we actually *need* a comprehensive, formal, and multilateral regime. Indeed, following Arthur Stein's model, the expression of interests among North American policy makers suggests that the issue of border management is one of a dilemma of common aversion rather than common interest—at least in this early post-9/11 period. Because unity of interest is centered on avoiding a particular outcome, we are most likely to see a continuation of the somewhat fragmented approach taken to date. A U.S. State Department official recently suggested that, "a piece-by-piece approach represents the best strategy for achieving a migration pact that's vital to both the United States security and its economy."[89] Instead of a multilateral security perimeter regime, the short-term focus needs to be placed on establishing a working security system and increasing ad hoc coordination among NAFTA countries.

Increased openness is in the economic interests of each NAFTA member country, yet American policy makers have made it clear that such openness cannot be achieved at the expense of homeland security. Because homeland security issues are now a necessary condition to forward liberalization, policy makers must focus on those elements most crucial to any security regime. These include gathering and organizing intelligence, creating effective infrastructure to disseminate this information, and ensuring that access to this system is secure and controlled. At this point, American efforts in this regard remain very much a work in progress. The creation of the Terrorist Threat Integration Center (now the National Counterterrorism Center or NCTC) represents a tremendous first step in building a better intelligence base, and the new Terrorist Screening Center (TSC) offers potential for expedited access to this information that is crucial if security is to be increased without creating backlogs at consulates abroad or ports of entry. It is important to include Canadian and Mexican officials in terror assessment and to promote the establishment of similar security infrastructure in those countries so that intelligence information can be effectively shared among them. Key issues that need to be addressed include: (1) what information will be made available to foreign security officials, (2) what process will be used to vet foreign officials for access to the American intelligence system, and (3) how security can be maintained in terms of access to the system. Multilateral consultations must also address the logistical demands that such international cooperation may make on the computer systems that process such information. If the United States makes TSC information available to Canadian and Mexican immigration officials, what effect will this have on the computer hardware system? Are current facilities adequate to process information requests?

Including Canadian and Mexican officials in threat assessment and providing access to antiterrorist intelligence also provides an incentive for their governments to improve screening procedures for those entering their countries. Increasing the probability that potential terrorists can be effectively identified prior to entry, or detained if they have already entered the country, is in everyone's best interests. What will be imperative, then, is making sure that access to this information is facilitated. Clearly, much work needs to be done regarding the role of information technology in providing access to intelligence information and facilitating screening processes. Promoting "harmonization" among NAFTA countries regarding information infrastructure and controlled access to this system will likely form the basis of movement toward a North American security perimeter in the short run. Once these necessary security conditions are in place, talks on regime formation can once again focus on the common interest: facilitating cross-border movement in North America to promote economic gains.

ACKNOWLEDGMENTS

Research for this chapter was made possible by a Canadian Studies grant from the Canadian Embassy, Washington, D.C.

NOTES

1. Steven A. Camarota, "The Open Door: How Militant Islamic Terrorists Entered and Remained in the United States, 1993–2001," *Center Paper 21* (Washington, DC: Center for Immigration Studies, 2002), 13.

2. Demetrios G. Papademetriou, "A Grand Bargain: Balancing National Security, Economic, and Immigration Interests of the U.S. and Mexico," typescript, Migration Policy Institute, Washington, DC, April 2002, 7.

3. Steven A. Camarota, "The Open Door, 2002."

4. See Christopher Rudolph, "Globalization and Security: Migration and Evolving Conceptions of Security in Statecraft and Scholarship," *Security Studies* 13, no. 1 (Fall 2004); Douglas S. Massey et al., *Worlds in Motion* (Oxford: Clarendon Press, 1998); James Mittelman, *The Globalization Syndrome* (Princeton, NJ: Princeton University Press, 2000); Saskia Sassen, "Beyond Sovereignty: De-Facto Transnationalism in Immigration Policy," paper read at the annual meeting of the American Political Science Association, Atlanta, GA, September 1–5, 1999.

5. Christopher Rudolph, "Sovereignty and Territorial Borders in a Global Age," *International Studies Review* 7, no. 1 (2005): 1–20; John Torpey, "States and the Regulation of Migration in the Twentieth-Century North Atlantic World," in *The Wall Around the West*, ed. P. Andreas and T. Snyder (Lanham, MD: Rowman & Littlefield, 2000); Cheryl Shanks, *Immigration and the Politics of American Sovereignty, 1890–1990* (Ann Arbor, MI: University of Michigan Press, 2001); Aristide R. Zolberg, "Changing Sovereignty Games and International Migration," *Indiana Journal of Global Legal Studies* 2, no. 1 (1994).

6. Wayne A. Cornelius, Philip L. Martin, and James F. Hollifield, eds., *Controlling Immigration: A Global Perspective* (Stanford, CA: Stanford University Press, 1994).

7. Much of the argument centered on replacing increasingly unwanted illegal immigration by facilitating more legal migration. Cf. Bimal Ghosh, ed., *Managing Migration: Time for a New International Regime?* (Oxford: Oxford University Press, 2000); James F. Hollifield, "Migration, Trade, and the Nation-State: The Myth of Globalization," in *Reconsidering Immigration in an Integrating World*, ed. Christopher Rudolph, *UCLA Journal of Int'l Law & Foreign Affairs* 3, no. 2 (1998), special issue; Kathleen Newland and Demetrios G. Papademetriou, "Managing International Migration: Tracking the Emergence of a New International Regime," in *Reconsidering Immigration in an Integrating World*, ed. Christopher Rudolph, *UCLA Journal of Int'l Law & Foreign Affairs* 3, no. 2 (1998), special issue; Howard F. Chang, "Migration as International Trade: The Economic Benefits from the Liberalized Movement of Labor," in *Reconsidering Immigration in an Integrating World*, ed. Christopher Rudolph, *UCLA Journal of Int'l Law & Foreign Affairs* 3, no. 2 (1998), special issue.

8. Wayne A. Cornelius, Thomas J. Espenshade, and Idean Salehyan, eds., *The International Migration of the Highly Skilled* (La Jolla, CA: Center for Comparative Immigration Studies, 2001); Wayne A. Cornelius, *The Role of Immigrant Labor in the U.S. and Japanese Economies* (La Jolla, CA: Center for U.S.-Mexican Studies, 1998).

9. Philip L. Martin, "Trade, Aid, and Migration," *International Migration Review* 26, no. 1 (1992); Sharon Stanton Russell, "Migrant Remittances and Development," *International Migration* 30, no. 3–4 (1992); Peter Gammeltoft, "Remittances and Other Financial Flows to Developing Countries," *CDR Working Paper 02.11* (Copenhagen: Centre for Development Research, August 2002).

10. Cf. Demetrios G. Papademetriou, "A Grand Bargain: Balancing National Security, Economic, and Immigration Interests of the U.S. and Mexico," typescript, Migration Policy Institute, Washington, DC, April, 2002; Deborah Meyers, "Security at U.S. Borders: A Move Away from Unilateralism?," *Migration Information Source* (August 2003); Deborah Waller Meyers, "Does 'Smarter' Lead to Safer? An Assessment of the Border Accords with Canada and Mexico," *Insight* (June 2003).

11. Remarks to the U.S. Conference of Mayors, Washington, DC, January 23, 2002, cited in Deborah Waller Meyers, "Does 'Smarter' Lead to Safer?," *Insight* (June 2003): 1.

12. Rey Koslowski, "Information Technology, Migration and Border Control," paper read at the Institute for Governmental Studies, University of California, Berkeley, April 25, 2002.

13. Jorge Castañeda, "The Forgotten Relationship," *Foreign Affairs* 82, no. 3 (2003): 67–81.

14. See Arthur A. Stein, "Coordination and Collaboration: Regimes in an Anarchic World," in *International Regimes,* ed. Stephen D. Krasner (Ithaca, NY: Cornell University Press, 1983), 115–140.

15. John Ashcroft, "The War Against Terrorism: Working Together to Protect America," testimony presented before the Committee on the Judiciary, United States Senate, March 4, 2003, available online at http://www.globalsecurity.org/security/library/congress/2003_h/03-04-03_ashcroft.htm.

16. Stephen Johnson and Sara J. Fitzgerald, "The United States and Mexico: Partners in Reform," *Backgrounder,* no. 1715 (Washington, DC: The Heritage Foundation, December 2003).

17. Canadian Embassy (Washington, DC), "Governor Ridge and Deputy Prime Minister Manley Issue One-Year Status Report on the Smart Border Action Plan," Press Release, October 3, 2003.

18. "North of the Border," *CBS News,* September 7, 2003, http://www.cbsnews.com/stories/2003/09/04/60minutes/ printable571584.shtml (accessed February 18, 2004); LaVerle Berry et al., *Nations Hospitable to Organized Crime and Terrorism* (Washington, DC: Federal Research Division, Library of Congress, October 2003).

19. Stephen Gallagher, "Canada's Dysfunctional Refugee Determination System," *Public Policy Sources* 78 (December 2003).

20. The White House, "United States-Canada Nexus Program," Press Release, September 9, 2002, available at http://www.whitehouse.gov/news/releases/2002/09/print/20020909-1.html.

21. Canadian Embassy (Washington, DC), "Governor Ridge and Deputy Prime Minister Manley Issue One-Year Status Report on the Smart Border Action Plan," Press Release, October 3, 2003.

22. Quoted in Jerry Seper, "Cooperation at the Border Bolsters Law Enforcement," *The Washington Times,* January 5, 2004, A7.

23. Canadian Embassy (Washington, DC), "Governor Ridge and Deputy Prime Minister Manley Issue One-Year Status Report on the Smart Border Action Plan," Press Release, October 3, 2003.

24. *Migration News* (July 2005), http://migration.ucdavis.edu (accessed October 5, 2005).

25. Stephen Gallagher, "Canada's Dysfunctional Refugee Determination System," *Public Policy Sources* 78 (December 2003): 5.

26. Quoted in "North of the Border," *CBS News,* September 7, 2003, http://www.cbsnews.com/stories/2003/09/04/60minutes/printable571584.shtml.

27. United Nations High Commissioner for Refugees, *UNHCR Population Statistics* (Geneva: UNHCR, August 4, 2003), table 5, reprinted in Stephen Gallagher, "Canada's Dysfunctional Refugee Determination System," *Public Policy Sources* 78 (December 2003): 18–19.

28. Peter Rekai points to several causes for this failure to detain potential "high-risk" applicants. These include lack of proper intelligence necessary for identifying "high-risk" applicants, lack of adequate detention facilities, and humanitarian considerations. See Peter Rekai, "U.S. and Canadian Immigration Policies: Marching Together to Different Tunes," *C.D. Howe Institute Commentary* 171 (November 2002): 13.

29. "North of the Border," *CBS News,* September 7, 2003, http://www.cbsnews.com/stories/2003/09/04/60minutes/printable/571584.shtml; James Bissett, "Canada's Asylum System: A Threat to American Security?," *Backgrounder* (Washington, DC: Center for Immigration Studies, May 2002).

30. Stephen Gallagher, "Canada's Dysfunctional Refugee Determination System," *Public Policy Sources* 78 (December 2003): 11.

31. *Migration News* (April 2003).

32. Gallagher, 14.

33. James Bissett, "Canada's Asylum System: A Threat to American Security?," *Backgrounder* (Washington, DC: Center for Immigration Studies, May 2002), 5.

34. LaVerle Berry et al., *Nations Hospitable to Organized Crime and Terrorism* (Washington, DC: Federal Research Division, Library of Congress, October 2003), 147.

35. Gallagher, 9.

36. "North of the Border," *CBS News,* September 7, 2003, http://www.cbsnews.com/stories/2003/09/04/printable571584.shtml.

37. Al-Sayegh was suspected in the 1996 Khobar Towers bombing in Saudia Arabia; Abu Mezer was apprehended with plans to detonate a bomb on a New York City subway in 1997; Al-Murabh has been identified as a key operative of Osama bin Laden; and Ressam was arrested trying to enter the United States from Canada with 100 pounds of high explosives intended for detonation at Los Angeles International Airport on New Year's Eve, 1999. "North of the Border," *CBSNews.com,* September 7, 2003, http://www.cbsnews.com/stories/2003/09/04/60minutes/printable571584.shtml.

38. LaVerle Berry et al., *Nations Hospitable to Organized Crime and Terrorism* (Washington, DC: Federal Research Division, Library of Congress, October 2003).

39. Ibid., 146.

40. Christian Joppke, "Asylum and State Sovereignty: A Comparison of the United States, Germany, and Britain," *Comparative Political Studies* 30, no. 3 (June

1997): 259–298; Christian Joppke, *Immigration and the Nation-State* (Oxford: Oxford University Press, 1999).

41. Quoted in James Bissett, "Canada's Asylum System: A Threat to American Security?," *Backgrounder*(Washington, DC: Center for Immigration Studies, May 2002), 4.

42. Gallagher, 15.

43. Howard Adelman, "Governance, Globalization and Security: The Harmonization of Immigration Policy," paper presented at a conference on "Globalization, Multilevel Governance, and Democracy: Continental, Comparative and Global Perspectives," Queens University, Kingston, May 3–4, 2002.

44. United States House of Representatives, Hearing on the U.S. and Canada Safe Third Country Pact, Judiciary Committee, Subcommittee on Immigration, October 6, 2002; also Gallagher, 15.

45. Canadian Foreign Minister Bill Graham was notified three days after Arar's arrest that he had been deported to Syria.

46. Andre Belelieu, "Canada Alert: The Smart Border Process at Two: Losing Momentum?," *Hemisphere Focus* 11, no. 31 (Washington, DC: Center for Strategic and International Studies, December 10, 2003), 7.

47. Citizenship and Immigration Canada, "Fact Sheet: Safe Third Country Agreement," December 29, 2004.

48. Paul Henry, Trade Policy Analyst, Ecnomic Policy and Programs Division, Selection Branch, Citizenship and Immigration Canada (CIC), put this priorities schema forward.

49. Cf. James F. Hollifield, *Immigrants, Markets and States* (Cambridge, MA: Harvard University Press, 1986); David Jacobson, *Rights Across Borders: Immigration and the Decline of Citizenship* (Baltimore, MD: Johns Hopkins University Press, 1996); Yasemin Soysal, *The Limits of Citizenship* (Chicago: University of Chicago Press, 1994).

50. Gallagher, 31.

51. Peter Andreas, "A Tale of Two Borders: The U.S.-Mexico and U.S.-Canada Lines After 9-11," *Working Paper No. 77* (La Jolla, CA: Center for Comparative Immigration Studies, UCSD, May 2003), 12.

52. Quoted in Paul Wells, "We Don't Pull Our Own Weight: Manley," *National Post*, October 5, 2001, A6; also cited in Donald Barry, "Managing Canada-U.S. Relations in the Post-9/11 Era: Do We Need a Big Idea?," *Policy Paper on the Americas Vol. XIV, Study 11* (Washington, DC: Center for Strategic and International Studies, November 2003), 11.

53. Quoted in Steven Frank and Stephen Handelman, "Drawing a Line," *Time* (Canadian edition), October 8, 2001, 45; also cited in Donald Barry, "Managing Canada-U.S. Relations in the Post-9/11 Era: Do We Need a Big Idea?" *Policy Paper on the Americas Vol. XIV, Study 11* (Washington, DC: Center for Strategic and International Studies, November 2003), 11.

54. Christopher Sands, "Terrorism, Border Reform, and Canada-United States Relations: Learning the Lessons of Section 110," paper presented at the conference "Linkages Across the Border: The Great Lakes Economy," held at the Federal Reserve Bank of Chicago, Detroit Branch, April 4, 2002, 12.

55. Howard Adelman, "Governance, Globalization and Security: The Harmonization of Immigration Policy," paper presented at a conference on "Globalization, Multilevel Governance, and Democracy: Continental, Comparative and Global Perspectives," Queens University, Kingston, May 3–4, 2002, 24.

56. Wayne A. Cornelius, "Controlling 'Unwanted' Immigration: Lessons from the United States, 1993–2004," *Journal of Ethnic and Migration Studies* 31, no. 4 (July 2005).

57. Referred to as the "Gap Hypothesis." See Wayne A. Cornelius, Takeyuki Tsuda, Philip L. Martin, and James F. Hollifield, eds., *Controlling Immigration: A Global Perspective,* 2nd ed. (Stanford, CA: Stanford University Press, 2004).

58. President's Commission on Migratory Labor, *Migratory Labor in American Agriculture* (Washington, DC: U.S. Government Printing Office, 1951).

59. See Christopher Rudolph, "Security and the Political Economy of International Migration," *American Political Science Review* 97, no. 4 (2003). Most recently, a highly controversial article by Samuel Huntington again defined the southern border as a societal threat. See Samuel Huntington, "The Hispanic Challenge," *Foreign Policy* (March/April 2004).

60. Cf. Peter Andreas, *Border Games: Policing the U.S-Mexico Divide* (Ithaca, NY: Cornell University Press, 2000); Christopher Rudolph, *National Security and International Migration,* typescript, UCLA, 2004.

61. Cited in Jon Dougherty, "Mexicans: Southwest is Ours," *WorldNetDaily.-Com,* June 13, 2002, http://www.worldnetdaily.com/news/printer-friendly.asp?ARTICLE_ID=27941 (accessed February 18, 2004).

62. Kevin O'Rourke and Jeffrey Williamson, *Globalization and History: The Evolution of a Nineteenth Century Atlantic Economy* (Cambridge, MA: MIT Press, 1999).

63. Alonso Urrutia, "Remesas de migrantes equivalen a 83 percent de la inversion de EU en Mexico," *La Jornada,* October 30, 2000, A1.

64. Marc R. Rosenblum, "Moving Beyond the Policy of No Policy: Emigration from Mexico and Central America," *Latin American Politics and Society* 46, no. 4 (Winter 2004): 10.

65. Interview with Vicente Fox, *The News Hour with Jim Lehrer,* March 21, 2000, http://www.pbs.org/newshour/bb/latin_America/jan-june00/fox_3-21.html (accessed March 13, 2006).

66. Christopher Rudolph, "Security and the Political Economy of International Migration," *American Political Science Review* 97, no. 4 (2003).

67. The White House, "Joint Statement Between the United States of America and the United Mexican States," Press Release, September 6, 2001, available at http://www.whitehouse.gov/news/releases/2001/09/20010906-8.html.

68. Peter Andreas, "A Tale of Two Borders."

69. *Migration News* (October 2002).

70. Jorge Castañeda, "The Forgotten Relationship," *Foreign Affairs* (May/June 2003): 70.

71. LaVerle Berry et al., *Nations Hospitable to Organized Crime and Terrorism* (Washington, DC: Federal Research Division, Library of Congress, October 2003), 171.

72. Quoted in Hugh Dellios, "Mexico Struggles to Secure Its Southern Border," *AberdeenNews.Com,* March 4, 2004, http://www.aberdeennews.com.

73. Hugh Dellios, "Mexico Struggles to Secure Its Southern Border," *Aberdeen-News.Com*, March 4, 2004, http://www.aberdeennews.com (accessed March 5, 2004).

74. Ariel Riva, local director for the UNHCR, quoted in Hugh Dellios, "Mexico Struggles to Secure Its Southern Border," *AberdeenNews.Com,* March 4, 2004, http://www.aberdeennews.com (accessed March 5, 2004).

75. Stephen Johnson and Sara J. Fitzgerald, "The United States and Mexico: Partners in Reform," *Backgrounder,* no. 1715 (Washington, DC: The Heritage Foundation, December 2003).

76. Peter Andreas, "A Tale of Two Borders," 10.

77. Quoted in Justin Gest, "Mexican Official Touts Amnesty as a Security Booster for the U.S.," *Los Angeles Times,* July 11, 2003, A8.

78. Ibid.

79. Available online at http://www.whitehouse.gov/infocus/usmxborder/22points.html.

80. Deborah Waller Meyers, "Does 'Smarter' Lead to Safer?," 9.

81. In terms of synchronizing operations, the action plan specifies "harmonizing" hours of operation, infrastructure improvements, and traffic flow management at adjoining ports of entry on both sides of the border.

82. U.S. Embassy in Mexico City, "Prepared Remarks by Secretary Ridge at Press Availability with Secretary Creel on the Border Between the United States and Mexico," Press Release, April 24, 2003, available at http://www.usembassy-mexico.gov/releases/ep030424remarks_ridge.htm.

83. Ricardo Alsonso-Zaldivar, "War on Terrorism Draws U.S. and Mexico Closer," *Los Angeles Times,* February 29, 2004, A14.

84. Quoted in Ricardo Alsonso-Zaldivar, "War on Terrorism Draws U.S. and Mexico Closer," *Los Angeles Times,* February 29, 2004, A14.

85. Quoted in Alfredo Corchado, "Possibility of Migration Accord with Mexico Revisited," *The Dallas Morning News,* November 12, 2003.

86. Quoted in Eric Green, "Powell Says U.S. Wants Movement on Immigration Issues with Mexico," *Usinfo.State.Gov,* June 2, 2003, http://www.usinfo.state.gov/gi/Archive/2003/Jun/04-808468.html.

87. Jorge Castañeda quoted in Tom Zoellner, "Mexico Says Legalize Crossers or No Deal," *The Arizona Republic,* June 22, 2001.

88. Peter Andreas, "A Tale of Two Borders," 12.

89. Roger Noriega, Assistant Secretary of State for Western Hemispheric Affairs, paraphrased by Alfredo Corchado, "Possibility of Migration Accord with Mexico Revisited," *The Dallas Morning News,* November 12, 2003.

CHAPTER 5

SECURING THE WESTERN HEMISPHERE: LATIN AMERICA AND THE FIGHT AGAINST TERRORISM OF GLOBAL REACH

Farid Kahhat

> If September 11 puts an end to the Post-Cold War era, as most analysts seem to believe, does that mean too the end of the debate about the concepts and phenomena of the Post-Cold War era, like 'human security', to the extent that they were a consequence of the imprecision you would expect from an international system going through a 'transitional' phase?[1]
>
> —Khatchik Derghoukassian

In the post-9/11 security environment, combating terrorism has taken center stage in public debates and policy making, in many cases providing a new source of incentives for multinational cooperation. Over the past century, nation-states in the Western Hemisphere have increasingly recognized the importance of security cooperation, and considerable efforts have been seen in areas of combating drug trafficking, piracy, and money laundering. Since the 1990s, increasing trade cooperation and economic interdependence has further cemented the cross-national cooperation throughout North and South America. This chapter explores the theoretical and practical dimensions of Latin America's role in the global fight against terrorism and suggests some areas in which these efforts can be strengthened.

THEORETICAL BACKGROUND

The causes of conflict and cooperation between states have historically been the main focus of study of international relations as an academic discipline. Theoretical approaches usually differ with regard to the level on which the analysis is focused, either the internal structure of the state or the characteristics of the international system.[2]

The approach that focuses on the characteristics of the international system, generally associated with the concept of balance of power, is the distinctive contribution of the academic discipline of international relations to the study of the causes of conflict and cooperation between states. After World War II, the concept of balance of power was subsumed by the realist school, which, with the beginning of the Cold War, began to predominate in schools of thought about international relations.[3]

Even though realism is a theory of international relations that attempts to explain the causes of both conflict and cooperation between states, the theory's premises also lead to a particular approach to security studies within this discipline. According to this approach, the ultimate purpose of security policies is to ensure the survival of the state as an independent political unit (which implies, at the very least, maintaining control over a certain geographic area). Threats to the state's survival are generally perceived as external military threats, represented by the regular armies of other states. Thus, military means are the most adequate to neutralize those threats.

The emergence of a bipolar world, in which the threat of a nuclear war seemed at times a distinctive possibility, helps to explain the preeminence of realist thought in the aftermath of World War II. In turn, the fact that most realist authors did not foresee the end of the Cold War, and that it did not take place through any of the mechanisms they would have anticipated (i.e., a change of alliances or a major war), seemed to open up a space for alternative perspectives on security issues. The main contentions of these perspectives, in turn, could be summarized as follows: the ultimate goal of security policies is to guarantee a certain quality of life within the state, and not the state's mere political survival. Security threats are not necessarily external in nature, and if they are, they are not necessarily posed by other states, but rather by private transnational actors. These actors do not necessarily pose a military threat, nor do they jeopardize the territorial integrity of the state. Thus, the use of military means may not be the most effective response to these threats.

Although at first glance the attacks that occurred on September 11, 2001, seem to vindicate the realist approach to security issues, they could as well provide some support for those alternative perspectives. For example, the aggressor was not a state, the aggression was not, *in strictu sensu*, a military attack, nor did it lead to a war in the conventional sense of the word. Unlike a territorial war, it is not clear what it means to "win" a confrontation of this type; also, neither the battle fronts nor the identity of the warring parties is known for certain. Nor do the private and transnational nature of the threat or the permeability of boundaries between political violence and organized transnational crime fall within the traditional concept of security.

Precisely for reasons of this type, the issue of terrorism tended to be absent from debates over military strategy, as realism would foresee. Especially in Europe, the subject was essentially viewed as a crime problem to be fought through police forces, justice ministries, and domestic intelligence services.[4] When the issue transcended the bounds of crime, it generally entered into political calculations without being the subject of military strategy debates. When this occurred, one of two questions was usually asked: the first was whether the demands made by organizations that used terrorism as a tactic[5] could be processed by the political system at an acceptable cost (for instance, in Northern Ireland); the second was whether there was some set of public policies that could deprive such organizations of their social base of support.[6]

When the issue of terrorism arose in debates over military strategy in the United States, it gave rise to two different positions. The first held that it was neither possible nor desirable to design a comprehensive strategy against a phenomenon that did not constitute a monolithic threat. Because the organizations that engage in terrorism as a tactic have different motivations (i.e., social, ethnic-religious, or ideological), different scopes (i.e., regional, national, or international), and different political objectives (i.e., autonomic, separatist, or revolutionary), each must be addressed on its own terms.

The opposing view held that it was not only necessary to use military means to fight terrorism, but it would also be helpful to develop a comprehensive global plan for doing so. This position was based on three premises. First, even in cases where terrorist actions are limited to the local level and do not target U.S. citizens or interests, they tend to restrict the U.S. government's freedom of action in such diverse areas as drug trafficking, national security or energy policy.[7] Second, international terrorist actions are increasingly designed to cause the greatest possible number of victims. Third, the organizations that perpetrate these actions could be trying to obtain weapons of mass destruction, with which their ability to produce casualties would increase exponentially.[8]

Probably the most lasting effect of the terrorist attacks of September 11, 2001, has been to give this latter view a prominence that it would not have had otherwise. As Oliver Roy recalls,

> Most of the analysis done after September 11 starts from the premise that it was a foundational event in geostrategic terms, comparable to the demise of

the Soviet Union. Thus, the metaphor of 'war' was used for the first time to designate a terrorist act and the American response that followed . . . The real new terrorist threat, feared by analysts, was the privatization of weapons of mass destruction (WMD), that is, their use by non-state actors.[9]

This understanding of the new threat from mass casualty terrorism underscores an emerging debate over the role that Latin America can or should have in combating terrorist groups of global reach.

WHAT ROLE COULD LATIN AMERICA PLAY IN THE FIGHT AGAINST TERRORISM OF GLOBAL REACH?

Latin America has never been particularly important in terms of global balance of power calculations. In a book about the United States' policies towards Latin America, based on interviews with officials from the State Department, Lars Schoultz stated: "Give these officials the opportunity to choose between the continued physical presence of our neighboring republics to the south, on the one hand, and a vast ocean broken only by the ice packs of Antarctica, on the other, and the probability is quite high that they would select the latter option."[10] While his remarks about State Department officials' world outlook were published in 1987, some would argue that they still reflect a common perception in contemporary Washington, D.C.

The logic of the argument underlying that choice was quite simple. On the one hand, the containment of Communist expansion was one of the overarching principles guiding U.S. foreign policy during the Cold War, and "historically the Latin American policy of the United States has never been separated from the global distribution of power."[11] On the other hand, Latin America was of marginal significance in terms of global power rivalry. A key argument provided during the Cold War in support of that claim derives from Halford Mackinder's view, according to which, the "Eurasian land-mass" constitutes the "pivot area" of world politics. In his own words, "Who rules East Europe commands the Heartland: who rules the Heartland commands the world Island: Who rules the World Island commands the World."[12]

Not being located in the Eurasian landmass, the United States was able to play a key role in world politics because of its economic and military potential. Lacking such a potential, Latin America was always condemned to dance to someone else's tune on the world stage: "Left to its own devices, Latin America can go nowhere, being as it is a strategically isolated place. And if it starts to go somewhere under the guidance of a global power, like the U.S.S.R., then the United States will deal with that global power, and not with Latin America."[13] In another instance, two influential authors on the subject argued that South America's southern cone was "essentially removed" from global distribution of power considerations, given "its southern remoteness, its internal economic and political fragmentation, its lack of strategic location and natural resources, and its isolation behind the protected southern flank of the United States."[14] Therefore, the concept of "strategic denial" defined the primary thrust of U.S. policies towards the region. In the words of Lars Schoultz, "it is not that policy makers want much of anything from Latin America but rather that they do not want the Soviet Union to have it."[15] This is the reason why the only security alliance in the Western Hemisphere—the Inter-American Treaty of Reciprocal Assistance (IATRA, also known as the Rio Treaty)—was created in 1947 to address interstate conflicts within the region through nonmilitary means. It was only later that it became the regional counterpart of other U.S.-led security alliances (like NATO and CENTO), that were part of the containment strategy during the Cold War.

However, even as a mechanism to deal with interstate conflicts within the Western Hemisphere, the Rio Treaty was not particularly useful. For instance, it was not invoked during the only interstate armed conflicts within the region that took place in the last 25 years (between Peru and Ecuador in 1981 and 1995), and it was simply ignored by the United States during the only armed conflict between a state from this hemisphere and an extracontinental power (the Malvinas/Falkland Islands War of 1982). Nevertheless, when the terrorist attacks of September 11 occurred, IATRA provisions calling upon members to come to the aid of an ally under attack were invoked for the first time in the treaty's history.

Furthermore, the Organization of American States (OAS) had already created an Inter-American Committee Against Terrorism in November of 1998. Its intended purpose was to reunite the "relevant national authorities" on terrorism of the member states in order to define a common approach. However, it barely functioned before September 11, 2001. As the Web site of the Organization of American States notes, "The first round of sessions of the Committee took place in Miami, Florida on October 1999, and developed a working plan. A second round of sessions, due to take place in Bolivia in 2000, had to be cancelled at the last minute. No session was programmed for 2001."[16] The Committee launched a new round of sessions just a month after 9/11, and its agenda was formed precisely by the kinds of issues that the U.S. Department of State considered to be the potential goals of international terrorism within the Western Hemisphere—i.e., the search for sources of financing, recruits, and illegal personal documents (particularly passports).[17]

In June 2002, during its XXXII General Assembly, the Organization of American States adopted an Inter-American Convention Against

Terrorism. Its intended purpose is to "prevent, sanction and eliminate terrorism."[18] It then defines both internal and regional policies that member states have to adopt in order to fulfill that purpose. At an internal level, member states commit themselves to adopting and implementing existing international instruments for the fight against terrorism. Regarding regional policies, the convention deals with the same topics identified above regarding the Inter-American Committee Against Terrorism, but it also adds specific commitments concerning cooperation on judicial matters, like the denial of political asylum to those who might be suspected of belonging to a terrorist organization.

Thus, the Western Hemisphere now has the institutional means necessary to foster interstate cooperation on security-related issues, such as intelligence sharing, money laundering, port and airport security, and immigration controls. There are no reasons, however, to assume that anything would have been different if the Rio Treaty was not invoked after September 11, 2001. In fact, it is doubtful whether anything would have been different if those treaties, conventions, and organizations did not exist. First of all, because the assistance that Latin America could provide in a strategy against terrorism of global reach (i.e., against al Qaeda-related organizations) would still be of marginal relevance. On that regard, not much has changed since the end of the Cold War.

One exception to that rule would be the case of the border between the United States and Mexico, which extends more than 3,100 kilometers (2,000 miles), and is one of the most dynamic border areas in the world. That is the case not only because Mexico is the second biggest trade partner of the United States, but also because over a million illegal immigrants cross that border every year.[19] Security issues in this arena are dealt with on a strictly bilateral basis, so hemispheric-wide initiatives are typically not seen as having relevance here. However, it should be noted that illegal immigration and human trafficking have important hemispheric dimensions. In a July 2005 hearing before the U.S. House Appropriations Subcommittee on Homeland Security, Border Patrol Chief David Aguilar said his agency has apprehended 919,000 illegal immigrants in the first six months of the year—119,000 of them were classified as "other than Mexicans" (OTMs), and of these the majority were from other Latin American countries.[20]

Another possible exception to the common perception of Latin America's marginal role in a strategy against terrorism of global reach would be the emergence of what the U.S. State and/or Defense Department would consider to be a "rogue state." However, if such a state is thus defined not just by its ideological hostility towards U.S. values or interests, but also by its support to irregular armed groups beyond its borders, then there is no evidence of such a process taking place in the Western Hemisphere. The only feasible candidate, the Cuban regime, was successfully contained in the past, and is absorbed by its internal problems in the present. And although the Venezuelan regime might have links with Colombian guerrilla groups, it seems to be motivated primarily by an interest to prevent the spillover into Venezuela of the Colombian conflict.

On the other hand, the support that the Venezuelan regime provides to radical populist organizations like Evo Morales' "Movement Towards Socialism" in Bolivia could produce security externalities, but for reasons that have nothing to do with terrorism of global reach: if Bolivia ends up turning into a failed state, that would be worrisome because of the effects it could have beyond that country's borders (for instance, among the Aymara population in neighboring Peru), or because it could lead to the fragmentation of the country amid political violence, but not because any al Qaeda-related organization might profit from it. On this regard, claims about the presence of violent Islamist organizations in the so-called "Tri-Border Area" between Argentina, Brazil, and Paraguay have yet to be substantiated. For instance, a press briefing that took place after the "Library of Congress Report on the Tri-Border Area" was made public is quite explicit on that issue: "At this time, the U.S. Government does not have credible information confirming an established al Qaeda presence in the Tri-Border Area, nor have we uncovered information that would confirm terrorist operational planning ongoing in this region. Terrorist supporters in the Tri-Border Area are primarily engaged in fundraising for Hezbollah and Hamas."[21]

Those organizations have no links to al Qaeda, are not known to operate outside the Middle East, and the people allegedly raising funds for them were actually indicted under tax evasion charges (because the funds they raised were devoted to charities that may or may not have links to Hamas and Hezbollah, and not to the militant organizations themselves). It seems, then, that what raises suspicion in this case is not what actually happens in the Tri-Border Area, but the potential security implications of a no man's land where smuggling thrives and which harbors a Muslim community. A suspicion that, needless to say, Muslim leaders in the region overtly resent.

The case of the Tri-Border Area leads us again to the issue of failed states. The key defining feature of a failed state would be the inability of its institutions to exert control over significant portions of its own territory and population. Then again, it all depends on what specifically the word "significant" entails in this context, since—as the case of the Tri-Border Area suggests—to a certain extent that lack of control takes place in just about every country of the region. We have to remember here that in the contemporary world, states that do not survive tend to perish by implosion, rather than foreign aggression. For example, between 1998 and 1999 there were 54 wars in the world, 50 of which were civil wars. And even in some instances of international war, interethnic conflicts have been the cause or detonator of the conflict (for instance, between India and Pakistan or between Armenia and Azerbaijan).

So far, Latin America has not experienced ethnic separatism, but it has not been free of other phenomena that, by adversely affecting social welfare and prospects for good governance, could eventually become threats to the state's capacity to survive as a sovereign political unit. The symbiosis between political violence and drug trafficking that has posed such a threat to the Colombian state is proof of this. While the Revolutionary Armed Forces of Colombia (known by its Spanish acronym, FARC) has been an insurgent group since the 1960s, it only became a belligerent force in the strict sense when its ties to drug trafficking gave it access to an annual budget of hundreds of millions of dollars. This turned Colombia into a country in which the synergies established between drug trafficking, on the one hand, and paramilitary groups and guerrilla factions on the other, undermined the authority and legitimacy of the state.

In cases like that, a military response would be only one component of a strategy for combating political organizations that use terrorism as a tactic, and would not necessarily be the most important one. Economic development and institutional building would be crucial goals, both in their own right and as part of a grand strategy devoted to addressing security concerns.[22] The case of the Peruvian state, facing during the 1980s and early 1990s the terrorist threat posed by the Peruvian Communist Party (commonly known as Sendero Luminoso, or the "Shining Path"), provides an illustration of this point. While the Peruvian army confronted the Maoist insurgency with a strategy of indiscriminate repression, the Shining Path's presence expanded like wildfire throughout the country. Only when the armed forces decided to build an alliance with peasant organizations did they succeed in isolating the Shining Path in the countryside.[23] Forced to flee to the cities, the leaders were captured by elite police intelligence units without shedding a drop of blood.

The governments of the Western Hemisphere do agree on the fact that actual or potential synergies between drug trafficking and political violence constitute a major security threat within the region. They, however, do not seem to agree on the nature of the strategy that would be needed to deal with it. In the case of drug trafficking, for instance, Andean countries tend to emphasize the socioeconomic dimension of the problem and, thus, the need to promote alternative crops within local development projects, in order to provide coca-growing peasants with an alternative source of income. They also emphasize the shared nature of the responsibility for creating the problem (i.e., between the countries that are the main source of supply for illegal drugs, and the countries that provide the main source of demand for those drugs).

The strategy of the United States' government on drug trafficking, on the other hand, tends to emphasize programs focused on interdiction and the forced eradication of crops, using for that purpose military personnel. That was the case of the "Coca Cero" program developed in Bolivia: it was successful in reducing coca crops in that country, but, as Columbia professor Jeffrey Sachs claims, it created in the process the kind of grievances that would make displaced peasants the social base of support of a populist leader like Evo Morales.[24] Furthermore, gains in terms of crop eradication proved to be ephemeral: according to a recent report by the United Nations Office on Drugs and Crime (UNODC), the area producing coca leafs in Bolivia has increased 17 percent during the year 2004.[25] These are the reasons why a comprehensive study by an independent commission sponsored by the Council of Foreign Relations concludes the following in terms of its policy recommendations: "Andes 2020 thus attempts to redress what the Commission considers to be a major weakness of current U.S. policy, as embodied in Plan Colombia and the Andean Counter Drug Initiative: too great an emphasis on counter narcotics and security issues, and too little emphasis on complementary, comprehensive, regional strategies."[26]

CONCLUDING REMARKS

In sum, with the exception of Cuba and probably Venezuela, all the governments of Latin America are willing to establish cooperative links on security issues with the United States. Most would even consider themselves to be allies of the United States. And the institutional means available to deal with regional security concerns are adequate for that purpose. The resources devoted by many agencies of the U.S. government to the fight against terrorism of global reach in the Western Hemisphere, though, seems to reflect the perceived level of threat that it poses within the region. For example, according to a statement posted to the Web site of the U.S. Embassy in Uruguay, "In February 2005 the U.S. Department of State added $1.6 million to reinforce and extend its cooperation against terrorism in the Western Hemisphere. The total contribution of the United States since the terrorist attacks of September 11 thus reach a total of $5 million."[27] That does not necessarily mean, though, that countries throughout the region share the security priorities of the United States, or its strategy for dealing with them. Latin America is the only region in the world in which terrorist networks of a potentially global reach (i.e., al Qaeda-related groups) do not have an organized presence. Furthermore, with the exception of Colombia, there have been no major armed insurgencies in the region since the early 1990s. And although there are pending territorial disputes between several states of Latin America, resort to force as a means to deal with them seems extremely unlikely. Thus, most of the security threats that the states of the region face are internal rather than external, and of a social and political nature, rather than a military one. In turn, their governments tend to emphasize non-military means to deal with those threats. These, though, are not the only differences between these countries and the United States when it comes to security issues. As the so-called "Estrada Doctrine" illustrated in the past for the case of Mexico, some Latin American countries (particularly those located in South America's southern cone), consider the preservation of an autonomous capacity to decide and implement their foreign and defense policies a national priority.

Those are the reasons why a report of the Center for Strategic and International Studies could reach the following conclusion: "Conventional wisdom among U.S. defense experts argues that too many key elite actors in South America remain averse to effectively confronting hemispheric security issues—especially those impelling the threat or actual use of force—to permit an explicit dialogue with the United States."[28] In the next paragraph, the document provides part of the explanation for that state of affairs: "An associate U.S. vision suggests that Washington's security-oriented articulation of regional policy only reinforces the traditional unease with Yankee heavy-handedness."[29]

Furthermore, a couple of pages later, the report identifies "four alternative policy futures for U.S. strategic engagement," one of which reads as follows: "Military minimization. A concerted effort to shrink threats and the role of conventional armed forces in attending to them."[30] Thus, beyond the elite consensus regarding the need to preserve an autonomous decision-making process on foreign and defense policies, this quote provides an explanation for a specific reluctance of the military establishment in some countries to fully engage in U.S.-conceived region-wide security strategies.[31]

Paradoxically, one reason why the U.S. government has not exerted major political clout in order to push forward its security agenda within the region seems to be that it partly agrees with the assessment articulated earlier in this chapter: since the region is not particularly important in terms of the fight against terrorism of global reach, there is no compelling reason to do so. As researcher Adrián Bonilla observed in 2003, "The American bureaucracy that deals with Latin American issues was not complete until 2002. For a year and a half, uncertainty prevailed regarding the bureaucratic chain of command in the State Department and the National Security Council. And yet, key staff positions were occupied by care-taker officials almost until the first half of the Bush administration had gone by."[32] This observation illustrates the true relevance of Latin

America within a U.S. foreign agenda in which the security issues described in this chapter tend to prevail.

NOTES

1. Khatchik Derghoukassian, "Human Security: A Brief Report on the State of the Art," The Dante B. Fascell North-South Center, Miami, FL, Working Paper Series, November 2001, 10.

2. See Kenneth Waltz, *Man, the State and War, A Theoretical Analysis* (New York: Columbia University Press, 1959); and Daniel Singer, "The Level of Analysis Problem in International Relations," in *American Foreign Policy: Theoretical Essays,* ed. John Ikenberry (New York: Harper Collins Publishers, 1989).

3. Hans Morgenthau refers to the concept of balance of power as a "necessary consequence" of "power politics," which is also the main focus of the realist school. See Hans Morgenthau, *Politics Among Nations: The Struggle for Power and Peace* (New York: Alfred Knopf, 1973), 161. In turn, from the anarchic nature of the international system and the assumption that states "are unitary actors who, at a minimum, seek their own preservation and, at a maximum, drive for universal domination," Waltz deduces that balances of power "must necessarily emerge." Robert Keohane, "Realism, Neorealism and the Study of World Politics," in *Neorealism and its Critics,* ed. Robert Keohane (New York: Columbia University Press, 1986), 15.

4. See Olivier Roy, *Las Ilusiones del 11 de Septiembre. El debate estratégico frente al terrorismo* (Buenos Aires: Fondo de Cultura Económica, 2003).

5. "Except in the unusual case of psychopathic nihilists, terror is a means, not an end." Richard Betts, "The Soft Underbelly of American Primacy: Tactical Advantages of Terror," *Political Science Quarterly,* 117, no. 1 (2002).

6. See Paul Pillar, *Terrorism and U.S. Foreign Policy* (Washington, DC: Brookings Institution Press, 2001).

7. Ian Lesser, "Countering the New Terrorism: Implications for Strategy," in *Countering the New Terrorism,* ed. John Arquila et al. (Washington, DC, Rand Corp., 1999), 86.

8. Ibid., 20–21.

9. Olivier Roy, *Las Ilusiones del 11 de Septiembre,* 10. See, for example, Jessica Stern, *El Terrorismo Definitivo, Cuando lo impensable sucede* (Buenos Aires: Ediciones Granica S.A., 2001), 35.

10. Lars Schoultz, *National Security and United States Policy toward Latin America* (Princeton University Press, 1987), 310.

11. The Committee of Santa Fe, "A New Inter-American Policy for the Eighties," Council of Inter-American Security, Washington DC, 1980, 3.

12. Halford Mackinder, *Democratic Ideals and Reality* (New York: W.W. Norton & Co., 1962), 150.

13. John Plank; quoted by Luis Maira, *América Latina y la Crisis de Hegemonía Norteamericana* (Lima: Desco, 1982), 134.

14. Philip Kelly and Jack Child "Geopolitics, Integration and Conflict in the Southern Cone and Antarctica," in *Geopolitics of the Southern Cone and Antarctica,*

ed. Philip Kelly and Jack Child (Boulder and London: Lynne Rienner Publishers, 1988), 7. In the case of the southern cone, we have to add its geographical distance from the United States to its geographical distance from the Eurasian landmass. For instance, one of the arguments put forward by the Reagan Administration to justify its policies towards Nicaragua was that Nicaragua was closer to Texas than Texas to Massachusetts, and that if the U.S. did not contain the spread of Marxist subversion north of Nicaragua, it would soon find itself trying to contain it south of Texas.

15. Lars Schoultz, *National Security,* 310.

16. El Comité Interamericano Contra el Terrorismo, "Historia del CICTE," Organización de Estados Americanos, http://www.cicte.oas.org/historia.htm (accessed October 29, 2005).

17. U.S. State Department, http://www.state.gov/documents/organization/45313.pdf.

18. "Convención Interamericana Contra el Terrorismo," Organización de Estados Americanos, http://www.oas.org/juridico/spanish/tratados/a-66.htm.

19. For more on this important issue, please see the introduction to this volume as well as the chapters by Jason Ackleson, Christopher Rudolph, and Margaret Stock.

20. "Illegal Entry by Non-Mexicans Rises," *Christian Science Monitor,* 26 (July 2005), http://www.csmonitor.com/2005/0726/p01s01-usfp.html.

21. "Library of Congress Report on the Tri-Border Area (TBA), Questions Taken at the February 9, 2004 Daily Press Briefing," http://www.state.gov/r/pa/prs/ps/2004/29240.htm.

22. For example, if Latin America were exposed to concerted efforts to spread anthrax spores, the region's main vulnerability in the area of security would not be either its armed forces or its intelligence services, but the lack of quality and coverage of its public health systems.

23. Carlos Iván Degregori, ed., *Las Rondas Campesinas y la Derrota de Sendero Luminoso* (Lima: IEP, 1996).

24. Jeffrey Sachs, "Bolivia—A World for Which Bush Cares Little," *The Financial Times,* April 8, 2003.

25. Oficina de las Naciones Unidas contra la Droga y el Delito (ONUDD), "Informe Mundial sobre las Drogas de las Naciones Unidas para 2004," http://www.un.org/spanish/Depts/dpi/boletin/drogas.

26. "Andes 2020: A New Strategy for the Challenges of Colombia and the Region," report of an independent commission sponsored by the Council of Foreign Relations, Washington, DC, 2004, 2.

27. "Senado de EE.UU. aprueba Convención Interamericana contra Terrorismo," Embassy of the United States of America in Montevideo, Uruguay, October 13, 2005, http://montevideo.usembassy.gov/usaweb/paginas/562-00ES.shtml.

28. The Center for Strategic and International Studies, *Thinking Strategically About 2005, The United States and South America* (Washington DC: CSIS, 1999), 9.

29. Ibid.

30. Ibid., 11.

31. This is an issue that appears constantly in South American literature on the subject. For example, "Civilian control over security forces, and the American conception about their appropriate size and structure are goals that Washington has not been able to achieve so far in the region." Adrián Bonilla, "Una Agenda de Seguridad Andina," in *Seguridad Hemisférica: un largo y tortuoso camino,* ed. María Cristina Rosas (México DF: Universidad Nacional Autónoma de México y Centro de Estudios de Defensa Hemisférica, 2003), 233.

32. Ibid., 231.

CHAPTER 6

GLOBAL TRADE AND FOOD SECURITY: PERSPECTIVES FOR THE TWENTY-FIRST CENTURY

Justin Kastner and Jason Ackleson

In today's age of globalization, the prosperity of the United States depends on international trade. Approximately 25 percent of the nation's gross domestic product comes from international trade.[1] The United States imports and exports large volumes of manufactured goods, raw materials, and food; these are projected to increase at approximately 8 percent annually until at least 2010.[2] Two-thirds of all U.S. wheat and wheat flour, one-third of U.S. soybean and rice production, and almost two-fifths of U.S. cotton production are exported via U.S. ports.[3] America's international borders facilitate much of this trade—particularly trade with Canada and Mexico (the United States's number one and number two trading partners, respectively). Approximately $1.8 billion in commerce occurs over the U.S.-Canada and U.S.-Mexico borders each day.[4]

In addition to facilitating trade, the U.S. border plays an obvious role in ensuring national security. National security demands not only the preservation of the United States, but also the realization of critical national interests, including the preservation of the U.S. way of life. Globalization presents many challenges for the U.S. government as it seeks to ensure this national security, even despite its status as "sole superpower." One challenge arises because the pursuit of free trade may compromise America's ability to secure its domestic security; on the other hand, a different challenge arises when demands for security threaten the essential cross-border flows needed for U.S. economic growth. Food security exemplifies these contrasting challenges; cross-border trade flows help ensure food security, but cross-border flows also potentially represent a security threat to America's food supply and agricultural base.

These security tensions often manifest themselves at the U.S. border; it is at America's land frontiers and other ports of entry where the U.S. government attempts to screen the vast flows of incoming goods and individuals. Given the massive volume of cross-border flows, traditional methods of border control are poorly suited for this task. Moreover, today there are new actors, such as transnational terrorist networks, which operate below and across the state. These realities have led to a redefinition of the task of border security to "good border management," which means facilitating the movement of legitimate goods and people while screening out dangerous people and materials. Accordingly, the United States is turning to new kinds of border management policies. These approaches begin by thinking of the border not as a material, static obstacle but rather as a flexible concept that begins when people or goods start their journey to the United States.

To illustrate the security dilemmas and current challenges facing policy makers in the post-9/11 world, this chapter examines regulatory frameworks for border and food security. It is helpful to adopt a multidisciplinary analysis of these issues, and this chapter follows such a course. The chapter begins with a historically-informed discussion of globalization, trade policy, and food security. The chapter then pauses to consider the homeland security language milieu in which the term "food security" today finds itself. Next, the chapter describes current policy responses to the challenges of terrorism, weapons of mass destruction (WMD), and threats to the food supply. The chapter argues that hedging against conventional, nonterrorist threats can have positive consequences for counterterrorism and food security policy. The chapter also touches on the key dilemma mentioned above: reconciling the competing pressures of globalization and national security. Finally, the conclusion details several policy trajectories and key recommendations.

HISTORICAL CONTEXT

The Road to Globalization

Globalization—commonly defined as the integration of financial, information, trade, and social networks to create a high-speed global marketplace—today plays a major role in American prosperity and security. How did this major international economic structure of today develop? Why is the United States caught up in globalization? To best understand the road to globalization, a brief review of history is in order.

In the later half of the nineteenth century and early part of the twentieth century, policies of protectionism and strategic trade increased dramatically. Before World War II, states acted to dominate their colonial possessions, protect their national industries, and compete with one another in a zero-sum game of economic strength and market control. This led to ever-increasing international trade barriers; for example, after the 1929 stock market crash, the United States imposed a 53 percent tax on imports. Similar taxes were imposed in other areas of the world, leading to a drastic reduction in trade flows and a depressed international economy. After World War II, the Allies sought to create a new international economic order that would prevent conflicts and increase prosperity. At the famous Bretton Woods meetings, new institutions were created to order this structure, which was largely committed to embedded liberalism and ever-freer trade. At Bretton Woods, the Allies established the General Agreement on Tariffs and Trade (GATT) which sought to manage international trade relations by liberalizing trade through multilateral negotiations. This was done on the basis of reciprocity and nondiscrimination: barriers would be lowered together and no nation's goods would be favored over any others.

"Rounds" of subsequent trade negotiations resulted in average world tariffs on nonagricultural products falling from 40 percent to around 4 percent. Importantly, the Uruguay Round of Multilateral Trade Negotiations (Uruguay Round, 1986–1994) culminated in the establishment of a new international organization, the World Trade Organization (WTO), as a successor to the GATT. In recent years, member countries of the WTO have pushed trade liberalization further than it has ever gone, based partly on the idea that forward momentum will avoid backsliding into economic protectionism. The WTO, a formal multilateral body based in Geneva, is made up of 150 member nation-states who negotiate agreements on international trade; its members engage in 97 percent of the world's trade.[5] When contrasted with other multilateral institutions, the WTO has a comparatively powerful dispute settlement body (panels of experts that investigate complaints about violations of trade agreements) to enforce international trade law. A number of high profile cases (such as the U.S.-European Union dispute over hormone-treated beef) have been heard by WTO panels.

The rise in global trade was underpinned ideologically by neoliberal economic theory and politically by powerful private economic interests (such as multinational corporations) as well as multilateral institutions (including the WTO, International Monetary Fund or IMF, and the World Bank). Scholars from the field of international political economy (IPE) note that these dynamics have favored the market over the state in some areas; they point to diminishing state sovereignty, the erasure of borders in favor of economies of scale, and a relatively widespread acceptance of liberal economic principles of free trade, competition, and integration. (These dynamics have also simultaneously led to regionalism whereby states agree to cooperate and share responsibility for common goals; NAFTA and the European Union offer noteworthy examples.)

Importantly, the increased flow of goods, services, and capital across borders can boost economic activity and enhance prosperity. Daalder and Lindsay point out that "during the 1990s the more globalized economies grew an average of 5 percent a year, while the less globalized economies contracted by an average of 1 percent a year."[6] But globalization is about more than just economics; some have argued that globalization has made the state a less important player in an international system defined by multinational corporations, communications technologies, and transnational networks (both licit and illicit). Joseph Nye's recent volume, *The Paradox of American Power*, points out some of the complex ways globalization has affected power in the international system today.[7] He argues that while American military power remains dominant, the transnational dimension of power—which involves nonstate actors such as multinational corporations and transnational criminal networks—is to a great degree widely dispersed and out of the state's ability to control.

International Trade Policy and Food Security

Historically, nation-states' food security policies have changed with evolving international trade, food safety, and border security policies. In nineteenth-century Great Britain, for example, food security problems prompted changes in agricultural trade policies. During the 1830s and 1840s, British politicians like Richard Cobden and groups like the Anti-Corn Law League (an activist group opposed to economic protectionism embodied in the so-called Corn Laws) campaigned for free trade in agricultural products. The logic of free trade in agricultural products became compelling when Britain experienced food crises in the mid-1840s. Substantial harvests were reaped in 1842, 1843, and 1844, but a poor yield in 1845 reminded British farmers and consumers of the elusiveness of plenty. In that year, Britain's food supply was beleaguered by bad weather, poor harvests, and, in Ireland, the beginnings of a potato famine. The woes of 1845 appeared to prove what free trade advocates had claimed; free traders had always argued that agricultural imports were needed to ensure a cheap, plentiful food supply for the working classes of an increasingly urban Britain. After the bad harvest of 1845, British Prime Minister Sir Robert Peel agreed. In 1846, Britain completely repealed the Corn Laws and also eliminated tariffs on livestock imports.

Twenty years after Britain's repeal of the Corn Laws, the spirit of free trade was alive and well not only in Britain but also in continental Europe. By the 1860s, American agricultural exports to Europe had noticeably expanded from the staple goods (e.g., cotton and tobacco) that had characterized transatlantic agricultural trading since colonial days. Richard

Cobden, still one of Europe's well-recognized advocates of free trade, explained this to textile manufacturers in October 1862: "You get an article even more important than your cotton from America—your food."[8] During the second half of the nineteenth century, Britain was well aware of the importance to food security of international supplies of food, particularly those from the United States. In May 1867, the food committee of Britain's Society of the Arts investigated the prospect of further increasing imports of American meat, particularly bacon. The committee interviewed a businessman and a professor acquainted with the transatlantic trade in preserved American meat. Both interviewees agreed that American meat could enhance Britain's food security—by supplying the working classes with nutritious, cheap food.[9] Eventually, due to increased competition and lower food prices, even the poor were able to improve their diets, consuming increased amounts of meat, milk, and vegetables in addition to bread, potatoes, and beer.[10]

Like nineteenth-century Britain, the United States today finds itself in an economic love affair with low food prices. Today, food is cheaper than it has ever been. Americans spend less than 6 percent of their after-tax income on groceries. In other countries like India, one-half of disposable income goes to food.[11] However, having a plentiful, inexpensive supply of food represents but one aspect of food security. Public health and agricultural security also matter; food-borne pathogens, animal diseases, and plant diseases have historically threatened food safety as well as nations' capacities to produce food. Agricultural trade, recognized in the early 1990s as one of the most problematic areas of world economic affairs, has in recent years been further complicated by import restrictions related to food safety, animal health, and plant health policy. These restrictions have precipitated trade disputes—even as countries have embraced globalization.

Food security-related trade disputes have emerged in part because of international economic policy. While tariffs, subsidies, import quotas, and other tools of economic protection have long resided at the root of agricultural trade disputes, agreements forged during the Uruguay Round began to reduce some of these agricultural trade-restricting practices. At the conclusion of the Uruguay Round (1994), governments across the world agreed to convert a number of economic protection measures, such as import quotas, into tariffs. This process, termed tariffication, transformed these trade measures into a clear, negotiable currency. (The word tariff has its origins in the Arabic "ta'rif," which means to make known; essentially, governments carried out tariffication so as to clearly inform each other of their respective import access barriers.[12]) After tariffication, further commitments were made to reduce the tariffs, and these commitments are reflected in the Uruguay Round Agreement on Agriculture.

In the wake of the Uruguay Round's tariffication and tariff reduction schemes, trade officials redirected their attention to nontariff trade barriers that might be susceptible to discriminatory or arbitrary application. One writer for the *Financial Times* has explained, "as border barriers, such as tariffs and quotas, fall, other obstacles to market access [emerge]."[13] Food security-related health regulations are especially illustrative of the nontariff barrier problem; while often legitimately employed to protect food security, food safety and animal/plant disease regulations can also simply be disguised barriers to trade.[14]

To address this very problem, governments worldwide adopted the Uruguay Round Agreement on the Application of Sanitary and Phytosanitary Measures (the SPS Agreement). (Measures to protect human or animal health are sanitary measures; measures to protect plant health are phytosanitary measures.) While recognizing nations' rights to adopt controls for the purposes of health protection, the SPS Agreement provides a framework for ensuring that such controls do not represent arbitrary, discriminatory, or scientifically unjustifiable trade restrictions. By requiring scientific risk assessment for SPS-related (sanitary- or phytosanitary-related) trade barriers, the SPS Agreement encourages members to base their trade restrictions on genuine public health and agricultural security considerations—not the impulses of economic considerations or risk perception biases. National governments decide the levels to which they seek to protect human, animal, and plant health from pest and disease threats. These are known as their Appropriate Levels of Protection (ALOPs). According to the SPS Agreement, ALOPs and the regulations adopted to achieve ALOPs must be consistently applied, nondiscriminatory, and not more trade-restrictive than necessary. The SPS Agreement also stipulates that the associated regulations be based on scientific risk assessment.

With a view to promote regulatory harmonization among governments, the SPS Agreement explicitly acknowledges three scientific bodies responsible for developing standards for international trade. The Codex Alimentarius Commission elaborates international food safety standards for human health, the Office International des Epizooties sets standards related to animal health, and the Secretariat of the International Plant Protection Convention establishes plant health standards. Aiming to protect health while facilitating trade, the SPS Agreement encourages countries to engage in multilateral harmonization; that is, national governments are to participate in standard-setting activities in the three international organizations and base their domestic regulations on the standards developed. The SPS Agreement encourages regulatory harmonization in other ways. The agreement requires countries to notify each other of new or anticipated health protection trade regulations, and importing countries are obligated to accept as equivalent the health regulations of exporting countries that, while different, demonstrably achieve the importers' ALOPs.

The SPS Agreement came into force with the establishment of the WTO, of which each signatory government is a member. The WTO delivers judgment in disputes related to the SPS Agreement, and it requires violating members to modify or withdraw their noncompliant SPS-related regulations. While the WTO is unable to force a member government to change its measures, it can authorize those countries adversely affected to retaliate by suspending tariff concessions previously granted to the violating country.[15] Aside from the tariff suspension provision, the WTO has no real enforcement power. It is therefore not surprising that the authors of the SPS Agreement believe the best path to food security dispute resolution is for the involved countries to discuss and settle the matters themselves. This confession, however, is of little worth in the absence of information about the forces that actually influence such resolution.

If forces beyond those provided by international law and multilateral standard-setting organizations are responsible for the resolution of SPS-related trade disputes, then it is worthwhile to consider the nature of these forces. In her book, *Interests, Institutions and Information: Domestic Politics and International Relations*, IPE scholar Helen Milner argues that domestic forces are more important determinants of international cooperation than are international structures.[16] That is, when the heat of international relations is turned up in such arenas as food security or border security, extralegal forces trump international agreements—such as the SPS Agreement—and institutions—such as the WTO or the three scientific standard-setting bodies. The essence of Milner's thesis has been confirmed by contemporary experience and studies touching on the forces that influence the resolution of SPS-related trade disputes. Domestic economic considerations represent one such determinant. Governmental policies are responses to the demands of people economically affected by those policies; as a result, domestic economic considerations play an obvious role in agricultural trade policy—and agricultural trade cooperation. While agricultural trade cooperation in general has earned a reputation amongst economists for being difficult, SPS-related food security disputes have proven equally troublesome. While economic protectionism is sometimes mistakenly used to explain governments' behavior in food security trade disputes, economic considerations do often play a determining role. For example, in 2002 the Russian Federation's President Vladimir Putin hinted at the influence of economic food security considerations when, during a U.S.-Russia dispute regarding sanitary concerns in poultry, he remarked, "We never had the intention of banning the import of agricultural products, including chicken meat, into Russia because unfortunately for the moment we cannot supply the necessary volume at the necessary price for our people."[17]

UNDERSTANDING FOOD SECURITY

Today's homeland security lexicon includes such terms as "foreign animal disease," "food protection," "food defense," and "food security." Since 9/11, references to each of these terms—but especially "food security"—have grown in noticeable frequency. Previously an expression used primarily in the international development community, the phrase "food security" has become a mainstay in U.S. homeland security discourse.

The meanings of ideas and words change over time. One historian explains why: "Ideas have a radiation and development, an ancestry and posterity of their own."[18] In the United States, the radiation and development of the idea of "food security" may be seen in the term's usage in the U.S. government. A 1996 position paper—co-authored by officials within the U.S. Department of Agriculture (USDA), the U.S. Department of State, and the U.S. Agency for International Development (USAID)—explained that food security amounted to having "physical and economic access to sufficient food to meet…dietary needs."[19] Three dimensions of food security were acknowledged: availability, access, and utilization. While national security interests were acknowledged, the importance of food security was couched largely in humanitarian, international-development terms; in the report, the national-security basis for food security efforts had little to do with protection of the U.S. food supply:

> Grain imports in Asia affect farmers' purchasing power in Kansas and the amount of food available for hungry children in Rwanda. Long-term U.S. strategic interests are also affected….Looking to the future, a food crisis in North Korea could threaten stability in a region vital to U.S. security.[20]

After the terrorist attacks of September 11, 2001, increased use of the term "food security" emerged within the agricultural and food safety communities. As Annette Beresford explains in her work on the ideology and terminology of "homeland security," the events of 9/11 prompted the reflection of a new meaning of homeland security: "the reduction of terrorism and the ability to pursue and maintain social practices and opportunities that Americans hold dear."[21] Similarly, the events of 9/11 awakened a new understanding of the food security mandate: to protect the U.S. food system from terrorists, food-borne pathogens, foreign animal diseases, and exotic plant pests. While previously food security meant ensuring enough food for a population, now food security covers every aspect of ensuring a safe, adequate, and cost-effective food supply.

Since 9/11, policy makers tasked with ensuring food security have directed renewed attention to agroterrorism. The Center for Food Security and Public Health at Iowa State University has adopted the following definition of agroterrorism:

> The use, or threatened use, of biological (to include toxins), chemical, or radiological agents against some component of agriculture in such a way as

to adversely impact the agriculture industry or any component thereof, the economy, or the consuming public.[22]

Agroterrorism threatens America's food security because it targets the very basis of American food security, the agri-food system. An agroterrorist attack would seek to significantly disturb this system—leading to higher food prices, increased unemployment, loss of export markets, and spillover effects in industries closely affiliated with agriculture. The U.S. agricultural infrastructure is uniquely susceptible to attack. Agricultural losses in crops illustrate America's vulnerability. Already, the United States loses $33 billion a year to plant diseases. American agriculture is a "soft" target, the protection of which is a monumental task. There are approximately one billion acres of farm land. Today, farms in the United States are fewer than ever before but are highly consolidated; the use of animal- or plant-targeting agents could be directed at relatively small regions and have widespread repercussions.[23]

Along with agroterrorism, food security officials are concerned about bioterrorism—the use of microorganisms or toxins derived from living organisms to cause death or disease in humans, animals, or plants in civilian settings.[24] This includes food-borne disease-causing pathogens intentionally introduced into the food supply.

MODERN-DAY CONCERNS, CHALLENGES, AND POLICY RESPONSES

Broadly speaking, a formidable challenge faces the United States: managing an international economic environment underpinned by free trade and the forces of globalization. Increasingly, prosperity in the Global North is linked to removing trade barriers, increasing efficiency, and generally encouraging regional economic integration. However, these dynamics can complicate the ability of nation-states to regulate a key element of their national infrastructure—international borders—for security purposes, such as preventing the entry of terrorists, agents that threaten food security, or WMD. In other words, more open borders increase the ability of the more nefarious elements of globalization to infiltrate states.

This section of the chapter borrows insights from the fields of IPE and food safety and security to summarize new challenges and policy responses. Significantly, the discussion highlights current food security policy trends, and explains the two main ways that the United States (specifically) and North America (generally) are seeking to balance the competing pressures of national security and globalization: "smart borders" and The Security and Prosperity Partnership of North America (SPP).

The Public Health Security and Bioterrorism Preparedness and Response Act of 2002

Regulation of the U.S. food supply has historically been fragmented, with various agencies gradually assuming regulatory responsibility for different segments of the U.S. agri-food system. For most of the twentieth century, there has been a "division of regulatory labor" between the U.S. Food and Drug Administration (FDA) and the U.S. Department of Agriculture (see Table 6.1).

Historically, the USDA Food Safety and Inspection Service (USDA-FSIS) has had more enforcement power than the FDA. However, this has changed post-9/11. In 2002, the United States adopted the *Public Health Security and Bioterrorism Preparedness and Response Act (Bioterrorism Act)*. The *Bioterrorism Act* features five sections, the third of which is titled "Protecting Safety and Security of Food and Drug Supply." Most significantly, the *Bioterrorism Act* confers onto the U.S. Food and Drug Administration many of the kinds of authorities (e.g., detention, registration, etc.) that previously only the USDA-FSIS had.

Table 6.1   Pre-9/11 Federal Legislative Authority for Food Safety[25]

	FDA	USDA-FSIS
Key legislation	Federal Food, Drug & Cosmetic Act	Federal Meat Inspection Act; Poultry Products Inspection Act; Egg Products Inspection Act
Foods regulated	Food and beverages for humans or animals	Meat, poultry, some egg products
Facilities regulated (food)	~57,000	~6,500
Inspectors	~770	~7,600
Inspector frequency	Once every 5–10 years	Each shift
Prior to Bioterrorism Act, authority to:		
Temporarily detain suspect food products	No	Yes
Require food processors to register	No	Yes
Ensure exporter's food safety system equivalent to U.S.	No	Yes

Source: GAO/T-RCED-99-256; Strongin, 2002.

The *Bioterrorism Act*'s food security provisions apply only to products regulated by the FDA. (USDA-FSIS continues to have authority over the meat and poultry industries.) Examples of products regulated by the FDA include dietary supplements and ingredients, infant formula, beverages, fruits and vegetables, fish and seafood, dairy products and shell eggs, canned or frozen foods, animal feeds and pet food, snack foods, candy, and bakery goods.

Key food security features of the *Bioterrorism Act* include rules for the registration of all facilities manufacturing, processing, packing, or holding food for human or animal consumption. Significantly, this registration requirement applies to both domestic and foreign facilities; over 400,000 facilities worldwide are expected to register. Another feature of the *Bioterrorism Act* is that of "prior notice." This requirement stipulates that the FDA must be notified in advance of all food import shipments so that the FDA can (a) review and evaluate information before a food product arrives in the United States, (b) better deploy resources to conduct inspections, and (c) help intercept contaminated products. Varying time requirements apply, but all prior notice submissions must occur no more than five days in advance of arrival. Other aspects of the *Bioterrorism Act* include the granting of detention authority to the FDA; the FDA can now, on its own, detain an article of food when there is credible evidence that the article presents a threat to humans or animals. The registration, prior-notice, and administrative-detention features of the *Bioterrorism Act* are far-reaching and illustrate how food security has become an elevated priority of the U.S. government.

Following adoption of the *Bioterrorism Act*, a new list of bioterrorism agents of concern was elaborated. The list is broken down according to regulatory authority and areas of overlap:

- *Department of Health and Human Service (HHS) agents (HHS has sole authority and responsibility to regulate).* Included in this list are select agents (Ebola virus, *Yersinia pestis* or Plague, etc.) and toxins (e.g., Ricin) that may affect public health and safety.

- *USDA-only agents (USDA has sole authority and responsibility to regulate).* Included in this list are agents (foot and mouth disease virus, rinderpest virus, Plum Pox Potyvirus, etc.) and toxins that may affect animal and plant health and animal and plant products.

- *Overlap agents (agents and toxins subject to regulation by both HHS and USDA).* Examples of agents and toxins from this list include *Bacillus anthracis* (anthrax) and botulinum neurotoxin.

A Special Concern for "Foreign Animal Diseases"

Throughout history, governments have been preoccupied with foreign sources of disease; this preoccupation has repeatedly been appropriated through international trade politics (import restrictions) and more recently the looming threat of terrorism. This preoccupation has fueled the current demand for food security policies such as those embodied in the *Bioterrorism Act*. The very term "foreign animal disease," used by not only the United States but also other countries, signals this preoccupation. Biases against foreign sources of food safety and animal disease risks are rampant. For example, during the 1990s, Australia, ostensibly for reasons of aquatic disease protection, restricted imports of Canadian salmon while ignoring other fish that carried the same diseases as salmon. During the dispute, which eventually was considered at the WTO under the terms of the SPS Agreement, it became evident that the root of the dispute was economic pressure and risk perception biases in the Tasmanian salmon industry.

More recently, a Canada-U.S. row over bovine spongiform encephalopathy (BSE, or mad cow disease) illustrated the preoccupation with foreign animal diseases. The Canada-U.S. border, like all borders, contains and causes certain political, social, and economic realities. However, food safety and animal disease problems do not bow to borders. Consequently, farmers, regulators, and consumers on both sides must be vigilant. That means being honest about food safety risks, implementing strategies to manage those risks, and keeping the public informed. BSE is a poorly understood phenomenon, the existence of which demands surveillance and regulatory sweat within each country. Fortunately, both the U.S. and Canadian governments understand this; but one U.S. producer group, fanning sentiments of the fear of foreign sources of disease, temporarily blocked resumption of live-cattle imports from Canada.

North American Challenges

In IPE, the "state-market tension" underpins the dynamics of the global economy. The state and the market exist in parallel; markets decide how scarce resources are allocated and how such resources are distributed. However, states allocate and distribute power, which in turn determines the distribution of wealth and the control of markets. The production structure of contemporary IPE—how goods and services get made and distributed—informs the relationships between state and market control, for example, through rules regulating international trade.

As the chapter has already discussed, since World War II the United States has embraced economic policies that emphasize free markets, free trade, and globalization. This decision was based on a strong belief in liberal economic theory and its core concepts of comparative advantage and efficiency. Indeed, the exceptional economic growth rate of the United States in the post-WWII era suggests that these arrangements have benefited the country. Scholars have argued, in fact, that the country's status today as the world's "sole superpower" has to do, in part, with its vast economic strength.

However, on a practical level, free markets constrain the ability of any state to unilaterally regulate commerce. This regulation generally includes the ability to control international borders; when free trade agreements (often made in the name of economies of scale) erase these barriers to the flow of goods and services, national economies tend to become more integrated with and dependent upon one another. Scholars argue that this is the case in North America; because many trade barriers between the United States, Canada, and Mexico are now removed under the North American Free Trade Agreement (NAFTA), the three countries are increasingly economically integrated.

For example, manufacturing processes in North America now often span the U.S.-Mexico and U.S.-Canada borders. For example, many goods are manufactured in Mexican border assembly plants (*maquiladoras*) for delivery and sale in the United States and Canada. Similarly, the typical automobile produced in North America has components that cross the U.S.-Canada border numerous times. The volume of commercial traffic across the border has exploded under NAFTA and has, in many cases, resulted in significant crossing delays due to the sheer weight of traffic and congested ports of entry. Containerized shipments in the United States doubled during the last ten years and are expected to double again every 10 to 15 years.[26]

Each year, 300 million people, 90 million cars, and 4.3 million trucks cross into the United States from Mexico. Flows between the two nations have more than tripled during the past decade, from $81 billion in 1993 to $247 billion in 2000, mostly in products moved across the border by truck.[27] $1.3 billion worth of trade takes place between the United States and Canada; 40,000 commercial shipments and 300,000 people cross the border every day.[28] These are formidable numbers to manage from a security point of view.

Reconciling the Competing Demands of Security and Trade: Smart Borders and The Security and Prosperity Partnership of North America

Despite the structural limitations in doing so, the United States and other states in the Global North are attempting to reconcile the competing demands of security and trade under globalization. To do so, the United States has embarked upon the development of a new border infrastructure it hopes is appropriate for the international security environment. This infrastructure includes elements of what are known as "smart border" systems. In addition, the United States has entered into bilateral and trilateral agreements with its northern and southern neighbors, an agreement known as The Security and Prosperity Partnership of North America (SPP). The SPP is designed to facilitate North American economic integration and regulatory cooperation on trade and security matters. The next section of this discussion briefly explores each of these policies.

Smart Borders

To better manage its international frontiers with Canada and Mexico, the Bush administration has negotiated bilateral smart border accords with each country.[29] The smart border plan has emerged as the preferred policy solution to the difficult problem of screening for terrorist incursions into the United States while maintaining flows of goods and individuals, key drivers of globalization. President George W. Bush seeks a border of the future that "poses little or no obstacle to legitimate trade and travel...keep[ing] pace with expanding trade while protecting the United States from the threats of terrorist attack, illegal immigration, illegal drugs, and other contraband."[30]

The United States has accordingly signed agreements with Canada and Mexico that involve limited cooperation on a number of policy issues related to border control, including inspections, preclearances of goods and people, database coordination, biometric identifiers, and other areas. For example, the accords call for new detection technologies, such as the U.S. Customs and Border Protection's (CBP) Vehicle and Cargo Inspection Systems. Components of these systems include radiation portals, explosives detectors, surveillance cameras, sensors, and databases to monitor entries and exits of individuals and facilitate trusted travelers and traders. The U.S. Department of Homeland Security is convinced that the proper deployment of these tools can greatly enhance border security while not slowing trade and commerce. Much work remains to be done on these fronts.

The Security and Prosperity Partnership of North America

Building on the cooperation fostered by the smart border accords, President Bush, President Vicente Fox of Mexico, and Canadian Prime Minister Paul Martin met in Texas in March 2005 to announce the establishment of the Security and Prosperity Partnership of North America (SPP). The SPP seeks to improve the "competitive position of North American industries in the global marketplace and to provide greater economic opportunity for all of our societies, while maintaining high standards of health and safety for our people."[31] The prosperity section of the SPP involves a three-tiered agenda: improving productivity, reducing the costs of trade, and enhancing quality of life. On the security front, the SPP seeks to protect North America from external threats, prevent and respond to threats within the continent, and further streamline the secure movement of low-risk traffic across shared borders.[32]

Since the first high-level meeting in March 2005, interagency working groups have made progress on many SPP-inspired initiatives. In late June 2005, the leaders announced further progress in a number of areas, including streamlining regulations on electronic commerce, a harmonized approach to BSE, border infrastructure development, land preclearance, energy, and coordination on food safety.[33] There are a number of other future policy directions for further cooperation and harmonization.

The SPP clearly acknowledges that some policy makers in the United States, Canada, and Mexico understand the complicated trade and security dynamics and dilemmas facing each country. Increasingly, some analysts rightly argue that only by cooperating as a North American community can each nation-state achieve the security that will preserve crucial cross-border relationships; in a highly integrated North America, unilateral action on border security is bound to fail and be counterproductive.[34]

From a policy formulation point of view, the SPP is somewhat unique in that it is proceeding through mid-level negotiations conducted between each state's bureaucratic structures *and* is backed by high-level political will provided by the leaders of Canada, Mexico, and the United States. For example, on food inspections, the Canadian Food Inspection Agency and Health Canada are working with the U.S. Department of Agriculture and the Food and Drug Administration on prior notice regulations for food shipments across North American borders. This process allows for progress to be made in a swifter way that is not as politicized as, for example, a debate over a major international trade treaty would likely be.

In addition, under the SPP, regulatory cooperation and creative harmonization may proceed at different levels, between and across the three partner countries; this allows for a unique degree of flexibility and adaptability as bureaucrats seek to accommodate the different circumstances of each country.

The chief premise behind both smart borders and the SPP is good border management, achieved through risk management. The systems being developed and implemented through the smart border agreements are largely based on these principles. To adapt the haystack metaphor, the idea behind risk management on the border is to systematically separate the "bad needles" (e.g., suspicious individuals, unsafe food, and potential weapons of mass destruction) from the "good straw" (e.g., low-risk travelers, routine freight shipments) of the North American haystack. By screening out low-risk goods and people, inspection resources can be redirected to where they ought to be: watch-list suspects, suspicious individuals, and shipments from untrustworthy firms within the international community. Elements of the SPP that, for example, may help the United

States, Canada, and Mexico move toward a more perimeter-oriented approach to North American border security, can facilitate trade between the three NAFTA partners and focus scrutiny on suspect foreign shipments.

CONCLUSIONS AND POLICY RECOMMENDATIONS

This chapter highlighted the trade and security tensions in an age of globalization. Food security classically illustrates these tensions, particularly in the wake of 9/11. Previously an expression used primarily in the international development community, the phrase "food security" has become a mainstay in U.S. homeland security discourse. While previously food security meant ensuring enough food for a population, in the United States food security now seems to cover every aspect of ensuring a safe, adequate, and cost-effective food supply. Policy makers tasked with ensuring food security are concerned with agroterrorism and bioterrorism. Their job is not easy; they must conduct their tasks within a complex milieu of unilateral, bilateral, and multilateral arrangements regulating trade, food safety, and border security. Regulation of the U.S. food supply has historically been fragmented, with various agencies assuming over time various segments of the U.S. agri-food system. New powers, conferred upon the FDA by the 2002 *Bioterrorism Act*, are far-reaching and illustrate how food security has become an elevated priority of the U.S. government. In addition to granting new authorities, the *Bioterrorism Act* identifies bioterrorism and agroterrorism agents of concern.

Both smart borders and the SPP represent progressive steps towards managing the competing demands of security and trade under globalization. To capitalize on progress made, the following observations and policy trajectories should also be considered:

- Policy makers and stakeholders should recognize and promote border/food supply protection as key elements of the national infrastructure.
- We should remember that policies and tools for protecting against conventional, nonterrorist threats can have positive consequences for counterterrorism and food-security policy.
- Improved border infrastructure and regulatory mechanisms will help realize the goals of both prosperity and security in North America.
- Policy makers should continue their dialogue to advance the SPP agenda.
- Only through multilateral cooperation can the United States mitigate the trade/ security dilemma.
- We must increase public awareness and develop stakeholder buy-in on the SPP.

The United States is in a position to address the formidable trade and security challenges of the twenty-first century. While fail-safe border and food security policies remain elusive, real progress has been and will continue to be made in the protection of these critical components of North America's infrastructure.

NOTES

1. U.S. import and export trade represented 25.1 percent of U.S. gross domestic product in 2004. See U.S. International Trade Administration, "Foreign Trade Highlights GDP and U.S. International Trade in Goods and Services, 1976–2004," http://www.ita.doc.gov/td/industry/otea/usfth/aggregate/H04T05.html (accessed August 31, 2005).

2. Betty W. Su, "Employment Outlook: 2000–10: The U.S. Economy to 2010," (Washington, DC: U.S. Bureau of Labor Statistics, 2001), http://www.bls.gov/opub/mlr/2001/11/art1full.pdf (accessed August 31, 2005).

3. American Association of Port Authorities, "America's Ports: Gateways to Global Trade,"http://www.aapa-ports.org/industryinfo/americasports.htm (accessed August 18, 2005).

4. Data is from 2002. See Rebecca Jannol, Deborah Meyers, and Maia Jachimowicz, "U.S.-Canada-Mexico Fact Sheet on Trade and Migration" (Washington, DC: Migration Policy Institute, 2003), http://www.migrationpolicy.org/pubs/US-Canada-Mexicofact percent20sheet.pdf (accessed June 1, 2005).

5. World Trade Organization, "The WTO In Brief." (Geneva: World Trade Organization, 2005), http://www.wto.org/english/res_e/doload_e/inbr_e.pdf (accessed August 30, 2005).

6. Ivo H. Daalder and James M. Lindsay, "The Globalization of Politics: American Foreign Policy for a New Century," *The Brookings Review* 21, no. 1 (2003): 12–17.

7. Joseph S. Nye, *The Paradox of American Power: Why the World's Only Superpower Can't Go It Alone* (Oxford: Oxford University Press, 2003).

8. Speech of October 25, 1862, quoted in Charles S. Campbell, *From Revolution to Rapprochement: The United States and Great Britain, 1783–1900* (New York: John Wiley & Sons, Inc., 1974), 106. Cobden was indeed popular; years before he was one of the most celebrated British politicians in Europe, "fêted in capital after capital." Christopher Harvie, "Revolution and the Rule of Law (1789–1851)," in *The Oxford History of Britain*, ed. Kenneth O. Morgan (Oxford and New York: Oxford University Press, 1988), 513.

9. "Proceedings of the Society: Food Committee," *Journal of the Society of Arts* XV, no. 756 (1867): 414–16.

10. H.C.G. Matthew, "The Liberal Age (1851–1914)," in *The Oxford History of Britain*, ed. Kenneth O. Morgan (Oxford and New York: Oxford University Press, 1988), 540.

11. Daniel Akst, "Cheap Eats," *The Wilson Quarterly* 27, no. 3 (2003): 30.

12. For the insightful explanation of the history of the term "tariff," the authors credit Dr. Lester Crawford, former Commissioner of the Food and Drug Administration.

13. Guy de Jonquières and Nancy Dunne, "A Partnership in Peril," *Financial Times,* March 8, 1999.

14. G.G. Moy, "Food Safety and Globalization of Trade: A Challenge to the Public Health Sector," *World Food Regulation Review* 8, no. 9 (1999).

15. Michael Trebilcock and Robert Howse, *The Regulation of International Trade* (London: Routledge, 1999), 37. For example, in its hormone-treated beef dispute ruling, the WTO permitted the U.S. to retaliate in an amount up to US$117 million; the U.S. applied tariffs in this amount to a variety of products, mostly from France, Italy, Germany, and Denmark.

16. Helen Milner, *Interests, Institutions and Information: Domestic Politics and International Relations* (Princeton, NJ: Princeton University Press, 1997), 9–15.

17. "No US-Russian 'Chicken War': Putin," via *Agence France Presse English,* April 22, 2002, http://archives.foodsafetynetwork.ca/animalnet/2002/4-2002/animalnet_april_23-2.htm (accessed October 21, 2005).

18. Letter of Lord Acton, dated March 15, 1880, quoted on page 8 of Gertrude Himmelfarb, "Introduction to John Stuart Mill's *On Liberty,*" in *On Liberty* (London: Penguin Books Ltd, 1974).

19. U.S. Department of Agriculture, U.S. Department of State, and U.S. Agency for International Development, "The U.S. Contribution to World Food Security (the U.S. Position Paper Prepared for the World Food Summit)," (1996), 2.

20. Ibid., 3.

21. Annette D. Beresford, "Homeland Security as an American Ideology: Implications for U.S. Policy and Action," *Journal of Homeland Security and Emergency Management* 1, no. 3 (2004): 16.

22. Radford G. Davis and Danelle Bickett-Weddle, "Agroterrorism Awareness," in *Agroterrorism Awareness Education,* version 1.2 (Ames, Iowa: Iowa State University Center for Food Security and Public Health, 2004).

23. Ibid.

24. Glenda Dvorak, "Definitions," in *Bioterrorism Awareness Education,* version 1.2 (Ames, Iowa: Iowa State University Center for Food Security and Public Health, 2003).

25. Table prepared by Dr. Abbey Nutsch, Assistant Professor of Food Safety & Security at Kansas State University, using data from R.J. Strongin, "How Vulnerable Is the Nation's Food Supply? Linking Food Safety and Food Security," National Health Policy Forum Issue Brief, no. 773 (2002); and U.S. General Accounting Office, "Food Safety: U.S. Needs a Single Agency to Administer a Unified, Risk-Based Inspection System," Report no. GAO/T-RCED-99-256 (Washington, DC: U.S. Government Printing Office, 1999).

26. American Association of Port Authorities, "Current Issues Facing the Industry," http://www.aapa-ports.org/industryinfo/currentissues.html. More than 31 million containers enter the U.S. each year.

27. Peter Andreas, "A Tale of Two Borders: The U.S.-Mexico and U.S.-Canada Lines After 9-11," Working Paper No. 77 (May 2003), The Center for Comparative Immigration Studies, University of California, San Diego.

28. Ibid.

29. For a more detailed discussion of smart borders, see Jason Ackleson, "Migration and the 'Smart Border' Security Environment," in this volume. See also Deborah Waller Meyers, "Does 'Smarter' Lead to Safer? An Assessment of the Border Accords with Canada and Mexico," *Migration Policy Institute Insight*, no. 2 (June 2003), http://www.migrationpolicy.org/pubs/6-13-0~1.PDF (accessed October 15, 2005).

30. George W. Bush, "Securing America's Borders Fact Sheet: Border Security" (Washington, DC: The White House, 2002), http://www.whitehouse.gov/news/releases/2002/01/print/20020125.html (accessed November 19, 2002).

31. Prosperity Agenda, Security and Prosperity Partnership of North America. Available at http://www.spp.gov/prosperity_agenda/ (accessed April 2, 2006).

32. Security Agenda, Security and Prosperity Partnership of North America. Available at http://www.spp.gov/security_agenda/ (accessed April 2, 2006).

33. Security and Prosperity Partnership of North America, "Report to Leaders: June 2005," http://www.spp.gov/report_to_leaders/ (accessed April 2, 2006).

34. See Jason Ackleson and Justin Kastner, "Partnership on Border Is a Big Step," *The El Paso (TX) Times,* July 1, 2005, B7.

CHAPTER 7

IMMIGRATION AND NATIONAL SECURITY: POST-9/11 CHALLENGES FOR THE UNITED STATES

Margaret D. Stock

Post-September 11, most policy makers and pundits view the immigration aspects of national security very simply: they believe that immigration policy can enhance national security by focusing on keeping people out of the United States. Thus, when speaking of immigration and national security, most people think of hiring more border patrol agents, tightening up the laws to make it harder for people to get into the United States, and quickly deporting those who violate their status while they are here.

The relationship between immigration and national security, however, is much more complicated than that. Rather than focusing on "keeping people out," an effective national security oriented U.S. immigration policy must focus on letting in the right people. Immigrants are a key asset in fighting the global war on terrorism and maintaining U.S. military dominance. They are also key to the United States maintaining its economic dominance, which is necessary to support our military power.

Yet the United States has no national security strategy for immigration. Immigration policy must be an explicit part of such a strategy, not an afterthought. A key aspect of our national security is a comprehensive immigration policy that allows us to distinguish between legitimate immigrants and the small number of people who intend to do us harm.

REACTION TO 9/11: A BACKLASH AGAINST IMMIGRANTS

Following the September 11 terrorist attacks on the World Trade Center and the Pentagon, many were quick to blame lax U.S. immigration policies.[1] Because all 19 terrorists were foreigners, such scrutiny was predictable, but inevitably resulted in overreaction. There were calls to halt immigration altogether;[2] stop the issuance of student visas;[3] close the borders with Canada and Mexico;[4] eliminate the Diversity Lottery visa program,[5] and pass ever-harsher immigration laws. One commentator even suggested setting up internment camps and profiling immigrants based on race and religion.[6] Typical was this comment from one restrictionist organization: "September 11 exposed the serious breaches in our immigration policies and laws that could be exploited with relative ease and deadly consequences."[7]

These extreme proposals reflect much popular thinking post-September 11 about the supposed connection between immigration and security: security is said to involve keeping people out of the United States—whether those people are terrorists coming on a flight, or illegal aliens in search of work trekking across the Arizona desert in an attempt to avoid the Border Patrol.

The relationship between immigration and security is far more complex, however, than just a matter of keeping people out. The "keeping people out" approach is not an appropriate or helpful way to link the two together. In fact, maintaining and enhancing our national security increasingly requires taking affirmative steps to let the right people in because immigrants are a national asset and are critical to success in the global war on terrorism.

Because American national, military, and homeland security strategies have failed to take into account the vital role that "letting people in" should play in maintaining our security, the U.S. government has missed key opportunities to enhance its security posture. American policy makers must reorient their thinking about the connection between immigration and national security, and develop a forward-thinking immigration policy as an explicit part of our national security strategy.

Defining National Security

Amos A. Jordan, William J. Taylor Jr. and Michael J. Mazarr have pointed out that "national security" is a "marvelously elastic term that has been stretched at times to cover a multitude of different issues and activities."[8] Jordan, Taylor, and Mazarr note that the term does not just mean protection from physical harm, but also implies protection, through a variety of means, of vital economic and political interests, the loss of which could threaten the fundamental values and vitality of the state.[9] If one thinks of national security this way, the complex relationship between immigration and national security becomes apparent. Immediately after the September 11 attacks, however, all eyes were on the issue of physical harm. Thus, the goal of nearly all of the immigration initiatives the

U.S. government took in the first year following the attacks was to keep people out.

The Reaction to 9/11: Immigration Policies Aimed at Keeping People Out

Immigration issues took center stage immediately after the September 11 attacks. All 19 of the hijackers were foreigners, and, it soon became apparent, all had entered the United States by applying for visas at American consulates overseas, boarding commercial aircraft, and passing inspection by U.S. immigration agents at various airports in the United States.[10] Although U.S. immigration officials looked closely at some of the hijackers' paperwork, all but one of the hijackers were permitted to enter the United States.[11]

Clearly, had the hijackers not been permitted to enter the United States, they could not have boarded the domestic U.S. flights that they hijacked and flew into the Twin Towers, the Pentagon, and a field in Pennsylvania. Many thus logically concluded that the most direct way to stop future attacks was to stop future hijackers from getting to the United States in the first place. The most obvious way to achieve that goal seemed to be to "crack down" on immigration. In the months after September 11, the immense pressure on U.S. security officials to "do something now" caused immediate changes in U.S. immigration law and policy.

Nearly all of these changes focused on the twin goals of finding terrorists who might still be inside the United States and deporting them quickly, and keeping future hijackers out of the United States. None of the immediate changes took into account the larger security implications of an immigration crackdown; instead, they reflected short-term thinking—"instant gratification" of the desire to "do something." Among the immediate initiatives were mass arrests of immigrants who met a certain profile; an enhanced emphasis on quickly deporting these immigrants by the use of secret hearings; new security checks and export controls; new tracking systems for foreigners entering the United States; interviews of certain immigrants; halting the flow of refugees to the United States until new screening procedures could be implemented; and enactment of new laws making it harder to enter the United States and easier to deport those who did. There was little focus, however, on how the immigrant community might be uniquely suited to assist in the effort to boost security, apart from a few initiatives to help immigrants who were serving in the U.S. military.

Mass Arrests

In the weeks following September 11, more than 1,000 people of Arab or Muslim origin were arrested as part of the investigation into the terrorist attacks. The government released very little information about these people, but eventually some of them were able to tell their stories. According to various media reports, "the handling of Muslims arrested on immigration charges after September 11 [was] fraught with delay and sloppy bookkeeping and [] due process [was] shortchanged...."[12] Immigrants were held for months without being charged, and at least one detainee died while in custody, apparently as a result of the stress of being detained.[13] "[D]etainees the government suspects least end up being held longest since they are low on the list of priorities. In the meantime, reputations are ruined, jobs are lost, families are kept apart, and lives are turned upside down."[14] While being held in detention, they were abused. "As innocent Muslim men swept up in the post-September 11 dragnet begin to emerge after being held in custody, often in secret, for weeks and months, they [told] embarrassing and sometimes horrifying tales of official indifference and, occasionally, abuse."[15]

Increased Deportations and Closed Hearings

On September 21, 2001, in apparent reaction to the September 11 terrorist attacks, Chief Immigration Judge Michael Creppy of the Executive Office for Immigration Review[16] (EOIR) issued a directive,[17] popularly known as "the Creppy memo," ordering that immigration judges hold secret hearings whenever the Attorney General of the United States deemed an immigrant to be "of special interest." Following issuance of the Creppy memo, the EOIR closed thousands of immigration court hearings, thereby excluding the immigrant's family, the press, and the public. Moreover, the very existence of the hearing was kept secret, and no information about the case could be found on the public docket or the public information telephone line.

The Creppy memo did not define what it meant by a "special interest" case. It was later revealed, however, that "special interest" cases invariably involved persons from a selected set of countries, most of which were Middle Eastern, Muslim, or Arab.[18] The Attorney General claimed the sole discretion to determine when a hearing would be closed, and his criteria were also secret.

The Creppy memo was immediately implemented, and its general terms were later made part of the Code of Federal Regulations.[19] Under post-September 11 "special interest" hearing procedures, many immigrants were arrested and tried in secret. The government refused to reveal their names or whereabouts, and their family and friends were often unable to locate them. In many cases, although the immigrants had attorneys, the government refused to reveal to their attorneys the clients' whereabouts. Lawyers and family members reported that the "special interest" immigrants were being "denied legal counsel, held indefinitely without charges, suddenly moved to new locations, or kept in prison even after a judge had ordered them released."[20]

An apparently typical case involved Malek Zeidan.[21] Mr. Zeidan, a Syrian who worked as an ice cream truck driver, was arrested on February 14, 2002. He had entered the United States more than a decade earlier on a visa, and had stayed well beyond his period of admission. Immigration authorities came across him accidentally in the course of investigating another case, and held him in detention for about 40 days before releasing him. Ultimately, he was freed on bail, but his removal hearing remained closed to the public. He had no known connections to terrorists of any kind, was not charged with a crime, and was apparently of so little danger to the safety of Americans that he was not held in custody. He was labeled a "special interest" case apparently solely as a result of his Syrian nationality. Later, after Mr. Zeidan sued to have his hearing opened to the public, the government suddenly redesignated his case so that it was no longer of "special interest."[22]

Other "special interest" detainees told similar tales. Mohammed Irshaid, a New York civil engineer, reported being arrested by federal agents who accused him of being a terrorist, threw him in jail in Passaic, New Jersey, mistreated him badly, and then released him three weeks later without ever filing any charges against him. Syed Jaffri, a Pakistani who had had a dispute with his Bronx landlord, reported being arrested, thrown into solitary confinement, beaten up, verbally abused, never advised of his right to a lawyer, and summarily deported (without his money or papers) to Canada after being held for six months.[23]

In one of the worst cases, Al-Badr Al-Hazmi, a doctor from Texas, answered his door one day to find federal agents armed with guns. The agents arrested him, taking him first to the FBI office in San Antonio, and then transferring him to New York, where he was held in the Metropolitan Correctional Center. He alleges that he was subjected to physical abuse and not permitted to contact his family for more than a week. Finally, after 12 days in jail, he was released, without his glasses and wearing only prison clothing. His apparent transgression was to have the same last name as one of the September 11 hijackers—although that name is apparently as common in Saudi Arabia as "Smith" is in the United States.[24]

Halting Refugee Admissions

After September 11, the government called a temporary halt to refugee admissions, asserting the need to increase security measures to thwart terrorists. This moratorium was implemented despite the fact that extensive security measures already were in place, none of the 9/11 hijackers entered the United States as refugees, and the difficult conditions that refugees endure make the program an unlikely conduit for terrorists. When refugee admissions began again in December 2001, the number of admissions remained abnormally low. During fiscal year 2002, the United States admitted the lowest number of refugees in more than 20 years— only 27,500 of the 70,000 slots available.[25] Many said that the United States had "closed its doors" to refugees, and the new security measures implemented in November 2001 significantly increased processing times.

New and Tougher Laws

President George W. Bush on October 26, 2001 signed into law the *Uniting and Strengthening America by Providing Appropriate Tools Required to Intercept and Obstruct Terrorism (USA PATRIOT) Act* of 2001.[26] The *USA PATRIOT Act* contains three sections relating to immigration: one has "stopgap" measures designed to enhance security at the border between the United States and Canada; a second has provisions relating to the admissibility of terrorists and those who sponsor them; and a third has provisions designed to help the family members of the noncitizen victims of the September 11 terrorist attacks.

Uncontroversial immigration sections of the *USA PATRIOT Act* include those designed to enhance border security and intelligence collection in the short term. Among other things, these provisions waive certain caps on personnel on the northern border, allow the U.S. Immigration and Naturalization Service (INS) and Department of State (DOS) to access FBI criminal history records through the National Crime Information Center, and mandate development and certification of technology to verify the identity of people applying for visas or otherwise seeking to enter the United States. Changes designed to help noncitizen victims of the September 11 attacks, such as provisions granting posthumous citizenship to lawful residents who died in the attack, were also uncontroversial.

One significant portion of the *USA PATRIOT Act*, however, makes substantive changes to the law to enhance the government's ability to identify and deport terrorists or potential terrorists. One provision makes it possible to deport foreigners who engage in mere association with persons who turn out to be terrorists. Another gives sweeping new power to immigration authorities to deport foreigners who are accused, but not convicted, of threatening a single person.

Section 411 of the law adds new grounds of inadmissibility for representatives of foreign terrorist organizations or any group that publicly endorses acts of terrorist activity, and spouses and children of aliens who are inadmissible on any of the terrorism-related grounds. It provides new, unreviewable authority to the Secretary of State to designate any group, foreign or domestic, as a terrorist organization, upon publication in the Federal Register; makes a deportable offense any fundraising, solicitation for membership, or material support—even for humanitarian projects—for groups that are designated terrorist organizations by the Secretary of State (without regard to whether such activities further actual terrorist activity); and makes a deportable offense any solicitation of funds or other material support for groups engaging in terrorism, though not officially designated as "terrorist organizations," unless the person can prove that he "did not know, and should not reasonably have known, that the solicitation would further the organization's terrorist activity."

In perhaps the most startling change to immigration law, however, the *USA PATRIOT Act* redefines "terrorist activity" to include the threat to use, or the use of, any "dangerous device (other than for mere personal monetary gain), with intent to endanger, directly or indirectly, the safety of one or more individuals or to cause substantial damage to property." Lawmakers apparently passed this provision in the belief that airline hijackers possessed of box cutters would not be covered sufficiently by the specific hijacking language already in law. Ironically, however, under this new, broader definition of a terrorist, the September 11 hijackers would not have been screened out, because they had no apparent previous criminal history and had not publicly announced their intention to attack anyone. The new legislation would, however, deny visas to any foreigners ever involved in a knife fight in a bar.

New Security Checks

The State Department in November 2001 implemented a new visa approval process for young men, age 16 through 45, from 26 Arab or Muslim countries.[27] The countries affected included Afghanistan, Algeria, Bahrain, Djibouti, Egypt, Eritrea, Indonesia, Iran, Iraq, Jordan, Kuwait, Lebanon, Libya, Malaysia, Morocco, Oman, Pakistan, Qatar, Saudi Arabia, Somalia, Sudan, Syria, Tunisia, Turkey, the United Arab Emirates, and Yemen. The new checks, which were supposed to take about 20 days to process, sometimes took months, and visa applications from those countries dropped sharply. A State Department official admitted in October 2003 that although more than 125,000 visa applications had been screened using these checks, not a single application had been denied because of them.[28]

NSEERS Special Registration

Other immigration initiatives after September 11 included the National Security Entry Exit System (NSEERS) and a related program called Special Registration. NSEERS and Special Registration both require foreign men between 16 and 45 who come from certain countries to provide fingerprints, photographs, and substantial personal information to immigration authorities. They are also required to complete special checks upon entering and leaving the United States, and to report to immigration authorities at regular intervals while here. Billed as a tool to locate terrorists, these programs were implemented in several waves. More than 100,000 aliens complied with orders to report for registration; when immigration authorities began to file deportation charges against some 13,800 who had registered, however, many immigrants began leaving the United States rather than trying to comply.[29] After the program was roundly criticized for poor implementation, government officials suspended most of the interior aspects of the program—Special Registration—in December 2003. They continue to implement NSEERS at ports of entry and deport persons who have not complied with it. In addition, some foreigners residing within the United States are still subject to it.

US-VISIT

The government after the terrorist attacks also refocused efforts to implement US-VISIT, an extremely costly computer network entry/exit system designed to track foreign visitors. Towards the end of 2005, US-VISIT had been implemented at more than 100 airports and seaports and 50 land ports of entry. (December 31, 2005 was the mandated deadline to implement US-VISIT at all other ports.) The system does not apply to a significant number of foreign visitors, including Canadians and Mexicans, who have been exempted from participating, at least temporarily.

The US-VISIT process involves visa applicants at foreign consulates providing two fingerprints and a digital photograph. When the visa holder arrives in the United States, he or she provides the same two fingerprints again, and another photo, which are compared digitally with the biometric information previously provided at the consulate. The system then tells immigration inspectors whether the person standing before them is the same person who applied for the visa overseas. Recently the Department of Homeland Security (DHS) announced that it would in the future collect all ten fingerprints of every applicant for admission.

The system is also supposed to compare fingerprints and photos with criminal and other databases. Eventually, the system is supposed to track people's exits from the country so that "overstays" can be identified. At the time of this writing, however, US-VISIT's exit function is almost nonexistent.

While this initiative is supposed to be the new centerpiece of efforts to improve national security through new immigration initiatives, it has been beset by poor management and insufficient funding. While US-VISIT is projected to cost in excess of $7 billion, according to DHS estimates, Congress and the Administration have not indicated a willingness to appropriate the necessary funding. In fiscal year 2006, the

Administration requested $390 million for the program, and Congress appropriated $376 million. In a report issued last year, however, the General Accounting Office—now known as the Government Accountability Office (GAO)—said that the true cost of the program is likely to be twice the estimate given by DHS and that DHS does not have the staff to manage US-VISIT.

Thus far, DHS has announced that this system has "flagged" about 1,300 people out of 10 million applying for visas to enter the United States since it was implemented; it is unclear, however, what "flagged" means. Recent testimony on Capitol Hill pointed out that the system only notices attempts to change fingerprints about 53 percent of the time.[30]

SEVIS

On May 14, 2002, the President signed into law the *Enhanced Border Security and Visa Entry Reform Act of 2002*.[31] Under this law, all U.S. institutions with foreign students or exchange visitors were required, by August 1, 2003, to comply with a new tracking system called the Student Exchange Visitor Information System (SEVIS). SEVIS is an Internet-based software application designed to transmit electronic information about foreign students and exchange visitors to both the Department of Homeland Security and the State Department. American colleges and universities are required to keep immigration officials constantly apprised of the whereabouts and status of their foreign students and exchange visitors, or risk losing the ability to enroll foreign students altogether. Although the SEVIS system is now functioning more smoothly than when it was first implemented, many people have raised security concerns due to its vulnerability to hackers, who have stolen valuable personal information from the SEVIS database.[32]

Deportation for Failure to File a Change of Address

The Justice Department on September 22, 2002, announced that it would begin prosecuting foreigners in the United States who fail to notify the government within ten days of any address change. While the statutory authority to do this had existed for decades, the law had not been enforced. Furthermore, the agency has repeatedly been criticized for maintaining obsolete addresses in its databases because of problems entering new information. When this initiative was announced, the federal government was swamped with hundreds of thousands of change of address notices, which it was unable to process.[33] The law apparently provides a convenient pretext to remove aliens thought to be suspicious but against whom no serious charges can be sustained.[34]

Expedited Removals

Immigration authorities announced in August 2004 an expansion of the "expedited removal" program, whereby immigration officers can summarily return immigrants to their countries of origin.[35] Under this program, the immigrants do not get a hearing with a judge or other neutral adjudicator unless they convince the officers that they should be permitted to apply for asylum. At the same time, the speed of the process means that U.S. government authorities have very little time to collect information and exploit possible intelligence sources. Immigration authorities brag about their newly-acquired ability to remove suspicious foreigners speedily, but others question whether it makes any sense to quickly release a suspected terrorist to freedom in another country. In at least one case, a person removed expeditiously committed a suicide attack in Iraq.

NEGATIVE NATIONAL SECURITY CONSEQUENCES POST-SEPTEMBER 11

Cumulatively, these post-September 11 immigration policies, intended to enhance U.S. national security, have had significant negative effects on security.

Alienating the Immigrant Community

According to many experts, some of the measures implemented by the U.S. government after September 11—particularly those that target Muslims and Arabs—have been too unfocused to enhance security effectively and, by fostering resentment among these groups both within the United States and abroad, may actually hinder intelligence investigations.[36] In some cases, the government has used terrorism grounds to bar well-known Muslims from the United States—including pop star Cat Stevens and prominent scholar Tariq Ramadan—thereby creating substantial negative publicity in the Muslim and Arab world. In other cases, immigrants have refused to cooperate with the government in antiterrorism efforts after being targeted by a "zero tolerance" policy for minor immigration violations.[37]

Economic Harm

Many of the post-9/11 initiatives have harmed the U.S. economy—and continue to do so. Inevitably, the policies and laws designed to keep terrorists out have cast a much wider net. Many foreigners have been excluded as "national security threats" although there is no reasonable probability that they truly constitute such threats. As word got out that the United States was behaving harshly towards foreign visitors, many simply stopped coming. Visa applications dropped substantially and American businesses reported billions of dollars in losses as a result of the new, harsher security regime.[38]

Loss of Foreign Students

Foreign students have been significantly affected by the post-9/11 regime. Turned off by post-September 11 security measures, many have elected to study in more hospitable countries. Despite a small recent rise in student visa numbers, a significant number of the best and brightest are going elsewhere. The Institute of International Education, which tracks foreign students in the United States, has noted that foreign student enrollment in U.S. colleges and universities is flat after years of steady growth, with significant declines in 13 of the top 20 sending countries, including Indonesia, Thailand, and Malaysia. A recent report by the Council of Graduate Schools found that nine out of ten U.S. graduate programs have seen a significant drop in international applications, particularly in areas like engineering and science. In April 2004, Harvard president Lawrence Summers, in writing a letter to U.S. Secretary of State Colin Powell, noted that applications from Chinese students were down as much as 40 percent in certain Harvard departments.[39] "[W]e risk losing some of our most talented scientists and compromising our country's position at the forefront of technological innovation," he wrote. "If the next generation of foreign leaders is educated elsewhere, we also will have lost the incalculable benefits derived from their extended exposure to our country and its democratic values."[40]

Other nations have directly benefited from America's unwillingness to recognize the downside of harsher immigration rules. "The European Union overtook the United States as the most popular destination for the growing numbers of middle-class Chinese students seeking a Western high school or university education in 2002, and the trend continued to gain momentum through this fall semester," according to a report by the American Immigration Law Foundation.[41] The report also noted that Britain, Australia, and Canada—in stark contrast to the United States—have chosen to boost their foreign-student populations aggressively since September 11.[42]

Outsourcing

Post-September 11, the United States developed procedures for entry into the United States that are so complicated and time-consuming that many of the world's brightest scientists, engineers, and foreign students cannot enter in a timely fashion to conduct research or pursue studies.

As a result, major research projects have been delayed and investments wasted when the lengthy processing times of visa applications and the uncertainty whether the applications even will be approved discourage, if not prevent, key personnel from entering the country. Richard Florida, the author of a book entitled *The Rise of the Creative Class* and a professor at Carnegie-Mellon, says that our harsher immigration regime has helped spur an exodus of the best and brightest from the United States: "[F]ewer educated foreigners are choosing to come to the United States....They now complain of being hounded by the immigration agencies as potential threats to security, and they worry that America is abandoning its standing as an open society."[43]

The anti-immigrant climate after September 11 has forced some American companies to shift projects and operations overseas. Unable to bring needed foreign workers to the United States, they have begun to move their work abroad and rely more heavily on overseas subsidiaries. Consequently, Americans desiring jobs in certain high-tech sectors have begun to relocate overseas.[44] In addition, American jobs that these projects and operations would have created here are created elsewhere instead.

Excluding the Wrong People

Overbroad immigration security measures intent on keeping people out can harm national security if they exclude the wrong people. In the past, the United States has had a poor record of distinguishing people who are true threats from those who are not, but who may be deemed so by overly broad statutory language and a failure by immigration agents to use reasonable discretion. The post-September 11 world was not the first time that the United States demonstrated an inability to discern those who are true threats from those who are not.

In December 1932, Albert Einstein, the world famous scientist, sought a visa to escape Nazi Germany and come to the United States. But there was a problem—a U.S. government file showed that Einstein was a suspected socialist, and had ties to socialist groups. A conservative organization had sent a 16-page report on Einstein to the State Department, urging that Einstein be denied entry to the United States because of his ties to socialist groups. Einstein was only able to obtain a visa after applying media pressure through the *New York Times* and the Associated Press. He escaped Germany just a few weeks before Hitler seized power in Berlin.[45]

In 2003, 70 years later, if Einstein had made the same application, he would no doubt have been excluded from the United States—inadmissible as a terrorist sympathizer. Einstein's documented ties to various subversive groups would have marked him as someone barred from entry to America.[46] He would have been left in Nazi Germany, probably to become a victim of the Nazi Holocaust. If he had not been imprisoned and executed, his scientific talents would surely have been put to use by the Nazis to develop nuclear weapons before the United States did.

Reflecting on Einstein should help American policy makers focus with greater clarity on post-9/11 immigration law measures taken in the name of "national security." By adopting blanket rules whereby whole classes of people are excluded without any individualized threat assessment, the United States may be excluding people who could make invaluable contributions to our security.

Loss of "Soft Power"

One of the greatest national security assets is the "soft power" of America's image.[47] Like the "goodwill" of a corporation, this asset cannot easily be measured. But one knows when it is being weakened. America is safest when others view her favorably, exhibiting values and virtues that make her worthy of support rather than attack. The image of America as a land of freedom is an invaluable national security asset that makes Americans and others willing to fight and die for her. Preserving this image is in large part a function of keeping America a country where the "rule of law," fairness, and justice prevail.

One of the overlooked "soft power" aspects of U.S. national security can be U.S. immigration policy. Those who perceive America as a land of opportunity and freedom are likely to join with Americans in the war on terrorism. The United States should not squander this asset by creating an image of America as xenophobic and isolationist.

Harsher laws also make it more likely that government power will be abused and misdirected. While harsher immigration laws will not stop terrorists, they will stop legitimate visitors who come to the United States and are exposed to our country; foreign students who seek to study here; investors who could increase U.S. productivity; and low-wage "essential" workers who work long hours in jobs that most Americans don't want. These laws will also keep families separated, causing untold hardship to American citizens and their children. Legitimate refugees will be denied a refuge on American shores. More and more citizens are likely to be deported or excluded erroneously.

Creating New Security Threats

Many of the measures that the government has taken also have the potential to harm American security directly. For example, the government is in the process of creating huge databases on both foreigners and Americans, on the theory that collecting this data may help identify and locate terrorists. While this concept in theory has merit, the implementation has been nothing short of alarming. New computerized databases are being created, and yet the agency charged with creating them has one of the poorest computer security programs in government. Its vulnerability to hackers has been well-publicized.[48] Employees of this agency have already begun to use its databases to engage in criminal acts.[49] As more and more sensitive personal data is compiled in these government databases, the likelihood that this data will be abused or stolen—and the magnitude of the resulting harm—increases dramatically. Past performance of government law enforcement agencies on this issue is not encouraging.

Overspending on Security

Throughout this process, there has been a sense that "national security" requires the government to spend as much as it can—as if it had unlimited resources—on all of these initiatives. There has been no effort to do an overall cost-benefit analysis of U.S. national security immigration measures and to prioritize accordingly. Nor, beyond blindly targeting the "types" of people who participated in the September 11 attacks, has there been any sort of comprehensive immigration strategy developed as part of our overall national security strategy. History teaches that overspending on ill-focused types of security measures can be counterproductive.

Other nations have overspent on similarly ill-conceived security measures, to their detriment. In fact, the former Soviet Union had many low-technology versions of the same "national security" immigration measures that the United States is now attempting to implement. Unfortunately for the Soviet Union, it spent so much on these and other security measures that it eventually disintegrated—and lost its superpower status. At the same time, it did not solve the terrorism problem within its borders.

More immediate harm to national security comes, however, when such harsh and counterproductive laws and policies are enacted that a nation finds itself unable to defend against the real threat. As the 9/11 Intelligence Joint Inquiry[50] found, the attacks of September 11 might have been prevented with better intelligence and interagency cooperation. A comprehensive immigration policy designed to enhance national security—rather than disjointed and unfocused initiatives—can provide the tools essential in this new kind of war.

U.S. SECURITY STRATEGIES ARE SILENT ON IMMIGRATION

The U.S. national security strategy, the national military strategy, and the homeland security strategy do not recognize the key role that immigration can play in enhancing our security. The first post-September 11 explicit recognition of the potential role can be found in a few comments made by the 9/11 Commission in its final report:

Our borders and immigration system, including law enforcement, ought to send a message of welcome, tolerance, and justice to members of immigrant communities in the United States and in their countries of origin. We should reach out to immigrant communities. Good immigration services are one way of doing so that is valuable in every way—including intelligence.[51]

We advocate a system for screening, not categorical profiling. A screening system looks for particular, identifiable suspects or indicators of risk. It does not involve guesswork about who might be dangerous.[52]

Our border screening system should check people efficiently and welcome friends. Admitting large numbers of students, scholars, businesspeople, and tourists fuels our economy, cultural vitality, and political reach.[53]

The border and immigration system of the United States must remain a visible manifestation of our belief in freedom, democracy, global economic growth, and the rule of law, yet serve equally well as a vital element of counterterrorism.[54]

[L]ong-term success demands the use of all elements of national power: diplomacy, intelligence, covert action, law enforcement, economic policy, foreign aid, public diplomacy, and homeland defense. If we favor one tool while neglecting the others, we leave ourselves vulnerable and weaken our national effort.[55]

As the 9/11 commission implicitly recognizes, immigrants and a welcoming immigration system are potential assets in a comprehensive national security strategy designed to fight a global war on terrorism.

APPLYING A FORWARD-THINKING APPROACH TO THE IMMIGRATION AND SECURITY ISSUE

How such a comprehensive strategy might work can be illustrated with the issue of whether or not to "regularize" the status of illegal immigrants. Some critics have argued that such regularization is equivalent to granting an amnesty to illegal aliens—a controversial proposal in today's overheated political climate—and will harm national security.[56] In fact, a comprehensive reform proposal that includes provisions allowing undocumented immigrants the opportunity to adjust their status to legal permanent residence is likely to enhance national security.

There currently are somewhere between 8 and 20 million illegal aliens in the United States, with these numbers growing daily.[57] The federal government has admitted that it cannot stop people from coming, and it cannot deport them all; in fact, less than 1 percent are actually deported annually. The inflow exceeds the outflow by a large magnitude. Mass illegal migration of people—whether Haitians fleeing the crime and poverty of their homeland or Mexicans coming here for jobs—may threaten security if the migrants disrupt communities, overwhelm social services, or perhaps—as Samuel Huntington has recently alleged[58]—threaten national identity. If even a few of these illegal immigrants mean to do physical harm, they can be seen as a national security threat.

Thus, some look at this problem and think: illegal immigration is a threat to national security. The government must do everything it can to stop this threat. Government must round up all the illegal aliens and deport them; military forces must be deployed to the border alongside citizen militias; government must hire more border patrol agents; government must crack down on employers who hire illegal aliens. Those who think in simple ways about immigration and security issues will call for unlimited spending on these programs.

Those who think more carefully about this issue will consider the real security costs and benefits of such initiatives. Does the United States have the resources to deport 8 to 20 million illegal aliens, while at the same time pursuing other government goals? No. Are these people harming the United States? Again, no. Luckily, nearly all are in the United States to work or to be with their families—if they planned to attack or cause Americans physical harm, the entire Department of Defense would not be large enough to stop them. And who are these people? Many of the illegal aliens in the country today are the parents, children, spouses, brothers, sisters, grandparents, cousins, uncles, and aunts of U.S. citizens and lawful permanent residents. What do they contribute? Many are hardworking, tax-paying workers who are essential to our economy because they take jobs Americans do not want, or provide necessary labor in occupations where there are worker shortages. They are nannies, janitors, hotel workers, bus drivers, health care workers, construction workers, factory workers, airport workers, computer programmers, guards at the front gate of U.S. military installations, even contractors working at the White House. They are married to members of the U.S. Armed Forces, engaged to be married to military members, or even military members themselves—several illegal aliens have died in combat in the U.S. military in the past three years, and many have served in Iraq and Afghanistan. A former illegal alien[59] is today the Republican governor of California. While those who criticize their illegality opine that they should "go get legal," there is no way under today's draconian U.S. immigration laws for them to do so.

Comprehensive reform that includes a provision giving illegal aliens the opportunity to earn their legal residency would mean that a significant number would no longer be illegal, and immigration officials would not have to waste limited resources on finding and deporting them. Second, such a policy would encourage these aliens to come forward to be fingerprinted, interviewed, have their backgrounds checked, pay taxes, and provide information to authorities about their existence and means of entry into the United States. Most are hard-working and have no criminal record, and the government has been completely unable to deport them in any effective fashion. An initiative that encourages undocumented aliens to come out of the shadows would create a new source of intelligence as well as generate vast economic benefits to this country.

From a security perspective, it is much better to have comprehensive records on these people than to continue the current situation, where locating them is entirely hit or miss—and for what purpose? If the United States had an explicit national security strategy in mind when approaching undocumented immigrants, policy makers would probably conclude that rather than seeking to deport them all, it makes a lot more sense to bring them out of the shadows and "regularize" them, allowing them to pay taxes, get driver's licenses, and otherwise participate openly in the national community. Regularization would speed their integration into U.S. society, making them less of a threat to security or national identity. Deporting them does not make Americans safer, and the effort to do so would squander precious law enforcement resources.

Along the same lines, a forward-thinking immigration strategy would call for enactment of legislation like the *DREAM Act*,[60] a bipartisan bill that has yet to pass Congress despite widespread support. The *DREAM Act* addresses the fact that many illegal aliens are undocumented children who have grown up in America, attended local schools, and demonstrated a sustained commitment to learn English and succeed in our educational system. They cannot be readily distinguished from native-born American citizen children, and yet U.S. immigration laws provide no avenue for these U.S.-educated and acculturated children to become legal. Many were brought to the United States by their parents at an age at which they were too young to understand the legality of their arrival. The *DREAM/Student Adjustment Act* would allow immigrant students who have grown up in this country, graduated from high school, been acculturated as Americans, and have no criminal record, to go to college or serve in the military and legalize their immigration status. Interestingly, it would also likely help the U.S. military meet its recruiting goals, making hundreds of thousands of teenagers eligible to enlist. Would it enhance American national security to regularize these children, rather than deport them? Probably. This is an example of a case where it makes more sense to have an approach that lets these people "in," rather than concentrating on kicking people out.

HOW IMMIGRATION HELPS ACHIEVE OUR NATIONAL SECURITY GOALS

There are many other ways in which "letting people in" enhances our national security. Consider that immigrants play a vital role in the U.S. health care system, a system that is one of the foundations of American national security, because it keeps the U.S. population healthy and is key to responding to national security emergencies such as terrorist attacks and natural disasters. More than a million immigrants work in the American health care system—13 percent of the workforce. The foreign-born comprise 25.2 percent of U.S. physicians; 17 percent of nursing, psychiatric, and home health care workers; and 11.5 percent of registered nurses.[61] The United States currently has a national shortage of 126,000 nurses[62]—a shortage that could be met by foreign nurses, except that restrictive immigration policies bar most of them from coming here legally. Health care workers are vital to American security; the United States is not producing enough of them among its native population, and yet the United States has no explicit national security policy about the immigration of health care workers.

Other critical national security assets are scientists and engineers.[63] The foreign-born comprise 11.1 percent of the U.S. population, but they comprise 16.6 percent of American scientists and engineers.[64] Foreign-born scientists and engineers comprise 38 percent of all scientists and engineers in the United States with a doctorate; specifically, they are 51 percent of engineers with a doctorate and 45 percent of life scientists, physical scientists, and mathematicians with a doctorate. Robert Paarlberg, a professor of political science at Wellesley College, published an article in a recent issue of *International Security*, entitled "Knowledge is Power: Science, Military Dominance, and U.S. Security."[65] Paarlberg points out that the United States dominates the world militarily because the United States is a net importer of scientific talent and knowledge from abroad. He argues that post-9/11 security measures aimed at immigrants have actually hurt American security because they have cut back significantly on the "vital net flow of scientific assets" that undergird U.S. military dominance. In his view, the United States should bring more talented foreigners into the United States in order to maintain its lead.

Social Security

According to Alan Greenspan, the chairman of the Federal Reserve, the U.S. Social Security system will go broke as baby boomers retire—unless America brings in more young, working immigrants to pay into the system. In the words of Mr. Greenspan, "The aging of the population in the United States will have significant effects on our fiscal situation. In particular, it makes our Social Security and Medicare programs unsustainable in the long run, short of a major increase in immigration rates, a dramatic acceleration in productivity growth...a significant increase in the age of eligibility for benefits, or the use of general revenues to fund benefits."[66] Greenspan has also said that immigration is the key to whether the U.S. labor force will experience growth or become stagnant.

Military Manpower

Immigrants play a key role in military operations. Thousands of immigrants serve in all branches of the military. Without them, the U.S. military could not meet its recruiting goals, and it could not fill the need for foreign language translators, interpreters, and cultural experts. Immigrants add valuable diversity to the armed forces, and do extremely well, often having significantly lower attrition rates than other recruits.[67]

Intelligence and Translation

An even more important problem, however, is that the U.S. government has failed to use immigration as an intelligence tool in the war on terrorism. The 9/11 Commission identified two key intelligence shortcomings that immigration can address—the need for human intelligence sources who can infiltrate terrorist groups and the communities from which terrorists come, and the need for translators who speak the language of the terrorists.

The best defense against terrorism, to quote Jack Dempsey and to paraphrase George Washington, is a good offense. In the immigration law and policy arena, that means exploitation of human intelligence about terrorism. Human intelligence (HUMINT) must come from immigrants, members of the communities in which the terrorists live. The United States needs reliable sources who can provide information about terrorists' plans. Immigrants can provide this intelligence.

Four years after 9/11, the United States still lacks the human assets to analyze what intelligence about terrorists it does collect. Why does the United States lack these assets? To a great extent, America simply doesn't have enough people who speak the language.[68] Margaret Gulotta, chief of the FBI's Language Services Section, has said that most intelligence analysts may not recognize terrorist threats because of language barriers. Although the FBI has hired hundreds of linguists since September 11, there is still a severe shortage.[69] Several years after 9/11, the FBI admitted that it had more than 100,000 intelligence intercepts that have gone untranslated because of a lack of interpreters. "Warnings of terrorist attacks may not be translated in time unless more people are hired by the nation's defense and intelligence agencies," Gulotta has said.[70] Only about American students are now studying Pashto, Dari, Farsi, and

Uzbek at U.S. colleges, although 40 million people worldwide speak those languages.[71] America simply does not produce enough speakers of many critical languages.[72]

The State Department—responsible for translating the U.S. message to the Arabic-speaking world—has only 54 fluent Arabic speakers, an appalling deficiency.[73] Very few American schools even teach the languages that the United States needs for the war on terror. Even the Defense Language Institute in Monterrey, California, does not teach some of them. So where can the United States get sufficient foreign language speakers to translate the massive amounts of intelligence that the intelligence community gathers each day? Answer: it's not possible—unless the United States relies on immigrants, or outsources the translation overseas.

One can draw similar conclusions about human intelligence. Very few native-born Americans have the ability to infiltrate al Qaeda camps. The few who have done so—John Walker Lindh and Jose Padilla, for example—have not been used as counterintelligence assets. It will take years to train native-born Americans to infiltrate terrorist organizations. In the meantime, where will the United States get its human intelligence sources? Again, America must recruit immigrants. But if immigrants are terrified and therefore unsympathetic to the U.S. cause, what is the likelihood that America will gain their cooperation?

The federal government has sometimes lacked sensitivity to this key security issue. For example, shortly after September 11, U.S. Attorney General John Ashcroft announced that he was cracking down on immigrants. A few days later, he announced that any immigrants who came forward and provided useful information would be rewarded with a visa.[74] Inconsistent messages like this do not encourage immigrants to help in the war on terror.

The Government has also summarily deported many who could have provided intelligence, or acted as counterintelligence agents. Rather than dumping immigrants in Somalia,[75] where they are likely to be killed or turned into future terrorists as a matter of survival, it might have been smarter to consider their value as intelligence sources, and treat them accordingly. Creating future terrorists—more angry people who have nothing to lose by attacking the United States—is not a logical strategy.[76] Part of a new U.S. national security strategy should include reform of deportation and removal laws so that an alien is not removed from the United States until a government official certifies that his removal will not harm the United States.

CONCLUSION

Unfortunately, the history of the U.S. federal government's immigration policies and initiatives after the September 11 terrorist attacks has reflected a philosophy that enhancing security demands keeping people out. The underlying assumption behind this approach is that stricter laws will inevitably increase security, because restrictive laws and initiatives can somehow prevent terrorism. In fact, harsher immigration laws harm security if they cause the United States to exclude the wrong immigrants, deprive America of the human intelligence it needs to learn of the terrorist threat, waste resources by focusing on deporting people who are no threat to U.S. security, and lead Americans falsely to believe that the threat of terrorism can be solved by limiting the number of foreigners who come to American shores.

U.S. immigration laws are already tougher than most people appreciate, and making them even harsher will do little to enhance security, and far more to harm it. Making immigration laws tougher can exclude the wrong people, people the United States needs to fight the war on terrorism. Tougher laws must be enforced, and thus additional law enforcement resources—already in short supply—must be devoted to enforcing these tougher laws. While such increased enforcement can enhance security if the harsher laws themselves are carefully focused on security, increased enforcement of harsher, ill-focused laws do not enhance security, but further diminish the limited resources available to target terrorism effectively. And finally, harsher laws give a false sense of security, a lesson American policy makers have already failed to learn from prior terrorist attacks.

It is also important to note that the United States is not just in a global war on terrorism. The United States is also in a global battle for people.[77] The United States became a superpower because it attracted the best and the brightest to American shores. Smart people from all over the world have sought to come to America for hundreds of years, have fought to come here, and have even died to come here. Current U.S. military dominance is a direct result of the fact that the United States has been the destination of choice for immigrants.

America's post-September 11 approach to immigration directly threatens that dominance. In the name of national security, the United States has instituted policies that have made many foreigners feel unwelcome in America. The United States is even starting to experience a "reverse brain drain" as Americans move to other countries that they deem to be more supportive of their creative needs. There has been a direct—and negative—economic impact from all this "security."

When most people think of immigration and national security, they think of harsher laws that keep people out. Instead, we should be thinking of immigration as a national security asset. We need a forward-looking immigration strategy that capitalizes on the national security benefits that immigrants provide. Keeping people out actually harms American national security if it hurts the U.S. economy and "soft" power, deprives

America of the human resources that the United States needs for the fight against terrorism, and allows other nations with more generous policies to pull ahead. "Implicit in the term 'national defense' is the notion of defending those values and ideals which set this nation apart...."[78] Before enacting new and harsher laws and policies, U.S. policy makers must ask whether those laws and policies will actually make Americans safer, and whether they will actually prevent future terrorism. In taking measures to enhance American security after the September 11 attacks, policies must be focused and effective, rather than a vast expenditure of resources to hit nonthreatening targets.

The United States is now the most powerful nation in the world, but history teaches that powerful nations do not always remain powerful. The United States does not have unlimited resources, and this war against terrorism must be fought with focus and intelligence. The United States did not have focus or adequate intelligence on September 11. Poor intelligence and information sharing allowed the attacks to happen when they could perhaps have been stopped. While September 11 clearly revealed the need for improved counterterrorism and security policies, it should not serve as a pretext to abandon America's traditional openness to newcomers. This openness is not just a reflection of American history and traditions—it is vital to American security. Post-September 11, American policy makers must think more imaginatively about immigration and national security, making immigration policy an explicit part of the U.S. national security strategy.

NOTES

1. Most prominently, the Center for Immigration Studies published a series of papers in which it claimed that current laws were inadequate to meet the threat of terrorism. See, e.g., Mark Krikorian and Steven A. Camarota, "Immigration & Terrorism: What Is To Be Done?" (Washington, DC: Center for Immigration Studies, 2001), http://www.cis.org/articles/2001/back1601.html.

2. Steven Camarota, "Safety in (Lower) Numbers: Immigration & Homeland Security" (Washington, DC: Center for Immigration Studies, 2002). Camarota argues that the best way to give INS "breathing room" and to address homeland security concerns is to reduce temporary and permanent immigration.

3. Holly Step, "Curbs Feared On Foreign Student Body," *Miami Herald*, September 26, 2001, 3B.

4. Thomas Ginsburg, "U.S. Immigration Policy to Undergo Scrutiny," *Philadelphia Enquirer*, September 18, 2001, A17 ("We must close the borders now, and have all illegal aliens deported.").

5. Mark Krikorian, "Feel Safer Yet?," *National Review Online*, September 10, 2002, http://www.nationalreview.com/script/printpage.p?ref=/comment/comment-krikorian091002.asp.

6. Michelle Malkin, *In Defense of Internment: The Case for Racial Profiling in World War II and the War on Terror* (Washington, DC: Regnery Publishing, 2004).

7. Federation for American Immigration Reform, "Invitation to Terror: How Our Immigration System Still Leaves America At Risk—Executive Summary," http://www.fairus.org/site/PageServer?pagename=research_research517a (accessed March 16, 2006).

8. Amos A. Jordan, William J. Taylor Jr. and Michael J. Mazarr, *American National Security,* 5th ed. (Baltimore, MD: Johns Hopkins University Press, 1999).

9. Ibid.

10. For a detailed discussion of how the September 11 hijackers got into the United States, see National Commission on Terrorist Attacks on the United States, *The 9/11 Commission Report: Final Report Of The National Commission On Terrorist Attacks Upon The United States* (2004), 168–69, 235.

11. Ibid. The one hijacker turned away was Mohammed al-Khatani, a Saudi who later turned up in U.S. custody as a result of the global war on terrorism. See "U.S. Says Guantanamo Detainees Give Best Al-Qaeda Intelligence," *Agence France Presse,*, April 18, 2005.

12. Jim Edwards, "Data Show Shoddy Due Process for Post-September 11 Immigration Detainees," *New Jersey Law Journal,* February 4, 2002.

13. Somini Sengupta, "Ill-Fated Path to America, Jail & Death," *New York Times,* November 5, 2001 (describing how a Pakistani detainee died of a heart attack after being inexplicably held in a U.S. jail after he agreed to depart the United States).

14. Tamara Audi, "Secrecy Veils Arrests, Jailings in Terror Probe," *Detroit Free Press,* October 22, 2001, 1A.

15. "Justice Kept in the Dark," *Newsweek,*, December 10, 2001, 37.

16. The Executive Office for Immigration Review (EOIR) is part of the U.S. Department of Justice. EOIR is responsible for all deportation and removal hearings. EOIR is independent of the Immigration and Naturalization Service (INS).

17. Creppy Memo of September 21, 2001, regarding cases requiring special procedures, http://news.findlaw.com/hdocs/docs/aclu/creppy092101memo.pdf.

18. See, e.g., Matthew Purdy, "Their Right? To Remain Silenced," *New York Times,* May 1, 2002 (recounting how an INS trial attorney told an immigration judge that a hearing was "special interest," and quoting a defense attorney saying, "That's a long way of saying he's Arab."), available at http://www.nytimes.com/2002/05/01/nyregion/01TOWN.html.

19. 67 Federal Register 36799; see also 67 Federal Register 19508.

20. Tamara Audi, "Secrecy Veils Arrests, Jailings in Terror Probe," *Detroit Free Press,* October 22, 2001, 1A.

21. Jim Edwards, "Letter From Newark; Keeping Court Proceedings Secret At New Jersey Immigration Courts," *Nation,* 275, no. 19 (December 2002): 7, 2 .

22. See *North Jersey Media Group, Inc. v. Ashcroft,* 205 F.Supp.2d, pp. 288, 291, note 1 (D.N.J. 2002).

23. Steven Brill, *After* (New York: Simon and Schuster, 2003), 145–46, 404 .

24. "Justice Kept in the Dark," *Newsweek,* December 10, 2001, 37.

25. Mae M. Chang, "Security Roadblock to Refugees: U.S. Admission Rate Looks to Remain Low," *N.Y. Newsday,* September 26, 2002; George Lardner Jr.,

"U.S. Welcomes Fewer Refugees: '02 Admissions Had Ripple Effect in Post-9/11 World, Report Says," *Washington Post,* May 30, 2003.

26. *USA PATRIOT Act,* Public Law No. 107-56, Stat. 272, p.115 (2001).

27. Neil Lewis and Christopher Marquis, "Visa Approval Tightened for 26 Countries: FBI Scrutiny for Men from Arab, Muslim Nations," *San Francisco Chronicle,* November 10, 2001.

28. Edward Alden, "Security Screening Hurts U.S. Interests," *Financial Times,* October 24, 2003, 13.

29. Sam Stanton and Emily Bazar, "Immigrants Flee From Fear in America," *Sacramento Bee,* September 23, 2003.

30. Caitlin Harrington, "DHS Defends Deployment of Leaky Border Fingerprint System," *CQ Homeland Security-Technology,* October 20, 2004.

31. Public Law 107-173.

32. Michael Arnone, "Hacker Steals Personal Data on Foreign Students at U. of Kansas," *Chronicle of Higher Education,* January 24, 2003, http://chronicle.com/free/2003/01/2003012403n.htm.

33. Julie Sullivan and Richard Read, "INS Crumbles Amid 9/11 Reforms," *Portland Oregonian,* September 10, 2002, A01 (stating that when INS announced it was going to enforce the change-of-address notification requirements, "[f]oreigners complied, flooding the INS with more than 700,000 change of address cards, which the agency announced last week it had no time to process"); see also "INS Backlog Shows Folly of Casting Too Large A Net," *Portland Press Herald,* August 7, 2002, 8A (describing how INS officials admitted that a Missouri warehouse held two million unprocessed documents, including change of address cards, that the agency was unable to manage).

34. Mary Beth Sheridan, "Immigration Law As Anti-Terrorism Tool," *Washington Post,* June 13, 2005, A01.

35. 69 Federal Register 48877, August 11, 2004.

36. John N. Paden and Peter W. Singer, "America Slams the Door (On Its Foot): Washington's Destructive New Visa Policies," *Foreign Affairs* (May/June 2003).

37. Mary Beth Sheridan, "Immigration Law As Anti-Terrorism Tool," *Washington Post,* June 13, 2005, A01.

38. Edward Alden, "Security Screening Hurts U.S. Interests," *Financial Times,* October 24, 2003, 13.

39. Letter from Lawrence H. Summers, President, Harvard University, to Colin Powell, U.S. Secretary of State (April 19, 2004), available at http://www.president.harvard.edu/speeches/2004/powell.html.

40. Ibid., 1.

41. "America Closes Its Doors," *Newsweek,* October 21, 2004 (discussing report by the American Immigration Law Foundation).

42. Immigration Policy Center, *Maintaining a Competitive Edge: The Role of the Foreign-Born & U.S. Immigration Policies in Science and Engineering,* vol. 3, no. 3 (Washington, DC: American Immigration Law Foundation, August 2004).

43. Richard Florida, "America's Best and Brightest Are Leaving...and Taking the Creative Economy With Them," *Conference Board: Across the Board*

(September-October 2004), http://www.conference-board.org/articles/atb_article.cfm?id=269.

44. Jonathan Krim, "Intel Chairman Says U.S. Is Losing Edge," *Washington Post*, October 10, 2003, E01 ("India's booming software industry, which is increasingly doing work for U.S. companies, could surpass the United States in software and tech-service jobs by 2010, he said.").

45. Fred Jerome, *The Einstein File* (New York: St. Martin's Press, 2002).

46. Recently, the Center for Immigration Studies (CIS), a restrictionist organization based in Washington, DC, called for the revival of ideological exclusion grounds for aliens; CIS cited with approval such historical examples as the deportation and exclusion of subversive Catholic priests in the 1800s and the removal of Emma Goldman and other socialists in the early twentieth century. See James R. Edwards Jr., "Keeping Extremists Out: The History of Ideological Exclusion, and the Need for Its Revival" (Washington, DC: Center for Immigration Studies, September 2005).

47. Joseph S. Nye is credited with having devised the concept of "soft power." See, e.g., Joseph S. Nye, *Soft Power: The Means to Success in World Politics* (Cambridge, MA: Public Affairs, 2004).

48. Alfonso Chardy, "Miami International Airport System Revived After Big Delays," *Miami Herald*, August 20, 2005, 1 (describing how a computer virus had "disrupted critical databases" at U.S. international airports).

49. "Customs Officials Accused in Drug Ring," *Associated Press*, October 20, 2004 (describing how customs agents involved in drug smuggling used law enforcement databases to determine if agents were investigating members of the drug ring).

50. Findings of the Final Report of the Senate Select Committee on Intelligence and the House Permanent Select Committee on Intelligence Joint Inquiry into the Terrorist Attacks of September 11, 2001 (December 2002), the Context, Part 1, Findings and Conclusions, 5. The entire report of the Joint Inquiry is available at http://intelligence.senate.gov/pubs107.htm.

51. National Commission on Terrorist Attacks on the United States, *The 9/11 Commission Report: Final Report Of The National Commission On Terrorist Attacks Upon The United States* (New York: W.W. Norton, 2004), 390; (hereinafter, *9/11 Commission Report*).

52. *9/11 Commission Report*, 387.

53. *9/11 Commission Report*, 389.

54. *9/11 Commission Report*, 387.

55. *9/11 Commission Report*, 363–64.

56. Jerry Seper, "Bush's 'Open Door' Slammed; Tancredo Calls His 'Altruistic Views' a Threat to Security," *Washington Times*, April 19, 2002, A01.

57. Stephen Dinan, "Illegal Aliens Outpace Legals; Large Increase From '03 to '04," *Washington Times*, September 28, 2005, A01.

58. Samuel Huntington, *Who Are We? The Challenges to America's National Identity* (New York: Simon and Schuster, 2004).

59. If you define an "illegal alien" as a "status violator"—someone who has worked in violation of his visitor status. See Charlie LeDuff, "Ethnic Issues in

California Recall Play Out at Latino Parade," *New York Times,* September 8, 2003, A17 ("Mr. Schwarzenegger has yet to clear up confusion as to whether he briefly worked illegally when he first came to California in the late 1960s.").

60. *Development, Relief, and Education for Alien Minors Act of 2003,* S. 1545, 108th Cong. (2003).

61. Rob Paral, "Health Worker Shortages & the Potential of Immigration Policy," *Immigration Policy in Focus* 3, no. 1 (February 2004): 1 (Washington, DC: American Immigration Law Foundation).

62. Ibid.

63. U.S. Commission on National Security/21st Century, "Road Map for National Security: Imperative For Change" (Phase III Report) (Washington, DC: 2001).

64. Rob Paral and Benjamin Johnson, "Maintaining a Competitive Edge: The Role of the Foreign-Born & U.S. Immigration Policies in Science & Engineering," *Immigration Policy in Focus* 3, no. 3 (August 2004): 1 (Washington, DC: American Immigration Law Foundation).

65. Robert L. Paarlberg, "Knowledge as Power: Science, Military Dominance, and U.S. Security," *International Security* 29, no. 1 (Summer 2004): 122–151.

66. Testimony of Alan Greenspan before the Special Committee on Aging, U.S. Senate, February 27, 2003.

67. Anita U. Hattiangadi, Aline O. Quester, Gary Lee, Diana S. Lien, Ian MacLeod, David L. Reese, and Robert W. Shuford, *Non-Citizens in Today's Military: Final Report* (Alexandria, VA: Center for Naval Analyses, April 2005).

68. Rowan Scarborough, "Troops Lack Intel Support," *Washington Times,* September 4, 2002 ("[A]gencies on which they depend to provide enemy locations, such as the Defense Intelligence Agency and the CIA, lack reliable human sources and enough foreign-language speakers.").

69. Daniel Klaidman and Michael Isikoff, "Lost in Translation," *Newsweek,* October 27, 2003, 26 ("hundreds of hours of tapes from wiretaps and bugs pile up in secure lockers, waiting, sometimes for months on end, to be deciphered.").

70. Mark Niesse, "Translator Shortage Hampers Intelligence," *Associated Press,* November 8, 2002.

71. Ibid.

72. See Richard D. Brecht and William P. Rivers, "Language & National Security in the 21st Century" (National Foreign Language Center, 2000), 119 ("The nation's capacity in the so-called LCTLs [Less Commonly Taught Languages] is shockingly thin, particularly outside of Arabic, Chinese, Japanese, and Russian.").

73. Charles Leroux, "U.S. Not Using Its Technical Edge To Win 'Public Diplomacy' War," *Chicago Tribune,* October 14, 2003, 1C.

74. Thomas Ginsburg, "Visa Program Sees Few Post-9/11 Takers," *San Diego Union-Tribune,* February 12, 2003, A18.

75. See, e.g., Janine di Giovanni, "How American Dream Faded In Downtown Mogadishu," *Times Newspapers Limited,* February 26, 2002 (describing how the United States Government deported a group of men—including an Intel Corporation employee—to Mogadishu, Somalia, where there is no functioning government).

76. Ironically, we have also created a threat to other nations' security by deporting large numbers of American-trained criminals. See, e.g., Randall Richard, "Criminal Deportees from U.S. Wreak Havoc around World," *Chattanooga Times Free Press,* October 26, 2003, A10.

77. Stuart Anderson, "The Global Battle for Talent and People," *Immigration Policy Focus* 2, no. 2 (Washington, DC: American Immigration Law Foundation, September 2003).

78. *United States v. Robel,* 389 U.S. 258, p. 264 (1967).

CHAPTER 8

MIGRATION AND THE "SMART BORDER" SECURITY ENVIRONMENT

Jason Ackleson

2005 was a watershed year in the history of a crucial component of the nation's infrastructure. In April of that year, the "Minutemen," a group of civilian volunteers, began watching a small section of the Arizona border with Sonora, Mexico for illegal crossings by migrants. This group, while limited in number, attracted a large media presence and focused attention on the issue of undocumented migration in the United States. In August, Governor Bill Richardson of New Mexico declared a "state of emergency" along that state's international boundary with Mexico, arguing the border had become "devastated by the ravages and terror of human smuggling, drug smuggling, kidnapping, murder, destruction of property and the death of livestock."[1] The action released $750,000 in emergency funding for law enforcement along the border. Just days later, Governor Janet Napolitano of Arizona followed suit in her state.

The Minutemen presence and the governors' declarations came in the midst of one of the deadliest-ever summer crossing seasons in the U.S.-Mexico borderlands; over 389 undocumented migrants, most of whom were from Mexico, died attempting to cross into the United States during fiscal year (FY) 2005.[2] Deterred by U.S. border patrol strategies that protect urban areas through bolstered law enforcement, migrants increasingly move through evermore desolate and dangerous desert areas and use smugglers (known as "coyotes") to help guide them into the United States. Increasingly, these migrants are caught up in transnational criminal networks that shuffle drugs into the United States. These criminal outfits are becoming increasingly bold, and as a result, lawlessness is a growing feature of a number of some U.S.-Mexico border communities.

As U.S. Border Patrol efforts work in one area of the border to stem the flow of migrants and drugs, smugglers react and shift their areas of operations elsewhere. This is what happened in the U.S. southwest in 2005: enforcement in Arizona shifted flows to New Mexico and this is what, in part, prompted Governor Richardson's declaration.

One of the main factors clearly driving the current border crisis is the major issue of undocumented migration. While many migrants fail to make it to the United States, many do manage to cross the frontier. Border Patrol agents anecdotally suggest that for every apprehension in the field, two to three other migrants make it through. Approximately 1.1 million migrants were apprehended on the U.S.-Mexico border in FY 2004.[3] A study released in March 2005 by the Pew Hispanic Center estimates the number of undocumented immigrants resident in the United States at 10.3 million as of March 2004, an increase of 23 percent from 8.4 million in 2000 and growth of nearly half a million each year.[4] These numbers are part of a short- and medium-term trend towards increased immigration from Mexico to the United States. Most are lured by a plethora of low-paying jobs, many in the agricultural and service sectors of the American economy.

Against this backdrop of migration are loud calls for additional security on the nation's borders to protect against the threat of terrorism. Among some policy makers and members of the American public, there is a sense that borders open to undocumented migration are also vulnerable to terrorists and weapons of mass destruction (WMD). As this chapter will illustrate, the national security dynamic introduced by the events of September 11, 2001, prompted this perception and indeed changed the immigration debate in the United States rather significantly.

Given this political context, one of the main solutions to border security in the post-9/11 period is known as "Smart Borders." This term refers to bilateral accords signed by the Bush administration, Canada, and Mexico in 2001 and 2002.[5] The agreements involve limited cooperation on a number of policy issues related to border control, including inspections, preclearances of goods and people, database coordination, and biometric identifiers. The Smart Border Plan has emerged as the preferred policy solution to the difficult problem of screening for terrorist incursions into the United States while maintaining flows of goods and individuals, key drivers of globalization.

Just as the Smart Border initiative is advanced by the U.S. government, prominent members of Congress—and President Bush himself—have sought answers to the issue of undocumented migration to the United States. Several lawmakers have introduced legislative solutions to this problem, most notably in the guise of a guest worker program. How do these migration reform initiatives—and the migration flows themselves—fit into the larger Smart Border policy regime? What components of the Smart Border Plan will be applied to screen and track foreign nationals? What are the socioeconomic implications of such initiatives? What realistic political, social, and security outcomes can be expected?

This chapter seeks to answer these questions by providing an analysis of migration and migration reform in the new Smart Border security environment of the post-9/11 era. It begins by examining the international political context of these issues, namely border security and U.S.-Mexico bilateral relations in the post-9/11 period. It then turns to major policy options that seek to facilitate the movement of goods, services, and people into the United States—including workers—while also providing adequate security for a key part of America's infrastructure, its international borders. Special emphasis is placed on efforts to enact some kind of migration reform in the United States. The chapter concludes by offering several policy recommendations to help deal with the question of undocumented migration and border security in the post-9/11 era.

BORDER SECURITY IN THE POST-9/11 PERIOD AND CONTEMPORARY U.S.-MEXICO RELATIONS

The terrorist attacks of September 11, 2001, put a halt to the progress on U.S.-Mexico relations and border issues fostered by high-level meetings between President Vicente Fox of Mexico and U.S. President George Bush held just days before. Agreements on problematic bilateral issues such as trade and migration were apparently in the offing. Unfortunately, the events of 9/11 intervened, effectively closing the U.S.-Mexico and U.S.-Canada borders: different levels of alert status issued by the U.S. government triggered intense inspections of incoming vehicles and persons. For a time, even the U.S. National Guard assisted with border operations. On occasion, these efforts brought traffic bound for the United States to a virtual standstill. At both frontiers, multihour delays were reported. At the San Ysidro-Puerta border between San Diego and Tijuana, for example, travelers and truckers faced waits of up to four hours.[6] The delays had a major economic impact; at the time, daily cross-border U.S.-Mexico trade averaged $670 million but declined by an average of 15 percent in the weeks after the attacks.[7] Local retailers in border cities like El Paso, Texas reported sales fell up to 50 percent due to fewer Mexican customers.[8]

As border security conditions shift—especially if another terrorist attack on the United States occurs—future slowdowns or even closures are a very real possibility. With American law enforcement agencies now concerned with a new priority—counterterrorism—there has been a subtle shift in emphasis away from drug and migrant interdiction. While these two objectives are still important and pursued by agencies such as U.S. Customs and Border Patrol (CBP), border security officials often maintain that their number one objective today is homeland security.

Accordingly, September 11 and the U.S. security response to it, had, and continues to have, a significant impact on North America's border communities as well as wider U.S.-Mexico and U.S.-Canada political and economic relations.[9]

The challenge facing these officials on the ground and policy makers in Washington is the problem of ensuring adequate border security in light of the new security environment posed by the threat of transnational terrorism. The problem is that threats to border security are at one level from terrorists networks but also in effect by the processes of globalization—particularly transnational industrialization, trade, and low-wage labor demands.[10] The United States thus faces a new kind of "security dilemma"—how to balance the risks of terrorist incursions into the United States versus the risks of high micro/macroeconomic and social costs if globalization and cross-border interaction is overly slowed or cut off by stringent border security measures.[11]

To understand both the benefits and constraints globalization puts on the security equation, and on U.S. ports of entry, one need only look at cross-border interaction between Mexico, Canada, and the United States. More than 100 million people cross the U.S.-Canada frontier each year; over 300 million pass annually through the U.S.-Mexico border.[12] The United States has 361 commercial ports of entry, 7,500 miles of land boundaries, and 95,000 miles of shoreline; over 11.6 million trucks and 16 million containers cross American land borders alone each year.[13] Canada and Mexico are the respective number one and two trading partners of the United States, accounting for $653 billion worth of trade in 2000.[14] On the northern frontier, nearly $1 billion in commerce takes place each day between the two countries.[15] Added to this huge volume of legal commerce are the flows of hundreds of thousands of undocumented workers who, as noted above, enter the country through often desolate and dangerous rural areas of North America's land borders. Borders clearly represent a key piece of America's trade and commerce infrastructure. Closure or damage (for example, from a terrorist attack) to any part of this system would have major economic ramifications.

Because nearly all trade barriers between the United States, Canada, and Mexico are now removed under the North American Free Trade Agreement (NAFTA), many scholars assert the continent is increasingly integrated economically. This can be observed in a variety of markets and manufacturing processes. For example, goods manufactured in border assembly plants (*maquiladoras*) for delivery into the United States constitute millions of truckloads annually. The volume of commercial traffic, in fact, has exploded under NAFTA and has, in many cases, resulted in significant crossing delays—even under normal conditions. The number of 20-foot shipping containers entering U.S. border crossings and seaports, for instance, doubled in the last ten years, and are expected to do so again in the next ten years.[16] Containerized shipments into the United States doubled in the last ten years and are expected to double again every 10 to 15 years.

Against this backdrop of flows of goods and people has come the new mandate for law enforcement agencies concerned with border control. As one Customs and Border Protection officer suggested, "Since 9/11... the biggest change in our mission is to defend our border from terrorism and weapons of mass destruction."[17] Despite this, most people, goods, and containers coming into the United States either receive a cursory inspection or are not inspected at all, creating a clear opening for the smuggling of a weapon of mass destruction.[18] To facilitate speedy clearances, only if a security agent notes a problematic shipping manifest or other suspect details is a physical inspection generally conducted. This occurs in a very small percentage of all shipments.

While much discussion about NAFTA has centered on its economic dimensions, surprisingly little empirical work has dealt with these security issues and the risks a liberalized trade regime partly fosters.[19] The problem is that transnational criminal networks utilize the same legal channels of globalization to move goods (e.g., drugs or possibly WMD) and people (e.g., migrants) across borders, thus aggravating these public policy problems.[20] As Stephen Flynn argues, "terrorists and the tools of terrorism do not spring up at the border...instead they generally arrive via hemispheric and international trade and travel networks."[21]

This is by no means a new phenomenon; U.S. borders have long been the main conduits for smuggling illicit flows of drugs and people. While little historical or empirical indications establish them as portals for terrorist movement, as noted in the 9/11 Commission report, there is clearly concern in the policy community that they may become such a mechanism.[22]

To prevent this, both international cooperation and risk management strategies are crucial. On the bilateral front, Mexican officials and the public have, for the most part, been fairly understanding of changing security conditions at ports of entry along the border. At the larger bilateral level, however, in the four years that have followed 9/11, U.S.-Mexico relations have ebbed and flowed. At least three major events seem to characterize the recent trajectory of this relationship: misperceptions about terrorist incursions into the United States from Mexico (despite popular perception, none of the 9/11 hijackers entered the United States from Mexico or Canada); disagreements about the course of the "war on terrorism" (particularly in regard to the war in Iraq); and the escalating drug violence along the U.S.-Mexico border. Over 800 drug-related killings occurred in Mexico during 2005 as narco-traffickers increasingly battled one another and law enforcement in several border cities and did so with evermore dangerous weapons, such as automatic weapons, bazookas, and hand grenades. The situation prompted the United States to close its consulate in Nuevo Laredo in July 2005.

On a more structural level, Mexico continues to experience a major demographic bubble that has resulted in large numbers of people in the age groups who tend to be willing to migrate. More importantly, neoliberal economic restructuring (in part due to NAFTA), wealth disparities, and corruption all combine to create a continuous displacement effect in the Mexican economy which "pushes" migration outward. On the demand or "pull" side of the equation, many sectors of the U.S. economy continue to seek workers that are willing to accept low wages for difficult work. Absent significant reforms and economic development in Mexico, migration flows to the United States will persist—even with heightened U.S. border security—necessitating some sort of solution to undocumented migration. The issue, along with the drug trade, puts tension on the U.S.-Mexico relationship.

Accordingly, many experts agree that the U.S.-Mexico border, and the U.S.-Mexico bilateral relationship more generally, is under some strain. This political climate tends to handicap mutual efforts between the two governments on counterterrorism and border security issues. While cooperation has increased in the wake of 9/11, particularly at the local and regional level, there are still several important U.S. border security initiatives that remain largely unilateral in nature. These fall under the category of "risk management" systems and are discussed in the next section. The subsequent part of the chapter deals with the question of migration reform.

SMART BORDERS: MANAGING RISK POSED BY INDIVIDUALS

Some have characterized the problem of border security under globalization as akin to looking for needles in a haystack: law enforcement is faced with facilitating the huge volumes of economic and social interaction across U.S. frontiers—including structural migration flows—but has to somehow screen for illicit individuals, narcotics, and weapons at the same time. To solve this dilemma, policy makers are seeking ways to better protect and manage U.S. borders, most of which employ some sort of screening technology. The chapter now turns to explore some of these solutions to border security in the post-9/11 period. It will then evaluate current policy options such as a guest worker accord that would attempt to track and at least partly regularize migrant flows from Mexico into the United States.

The systems being developed and implemented through the Smart Border Agreements are largely based on the principle of risk management. To adapt the haystack metaphor, the idea behind risk management on the border is to systematically separate the "bad needles" (e.g., suspicious individuals, unsafe food, and potential weapons of mass destruction) from the "good straw" (e.g., low-risk travelers, routine freight shipments) of the North American haystack. By screening out low-risk goods and people, inspection resources can be redirected to where they ought to be: watch-list suspects, suspicious individuals, and shipments from untrustworthy firms within the international community.

These systems are also meant to be fast: ideally implemented, they would not significantly increase the transit times for people and commerce through a lengthy inspection process. President Bush has advanced this vision, seeking a border which

> poses little or no obstacle to legitimate trade and travel... [while] keep[ing] pace with expanding trade while protecting the United States from the threats of terrorist attack, illegal immigration, illegal drugs, and other contraband.[23]

The United States has consequently signed separate 22- and 32-point Smart Border Agreements with Mexico and Canada, respectively.[24] In the Canadian case, the agreement builds on previous bilateral arrangements. The accords, somewhat different in the case of each bilateral partner, involve cooperation on a number of bilateral policy issues related to border control, including inspections, preclearances of goods and people, database coordination, biometric identifiers, and other areas.[25]

The agreements indeed cover a broad set of policy areas, including a wide set of initiatives designed to facilitate trade (for example, Fast and Secure Trade (FAST) lanes for cargo on both the northern and southern frontiers which allow prescreened and prequalified companies to expedite their transborder shipments).[26] There are similar programs for the prescreening of travelers—but not migrants—who pass background checks.[27] For the purposes of this chapter, however, the focus is on security technologies that impact the movement, monitoring, and admission of people, such as biometrics and information technology, because they have particular implications for foreign nationals and the North American border infrastructure.

Biometrics

Biometrics are automated methods of recognizing humans, based on unique physiological characteristics, including the face, fingerprints, hand geometry, handwriting, and retinal and voice features.[28] These immutable characteristics allow security officials using biometric technologies to recognize *and* authenticate people so theoretically they are highly secure. When this biometric information is compared against a computerized database, the systems can serve an identification purpose, for example, at an inspection booth.

Biometric technologies have a counterterrorism role in providing a tool to identify and authenticate terrorists, prevent identity theft, and control entry into the United States.[29] They play a key role in Smart Border systems. Policy makers have shown marked interest in this arena (the federal government has incorporated it into many of its own security systems) and major government research projects on it are underway. German authorities have recently installed an iris recognition system for biometric border checks at the Frankfurt airport.[30] The United States and the European Union are planning to harmonize identity standards by using biometric identification.[31] Biometric components will soon be required for both new U.S. and foreign passports; while it has missed previous mandates dictated by the *USA PATRIOT Act,* the State Department will eventually (possibly by October 2006) require the 27 "visa-waiver" countries to issue "e-passports" with these technological enhancements. Biometric identifiers are the first point in the U.S.-Canada Smart Border Agreement and are part of several U.S.-Mexico initiatives, including US-VISIT, as discussed below.[32]

Other policy proposals include expanding biometrics to include facial recognition, which captures distinctive visual images and compares them to photographic records.[33] It is clear that this technology will likely be a long-term component of the policy process, but operational considerations and the false-negative problem still remain problematic.[34]

Biometric technology is also already in place in some of the United States' immigration structure as it is embedded in some permanent resident ("green") cards. But the major test case of this technology is the issuance of over 7 million Border Crossing Cards (BCC), also known as *matriculas consulares* or *micas*. Micas are versions of the regular "B" visa, typically used for short-term tourist entries but not work. The Department of Homeland Security (DHS) and the State Department issue these cards to Mexican citizens who wish to cross into a limited (25-mile) border zone for up to 30 days. Embedded in each card is an array of unalterable personal data (80,000 bytes of information), including fingerprints and a digital photo. At the moment, BCC holders, along with visa-exempt Canadians, are not required to enroll in US-VISIT (discussed below).

U.S. law requires Mexicans wishing to transit to the border zone to carry and use BCC cards. The biometric data can be checked against immigration and criminal databases and thus authenticate the individual (cutting down on counterfeiting) and determine if he or she may be wanted by law enforcement. In practice, however, at many ports of entry, most Mexicans and their BCCs are generally just given a quick visual inspection at the primary inspection; the cards are generally not swiped through the computer system.[35] This implementation gap is indicative of the fact that new technologies do not, by definition, translate to improved conditions in real-world scenarios for a variety of political and operational reasons.

US-VISIT

For nearly ten years, policy makers have sought an information technology system that would allow law enforcement to track entries and exits in and out of the United States made by foreign nationals. The United States Visitor and Immigrant Status Indicator Technology (US-VISIT) program is a revision and extension of previous legislation on immigration control. That act, the *Illegal Immigration Reform and Immigrant Responsibility Act of 1996* (IIRIRA), contained a prevision known as "Section 110: Automated Entry-Exit Control System."[36] Section 110 required the government to implement, within two years, an "automated entry and exit control system that will collect a record of departure for every alien departing the United States and match the records of departure with the record of the alien's arrival in the United States."[37] However, the implementation of the 1996 law proved politically and practically impossible for a variety of economic, political, and practical reasons (chiefly revolving around concerns about slowing flows of goods and people across U.S. borders).[38]

Under the national security demands created by the events of 9/11, Section 110 was revised as US-VISIT and it began to be implemented to track entries and exits of many foreign visitors, students, and business travelers. Such individuals have to use two biometric identifiers—digital fingerprints and digital photographs—when entering and leaving the country. This information is checked against a number of linked law enforcement databases.

US-VISIT is being implemented in several phases. In the first phase, the system was deployed at U.S. airports in early 2004. It was then extended to the 50 largest land border crossings by December 2004, but only to non-BCC-carrying Mexicans and Canadians who require a visa (mainly students and guest workers), approximately 3 percent of all foreign visitors.[39] (The Bush Administration decided in early March 2004 to exempt BCC-holders.)[40] The next major step will be the implementation of a limited exit program at all points of entry. The DHS plans to use small radio frequency tags to "automatically, passively, and remotely" record the entry and exit of covered individuals.[41] While the President's FY 2006 budget included $50 million to accelerate the deployment of US-VISIT, currently only a limited percentage of foreign nationals entering the country are subject to the screening provided by the system.[42]

The U.S. Government Accountability Office has concluded full deployment of US-VISIT (complete entry and exit recording) will be very costly and potentially impractical.[43] As Rey Koslowski has also argued, it is

"not clear that US-VISIT's potential benefits justify the necessary investments in border infrastructure, data acquisition, human resources, and
other resources to make it work as envisioned…it may be better to scale
back the requirements—and expectations—of the program rather than
develop a problem-ridden, partially deployed system that cannot accomplish the unrealistic goals set out for it."[44] Enormous technical challenges
in managing the data exist, given the approximately 700 million foreign
national arrivals annually.

More importantly, even if accurate entry and exit records are available,
this does not guarantee that U.S. law enforcement can find wayward aliens who may have overstayed their visas. While several of the September
11 terrorists had overstayed their visas, none of them was targeted for
investigation as an absconder. Millions of individuals in the United States
have overstayed their visas, making thorough investigations nearly
impossible. A recent Department of Justice Inspector General investigation into several high-profile cases of criminals being admitted into the
United States concluded that full integration of the immigration and FBI
databases to check all undocumented migrants who are apprehended by
the CBP is at least three years away.[45]

US-VISIT is but one of several information technology programs now
underway to collect, track, and coordinate data on individuals passing
through U.S. borders. As noted below, these systems would likely include
any potential guest workers. Legislation such as the *Enhanced Border
Security and Visa Entry Reform Act of 2002* now mandates interoperational
databases (which requires integrating up to 28 different databases
which can have inaccurate information such as misspelled names[46]), intelligence sharing about students and aliens between the DHS and other
government agencies, and the biometric features on travel documents
mentioned above.[47] Moreover, the larger political issues of privacy and
control must be integrated into the policy debate. This issue derives from
the question of whether (and how) to incorporate additional information
into the National Crime Information Center (NCIC), intelligence, or private sector data (such as credit card transactions).

MIGRATION REFORM IN THE SMART BORDER ENVIRONMENT

While undocumented migrant flows from Mexico to the United States
initially declined in the wake of 9/11, the current of these individuals
entering the United States has now returned to historically high levels.
The current state of play on migration represents a short- and medium-
term trend towards increased immigration from Mexico to the United
States. The flows are a response to strong economic and social structures
that encourage migration. These forces include the significant economic
disparity that exists between Mexico and the United States. In addition,

development needs in Mexico tend to encourage migration because workers send billions of dollars of critical remittances back to their home communities each year. Moreover, NAFTA created an economic system that chiefly serves the interests of large U.S.-based multinational firms such as agribusinesses. Such interests tend to favor the existence of illegal immigration, because labor is generally cheaper when it is undocumented.

Just as the initial Smart Border security initiatives were being rolled out, President Bush unveiled a new proposal that may revive the momentum on migration reform he shared with President Fox back in 2001. This program would allow millions of employed undocumented migrants to remain in the United States as guest workers for up to two, three-year periods. If sponsored by their employer, the plan would allow migrants to apply for a limited number of permanent resident slots. Bush's plan, although stalled in Congress, marks the highest-level migration reform proposal in nearly a decade.

Given the economic, political, and ethical realities of migration flows, the current size of the undocumented population in the United States, the deaths suffered by border crossers, and the vital role such workers play in the American economy, many scholars believe policy reform to address the issue is long overdue.[48] Ahead of President Bush's 2004 State of the Union address, reports surfaced from the White House that the President would, somewhat surprisingly, propose a new guest worker program. On January 7, 2004 Bush formally announced some of his general ideas for the program.

The President seeks to admit migrants on a temporary work visa for a three year-period. Such guest workers would be able to renew this temporary visa once. It remains unclear how many guest workers would be eligible for permanent residency status upon the expiration of their temporary visas. To be eligible, they would require sponsorship by their employer and would have to apply for an as-yet undetermined but "reasonable" number of green card slots. The visas would, however, be portable and nonsector specific. Employers would have to demonstrate that a U.S. national would not take the job that is being given to the migrant. Financial incentives (such as allowing migrants who return home to earn credit in foreign pension plans) are intended to ensure workers return home after their visas expire—a potentially unfair and unrealistic expectation.

Much debate followed the President's unveiling of this proposal. Many conservatives see the program as a *de facto* amnesty which will fuel additional illegal immigration; some liberals warn of historical problems such as exploitation that come with guest worker plans and are concerned that the policy is not a real path to permanent residency.[49] Surveys and initial apprehension figures obtained by the CBP in the month following the announcement of the immigration reform initiative suggest that some migrants have been motivated to travel to the United States in anticipation of this policy change.[50]

The guest worker proposal is being considered in the 109th Congress. In fall 2005, two major but competing immigration bills began their journey on the Hill: the McCain-Kennedy-Kolbe-Flake proposal (known as the *Secure America and Orderly Immigration Act*)[51] and the Kyl-Cornyn proposal *(Comprehensive Enforcement and Immigration Reform Act of 2005).*[52]

The *Secure America and Orderly Immigration Act,* in the words of its chief sponsor Senator McCain, is "a comprehensive bill that doesn't try to solve the hemorrhaging immigration problem with a band-aid—this bill is major surgery."[53] The bill will "establish a new market-based temporary worker program so that when there is no U.S. worker to fill a job, employers will be able to hire willing and able foreign workers who have gone through security background checks, medical exams, and paid a fee for their visa."[54] The bill would create 400,000 three-year visas for guest workers, but more could be added in the future and undocumented workers could stay in the United States during the application process.[55] Importantly, and in contrast to the Kyl-Cornyn bill, this legislation includes a route for immigrants who wish to become permanent residents. It recognizes that a guest worker proposal that seeks to track and regularize migrants must have this possibility attached to it. As McCain argues, "anyone who thinks this goal can be achieved without providing an eventual path to a permanent legal status is not serious about solving this problem."[56]

The McCain bill interfaces with a number of Smart Border provisions, including requiring the development and implementation of a mandatory employment verification system using tamper-resistant, biometric, machine-readable identification. It would strengthen internal enforcement, doubling the fines on employers who hire illegal immigrants.

Bearing some similarities but also important differences to the McCain proposal, the Kyl-Cornyn *Comprehensive Enforcement and Immigration Reform Act of 2005* would allow undocumented immigrants to obtain work permits and apply for legal residency and citizenship after they pay fees and a fine and pass background checks. They could stay in the United States for two years; then they would have to return home for at least one year. They could participate in the program three times. There is no route to permanent status under this plan.

At the same time as creating a guest worker proposal, the bill seeks a major injection of border security resources, including 10,000 Border Patrol agents and 1,250 new Customs and Border Protection officers (working at ports of entry). It would authorize $5 billion over five years for security technology and infrastructure along the border.

In terms of an interface with Smart Border initiatives, this proposal also requires the completion of background checks, health screening, and issuance of "secure, biometric identity documentation" to participating foreign nationals. Employers would use document readers to verify identity and employment authorization.[57] It also requires that within one year, secure machine-readable, tamper-resistant Social Security cards be issued and that all new hires participate in a Social Security-based electronic employment eligibility verification system.

In evaluating the proposals, at least three points can be made. First, in the short term, the prospect of a guest worker proposal making it into law is somewhat unclear. The divisive politics of the issue make agreement very problematic. This could change if the pressure building due to the events mentioned in the introduction to this chapter forces lawmakers and President Bush to take action. Second, the administrative requirements of these reforms, and the Smart Border program more generally, are daunting. Given the U.S. government's past record on immigration management, the current bureaucratic environment, and the massive implementation issues with such a program, it is unclear how well and how secure the migration program, and indeed the border itself, would be. The current DHS and State Department infrastructure would be strained with the work on security checks and visa issuing for guest workers. Additionally, a realistic guest worker program will have to include some sort of route to permanent residency. Structural economic conditions require liberal democracies to periodically issue amnesties to undocumented workers.[58]

Given the international and domestic political realities of 2006, the prospects for Bush's guest worker plan, or a similar initiative from Congress, look rather uncertain.[59] From his initial proposal, Bush in principle seeks at least two possibly contradictory objectives: "protect the homeland by controlling the borders [and] serve America's economy by matching a willing worker with a willing employer"; and "promote compassion for unprotected workers."[60] As former Under Secretary for Border and Transportation Security Asa Hutchinson maintained in a recent hearing on the matter, "In order for a temporary worker program to work effectively, border enforcement will be critical."[61] Some of these new resources were approved for FY 2006; President Bush's budget request included a nearly 4.8 percent increase in funding for U.S. Customs and Border Protection, bringing the agency's total to $6.7 billion.

The temporary worker proposals thus can be seen as part of an *antiterrorism* effort that drives Smart Border initiatives and fits into the risk management framework: by regularizing and tracking those who are undocumented, the government would attempt to focus security resources on those who are not in the country legally, as well as smugglers and potential terrorists between legal ports of entry. In other words, the polices would attempt to manage the risk generated by structural neoliberal policies that favor undocumented migration.[62] As Senator McCain suggests, "We have a national interest in identifying these individuals, incentivizing them to come forward out of the shadows, go through security background checks, pay back taxes, pay penalties for breaking the law, learn to speak English, and regularize their status."[63]

CONCLUSIONS AND POLICY RECOMMENDATIONS

Record migrant deaths, violence, the Minutemen, media attention, and the state of emergency declared by border state governors in August 2005 all signal a major chasm in the politics of a key piece of U.S. infrastructure: America's international border with Mexico. Protecting that infrastructure has become increasingly difficult, given the new security dilemma of the post-9/11 era set out in this chapter: how can the United States maintain the massive cross-border flows of migrants and goods that help sustain its economic growth while at the same time apply increased security at boundaries against the threats of terrorism, weapons of mass destruction, and transnational criminal activity? This security dilemma presents difficult choices, particularly because, increasingly, security risks are introduced and complicated by economic integration policies and the open society Americans enjoy.

In an attempt to escape the dilemma, the Bush administration favors Smart Border accords that rely on bilateral cooperation and new security technologies. These systems are designed to efficiently screen for terrorists and illicit items (e.g., WMD) being shipped or transited into the United States while simultaneously not deleteriously affecting the flows of legitimate goods, visitors, and workers so vital to regional and national economies.

Smart Border policies remain a work in progress. They offer a partial solution to the dilemma, but alone they do not constitute a comprehensive border security policy. The systems and policies detailed here are still rather young and although they offer some additional screening and surveillance as well as hold significant symbolic and political appeal, it is not terribly clear they offer solid protection against determined terrorists or the smuggling of destructive weapons into the country, given the macroeconomic pressures and flows under globalization and free trade and the still relatively open nature of U.S. borders. As noted above, only a limited percentage of foreign nationals currently entering the country are subject to Smart Border screening via US-VISIT.[64] The systems themselves have major limitations, including implementation and privacy issues, and are often not cost-effective.[65]

The increased flow of economic migrants into the United States, most of whom operate in the shadows of society and the economy, is an often neglected part of the security discussion. As this chapter has indicated, the question of undocumented migration must also be integrated into the debate. Given the major immigration reform bills currently under consideration in Congress, it appears that some lawmakers are now recognizing this reality. They seek to integrate a guest worker program within the larger framework of managed border control, namely using biometrics and information technology to screen and track workers. Therefore, the guest worker initiatives, as they are currently constructed, fit into a national security rationale of electronically documenting all foreign nationals to try to screen out threats. However, the political future of the competing guest worker plans and their potential implementation are uncertain. Migrants will continue to chance everything to enter the United States—no matter if the border they cross is seemingly "smart."

Given this analysis, the following are some policy recommendations that may strengthen U.S. border policy and enhance key infrastructure:

- The situation on the border demands comprehensive migration reform. The current guest worker proposals do not include a sustainable development policy in Mexico and the U.S.-Mexico border region. An investment fund should be created that builds infrastructure, protects the environment, and encourages equitable economic development in Mexico. When this happens, migration flows to the United States will decrease. In the meantime, Mexican migration to the United States must be addressed in a humane way that acknowledges the contributions of migrants and the current economic needs of all three NAFTA partners.

- The U.S. government needs to prepare for a guest worker program by bolstering Department of State and Department of Homeland Security capabilities for processing guest worker background checks and visas.

- Through the guise of trilateral agreements like the Security and Prosperity Partnership of North America, policy makers need to seek out alternative and cooperative approaches to border security that take into account the transnational nature of trade and migration, as well as terrorism. Multilateral cooperation with Canada and Mexico on security and trade can go far towards achieving U.S. national interests in these areas. This involves sharing key information on threats and additional law enforcement cooperation.

- Wherever possible, it is important that the United States pushes its borders "out"—conducting intelligence, inspections, and prescreening far away from the physical frontier. This is occurring in a limited way through the Container Security Initiative, but such efforts should be expanded. Good border security should not begin at the frontier. Counterterrorism policy is most effective *before* a terrorist hits the vast mix of people and commodities trying to expeditiously cross into the United States.

- The United States should expand and protect border infrastructure, ensuring the new infrastructure is "smart." Many border crossings are crowded and outdated. The U.S. government should engage in a strategic plan to expand

and protect its crossings and do so with the underpinning of Smart Border technologies.

The problem of ensuring that the large flow of individuals—including visitors, businesspeople, and migrant workers—into the United States in an efficient and secure process is a complicated task, fraught with dilemmas and trade-offs. Policy makers and the public should recognize this reality. To mitigate the compromises that inevitably have to be made when the United States seeks both trade and security in an era of globalization, comprehensive policy reforms that address migration and America's international borders are vital. While not the sole solution, such reforms would help develop a secure infrastructure, both by increasing security at physical ports of entry and by implementing a reasonable immigration policy, and thus promote a system of borders that can adequately and safely facilitate legitimate travelers, workers, and goods, while screening out terrorists and weapons of mass destruction.

NOTES

1. Bill Richardson, "Executive Order 2005-040: Declaring a Disaster in Hidalgo, Luna, Dona Ana, and Grant Counties Due to Border Security Concerns," (Santa Fe, NM: Office of the Governor, 2005), http://www.governor.state.nm.us/orders/2005/EO_2005_040.pdf (accessed August 18, 2005).

2. Leslie Berestein, "A Grim Record at the Border: This Year Likely to be Worst in Migrant Deaths,"*San Diego Union-Tribune,* August 10, 2005, http://www.signonsandiego.com/news/mexico/20050810-9999-1n10deaths.html (accessed August 18, 2005).

3. U.S. Department of Homeland Security, "Southwest Border Apprehensions" (May 2005), http://uscis.gov/graphics/shared/aboutus/statistics/msrjuly05/SWBORD.HTM (accessed August 1, 2005).

4. Jeffrey S. Passel, *Estimates of the Size and Characteristics of the Undocumented Population* (Washington, DC: Pew Hispanic Center, 2005), http://pewhispanic.org/files/reports/44.pdf.

5. For a general review of the Smart Border Accords, see Deborah Waller Meyers, "Does 'Smarter' Lead to Safer? An Assessment of the Border Accords with Canada and Mexico," *Migration Policy Institute Insight,* no. 2 (June 2003), http://www.migrationpolicy.org/pubs/6-13-0~1.PDF.

6. See also U.S.-Mexico Border Governors Conference, "U.S.-Mexico Border States September 11 Border Impact Report" (January 2, 2002), http://www.agr.state.tx.us/border/activities/iga_911_border_impact.htm (accessed November 30, 2003).

7. Peter Andreas, "A Tale of Two Borders: The U.S.-Mexico and U.S.-Canada Lines after 9-11," (The Center for Comparative Immigration Studies Working

Paper 77) (San Diego: University of California, San Diego, 2003), http://www. ccis-ucsd.org/PUBLICATIONS/wrkg77.pdf.

8. The Hispanic Council on International Relations, "The Post-9/11 Effects on Immigration and Economic Development in the Americas," http://www. hcir.org/eventreport_911effects.htm (accessed November 10, 2003).

9. For example, the new national security dictates disrupted high-level talks between U.S. President Bush and Mexican President Vicente Fox on "softening" border policies to possibly regularize or legalize migrants.

10. Ibid., 12.

11. For a related discussion of the new security dilemma, see Philip G. Cerny, "Terrorism and the New Security Dilemma," *Naval War College Review* 58, no. 1 (2005): 11–33. On the impact of security measures, see Jason Ackleson, "Border Security Technologies: Local and Regional Implications,"*Review of Policy Research* 22, no. 2 (2005): 137–155.

12. Demetrious Papademetriou and Deborah Meyers,*Caught in the Middle: Border Communities in an Era of Globalization* (Washington, DC: Carnegie Endowment for International Peace, 2001), 62.

13. Abraham McLaughlin, "U.S. Port Security: Is X-ray Enough?," *The Christian Science Monitor,* May 8, 2003, http://www.csmonitor.com/2003/0508/p02s01-usgn.html (accessed November 20, 2003).

14. Nancy Kingsbury, "Border Security: Challenges in Implementing Border Technology," *GAO Report 03-546T* (Washington, DC: Government Printing Office, 2003).

15. See Arlene Wilson, "NAFTA's Effect on Canada-U.S. Trade and Investment," *Congressional Research Service Report for Congress 97-889 E* (Washington, DC: Congressional Research Service, 1997).

16. American Association of Port Authorities, "Current Issues Facing the Industry," http://www.aapa-ports.org/industryinfo/currentissues.html. More than 31 million containers enter the U.S. each year.

17. Gilbert Aldaz, quoted in James Pinkerton, "More Eyes, Gadgets Watch Border: Inspectors, High-Tech Equipment Are Added to Crossings Large and Small,"*Houston Chronicle,* September 14, 2003.

18. The U.S. Customs and Border Protection is quick to point out its "multilayered" approach to screening (e.g., cargo manifests) but, given time and volume constraints, clearly a very small percentage of cargo is inspected. See U.S. Customs Service's Fact Sheet, "The 2 Percent Myth: Automated System, Technology, People Screen Cargo for Contraband" (May 2002), http://www.customs.ustreas.gov/news/safeguarding/2percent.htm (accessed October 18, 2002). See also Stephen Flynn, "America the Vulnerable," *Foreign Affairs* 81, no. 1 (2002): 60–75.

19. See Jason Ackleson, "Directions in Border Security Research," *The Social Science Journal* 40, no. 4 (2003): 1–9.

20. See David Dye, "Sensors for Screening and Surveillance," article presented at the Hoover Institution National Security Forum Conference on Technology for Preventing Terrorism (March 12–13, 2002), http://www-hoover.stanford.edu/research/conferences/nsf02/dye.pdf (accessed March 2, 2004).

21. Stephen Flynn, "End of the Joyride: Confronting the New Homeland Security Imperative in the Age of Globalization," article prepared for the Colloquium Series on Border Control and Homeland Security at Rutgers University (April 7, 2003).

22. *The 9/11 Commission Report: Final Report of the National Commission on Terrorist Attacks upon the United States* (Washington DC: National Commission on Terrorist Attacks upon the United States, 2004), http://www.9-11commission.gov/report/index.htm. A notable exception to the case of terrorist incursions across U.S. borders is the case of Ahmed Ressam, an Algerian terrorist who was arrested at the U.S.-Canada border in 1999. His professed plan was to bomb Los Angeles International Airport. The Department of Homeland Security has indicated no chemical materials, explosives, or terrorists have been seized at the U.S.-Mexico border since 9/11. Tom Ridge indicated this in his remarks made in El Paso, Texas (December 4, 2003). See Louie Gilot, "Balance Trade and Security, Ridge Says,"*El Paso Times*, December 5, 2003.

23. George W. Bush, "Securing America's Borders Fact Sheet: Border Security" (Washington, DC: The White House, 2002), http://www.whitehouse.gov/news/releases/2002/01/print/20020125.html (accessed November 19, 2002).

24. See Department of Homeland Security, "Specifics of Secure and Smart Border Action Plan" (January 2, 2002), http://www.whitehouse.gov/news/releases/2002/01/20020107.html (accessed July 6, 2003). Department of Homeland Security, "Smart Border: 22 Point Agreement: U.S.-Mexico Border Partnership Action Plan," http://www.whitehouse.gov/infocus/usmxborder/22points.html (accessed November 20, 2003).

25. See Deborah Walter Meyers, "Does 'Smarter' Lead to Safer? An Assessment of the U.S. Border Accords with Canada and Mexico," *International Migration* 41, no. 4 (2003): 5–35.

26. Jerry Pacheco, "As the Maquiladoras Go, So Goes the Border," *Albuquerque Journal*, June 19, 2003, http://abqjournal.com/biz/outlook/52722biz06-19-03.htm (accessed October 20, 2003). See also U.S. Customs and Border Protection, "FAST Overview," http://www.cbp.gov/linkhandler/cgov/import/commercial_enforcement/ctpat/fast/fast.ctt/FASTBrochure.doc.

27. Dedicated commuter lanes on international bridges have existed since 1995 and have gradually increased in number since then. These lanes use the Secure Electronic Network for Travelers Rapid Inspection (SENTRI) system which lets low-risk users generally bypass the inspection process, thereby allowing security agents to focus on higher risk travelers. Participants must pass criminal background checks and pay a fee to enroll. Nearly 60,000 travelers participate in the SENTRI program along the U.S.-Mexico border. Analogous programs are in place along the Canada-U.S. border (the PACE and NEXUS programs). Recent iterations of the policy involve modified transit cards with biometric information which can be quickly read by inspectors or employ vehicle-based tags similar to those in use on toll roads. Facial recognition or voice recognition is seen as a needed enhancement given the terrorist threat. See Chris McGann, "Travelers at U.S.-Canadian Border Eager for New Pass Card," *Seattle Post-Intelligencer*, June 25, 2003, http://seattlepi.nwsource.com/local/75946_nexus25.shtml (accessed July 7, 2003).

28. Biometric Consortium, "Introduction to Biometrics" (November 2002), http://www.biometrics.org/html/introduction.html (accessed November 10, 2002).

29. John D. Woodward Jr., *Biometrics: Facing Up to Terrorism* (Santa Monica, CA: RAND Corporation, 2001), 4.

30. Oki Electric Industry Company, "Iris Recognition System is Selected for Border Control at Frankfurt/Main Airport by the German Federal Ministry of the Interior," http://biz.yahoo.com/prnews/040213/lnf006_1.html (accessed February 20, 2004).

31. "U.S., E.U. Seek Common Border Security Guidelines," *EU Business* (October 29, 2003), http://www.eubusiness.com/afp/031029143422.moekgtd5 (accessed October 29, 2003).

32. One of the largest is the Biometrics Fusion Center, a major center for research tied with FBI and other law enforcement data projects. In addition, the Biometric Consortium, another epistemic community, is a focal point for these technologies. It also appears the new DHS will have a large, but yet unknown, role to play in the formulation of biometrics policy to combat terrorism; this is a question requiring future research. See Ibid.

33. Warren Webb, "Friend or Foe: Face Recognition Goes to War," *EDN Magazine* (December 20, 2001), http://www.ednmag.com (accessed September 9, 2002). This system, however, depends on good environmental conditions (such as lighting) and also can be foiled by factors like hair and weight when used in real environments; this has led to fairly high false-positive results in some tests. See Paul Skokowski, "Can Biometrics Defeat Terror?," Hoover Institution National Security Forum Conference on Technology for Preventing Terrorism, Stanford University (March 12–13, 2002).

34. Frank Baumgartner and Bryan D. Jones, *Agendas and Instability in American Politics* (Chicago: University of Chicago Press, 1993).

35. Elliot Spagat, "Border Security Plan Faces Big Questions as Deadlines Loom,"*USA Today,* December 1, 2003, http://www.usatoday.com/tech/news/techpolicy/2003-12-01-border-biometrics_x.htm (accessed December 1, 2003).

36. Division C of U.S. Public Law 104-208, 104th Cong., 2d sess., September 30, 1996.

37. Ibid.

38. See Lance Bronwyn, "Border-Crossing Boondoggle," *Christian Science Monitor,* October 26, 1999, http://www.csmonitor.com/durable/1999/10/26/fp11s1-csm.shtml (accessed November 1, 2002).

39. Department of Homeland Security, Office of Inspector General,*Implementation of the United States Visitor and Immigrant Status Indicator Technology Program at Land Border Ports of Entry,* OIG-05-11 (February 2005), 3, www.dhs.gov/interweb/assetlibrary/OIG_05-11_Feb05.pdf (accessed March 3, 2005).

40. Asa Hutchinson, Testimony Before the House Committee on Government Reform (March 4, 2004), http://www.dhs.gov/dhspublic/display?content=3287 (accessed March 4, 2004).

41. Notice of Privacy Act: Systems of Records, 70 Fed. Reg. 38699 (July 5, 2005), http://a257.g.akamaitech.net/7/257/2422/01jan20051800/edocket.access.gpo.gov/2005/05-13215.htm.

42. Budget of the U.S. Government, FY 2006, http://www.whitehouse.gov/omb/budget/fy2006/protecting.html; Department of Homeland Security, Office of Inspector General,*Implementation of the United States Visitor and Immigrant Status Indicator Technology Program at Land Border Ports of Entry,* OIG-05-11 (February 2005), www.dhs.gov/interweb/assetlibrary/OIG_05-11_Feb05.pdf.

43. U.S. General Accounting Office, "Homeland Security: Risks Facing Key Border and Transportation Security Program Need to Be Addressed," GAO Report 03-1083 (September 2003) (Washington, DC: Government Printing Office, 2003).

44. Rey Koslowski, "Real Challenges for Virtual Borders: The Implementation of US-VISIT," Migration Policy Institute Report (June 2005), http://www.migrationpolicy.org/pubs/Koslowski_Report.pdf (accessed August 26, 2005).

45. Department of Justice Office of the Investigator General, "IDENT/IAFIS: The Batres Case and the Status of the Integration Project" (March 2, 2004), http://www.usdoj.gov/oig/special/0403/final.pdf (accessed March 2, 2004).

46. Chris Strohm, "Inaccurate Databanks Pose Challenge for New Visitor Tracking System," *Government Executive Magazine* (January 7, 2004), http://www.govexec.com/dailyfed/0104/010704c1.htm (accessed March 1, 2004).

47. The chief legislation that authorized these policy reforms is the *Enhanced Border Security and Visa Entry Reform Act of 2002,* Public Law 107-173, 116 Stat. 543 (May 14, 2002). See also *Homeland Security Act,* sect. 442, p. 148; sect. 461, p. 172.

48. Demetrios Papademetriou, "Converging Realities of the U.S.-Mexico Relationship," *Migration Policy Institute Report* (July 1, 2002), http://www.migrationinformation.org/USfocus/display.cfm?ID=35 (accessed November 15, 2003).

49. See Daniel Wood, "Past Has Cautionary Lessons for Guest-Worker Programs," *Christian Science Monitor,* January 27, 2004, http://www.csmonitor.com/2004/0127/p03s01-usfp.html (accessed February 20, 2004); Stuart Anderson, "When a More Open Border is Better," *Washington Post,* January 26, 2004, http://www.washingtonpost.com/wp-dyn/articles/A47658-2004Jan25.html (accessed February 28, 2004).

50. Assessing and assigning causation to migrant flows is a problematic matter; however, the number of illegal immigrants apprehended by authorities has increased steadily in recent years. See U.S. Customs and Immigration Service, "Southwest Border Apprehensions,"http://uscis.gov/graphics/shared/aboutus/statistics/msrdec03/SWBORD.HTM (accessed February 20, 2004). See also Louie Gilot, "Survey Finds Migrants Crossing for Amnesty," *El Paso Times,* January 24, 2004, http://www.elpasotimes.com/stories/borderland/20040124-72385.shtml (accessed February 2, 2004).

51. The Senate Bill is S.1033 and the House version is H.R.2330.

52. S.1438.

53. John McCain, "Members of Congress Introduce Comprehensive Border Security & Immigration Reform Bill," Press Release, May 13, 2005, http://kennedy.senate.gov/~kennedy/statements/05/05/2005512A04.html (accessed March 8, 2006).

54. John McCain, Remarks in the *Congressional Record,* May 12, 2005, S.5169.

55. Ron Fournier, "Split Policy Considered on Immigrants," *Seattle Post-Intelligencer,* August 27, 2005, http://seattlepi.nwsource.com/national/apwashington_story.asp?category=1151&slug=Immigration percent20Divides (accessed August 29, 2005).

56. McCain, "Members of Congress Introduce Comprehensive Border Security & Immigration Reform Bill."

57. John Coryn and Jon Kyle, "Comprehensive Enforcement and Immigration Reform Act – Short Summary," http://www.cornyn.senate.gov/doc_archive/CEIRA percent20Short percent20Summary.pdf (accessed August 29, 2005).

58. Ferruccio Pastore, "To Regularize or Not to Regularize: Experiences and Views from Europe Events," Migration Policy Institute Briefing (June 30, 2004), http://www.migrationpolicy.org/events/063004.php (accessed August 20, 2005).

59. James G. Lakely, "Bush Studies New Immigration Plan," *Washington Times,* January 24, 2004, http://www.washtimes.com/national/20040123-102052-9037r.htm (accessed January 24, 2004).

60. The White House, "Fact Sheet: Fair and Secure Immigration Reform," (January 7, 2004), http://www.whitehouse.gov/news/releases/2004/01/20040107-1.html (accessed February 26, 2004).

61. Asa Hutchinson, Testimony Before the Subcommittee on Immigration, Border Security, and Citizenship Committee on the Judiciary U.S. Senate (February 12, 2004), http://judiciary.senate.gov/testimony.cfm?id=1034&wit_id=2961 (accessed February 20, 2004).

62. Stewart Verdery, "Building 21st Century Borders: Policy Development to Meet New Threats," remarks at the Heritage Foundation, February 18, 2004, http://www.heritage.org/Press/Events/ev021804a.cfm (accessed February 20, 2004).

63. McCain, "Members of Congress Introduce Comprehensive Border Security & Immigration Reform Bill."

64. Department of Homeland Security, Office of Inspector General, *Implementation of the United States Visitor and Immigrant Status Indicator Technology Program at Land Border Ports of Entry,* OIG-05-11 (February 2005), www.dhs.gov/interweb/assetlibrary/OIG_05-11_Feb05.pdf.

65. For example, expensive facial recognition pilot programs deployed in some public areas in the United States were discontinued after failing to find a single match.

CHAPTER 9

INTERNATIONAL HUMAN TRAFFICKING AND HOMELAND SECURITY

Matthew T. Kenney

At first blush, human trafficking might not appear to pose a threat to homeland security in the United States. However, as this chapter will argue, it poses moral and practical challenges to U.S. security interests at home and abroad of a very high order indeed. Contemporary human trafficking is slavery, and it exhibits features that are every bit as brutal and terrorizing as the worst forms of slavery from past eras. According to U.S. President George W. Bush, "trafficking is nothing less than a modern form of slavery, an unspeakable and unforgivable crime against the most vulnerable members of the global society."[1]

DEFINING TERMS

To begin, it is necessary to define clearly what human trafficking is. A recent United Nations report defines the trafficking of human beings as:

> …the recruitment, transportation, transfer, harbouring or receipt of persons, by means of the threat or use of force or other forms of coercion, of abduction, of fraud, of deception, of the abuse of power or of a position of vulnerability or of the giving or receiving of payments or benefits to achieve the consent of a person having control over another person, for the purpose of exploitation. Exploitation shall include, at a minimum, the exploitation of the prostitution of others or other forms of sexual exploitation, forced labour or services, slavery or practices similar to slavery, servitude or the removal of organs.[2]

The 2005 U.S. Department of State *Trafficking in Persons Report* endorses this definition and adds to it a definition of "severe forms of trafficking" (borrowing from the *U.S. Trafficking Victims Protection Act of 2000*) as constituting:

a. sex trafficking in which a commercial sex act is induced by force, fraud, or coercion, or in which the person induced to perform such an act has not attained 18 years of age; or

b. the recruitment, harboring, transportation, provision, or obtaining of a person for labor or services, through the use of force, fraud, or coercion for the purpose of subjection to involuntary servitude, peonage, debt bondage, or slavery.[3]

According to the U.S. Department of Justice, "Traffickers often prey on individuals who are poor, frequently unemployed or underemployed, and who may lack access to social safety nets, predominantly women and children in certain countries."[4]

Most policy and scholarly treatments of human trafficking make a technical distinction between trafficking and smuggling of human beings, with the latter referring to a more voluntary, contractual arrangement between the smuggler and the person being smuggled, while the former is characterized by high degrees of coercion, victimization, and other forms of violence.[5] The most common example of smuggling in the U.S. context is the widespread hiring of *coyotes* by Mexicans seeking to enter the United States illegally. However, the distinction between smuggling and trafficking is frequently blurred as individuals discover upon being smuggled into other countries that they are forced to work in the local sex industry or some other form of bondage. When this happens, individuals often unwittingly pay their own transit costs in being delivered to their captors. Still, according to Raimo Väyrynen of the World Institute for Development Economics Research, a key implication to the distinction between human smuggling and trafficking in terms of policy approaches "is that 'smuggling' is a migration issue that has to be dealt with by legal and bureaucratic means, while 'trafficking' is a human rights issue and, as a consequence, the victim deserves protection."[6]

As the above definitions suggest and as will be seen below, much of the thriving business—and it is big business on a global scale—in the sale and ruthless exploitation of human beings today feeds a seemingly insatiable demand for commercial sex in rich and poor countries alike. This discussion deliberately avoids using the word prostitution, though one encounters it often in the literature on human trafficking, because this term carries with it considerable baggage and can be highly misleading. According to the fourth edition (2000) of *The American Heritage Dictionary of the English Language,* a prostitute is defined as "One who solicits and accepts payment for sex acts." When trafficked persons, usually women and girls, are forced against their will to have sex, they are not so much prostitutes as sex slaves. By referring to them as prostitutes, we distort what is actually occurring and, most perniciously, transfer responsibility and blame to the victims rather than the criminals. This is especially true in societies such as Japan, where prostitution is illegal but only the prostitute is guilty of a crime. In its 2005 report on human trafficking, the U.S. State Department concluded that even "Where prostitution is legalized or tolerated, there is a greater demand for human trafficking victims and nearly always an increase in the number of women and children trafficked into commercial slavery."[7]

Before looking more closely at the problem of human trafficking today, it is also worth considering what constitutes terrorism. Terrorism is the "unlawful use or threatened use of force or violence by a person or an organized group against people or property with the intention of intimidating or coercing societies or governments, often for ideological or political reasons."[8] Although many other definitions of the term can be found, this definition is representative of nearly all in its focus on the inherent political nature of terrorism. This being the case, one might reasonably conclude that human trafficking, as horrific as it is for its victims, falls short of a definitional requirement of terrorism. This discussion will return to this point in the conclusion of this chapter.

HUMAN TRAFFICKING IN THE TWENTY-FIRST CENTURY: THE SCOPE OF THE PROBLEM

Obtaining reliable data on human trafficking is difficult for a variety of reasons. First, the illegality of the practice means that the criminal networks that conduct it try, as much as possible, to disguise and conceal their activities. Second, trafficked persons are often so terrorized and traumatized that they are reluctant to report their situation to local authorities. In many instances, sex slaves in particular are threatened with physical retribution (including death) against themselves and their families. Also, because they have been transported to and sold in societies where they have few rights and are usually unfamiliar with the local language and customs, they are further trapped. Third, even if they are freed, formerly trafficked persons (once again, especially former sex slaves) carry with them debilitating physical and emotional scars that make the idea of publicizing in any way their past bondage too shameful and unbearable. Fourth, public perceptions and attitudes (which of course vary across regions and countries) toward prostitution, illegal immigration, and foreigners can have the perverse effect of causing many to turn a blind eye to the presence of human trafficking in one's society. In a culture like that of the United States, with its heightened emphasis on individualism, tolerance, and personal responsibility, an unintended consequence can be a weakened sense of community from which alarms might go off when deviant behaviors are sighted or suspected.[9] Fifth, weak institutions and corrupt law enforcement officials, especially (though not exclusively) in impoverished countries, mean that the latter can be bought off and even brought into trafficking networks, making enforcement and reporting of laws both lax and suspect.

Given the above qualifications, we need to view statistics on the prevalence of human trafficking as modest estimates. Not surprisingly, ranges vary considerably, depending on the sources consulted. For recent years, the U.S. Department of State has estimated "600,000 to 800,000 men, women, and children [are] trafficked across international borders each year."[10] The authors of the *Trafficking in Persons Report* go on to note that "approximately 80% [of those trafficked each year] are women and girls and up to 50% are minors. The State Department's estimate is conservative when compared with those of the United Nations and many nongovernmental organizations. Yet even taking the lower figure of 600,000 means that an average of 1,643 people are trafficked every day of the year throughout the world.

Together with U.S. State Department reports, perhaps the best source for information on human trafficking today is The Protection Project.[11] This institute, which was founded in 1994 at the Foreign Policy Institute at The Johns Hopkins University School of Advanced International Studies in Washington, D.C., with the purpose of promoting human rights around the world, has published detailed reports on human trafficking activities in nearly every country in the world. Its highly-trained staff produces both original research as well as pulls together data from governmental and nongovernmental sources.

According to a special report released in 2004, human trafficking "has become a $12-billion-a-year global industry that touches virtually every country."[12] A recent *National Geographic* article reports that an Israeli brothel with as few as ten sex slaves (in Israel, they frequently are brought from Eastern European countries) can generate revenues of $1 million per year.[13] The laws of supply and demand are very much in evidence when we examine human trafficking. This highlights, among other things, the need to address this problem both at the source and destination as well as disrupting and shutting down the networks that engage in human trafficking.

CAUSES

Slavery, alas, has been a feature of the human experience since the beginning of recorded history. In the United States, with its own bitter legacy of this "peculiar institution," the general view among its citizens is that slavery came to an end with the conclusion of the U.S. Civil War.

Many would no doubt be surprised that as many as 20,000 people are trafficked into the United States each year, most of whom are forced to work as sex slaves. While there are isolated cases of native-born Americans being trafficked as sex slaves, the United States is overwhelmingly a receiver state because of the strong demand for inexpensive sex in the domestic market.

Human trafficking, whether for purposes of the sex industry or other forms of forced labor, shows globalization and economic interdependence at its worse. As such, it poses acute challenges to defenders of economic interdependence who see it, *ceteris paribus,* as leading to a beneficial and even optimal linking of states and peoples around the world. That is, international trade in a globalized free-market economy is viewed as a network of relations that builds upon and expands the individual freedom that lies at the heart of capitalist economic theory. When human beings are reduced to mere commodities and means, however, the theory collapses. Human trafficking today, as in the past, is compounded by the glaring inequalities in wealth and opportunities between rich and poor societies.[14] Traffickers, and the highly organized networks in which many operate, skillfully manipulate the desperation and hopes of individuals, especially the young and marginalized, in those societies where economic opportunities are severely limited. By promising jobs as nannies, maids, or waitresses in the West, they are able to lure unsuspecting individuals into future bondage.

Poverty and lack of economic opportunities, then, is one of the underlying causes of human trafficking, just as it is an underlying cause of terrorism by enhancing the recruitment opportunities of disaffected youth by organizations like al Qaeda. A key difference, of course, is that terrorist organizations, at least to date, display a marked (though not exclusive) preference for young men rather than young women.

We can point to other factors behind the recent increase in human trafficking. The collapse of the Soviet Union (and its satellites) and the end of the Cold War resulted in the relatively free movement of individuals across national borders in the region. This, together with the transition to market-based economies and the drastic scaling back of the social welfare states in the region, has created uncertainty and, as mentioned, desperation for many. Women, because of prevailing sexism in their societies, have been made more vulnerable than men during this transition phase. In fact, Russia today is a leading source and destination country for trafficked persons, with Russian trafficking networks active in many countries around the world.[15]

From a market perspective, as already alluded to, human trafficking networks have responded to this seemingly inexhaustible supply of young women willing to leave their home countries for greater economic opportunities in the West and the steady demand for commercial sex in the West. In this respect, human trafficking networks bear much in common with drug trafficking networks, though perhaps with even greater profit potential. "Most [human trafficking networks and organizations] operate without fear of reprisal because criminal sanctions against traffickers are often weak or not enforced. Unlike the trade in drugs and guns, the trade in women and children is virtually cost-free, and thus extraordinarily lucrative."[16] A reasoned strategy for dealing with the phenomenon of human trafficking must be multipronged, focusing on issues relating to supply, demand, rule of law, and, perhaps most importantly, international cooperation. In this respect also, human trafficking and drug trafficking share important points with international terrorism today. They are all global networks which seek, either directly or indirectly, to promote their particular interests—be they economic, religious, political, or a combination of these and other interests—by undermining the stability and cohesion of the societies in which they operate. And, as is apparent, all three place a premium on the use of violence to achieve their goals.

THE MORAL CHALLENGE OF HUMAN TRAFFICKING

Although a relative latecomer to the community of nation-states on the global stage, the United States, it is worth noting, is the world's oldest continuous representative democracy. Moreover, it was founded on core principles of freedom, respect for all human life, and equality of opportunity, among other values. Such values were revolutionary at the time, especially as foundational values for the establishment of a functioning system of government, and remain so to this day when one looks at the injustices and suffering of millions of the world's poorest members, many of whom live under authoritarian regimes of one stripe or another.

From its very inception, the United States was rightly seen by many as leading the way in the effort to safeguard individual freedom and other natural rights, or what today are more commonly referred to as human rights. Also from its inception, the United States fell short of its highest ideals, most notably and regrettably in permitting the institution of slavery to persist for nearly 100 years following its independence. Both the legacy of slavery and ongoing racial discrimination in America remain as hindrances to the full realization of its ideals.

Of course, to use as a practical standard the full realization of such lofty ideals as those which make up the American Creed is utopian. However, the general trend over the course of American history has, with notable exceptions, been a discernible movement toward these ideals. This is a redeeming quality, if one is needed, in the American experience and one that has served as a source of inspiration and hope for its own citizens and peoples from other parts of the world who view this land as one of possibilities and opportunities for a life lived with dignity, respect, and liberty.

Set against such ideals as these, human trafficking represents a degradation of and disregard for fundamental human rights that is certainly among the most egregious in the world today. It is, of course, reprehensible wherever it occurs. That it is as prevalent as it appears to be in the United States poses an especially grievous threat to American ideals and values. If history is to serve as a useful guide, as it certainly can in this instance, then this threat should rather be viewed as a challenge to be overcome and not merely a problem to be contained. Overcoming this challenge, as mentioned, will require a high degree of international cooperation with significant U.S. leadership. Failure to respond effectively to the individual and social destructiveness that results from the trafficking of human beings would signal moral capitulation and a dangerous return to a far less civilized world. Conversely, the only losers in bringing an end to human trafficking would be those who seek, to borrow from Immanuel Kant, the great moral philosopher of the Enlightenment Era, to treat people as means rather than as ends.

The United States has made great strides in removing obstacles to individual freedom over the course of its history. The contemporary form of slavery which we call human trafficking is a gross injustice to those, usually the poor and desperate, who are caught in its web. While it is certainly on the radar of many nongovernmental organizations and governments agencies, it has yet to reach the level of moral outrage it merits. As both the world's superpower and a nation with a rich tradition of promoting and protecting freedom, the United States has the resources and the moral fortitude to play a more prominent role in combating this scourge.

Writing in the late 1700s, Kant argued that history has a purpose, or at least can reasonably and constructively be thought to have a purpose, which is consonant with human freedom and autonomy and, hence, moral rectitude. He outlined this historical purpose in a short essay written in 1784, "Idea for a Universal History with a Cosmopolitan Intent."[17] Kant went on to argue that historical events, while frequently appearing random and more often evil than good, over the long term exhibit a pattern that is more consistent with moral and social progress. Far from taking a deterministic view of history, Kant instead maintained that human agency was crucial in advancing the course of history and the evolution of mankind along moral, political, and economic dimensions. While it may seem odd to some to draw on a figure such as Kant in a discussion of human trafficking and homeland security in the twenty-first century, his optimistic yet measured view of the human condition in fact exhibits many parallels to the American ethos (and to other liberal democracies where human rights figure prominently). Moreover, Kant remains to this day an important source for our understanding of and justification for the protection of human rights.

A more important reason, it can be argued, for drawing on Kant's thinking is because his view of history as progressive and not cyclical in nature accurately fits with the dominant view taken in the United States and still serves as a useful guide in resolving unacceptable social conditions in all societies and, indeed, in the nascent global society taking shape today. That is, in drawing on Kant, we view human beings as both products and agents of history. Kant believed that nature uses historical events, above all the antagonisms so characteristic of most human interactions—whether between two private individuals or among states on the international level—to prod us to turn to more rational and morally defensible resolutions to the injustices and suffering that flow from our antagonistic tendencies. Indeed, Kant argues that as our talents and rational capabilities are awakened and sharpened over time, we can each "transform the crude natural capacity for moral discrimination into definite practical principles and thus transform a *pathologically* enforced agreement into a society and, finally, into a *moral* whole."[18] The moral whole to which Kant refers is undoubtedly a high ideal, but even if it can never be realized its pursuit is still justified because it serves as an organizing principle both for law itself and those things which law-abiding citizens most value, chief among them their freedom.

HUMAN TRAFFICKING AND THE THREAT TO THE AMERICAN HOMELAND

As the above discussion indicates, a major threat to the American homeland posed by human trafficking is its potentially corrosive impact on American values and the related threat of a corruption of public officials, especially law enforcement officials. This is a speculative claim and not one that can at present be supported with empirical data, though there are many accounts of such corruption in countries like Mexico.

Throughout its history and especially since becoming a superpower in the mid-twentieth century, the United States has presented itself, especially in explaining its foreign policy actions and goals, as a promoter and defender of freedom and democracy around the world. As the very label demonstrates, Operation Iraqi Freedom, whatever one thinks of its underlying rationale or effectiveness, has from the outset been presented by the U.S. Administration as a mission to defend and promote freedom in Iraq, the United States, and around the world. In this sense, it reflects the U.S. rhetorical commitment to these ideals.

Human trafficking poses other threats to the American homeland. We see in many countries that illegal trafficking networks, whether of human beings or drugs (or other commodities, such as weapons), have the capacity to corrupt local and national law enforcement and government officials. "Corruption is," notes Väyrynen, "indeed a central element in human smuggling and trafficking because it makes it easier to get migrants across the borders."[19] It is not hyperbole to imagine that the threat of such corruption exists in the United States if efforts to end human trafficking are not pursued more aggressively than is currently the case.

Another very real potential threat to the American homeland posed by human trafficking networks is their ability to form linkages with terrorist organizations. In other parts of the world, examples of such linkages are known to exist between terrorist organizations and drug trafficking networks. The reasons for such a threat should come as no surprise. Many of those who are trafficked into the United States are brought into the country through the porous border with Mexico, even those whose country of origin is elsewhere. Human trafficking networks possess information and techniques about how best to bring individuals into the United States illegally that would be of high value to terrorist organizations seeking to do the same. As such, the formation of a symbiotic relationship between terrorist organizations and human trafficking networks, despite their widely differing goals, is not improbable. In fact, as pointed out in a 2001 U.S. government report, "The same networks that trade in weapons and narcotics are often also active in trafficking."[20]

Lastly, though there are no doubt other ways in which it threatens American society, human trafficking increases health risks to the American public. HIV/AIDS rates are higher among trafficked persons, especially those in the sex industry, as are other sexually-transmitted diseases. "The health implications of sex trafficking extend not only to its victims, but also to the general public, as well as those who frequent brothels and who can become carriers and/or core transmitters of serious diseases."[21]

As of 2005, the official U.S. commitment to eradicating human trafficking included the following main goals and activities:

- Vigorously enforcing U.S. laws against those who traffic in persons;
- Raising awareness about human trafficking and how it can be eradicated;
- Identifying, protecting, and assisting victims exploited by traffickers;
- Reducing the vulnerability of individuals to trafficking through increased education, economic opportunity, and protection and promotion of human rights; and
- Employing diplomatic and foreign policy tools to encourage other nations, the UN, and other multilateral institutions to work with us to combat this crime, draft and enforce laws against trafficking, and hold traffickers accountable.[22]

The major U.S. effort in the fight against human trafficking centers upon the *Trafficking Victims Protection Act of 2000* (P.L. 106-386) and the *Trafficking Victims Reauthorization Act* (P.L. 108-193). These two acts form the cornerstone of U.S. antitrafficking law today and are generally referred to by the acronym TVPA. The TVPA, which became law on October 28, 2000, accomplished the following:

- Provided for *victim assistance* in the United States by making trafficking victims eligible for federally funded or administered health and other benefits and services as if they were refugees; mandating U.S. Government provisions for victims of trafficking and, where applicable, their families; protecting certain trafficking victims who cooperate with law enforcement in investigation and prosecution of trafficking from removal; and allowing T nonimmigrant status holders to adjust to permanent resident status;

- Created *new crimes* and enhanced penalties for existing crimes including forced labor, trafficking with respect to peonage, slavery, involuntary servitude, or forced labor, sex trafficking of children or by force, fraud, or coercion, and unlawful conduct with respect to documents; mandatory restitution; and criminalized attempts to engage in these behaviors; and

- Provided *assistance to foreign countries* in drafting laws to prohibit and punish acts of trafficking, strengthening investigation and prosecution of traffickers, and creating programs to assist victims, and expand U.S. Government exchange and international visitor programs focusing on trafficking.[23]

ENDING THE TRAFFICKING OF HUMAN BEINGS: PROGRESS THROUGH COOPERATION

On the domestic level in the United States, much more needs to be done to reduce the demand for commercial sex and, though it is beyond the scope of this chapter, cheap immigrant labor. The demand for cheap labor, of course, is a major contributing factor to the related problems of illegal immigration and human smuggling in the country. In all cases, greater attention needs to be paid to the underlying causes of these problems. And, clearly, economic issues, especially severe poverty and glaring income inequalities in many parts of the world (and, perversely, the profit potential this creates for traffickers and *coyotes*, as already mentioned) are fundamental when talking about human trafficking and illegal immigration. Also needed is increased and improved training of law enforcement officials so that they can better identify and prosecute human traffickers.

The United States, most other countries, the United Nations, and innumerable nongovernmental organizations and individuals have all recognized the threats posed by human trafficking and the moral imperative to end it. Human trafficking by definition is a transnational problem.

Accordingly, it requires a coordinated, transnational response. To its credit, the work of various departments and agencies of the U.S. government generally reflect this reality, as is evidenced in the 2003 government report, "Assessment of U.S. Activities to Combat Trafficking in Persons." Within the government, efforts are being made to coordinate activities of the Departments of Justice, Health and Human Services, State, Labor, Homeland Security, and the U.S. Agency for International Development. Much more can be done, and on a practical level tackling this problem provides the United States, both its government and its people, an ideal opportunity to confront a contemporary social problem with devastating consequences, most clearly for its immediate victims but also for the broader societies in which it occurs.

Unlike decisions to go to war and other uses of military force, it is hard to imagine any respectable or respected governments and individuals opposing increased efforts to combat human trafficking and to bring to justice those who perpetuate it. The United States could reassert in no uncertain terms its genuine commitment to individual freedom, inviolable human dignity, and equality of opportunity by taking a far more proactive and decisive role in ending slavery once and for all. Devoting greater attention to ending human trafficking also provides the United States with an ideal opportunity to strengthen its ties to other countries, especially the world's poorer and weaker countries which at times resent the overwhelming economic and, especially, military power of the United States. Ties with traditional allies like France and Germany could also use mending. This is not to suggest that responding to the human and moral crisis of human trafficking will completely repair America's strained relations with other countries, but rather that it can be seen as part of a much-needed effort to demonstrate to the rest of the world that while the United States values democracy, freedom, and a free-market economy, it also understands the fundamental value and necessity of cooperation among peoples, and further recognizes that the most intractable problems facing most people in the world today cannot be solved with cruise missiles, smart bombs, or door-to-door raids by elite military units in impoverished parts of the world.

In short, the U.S. government can demonstrate its undying commitment to freedom as a universal value by promoting it in the most universal way possible at present; namely, through multilateral channels based on broad-based cooperation and not by acting unilaterally or with the support of a select few countries. This, as suggested in this chapter, will bolster U.S. credibility around the world, all the more so in that meeting the challenges posed by human trafficking cannot easily or accurately be depicted as motivated by the pursuit of financial interests on the part of the United States. This is an argument frequently made, whether rightly or wrongly, with respect to U.S. foreign policy in the Middle East.

Moreover, addressing the problem of human trafficking will require the U.S. government and its citizens to take a closer look at the underlying causes of this scourge. This spillover effect will enable us to take a more holistic and multidimensional approach to social problems, including security issues. In the process, it is highly probable we will discover that many of these causes contribute to terrorism and other threats to social stability and individual well-being in all parts of the world.

To a considerable extent, the U.S. government already has in place many well-designed programs and activities to address the problem of human trafficking. Not surprisingly, greater funding is needed to support these initiatives and increase the effectiveness. One relatively inexpensive measure, though, would be greater publicity on the part of the government, in tandem with organizations from civil society, of the peculiar challenges and opportunities for moral renewal and convergence posed by human trafficking. According to former U.S. Attorney General John Ashcroft, "Slavery, human trafficking, and sexual servitude are crimes that wrench our hearts. They rob human beings of freedom. They strike at our nation's belief in the potential of every life."[24] For champions of freedom, no greater practical distinction of this concept can be made in human societies, be they of the past or present, than that between slave and nonslave. History, it seems, at times does repeat itself, at least in broad contours. The evil of human trafficking once again presents the United States (and other countries) the opportunity to take a firm stand for or against slavery. More than 200 years ago, Kant wrote that "reason itself does not operate on instinct, but requires trial, practice, and instruction in order gradually to progress from one stage of insight to another."[25] How we respond to human trafficking today will test our reason and moral fortitude and determine whether we can move forward or backward as human beings.

NOTES

1. Quoted in U.S. Government, "Assessment of U.S. Activities to Combat Trafficking in Persons," August 2003, 1.

2. United Nations, *The United Nations Protocol to Prevent, Suppress and Punish Trafficking in Persons, Especially Women and Children, Supplementing the United Nations Convention Against Transnational Organized Crime* (New York: United Nations, 2000), 2.

3. U.S. Department of State, *2005 Trafficking in Persons Report* (Washington, DC, 2005), 12.

4. U.S. Department of Justice, Civil Rights Division, "Trafficking in Persons: A Guide for Non-Governmental Organizations," http://www.usdoj.gov (accessed February 25, 2004).

5. Raimo Väyrynen, "Illegal Immigration, Human Trafficking, and Organized Crime," World Institute for Development Economics Research, Discussion Paper No. 2003/72 (October 2003), 16.

6. Ibid.

7. *2005 Trafficking in Persons Report*, 19.

8. *The American Heritage Dictionary of the English Language* (Fourth Edition, 2000).

9. Peter Landesman, "The Girls Next Door," *New York Times Magazine* (January 25, 2004).

10. *2005 Trafficking in Persons Report*, 6.

11. The Protection Project Web site can be accessed at http://www.protectionproject.org.

12. "Human Trafficking and Slavery," *CQ Researcher,* March 26, 2004, http://library.cqpress.com (accessed April 6, 2004).

13. Andrew Cockburn, "21st Century Slaves," *National Geographic* (September 2003), 5.

14. For an excellent recent treatment of global poverty and inequalities among states, along with a host of statistical data, see Jeffrey D. Sachs, *The End of Poverty: Economic Possibilities for Our Time* (New York: Penguin Press, 2005).

15. For more on the Russian case, see the country report at The Prevention Project Web site.

16. United States Agency for International Development, "Trafficking in Persons: USAID's Response" (September 2001), 2.

17. The version of "Idea for a Universal History with a Cosmopolitan Intent" I use is from Immanuel Kant, *Perpetual Peace and Other Essays,* trans. Ted Humphrey (Indianapolis, IN: Hackett Publishing, 1983), 29–40.

18. Kant, "Idea for a Universal History," 32.

19. Väyrynen, "Illegal Immigration, Human Trafficking, and Organized Crime," 6.

20. USAID, "Trafficking in Persons: USAID's Response," 2.

21. *2005 Trafficking in Persons Report*, 49.

22. Ibid., 239.

23. U.S. Government, "Assessment of U.S. Activities to Combat Trafficking in Persons," 2–3.

24. John Ashcroft, "Prepared Remarks of Attorney General John Ashcroft Regarding Human Trafficking," U.S. Department of Justice, January 29, 2004, http://www.usdoj.gov (accessed February 25, 2004).

25. Kant, "Idea for a Universal History," 30.

CHAPTER 10

LAW ENFORCEMENT CHALLENGES AND "SMART BORDERS"

David A. Shirk

The context of U.S.-Mexican relations, particularly with regard to law enforcement and security issues, has been transformed by dramatic events in recent years. On the one hand, major changes in Mexico's political landscape have shifted the context for several key policy issues related to the rule of law and national security. On the other hand, the new post-9/11 security climate in the United States has fundamentally reshaped U.S. priorities with regard to law enforcement and security issues about the U.S.-Mexico border. While concerns about long-standing challenges —such as migration, narco-trafficking, arms trafficking, and other transborder crimes— have not abated, they have been superseded by new concerns related to international terrorism. The new law enforcement structures and agreements that have been devised to address post-9/11 border challenges may ultimately expand the scope of bilateral relations between the United States and Mexico. This chapter explores how the post-9/11 context has impacted U.S. and Mexican law enforcement and security relations, and how new policy directions may offer a framework to develop mutually beneficial practices and approaches to shared challenges. Drawing on insights from the San Diego-Tijuana region, this chapter evaluates recent developments in U.S.-Mexican border security and the prospects for improved binational collaboration.

THE SEARCH FOR SECURITY AND "COMMUNITY" ALONG THE BORDER

Experts have produced an ample body of research on border security issues such as immigration, narco-trafficking, and cross-border crime.[1]

This literature has traditionally focused on two broad sets of questions. The first set of questions deals with the objectives and effectiveness of existing border security arrangements. While there is considerable disagreement on the appropriate objectives of border security, there is a relatively widespread consensus and ample evidence that—despite enhanced law enforcement border security initiatives over the last decade—the U.S.-Mexico border remains highly permeable and suffers considerably high levels of crime and violence on both sides. While U.S. border security officials argue that their inability to protect the border is attributable to insufficient manpower and resources, scholars like Peter Andreas argue that U.S. initiatives are ineffective because they are intended to satisfy the political objectives of policy makers rather than seriously tackle the root causes of specific problems. In this context, the border itself becomes a highly visible symbol for complex policy problems, for which the enhancement of border security initiatives serves as an attractive panacea.

A second set of research questions is focused on the effectiveness of binational efforts to address cross-border security challenges and on whether there exists a binational "security community." That is, scholars of regional security question whether the United Sates and Mexico share a set of shared or common goals that facilitate cooperative security arrangements. Despite significant areas of cooperation and mechanisms that facilitate problem solving along the border, major challenges and obstacles exist. For example, as J. Z. García points out, binational cooperation in the U.S.-Mexican context is typically more focused on "reducing cross-border interagency irritants and misunderstandings" rather than on coordinated operations, and while occasionally stronger at the local level, interagency cooperation tends to vary "from place to place and time to time."[2] To the frustration of U.S. officials, persistent problems in Mexican law enforcement—from lack of resources to outright corruption—set limits on binational cooperation. Meanwhile, amidst a general sensitivity to ensuring respect for its sovereignty and policy priorities, authorities in Mexico have been frustrated by perceived U.S. unilateralism and hesitation regarding key Mexican priorities to promote immigration reform and economic integration. As a result of these challenges, the overwhelming conclusion of several major studies of binational cooperation in law enforcement is that there is no "security community" along the U.S.-Mexico border.[3]

In the post-9/11 context, an additional hurdle for border security and bilateral relations developed as the U.S. agenda became focused on the "war on terror" at home and abroad, and as tensions mounted over the debate on Iraq in the U.N. Security Council in 2002. In that context, Mexico found itself in the hot seat because it held one of the Council votes that could have provided greater legitimacy to the U.S.-led effort to oust Iraqi leader Saddam Hussein. Open admonishments from the U.S. Embassy and high-profile diplomats like Henry Kissinger raised concern in Mexico that its government and citizens would become victims of a backlash from Washington. After that debate and the defeat of the Iraqi regime, the United States and Mexico began working to reaffirm their ties. At the center of the agenda are efforts to reshape the policy framework for managing long-standing challenges and new terrorist threats along the border. In the next two sections, several different types of law enforcement and security challenges confronted in the U.S.-Mexican context are outlined. It is argued that the post-9/11 security environment adds a new and different conundrum, yet—like virtually all long-standing border security challenges—the key to preventing terrorism ultimately lies both beyond and within the border itself.

SUPPLY AND DEMAND: LONG-STANDING BORDER CHALLENGES

The border separates communities and markets in ways that produce anomalous economic pressures. In other words, were it not for the border, flows of people and goods would naturally conform to the market pressures of supply and demand. The border, however, creates separate markets where the distributions of supply and demand differ significantly due to contrasting policies, inconsistent regulation, and the distribution of productive factors on either side. For most of its existence, such market forces have driven legitimate cross-border economic activities. Mexican and U.S. border residents cross to the United States to work or shop because it is economically advantageous to do so. They cross the border to purchase goods and services that are cheaper or more available.

Likewise, most illegal border-related activities are conducted by individuals who are motivated by the same kinds of market forces. That is, long-standing border law enforcement and security "challenges" have been largely a reflection of illicit supply and demand dynamics. Accordingly, efforts to counter illegal cross-border activities have therefore targeted either supply or demand. To illustrate the economic nature of long-standing law enforcement and security challenges, below are discussed the trends in the key areas of immigration, narco-trafficking, and arms trafficking.

Undocumented Immigration

Historically, migration from Mexico to the United States has been driven by the lack of economic opportunities at home, and by the often cyclical draw of U.S. demand for low-wage laborers (especially in agriculture and labor-intensive industries). During much of the nineteenth and twentieth centuries, relatively open immigration policies and special programs to permit the entry of temporary guest workers brought large numbers of

Mexican laborers to the United States during cycles of economic prosperity. However, during times of low economic activity, migration from Mexico (and other countries) declined and was often discouraged through a variety of restrictive or even race-based exclusionary immigration policies.

The gradual evolution of the U.S. immigration policy regime over the course of the twentieth century progressively and subjectively set limits on the number of immigrants that were permitted legal entry from a given country. Although today Mexico is the country awarded the largest number of visas, it is also paradoxically the country that sends the largest number of undocumented immigrants to the United States (see Figure 10.1). According to a 2004 report by the Congressional Research Service, Mexicans represented an estimated 57 percent (5.3 million) of the roughly 9.3 million unauthorized residents living in the United States in 2002.

The so-called "push" and "pull" factors that have contributed to this massive wave migration are largely economic. On the one hand, the growth of the Mexican population seeking employment in the United

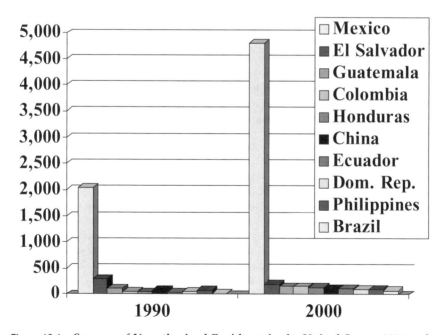

Figure 10.1   Sources of Unauthorized Residents in the United States, 1990 and 2000

Source: "Estimates of the Unauthorized Immigrant Population Residing in the United States: 1990 to 2000," Office of Policy and Planning, U.S. Immigration and Naturalization Service, 2003.

States is due to a series of economic crises in Mexico that has accompanied Mexico's economic restructuring in the era of globalization. Thus, Mexican laborers have left their home communities in large numbers to search for work because of "transitory poverty" associated with the deterioration of wages and the loss of employment, more so than because of problems of "chronic poverty." On the other hand, the large flows of Mexicans northward across the border have also been due in part to the demand for their labor in the United States, particularly during periods of strong economic growth such as that experienced in the late 1990s.

In reaction to these trends U.S. authorities initiated a series of concentrated border enforcement measures in the early 1990s, from Operation "Hold the Line" (also called the Blockade) in Texas to Operation "Gatekeeper" in San Diego. Such programs definitely contributed to a change in patterns of undocumented migration, primarily by driving migration away from more heavily populated segments of the border and into dangerous desert and mountain regions. However, such policies did not necessarily result in significant reductions in the number of undocumented Mexican migrants successfully entering the United States, who now crossed the border in larger numbers in central border states like Arizona (See Figure 10.2). Rather, the rate of undocumented Mexican migration

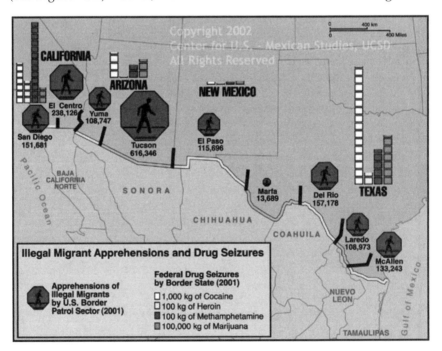

Figure 10.2   Detention of Undocumented Migrants and Seizures of Illegal Drugs along the U.S.-Mexican Border

into the United States—as measured by proxy through the number of apprehensions along the southwest border—increased with the demand for jobs in the strong economy of the late 1990s. Finally, after its peak of 1,643,679 in fiscal year (FY) 2000, undocumented migration appeared to decline to 929,809 (See Figure 10.2), though research suggests that this decline was related to the brief economic downturn following 9/11 rather than to enhanced border security. The distribution of immigration patterns along the border region is illustrated in Figure 10.3.

Meanwhile, government efforts to increase border security brought several paradoxical and unintended consequences. First, official government assessments of undocumented migration suggest that new barriers to entry (along with processing delays for persons awaiting legal residency) "created an incentive for those who succeed in entering the United States to stay."[5] In other words, rather than following traditionally cyclical patterns of migration for seasonal occupations (e.g., agriculture), many migrants opted to stay in the United States and/or bring their families across the border with them, as suggested by an increase in the number of women and unaccompanied minors entering the United States without authorization.

Another unintended consequence is that undocumented persons confronted with heightened security measures at U.S. ports of entry have increasingly relied on organized crime networks of "professional" smugglers (*coyotes*). The profits generated by providing access to the U.S. black market for labor can be extremely lucrative, often ranging between $1,000

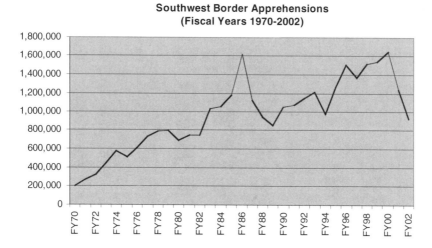

Figure 10.3   Southwest Border Apprehensions, 1970–2002

Source: Wayne Cornelius, "Evaluating U.S. Immigration Control Strategy, 1993–2003," Presentation at the Trans-Border Institute, University of San Diego, October 24, 2003.

to $2,000 per client. Moreover, some smuggling organizations appear to be increasingly diversified in their illicit activities, including narco-trafficking, auto theft, and even forced labor and sexual exploitation.[6]

Finally, as a direct consequence of new concentrated border enforcement efforts, there were significantly higher death tolls for migrants who were pushed to greater extremes—crossing the border in the deserts and mountains—in their efforts to fill employment demand on the U.S. side of the border, as illustrated in Figure 10.4. The number of migrant deaths reported by the Border Patrol and the Mexican government increased from a few dozen annually at the beginning of the 1990s to the current average of more than one person per day. In addition to the more than 2,500 migrant deaths that have occurred in the last decade, thousands more have suffered a wide range of injuries in their sojourns into the United States.

Drug Trafficking

For most of the twentieth century, the prohibition of drugs in the United States has created a black market that provides lucrative profit margins for domestic narcotics producers and those who illicitly smuggle drugs into the United States. Early production and distribution of narcotics to

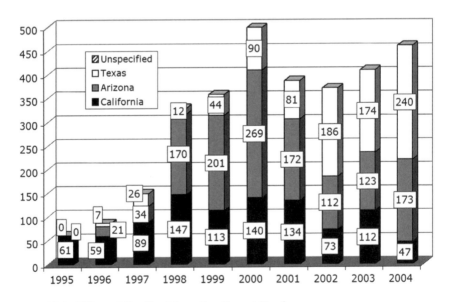

Figure 10.4   Migrant Deaths Along Southwest Border

Source: Secretaria de Relaciones Exteriores data collected by California Rural Legal Assistance Foundation. 2004 data from Rich Morosi, "Border Crossing Deaths Set a 12-Month Record," Los Angeles Times, October 1, 2005.

the United States was based in Asia (particularly China) and the Middle East (particularly Turkey). Immigrants to the United States from Europe (*La Cosa Nostra* and other organized crime organizations) were critical in establishing the linkages and networks of transport and distribution for narcotics, both before and after narcotics became illegal in the 1920s and 1930s. Additionally, smuggling networks operating in France helped facilitate the movement of drugs into the United States.

During WWII, Latin America experienced a brief surge in the export of narcotics to the United States, due to the interruption of European and Asian sources of production and distribution. However, it was not until the late 1960s and early 1970s that these networks were supplanted by Latin American producers, due to changes in European markets (such as the banning of production in Turkey) and new law enforcement initiatives to break the "French Connection" to the United States. The Nixon administration's declaration of a "war on drugs" in 1970 was accompanied by the consolidation of laws regulating narcotics under the *Controlled Substances Act,* and has set the basis for U.S. drug policy up to present day.[7]

Approaches that attempt to reduce drug trafficking target either the "supply side" or the "demand side" of the equation, though there has been considerably more emphasis on supply-side initiatives: (1) eradication, to destroy crops and production of illegal narcotics; (2) interdiction, to stop the flow of drugs while in transit through search and seizure; and (3) dislocation, to weaken or destroy narco-trafficking networks by bringing individuals involved in organized crime syndicates to justice.[8] Along the border, efforts to control the northbound flow of narcotics have centered primarily on interdiction through customs investigations of cross-border traffic. Some significant initiatives have been taken to dislocate organized crime networks along the border, particularly against the Tijuana-based Arrellano-Felix organization. Increased production of drugs in the border region, particularly the production of methamphetamines, has also led to new efforts to eradicate production. The differential distribution of drug trafficking and its effects along the border region is illustrated in Figure 10.2.

The problems associated with drug trafficking in Mexico and along the border have escalated in recent years as Colombian networks have deteriorated in that country's ongoing civil war. At different points over the last decade, the border region has seen a dramatic surge of violence as a result of territorial feuds between rival drug cartels, particularly when key cartel leaders are arrested or displaced. Such conflicts were extremely noticeable in 2005 when efforts by escaped drug lord Joaquin "El Chapo" Guzmán to move against imprisoned narco-traffickers Osiel Cárdenas and Benjamin Arrellano-Felix resulted in a wave of violence that included the retaliatory murder of half a dozen Matamoros prison guards, the brazen assassination of Nuevo Laredo's police chief only hours after being sworn in, and a series of kidnappings by masked commando units (known as *Zeta*) apparently comprising former military personnel. In response to these events, U.S. Ambassador Tony Garza issued two State Department warnings for visitors traveling to Mexico; these were followed by the closure of the U.S. Consulate in Nuevo Laredo in what Garza described as a U.S. effort to "punish" Mexico.[9]

Arms Trafficking

The prohibition of guns in Mexico and the legal availability of guns in the United States leads to the illegal southbound trafficking of arms at a profit. The United States effectively serves as a "gray market" for arms traffickers, and—ironically—a source of weapons for criminal organizations active in narco-trafficking and other cross-border crimes.[10] Law enforcement officials on both sides of the border have lobbied for stricter controls of arms flows from the United States. However, despite these efforts, there have been indications that arms trafficking in the border region continues in significant quantities. Moreover, while Mexican officials have been very vocal in addressing this issue, there has not been a corresponding increase in the scrutiny of border crossers into Mexico. Mexican officials typically do not individually evaluate southbound border crossers in a preliminary inspection process; instead, crossers are subjected to an ostensibly random process for indicating when a vehicle will be searched in a secondary inspection. This process is monitored by Mexican officials who are able to influence the electronic selection process by targeting specific vehicles for additional inspection. Individuals crossing south into Mexico by foot are not required to undergo any preliminary screening process and are therefore able to bring relatively small quantities of contraband (e.g., handguns) into Mexico without significant probability of revision. The primary concern, however, is the trafficking of arms on a larger scale.

Other Forms of Cross-Border Crime

A wide variety of cross-border criminal activity affects most communities throughout the borderlands. Communities located near the border are generally more likely than others to experience violence and property crime. For example, auto theft represents a significant portion of property crime in the border region, and approximately 20 percent of all major property crime in San Diego. In the nearby city of Chula Vista, law enforcement officials note that auto crime—the combination of theft of autos and theft from autos—is the leading category of crime. This trend is closely related to the city's proximity to the border and significantly inflates that city's ranking on the FBI index of serious crime. Autos stolen in the United States. are often smuggled into Mexico, where organized criminal networks frequently benefit from police protection. The legalization of *autos chocolates* (cars imported from the United States) in Mexico has contributed to this phenomenon. The result for many criminals and their accomplices is a high degree of impunity; indeed, some U.S. law enforcement officials have found evidence that many stolen cars have been "ordered" by used-car dealers in Mexico. Still, officials note that there is no evidence that such crimes are primarily committed by Mexican nationals, and that there are multiple variables that may contribute to the high rate of auto crime that do not relate to the city's proximity to the border. Moreover, it is also the case thatstolen cars in Mexico are frequently taken to the United States in order to evade Mexican law enforcement. Further research is needed in order to evaluate patterns of auto crime and determine whether there are similar trends across different regions along the border.

The state of the economy is highly relevant to cross-border indices of crime, particularly in Mexico where economic trends have a significant effect on the salaries of Mexican law enforcement personnel, the incidence of crime, and all other dimensions of the public security problem. Economic problems in Mexico also have spillover effects into the United States; in 1995, for example, an historic devaluation of the peso brought a major influx of Mexican citizens and exacerbated problems of crime in many U.S. border communities.

ECONOMIC MOTIVATIONS FOR VIOLENCE

Driving each of the illegal activities described above are the basic market forces of supply and demand created by the border or the policies on either side of it. As a result, the policies that can be designed to address these challenges are also necessarily market-oriented solutions. That is, solutions to these problems are targeted toward supply/demand reduction or accommodation.

For example, efforts to reduce the supply of undocumented workers can be directed toward physical prevention of entry (e.g., Operation Gatekeeper) or toward ameliorating the "push" factors in migrants' home communities (e.g., by promoting economic development in Mexico). Although it would certainly generate new challenges, an extension of the North American Free Trade Agreement (NAFTA) to allow the free flow of labor—in addition to the free flow of capital and goods—across the border would instantly eliminate the problem of illegal migration by accommodating the demand for labor.[11] A more likely and politically feasible option would be to accommodate that demand by developing a comprehensive temporary guest worker program. On the other hand, efforts to address the demand side of the equation could be directed toward more effective regulation of demand. That is, would-be employers of undocumented workers could be more carefully monitored and more harshly penalized for hiring undocumented workers.

With regard to narcotics, there is an emerging consensus that dealing with the demand side of the equation is the key to winning the war on drugs. In an unprecedented step forward in U.S.-Mexican relations, President George Bush stated publicly at the outset of his administration that U.S. demand was primarily to blame for the problem of narco-trafficking. In accordance with this new perspective, Drug Enforcement Administration (DEA) Director Asa Hutchinson significantly redirected agency resources to counter narcotics through preventative programs, with special emphasis on newly popular drugs (e.g., methamphetamines). Greater emphasis on treatment programs for drug users than on incarceration is another alternative that could help to mitigate demand.

Yet while the basic logic for combating long-standing border challenges is relatively simple, the debate over whether to prioritize demand over supply-side approaches has been more complex. There are strong political incentives for policy makers to externalize the "costs" of dealing with these challenges. On the immigration question, for example, policies that target the supply side place the burden on migrants who have no political rights and few resources, rather than on the employers who use their labor to generate tax revenue and campaign contributions. In narco-trafficking, Mexican suppliers have been the ones traditionally criminalized, much more so than U.S. consumers (and among consumers it is lower-class and ethnic minorities who are targeted, rather than white-collar Anglos).

However, while there appears to be a growing emphasis on addressing the demand side of the equation, there appears to be significant uncertainty and disagreement over whether demand should be accommodated through changes in the law (e.g., legalization of cross-border labor flows, drug legalization, legalized prostitution, etc.) or through better enforcement of the law. Regardless of the approach taken—whether addressing supply-side or demand-side logic—all these policy solutions are developed to address problems that are fundamentally economic at their core. The rise of international terrorism to the consciousness of U.S. policy makers and the American public with the events of September 11, 2001, has complicated this comparatively straightforward set of law enforcement and security priority challenges.

TERROR AND THE BORDER: NEW HARM-BASED CHALLENGES

The 9/11 terrorist attacks had an immediate impact on the long-standing law enforcement and security challenges along the U.S.-Mexico border. On the day of the attacks the U.S.-Mexico border was temporarily placed on a strict high-security alert that increased wait time for northbound border crossers from previous averages of 30 minutes to approximately 4 hours. The extended wait times continued in the weeks and months that followed, and resulted in a noticeable increase in effectiveness in the prevention and interdiction of contraband smuggling. Indeed, while waiting for a return to previous levels of alert, some smugglers grew desperate to move product as their inventories accumulated on the Mexican side of the border and as increased scarcity on the U.S. side drove prices higher than under "normal" black-market conditions. The pressure of inventories and rising prices was manifested in more brazen techniques for evading law enforcement, including the modification of sport utility vehicles (SUVs) with special armor and silicon-reinforced tires to crash through port of entry facilities.

Public anxiety about illegal immigration has also resulted because of fears that terrorists involved in the 9/11 attacks might have entered the country illegally or overstayed their visas. Indeed, despite nearly a decade of costly, concentrated border enforcement to combat long-standing challenges, there remains a general concern that the U.S.-Mexico border is still porous and largely unprotected from the new threats posed by terrorism. Yet there is no evidence that any of the 9/11 terrorists entered the United States through the U.S.-Mexico border.

The 9/11 attacks also had a significant impact on border enforcement efforts. The Border Patrol, for example, suffered a major drain on its available manpower because numerous agents were transferred to the Federal Air Marshals Program, leaving the organization below pre-9/11 staffing levels. This created major challenges because of the difficulty of recruiting, screening, and training responsible and qualified individuals for these positions; it takes a full year to train and deploy new agents. Most significant, however, was the November 2002 legislation that completely reorganized the structure of federal agencies responsible for border law enforcement and domestic security with the creation of a new cabinet-level agency, the Department of Homeland Security (DHS). This constituted the largest bureaucratic reorganization in the federal government since the creation of the Department of Defense.

While this new context has affected long-standing border law enforcement and security challenges in important ways, there is a fundamental difference between such challenges and the new dilemmas posed by the threat of international terrorism. That is, prior to 9/11 the main law enforcement and security challenges confronted along the U.S.-Mexico border—from drugs and immigration to auto theft and forced prostitution—were market-based and demand-driven. Accordingly, the responses to these challenges have been market-oriented solutions directed at supply and demand. While there is a contentious debate over whether supply-side approaches or demand-side approaches are more appropriate or effective, the end goal is to address market forces. Yet post-9/11, the threat of terrorism at and beyond the border has introduced a new set of motivations based on the ability to cause harm.

For most U.S. policy makers and citizens, terrorism is the "mother of all fears." That is, terrorism is a horrifying specter because of its infinitely unpredictable potential to cause harm. Yet, at its roots, terrorism is a form of organized political violence; one that exploits vulnerabilities and maximizes harms, often by targeting critical military installations, civilians, sources of economic production, and basic infrastructure. In this sense, terrorism is an especially efficient form of modern warfare. Traditional forms of warfare were more oriented toward the capacity to "win"; that is, the capacity to obtain territory, resources, or submission. While causing harm is often considered a necessary evil in such traditional approaches to warfare, it is typically not an end in itself. Terrorism, on the other hand, is explicitly directed toward the use of harm to advance the political objectives of an individual, group, or nation. Thus, short of accommodating the political demands of terrorists, attempts to address the threat of terrorism must be directed toward reducing vulnerabilities and the potential for harm. Given their focus on market-driven phenomena, past strategies for law enforcement and security along the U.S.-Mexico border were not at all oriented toward such objectives. Dealing with the new challenges created by terrorist threats therefore requires some significant reordering of priorities.

Along the border, the current policy response to this challenge is found in the 22-point Smart Border Agreement, which calls for "secure infrastructure," "secure flows of goods," and "secure flows of people." In the United States, most of the areas covered by the 22-point Smart Border Agreement fall under the jurisdiction of the Department of Homeland Security. According to Section 101(b1) of the act, the primary mission of DHS is to "prevent terrorist attacks within the United States; reduce the vulnerability of the United States to terrorism; minimize the damage, and assist in the recovery, from terrorist attacks that do occur within the United States." The new plan for domestic security created an entirely new cabinet-level department by integrating functions, agencies, and 180,000 employees from ten other cabinet-level departments.

In many ways, the tasks of the new department are defined by the structure of the Smart Border Agreement. Secure "flows" of both people and goods, for example, are to be achieved through a combination of approaches that seek to establish safe "supply chains" that will enable law enforcement personnel to distinguish potential threats from "known quantities" that have low probability of involvement in terrorist or other illicit activities. To address these tasks, the department is comprised of directorates organized around four major areas: border and transportation security; emergency preparedness and response; information analysis and infrastructure protection; and science and technology. The most relevant of these areas for U.S.-Mexican relations and border security is the Border and Transportation Security Directorate (BTSD), which includes most of the agencies transferred from the Department of Justice (DOJ) (See Figures 10.5 and 10.6).

Again, the purpose of this massive reorganization of departmental responsibilities was to streamline operations and provide a single "unified face" for domestic and border security in light of new terrorist threats. To this regard, the greatest gains in efficiency appear to be in operations related to immigration control, border protection, transportation security, and disaster response capability. In short, the continued diffusion of domestic security responsibilities among various agencies outside of DHS suggests that the reorganization has achieved only a partial rationalization of bureaucratic structures and operations for dealing with terrorism. The resulting "map" of U.S. agencies for addressing crime and security issues presents a fairly complex and overlapping matrix of institutions and programs. Overlapping responsibilities and jurisdictions persist in counterterrorism and drug enforcement efforts—two areas where agencies of the State Department; the Department of Justice (FBI, DEA); and the Executive Office of the President (CIA, Office of National Drug Control Policy) continue to play important roles alongside DHS.

Underscoring the persistence of bureaucratic overlap and the legal limits of DHS jurisdiction, Section 101(b2) of the *Homeland Security Act* clearly states that the department is restricted from primary responsibilities regarding counterterrorism efforts handled by other agencies at the federal, state, and local level:

> Except as specifically provided by law with respect to entities transferred to the Department under this Act, primary responsibility for investigating and prosecuting acts of terrorism shall be vested not in the Department, but

Border and Transportation Security Directorate

Bureau of Customs and Border Protection (BCBP)
Bureau of Immigration and Customs Enforcement (BICE)
Transportation Security Administration
Office for Domestic Preparedness
Federal Law Enforcement Training Center

Science and Technology Directorate (STD)

Homeland Security Advanced Research Projects Agency
Office for National Laboratories

Information Analysis & Infrastructure Protection

Information Analysis
Infrastructure Protection

Emergency Preparedness and Response Directorate

Figure 10.5   Directorates of the Department of Homeland Security

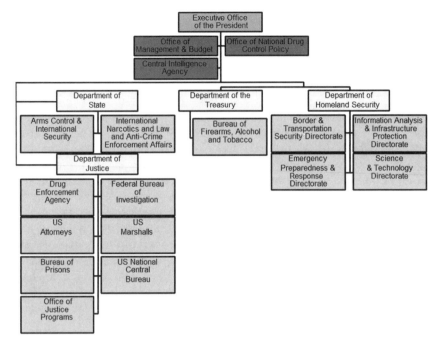

Figure 10.6 U.S. Federal Domestic Law Enforcement and Security Agency Mapping

rather in Federal, State, and local law enforcement agencies with jurisdiction over the acts in question.[12]

It is important to note that complexity and overlapping jurisdictions can hold important advantages and disadvantages for addressing law enforcement and security challenges. On the one hand, advocates of federal hierarchical organization suggest that the intricacy and overlap of the U.S. system has important advantages: promoting innovation in strategies, healthy competition between agencies, and more effective overall coverage of a variety of policy areas.[13] On the other hand, bureaucratic convolution and overlap can also allow for counterproductive interagency rivalries over scarce budgetary resources, inefficient duplication of efforts, and insufficient communication across agencies with similar responsibilities. In short, while allowing a broader and more diverse set of responses to key challenges, diffusion of responsibility creates unnecessary competition and allows some problems to fall through the cracks.

In addition to continued bureaucratic inefficiencies, critics of the new U.S. approach to domestic security point out that post-9/11 efforts have had disproportionately more impact on undocumented Latino immigration and drug trafficking than on terrorism. As a result, critics allege that the "red herring" of terrorism has created an immigration and border control system that negatively impacts Latinos and frequent border crossers and achieves only minimal gains in deterring terrorists.

Meanwhile, it is dubious whether Mexico will be able to fully adapt to the framework presented under the Smart Border Agreement without a significant reorganization of its own domestic law enforcement and security institutions. Upon taking office in December 2000, President Fox declared law enforcement and security issues to be among his administration's top priorities. Thus far, the Fox administration has focused on the restructuring and increased militarization of federal law enforcement agencies. Fox's most important reforms in the security area have been accomplished through the creation of a cabinet-level Ministry of Public Security (*Secretaría de Seguridad Pública* [SSP]), which is charged with the implementation of the National Public Security System (*Sistema Nacional de Seguridad Pública* [SNSP]) and the oversight of the newly recreated Federal Preventive Police (*Policía Federal Preventiva* [PFP]) (see Figure 10.7).[14]

Like the U.S.-side reorganization of federal law enforcement and security agencies, Fox's restructuring of law enforcement authorities was intended to achieve better coordination across agencies and areas. However, SSP is in some ways comparable to the Office of Homeland Security (which preceded the creation of DHS), given that the system it oversees is one of relatively diffuse jurisdictions. Within the framework of the SNSP, responsibilities for law enforcement and security are shared by agencies of the Executive Office of the President (e.g., Center for Research on National Security), Attorney General's Office (*Procuraduría General de la República*), Ministry of the Interior (*Gobernación*), Ministry of National Defense (*Secretaría de la Defensa Nacional*), Ministry of the Navy (*Secretaría de Marina*), Ministry of Foreign Relations (*Secretaría de Relaciones Exteriores*), and various subnational agencies. The diffusion of key functions across these agencies (e.g., immigration and border affairs, which reside in the Ministry of the Interior) prevents the SSP from functioning as a Mexican counterpart to DHS. Moreover, the SSP has recently appeared to pull away from border affairs, as the presence of Federal Preventative Police along key sections of the border has diminished.[15]

As a result of the lack of a direct counterpart, the DHS has tended to work more closely with the Ministry of the Interior. This cabinet-level department has extensive powers derived from its traditional role as an instrument of intelligence and political control under the previous regime. In other words, the persistence of a strong domestic security role for Mexico's Ministry of the Interior perpetuates structures that were traditionally designed to facilitate political oppression. As a result, critics argue that these powers should be redistributed to prevent a return to past abuses. In the meantime, even *Gobernación* lacks control of key policy areas—such

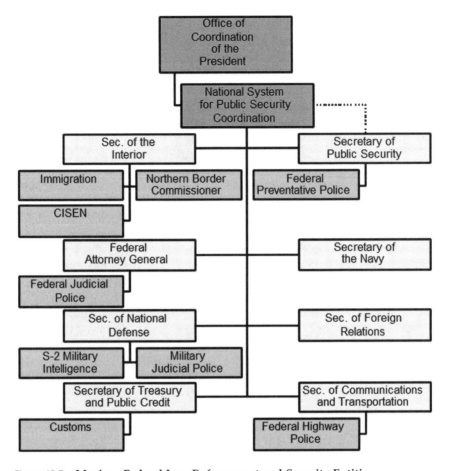

Figure 10.7 Mexican Federal Law Enforcement and Security Entities

as customs and transportation—that would enable it to function as a counterpart to DHS.

Still, the lack of a cognate to the DHS is not the only potential barrier to a more effective domestic security system or to U.S.-Mexican cooperation. On the one hand, recent trends suggest that the military and military personnel are being increasingly utilized to enforce public security and border protection. The Interior Ministry's announcement that 18,000 troops would be mobilized to secure the northern border region during the Iraq conflict was an important example. In addition to the concerns about human rights raised by domestic military involvement, there are important questions about the willingness and ability of the military to adapt to increasingly integrated security operations with its North American counterparts. For example, it is unclear whether the Mexican military would be willing to take on a role in NATO, but this seems unlikely.

On the other hand, there are important structural reasons to separate investigative and enforcement functions from prosecutorial and judicial functions which—under Mexico's system—reside in the Attorney General's Office; to function properly this system requires a greater separation of executive and judicial powers than currently exists. In short, the ability of Mexico to meet the demands of its own domestic security needs and the terms of the U.S.-Mexican Smart Border Agreement will undoubtedly require careful consideration of the current structuring of its domestic law enforcement agencies. In the process, close collaboration with the United States would be beneficial in identifying mutual concerns and opportunities for the sharing of best practices.

CASE STUDY IN CROSS-BORDER COLLABORATION: SAN DIEGO-TIJUANA

As the U.S. and Mexican federal governments move toward implementing the laws and administrative structures for dealing with law enforcement and security challenges, the concerns and experiences of state and local authorities on both sides of the border have been largely excluded from consideration in the federal-level policy making process. Perhaps more important, the centralization of responsibilities and resources for law enforcement under new federal-level agencies has not been accompanied by a corresponding increase in budgets for state and local law enforcement agencies.

This is troubling because state and local level authorities are typically the first responders to a wide array of public security challenges. In Mexico, where the vast majority of crimes pertain to state and local jurisdictions, law enforcement and security forces are dramatically undertrained and seriously underequipped compared to their U.S. counterparts. The disparity between U.S. and Mexican state and local law enforcement capabilities is attributable to both structural problems—including procedural restrictions that prevent over 75 percent of Mexico's estimated 400,000 law enforcement officers from conducting criminal investigations—and resource limitations faced in most state and local governments in Mexico. Lacking adequate training, performance standards, oversight, compensation, and civil service protections, the degree of professionalism among Mexican police is often below that of their U.S. counterparts.

Despite the asymmetry in capability, there appears to be a flourishing cross-border relationship between law enforcement and security agencies in the local and regional environments. In part, this appears to be linked to closer binational collaboration on a variety of fronts in the post-NAFTA environment. Three factors seem to be of benefit to binational collaboration in law enforcement and security in the San Diego-Tijuana border region. First is the existence of effective liaison mechanisms between different agencies and levels of jurisdiction for dealing with a variety of cross-border challenges. At every level—federal, state, and local—most U.S. and Mexican law enforcement agencies have liaison teams for dealing directly with their counterparts, though these tend to be staffed more heavily on the U.S. side. These liaisons have created the International Liaison Officer Association (ILOA), which meets monthly and includes liaisons from outlying areas such as Mexicali, Ensenada, and Los Angeles (see Table 10.1).

In contrast to the Binational Liaison Mechanism—a semiquarterly forum for high-ranking officials that is chaired by the region's U.S. and Mexican consulates—ILOA meetings provide important opportunities for agent-to-agent networking, and many officers and agents cite these meetings and contacts as highly beneficial for effective binational cooperation. In addition to opportunities presented by ILOA meetings, the members of the San Diego Police Department (SDPD) Border Liaison Unit work to maintain strong relationships with their single Tijuana Police Department counterpart and with other agencies on the Mexican side of the border. SDPD liaisons typically make at least one trip to Tijuana per day and also make random visits to maintain friendly ties. One liaison officer noted in an interview that San Diego/Tijuana liaison relations are the best they have been in at least eight years.

In addition to ILOA meetings, liaisons also benefit from a directory of the other U.S. and Mexican liaisons in the region, from Secure Electronic Network for Travelers Rapid Inspection fast lane passes for rapid border crossing, and from cell phones that allow direct communication to their counterparts. As a result of such mechanisms, local law enforcement officials in the San Diego-Tijuana region note that—in comparison to the pre-NAFTA era—today cross-border collaboration between agencies makes it significantly more difficult for transient criminal elements to perpetrate crimes on one side of the border and evade the law by crossing to the other side.[16]

A second factor that increases binational cooperation in the San Diego-Tijuana region is the use of Article 4 prosecutions. The San Diego-Tijuana region is unique in that the San Diego District Attorney's Office is the only local authority in California equipped to handle Article 4 prosecutions. Article 4 of the Mexican criminal code is used for prosecuting Mexicans who have committed a crime in the United States (or Americans arrested in Mexico for a crime involving a Mexican citizen in the United States). In such cases, U.S. authorities can file briefs providing evidence that can be used against the accused in Mexican court. U.S. authorities cannot retry the individual upon return to the United States because of the Fifth Amendment, even if the punishment is considered inadequate or the individual has evaded his or her complete sentence through bribery. Usually, San Diego's District Attorney will only use Article 4 to prosecute serious

Table 10.1   Agencies Represented in the International Liaison Officer Association

United States Agencies	Mexican Agencies
Arizona Department of Public Safety	Attorney General Representative in
Alcohol Tabacco & Firearms	Los Angeles (Agregaduria Regional
Binational Emergency Medical Care	Procuraduria De La Republica)
Committee	Attorney General Representative in
California Department of Corrections	San Diego (Sub-Agregaduria
California Department of Insurance	Regional Procuraduria General de
California Department of Justice California	la Republica)
Highway Patrol	Baja California State Attorney
Chula Vista Police Department	General's Office (Procuraduria
California Department of Motor Vehicles	Judicial Estatal)
Escondido Police Department	Juvenile Corrections (Consejo De
Federal Bureau of Investigation	Orientacion Y Rehabilitacion Para
Los Angeles Police Department	Menores)
Los Angeles County Sheriff's Department	Center for Women's Protection
Orange County District Attorney's Office	(DIF - Centro De Proteccion Social
San Diego County District Attorney's Office	de la Mujer)
San Diego County Probation Department	Ensenada Municipal Police
San Diego County Sheriff's Department	Department
San Diego Police Department	Grupo Beta Tecate
Sempra Energy	Grupo Beta Tijuana
U.S. Attorney's Office	Tijuana Customs (Aduana De
U.S. Border Patrol	Tijuana)
U.S. Consulate Tijuana	Mexicali Customs (Inspeccion
U.S. Customs	Fiscal Aduanera de Mexicali)
U.S. Department of Transportation	National Immigration Institute
U.S. Immigration & Naturalization Service	(Instituto Nacional De Migracion)
U.S. Marshal's Service	Mexican Consulate in San Diego
U.S. Navy Shore Patrol	State Investigative Police (Policia
U.S. Naval Criminal Investigative Service	Ministerial Del Estado De Baja
U.S. Postal Inspection	California)
U.S. Secret Service	Federal Preventative Police (Policia
City of El Monte Police Department	Federal Preventiva)
	Procuraduria General De La
	Republica (Tijuana)
	City of Tijuana - International
	Relations Office
	Tijuana Municipal Police
	Department

felonies, like murder or rape, when there is a strong indication that there will be adequate punishment.

A third factor enhancing U.S.-Mexican binational collaboration in the region is a history of good mayoral relations between the two cities. Beginning with the administrations of mayors Susan Golding and Hector Osuna, San Diego and Tijuana have placed a strong emphasis on cross-border collaboration. This represents important progress for San Diego which, despite being the city with the largest Anglo population on the border, has begun to emphasize and embrace its relationship with Mexico in ways that had not been done previously. Golding, for example, chaired a binational initiative on the region's shared engagement of the global economy and served as an outside observer during the 2000 Mexican elections. These kinds of political connections present a positive scenario for law enforcement and security collaboration by sending a message that cross-border relations are desirable and encouraged.

Still, the current fiscal environments for state and local governments present significant challenges on both sides of the border. Recent budget crises in two major U.S. border states—California and Texas—have had a direct impact on state and local law enforcement budgets. The San Diego Police Department's $4 million budget cut necessitated an across-the-board reduction in basic supplies (even toilet paper) and response capability.[17] As a result of such cutbacks, for example, the San Diego liaison team was reduced from a force of four full-time liaison officers to just one, part-time liaison officer. Local cost-saving measures such as these take place at a time when the U.S. federal government pours considerable human and fiscal resources into the new Department of Homeland Security. Thus, it appears that more effective law enforcement and security for the border region will require that state and local agencies have access to a larger share of the federal resources currently directed to DHS than is currently being contemplated.

CONCLUSION

The new security context has necessitated a reexamination of existing practices and mechanisms for cross-border collaboration in law enforcement and security. The pre-9/11 border law enforcement and security regime was designed to address primarily market-driven criminal activities and violations of the law. Naturally, the new policy regime is one in which such market-based infractions persist: migration has declined somewhat due to slackened demand for labor in the United States, but is likely to rise again with demand; meanwhile, other illegal activities (e.g., trafficking in persons and auto theft) have remained constant or increased. Yet in addition to these long-standing market-based challenges, there are a host of new challenges resulting from the threat of possible harm by political enemies of the United States. To meet this challenge, the Untied States has adopted a new strategy for border security and homeland defense, and will need to ensure that state and local agencies and corresponding agencies in Mexico are effectively integrated into the new system.

As the U.S. and Mexican federal governments move toward implementing the laws and administrative structures for dealing with law enforcement and security challenges, the 22-point Smart Border Agreement provides a helpful bilateral framework for addressing these priorities, and for building strong U.S.-Mexican ties in the aftermath of recent tensions over immigration and Iraq. However, the United States needs to take care to ensure that the Department of Homeland Security remains focused on its primary objectives of counterterrorism, and that it cooperates effectively with other federal, state, and local agencies sharing jurisdiction in this area.

At the same time, in order to ensure that Mexico can operate as an effective partner in this agreement, the United States will need to assist its neighbor by working toward the establishment of a mutually beneficial "security perimeter." The idea of extending the "perimeter" has been widely debated for over a decade, but 9/11 raised the stakes and increased the urgency of cooperation. Now is the time to consider increasing the spheres of cooperation between the United States and Mexico to involve thinking beyond NAFTA—an arrangement that some have begun to describe as "NAFTA-plus" security. The Smart Border Agreement framework—which also sets new terms of cooperation between Canada and the United States—may prove a useful basis for creating a parallel trilateral North American security regime to make "NAFTA-plus" a reality.

While critics may charge that increased collaboration on security would compromise standards in the United States, this view is shortsighted and fails to recognize the advantages of raising the security standards of our NAFTA partners. What is clear is that, at the local level, standards and practices for law enforcement and security collaboration have improved dramatically with our NAFTA partners, and present a microcosm that demonstrates how the possible advantages of increased cooperation outweigh the potential liabilities.

Over the long term, the harmonization of North American security standards would be beneficial to all three countries, and would constitute a positive step toward the creation of a stronger economic *and* security community in North America. This point merits future debate and discussion but as yet has been given insufficient consideration, as other issues have dominated the U.S.-Mexican agenda in recent months. What is clear at present, at least, is that the United States and Mexico currently have the basis for continued improvements in collaboration under existing bilateral agreements and emerging administrative structures. By building on the Smart Border Agreement, the United States and Mexico have a chance to become even better neighbors.

ACKNOWLEDGMENTS

The research presented in this chapter was first delivered as a paper at the 2003 International Studies Association meeting in Portland, Oregon, and was subsequently published in the *Journal of Borderlands Studies,* volume 18, no. 2 (Fall 2003). This revised piece constitutes part of the author's ongoing research on rule of law challenges in Mexico and along the U.S.-Mexico border, which has been generously sponsored by the William and Flora Hewlett Foundation, the Tinker Foundation, UC-MEXUS, and faculty research grants provided by the University of San Diego. The author wishes to acknowledge the important contributions of Arturo Alvarado, John Bailey, Robert Buffington, Wayne Cornelius, Athanasios Hritoulas, Armand Peschard-Sverdrup, Pablo Piccato, José María Ramos, Stéphane Roussel, Alejandra Ríos Casares, and Alexandra Webber. The author takes full responsibility for any errors or omissions.

NOTES

1. Georges Vernez, "Mexican Labor in California's Economy: From Rapid Growth to Likely Stability," in *The California-Mexico Connection,* ed. Abraham F. Lowenthal and Katrina Burgess (Stanford, CA: Stanford University Press, 1993), 147–164; Wayne A. Cornelius, Philip L. Martin, et al., *Controlling Immigration: A Global Perspective* (Stanford, CA: Stanford University Press, 1994); U.S. Congress, House, Committee on Government Reform and Oversight, Hearing before the Subcommittee on National Security, International Affairs, and Criminal Justice, *Counternarcotics Efforts in Mexico and along the Southwest Border,* 105th Cong., 1st sess., February 25, 1997; Wayne A. Cornelius, Yasuo Kuwahara, et al., *The Role of Immigrant Labor in the U.S. and Japanese Economies: A Comparative Study of San Diego and Hamamatsu, Japan* (San Diego, CA: Center for U.S.-Mexican Studies, University of California San Diego, 1998); Martha L. Cottam and Otwin Marenin, "International Cooperation in the War on Drugs: Mexico and the United States," *Policing and Society* 9 (1999): 209–40; John J. Bailey and Roy G. Godson, *Organized Crime and Democratic Governability: Mexico and the U.S.-Mexican Borderlands* (Pittsburgh, PA: University of Pittsburgh Press, 2000); Peter Andreas, *Border Games: Policing the U.S.-Mexico Divide,* (Ithaca, NY: Cornell University Press, 2000).

2. Jose Z. García, "Security Regimes on the U.S.-Mexican Border," in *Transnational Crime and Public Security: Challenges to Mexico and the United States,* ed. John Bailey and Jorge Chabat (La Jolla, CA: Center for U.S.-Mexican Studies, 2002).

3. E. Adler, and M. N. Barnett, *Security Communities* (Cambridge, UK; New York: Cambridge University Press, 1998); G. González and S. Haggard, "The United States and Mexico: A Pluralistic Security Community?," in *Security Communities* ed. M. N. Barnett (Cambridge, UK; New York: Cambridge University

Press, 1998); Jose Z. García, "Security Regimes on the U.S.-Mexican Border," in *Transnational Crime and Public Security: Challenges to Mexico and the United States,* ed. John Bailey and Jorge Chabat (La Jolla, CA: Center for U.S.-Mexican Studies, 2002).

4. Ruth Ellen Wasern, "Unauthorized Aliens in the United States: Estimates Since 1986," Congressional Research Service, Order Code RS21938, September 15, 2004, 1–4.

5. Ibid., 6.

6. David Shirk and Alexandra Webber, "Slavery Without Borders: Human Trafficking in the U.S.-Mexican Context,"*Hemisphere Focus* XII, no. 5 (January 23, 2004): 2–3.

7. M. Celia Toro, *Mexico's "War" on Drugs: Causes and Consequences* (Boulder, London: Lynne Rienner Publishers, 1995); E. Bertram, M. Blachman, et al., *Drug War Politics: The Price of Denial* (Berkeley, Los Angeles: University of California Press, 1996); M. Cottam and O. Marenin, "International Cooperation in the War on Drugs: Mexico and the United States," *Policing and Society* 9 (1999): 209–40.

8. M. Celia Toro, *Mexico's "War" on Drugs: Causes and Consequences.*

9. Dudley Althaus et al., "Border Travelers Warned of Violence," *The Houston Chronicle,* January 27, 2005, 1; Reuters News Service, "Mexico Scolds U.S. Ambassador for 'Punish' Boast," *The Houston Chronicle,* August 18, 2005, 15.

10. L. Lumpe, "The U.S. Arms Both Sides of Mexico's Drug War," *Covert Action Quarterly* 61 (1997): 39–46.

11. For some, illegal behaviors are considered a problem, but for others it is the policies and their results that are considered problematic. To avoid bias, the author therefore deliberately avoids terminology that identifies behaviors or policies as "problems"; such language often unnecessarily complicates the development of effective policy responses.

12. U.S. Congress, Senate, *H.R. 5005: Homeland Security Act of 2002,* 107th Cong., 2d sess., 2002.

13. Morton Grodzins and Daniel Elazar, "Centralization and Decentralization in the American Federal System," in *A Nation of States,* ed. Robert A. Goldwin (Chicago: Rand McNally, 1961).

14. In April 2004, the Fox administration introduced new legislation which would significantly restructure Mexico's entire national security system by unifying the PFP and the Federal Investigative Police (*Agencia Federal de Investigación* [AFI]), though this legislation was sidelined due to executive-legislative deadlock.

15. An accidental shooting of civilians in Tijuana in 2003 by Federal Preventative Police, reported instances of corruption, and efforts to increase police presence in the Mexican interior may all be relevant factors in explaining this trend.

16. Interview with San Diego Police Department, Border Liaison Unit Officer, April 29, 2003.

17. J. Hughes, "Police are conserving supplies, but $4 million in cuts still needed," *San Diego Union Tribune,* February 14, 2003.

CHAPTER 11

VISA SECURITY FOR A POST-9/11 ERA

Daniella E. Bove-LaMonica

The terrorist attacks of September 11, 2001, have placed the U.S. immigration policy at the center of a heightened debate. Conservative factions, who want to close borders indefinitely, have grown increasingly vocal against immigration advocates who want amnesty granted to all illegal aliens. The dialogue, which began in light of the hijackers' ability to procure U.S. visas, has become a charged public policy issue and is quickly gaining momentum. However, despite accusations of harsher policies due to the new security environment, in 2004, nearly three-fourths of all applicants for a U.S. visa were successful.[1] An even greater majority of those seeking student visas—about 80 percent—received approval.[2] In addition, the United States had a 12 percent increase in the number of business and tourism travelers and a 4 percent increase in the number of students who came as non-immigrant visitors last year.[3]

Immigration policy is not only a question of national security. The question of who is allowed access into the United States and for how long affects international politics, trade, economic stability, and society at large. The purpose of this chapter is not to critique the errors and oversight which allowed for many of the events leading up to 9/11, especially given that most cases of terrorism within the continental United States have been caused by domestic agents. Rather, it is to look at the visa application process and demonstrate how, even four years after 9/11, the consular arena is still extremely vulnerable despite new security policies. New laws, harsher punishments for immigration violators, additional personnel, and smarter technology will not greatly improve our national defenses if the core of the visa training and adjudication process is not examined more closely.

THE CONSULAR CLIMATE

Visa issuance is a nuanced specialty that has lost favor in recent years with Foreign Service officers (FSOs). There are four "cones" which one can register for when he or she goes through basic FSO training: economic, public diplomacy, consular, and management & political.[4] There are so few career consular officers in today's Foreign Service that the Department of State (DOS) has begun prescribing consular tours for all new junior officers (JOs). The DOS Web site announces, "The Officers should anticipate doing an average of three years of consular work in their first five years, as over 60% of all entry-level positions have a Consular component. Some officers may not serve in positions related to their career track in their first two tours (four years)."[5]

The DOS defines the Consular Corps as those who

> solve problems for American citizens abroad. From crisis situations to lost passports, the objective of the Consular Officer is a quick response and creative solution in providing assistance to U.S. citizens. Wherever Americans are in residence or traveling abroad, Consular Officers are there as a support system for addressing the surprises that can arise. Consular Officers also review visa applications and make decisions on whether or not to issue the visa. To excel in this challenging position, Foreign Service Officers must demonstrate sharp attention to detail and exhibit a reassuring, agreeable nature.[6]

However, the reality is usually the inverse. In a practical breakdown, probably 90 percent of consular officers work with visas, and the remaining few are left to deal with American citizen services. As an example, the American Citizens Services (ACS) unit of the U.S. Consulate General in Monterrey, CA is staffed with (at the most) two officers at one time, and it has the largest ACS unit outside of the embassy in Mexico City. In the new security environment post-9/11, DOS needs to reconsider how it markets consular work to its employees if it wants to improve job performance and overall quality of its system.

The drafting of consular officers is resented by most new FSOs who grudgingly undertake their first posting with the knowledge that visas are an unwelcome but necessary step to their career advancement. Many officers become quickly disillusioned with visa work and have very low job satisfaction, which leaves room for careless or deliberate error. To add to the general frustration, many new officers are sent to posts with heavy visa traffic, or "visa mills," because these embassies and consulates have the most staffing gaps. Once at their assigned post, the new JOs are expected to acclimate themselves to visa work as quickly as possible because there is considerable pressure on DOS to keep wait times low and issuances high.

THE ECONOMICS OF VISAS

Pressure on visa officers comes from different arenas: internal policies in place to keep the applicant waiting time low, goals to satisfy the local business community and foster diplomatic good will, and directives from Washington to promote American ideals abroad. Big industry and tourism place a lot of stress on DOS to keep visa issuance as fluid as possible. The American economy, to a certain extent—especially in border cities—depends on the financial contributions from tourism and commercial transactions. Customs officials report that Laredo, TX, for example, has more than 10,000 commercial truck crossings daily, while other reports place this figure at 15,000 crossings. In 1999, the three bridges in Laredo collected $27.2 million dollars in tolls alone, and this is only one crossing point along the 2,000-mile U.S.-Mexico border.[7]

Many American companies—the automobile industry, for example—depend on shipments of parts produced in foreign factories to complete their assembly lines in the United States. Facilitation of the quick transportation of goods and services is mostly a border control issue, but it is also a visa issue, as truckers who drive for foreign firms require nonimmigrant visas to enter the United States. Many consular posts in countries such as Mexico receive over 100 faxes daily from companies asking for special consideration for their employees who need to travel to the United States on company business. Although DOS has regulated special appointment slots for both business travelers and students to expedite the application process, demand never falters, and usually only increases. In addition, for every bona fide applicant presenting a fax appointment, there is someone trying to manipulate the system by using important contacts to gain appointments for tourist visas alongside business-related travel. The vulnerabilities of the appointment process bog down the already overloaded system and cause additional backlogs of work for visa officers.

In addition, it is in the State Department's own best interest to stack as many appointments as possible into a given year because these generate high revenues. Visa mills, such as the consular posts in Mexico, serve as the economic backbone of DOS, as the majority of consular funding comes from visa applications. In 2003, DOS issued 4,881,632 nonimmigrant visas; 1,022,012 of these were issued in Mexico, with each application costing $100 for standard processing.[8] Therefore, there is great pressure placed upon visa officers, not only to uphold security requirements and determine the eligibility of visa applicants, but also to make this determination as quickly as possible (in approximately 90 seconds) in order to not delay bona fide applicants who might be serving the economic interests of the United States. However, it is critical to point out that as security concerns continue to expand they will eventually come into direct conflict with U.S. economic interests and trade policy.

CONSULAR TRAINING

Visa officer training consists of four weeks of consular training, "Congen," at the National Foreign Affairs Training Center (NFATC) in Virginia. This training usually takes place after an intense seven-week officer training course called "A-100," where all new junior officers (JOs) are instructed in the overall workings of the Foreign Service. If an officer is to be posted overseas where a language is required, after A-100 he or she will be placed in language training for up to nine months, in addition to the consular course. Officers are then tested for linguistic competence and, if able to prove proficiency, sent overseas. The typical sequence of training is usually A-100, Congen, and then language, though the order can vary depending on class availability and size. This pattern, however, usually has the new junior officer leaving for his or her consular tour approximately ten months after finishing the consular course, with nine months of rigorous language training in between.

Training Specifics

Consular training at NFATC is divided into four segments covering the principal areas of practice: non-immigrant visas (NIV), immigrant visas (IV), NIV/IV ineligibilities/security and fraud, and services for American citizens abroad (ACS). Of the four, NIV is the most rigorous because, within a week, new officers must learn the 26 different types of non-immigrant visas (spanning everything from diplomats to students to guest workers to opera singers) and what specific circumstances and conditions apply to each type. Many officers will never use half of what they learned in Congen during their first posting. A JO at a non-immigrant visa mill, for example, could spend two years working with NIV and never set foot in the ACS section of the consular building. Or, in the case of Mexico, unless assigned to Ciudad Juarez, an officer's IV training will not apply because no other post in this country handles immigrant visas.

The consular training division of the National Foreign Affairs Training Center publishes several self-instructional guides (SIGs) to be used by Foreign Service officers as part of the Congen program. While these documents are not published directly by DOS and are explicitly stated as non-policy documents, these books and the accompanying four-week consular course comprise the only training new officers receive before being sent into the field to work in the visa sections of consulates and embassies. Therefore, while these documents are not directly policy-specific, they do indirectly control visa procedure and protocol worldwide.

According to reciprocity and diplomatic treaties, non-immigrant visas are issued to foreign visitors for a certain number of years, the maximum time varying from a few months to ten years, depending on the applicant's country of origin. However, training in the United States does not give trainees time to explore the nuances of many visa specifics. For example, Congen does not provide training on the ten-year, multipurpose visitor for tourism/business visa (BBBCC) that is only issued to Mexican nationals, even though these visas account for over one-fourth of all NIVs issued annually.

The "Introduction and Statement of Objectives" section on page 2 of the "Non-Immigrant Visa (NIV) Interviewing" manual states:

> Officers working in non-immigrant visa units may have to process hundreds of applications each day from persons seeking to travel in the U.S...Given the high NIV caseload at many posts, the interviewing officers may have little time to adjudicate each case; he/she must quickly review the documentary evidence and focus on what information is still needed from the applicant to determine visa eligibility.[9]

Eligibility is determined by interview techniques, documentation, and post-specific visa trends which have been outlined by managers and training officers. Unfortunately, visa controls and standard operating procedures, although acting in accordance with policy determined by DOS in Washington, are largely post-specific due to time and space constraints. The disconnect between the policy makers and the men and women on the ground leaves a large gap open for interpretation and lack of quality control worldwide.

Interview Techniques

In Congen, new JOs learn interviewing skills as well as standard operating procedures for visa adjudication. Mock interview windows are set up, which allow officers to practice the technical as well as practical aspects of visa adjudication. Simulations and case studies, where instructors play the role of applicants, with mock passports and application materials in hand, are a major component of the Congen training exercises. The "applicants" have already been added to the simulated computer system, given a history and a profile, and the new officer must decide whether the tourist is a bona fide non-immigrant or whether the tourist does not meet standard requirements.

Interviewing techniques are the most important tool in a consular officer's repertoire. A good interviewer, with strong language skills, will be more adept at determining fraudulent applications and more useful to the office in helping to recognize fraud trends with documents and passports. While it is extremely important that new officers understand the multitasking required by visa adjudication, learning to interview within a safety net is doing them a disservice. To begin with, the majority of real-life visa applications are not in English. In addition, interviewing norms are post-specific. Some posts have a very light visa workload, allowing for longer interview times. Other posts, especially those in countries sustaining strained diplomatic relations with the United States, will have other security measures in place which require additional information and processing times.

Documentation

Part of the training process involves teaching JOs to quickly review documentation materials. Although documentation is not the first priority of visa interviewing, it enables consular officers to gain a well-rounded perspective of their applicants. Job training encourages JOs "to interview the applicants and not their documents," but documentation can be an important element in the adjudication of a case. The antifraud SIG states:

> Most commonly, non-immigrant visa fraud is associated with B1/B2 (tourist) applications and seeks to create the illusion that the applicant is much more permanently established in the host country than is the actual case. In typical NIV fraud cases, applicants provide evidence of ties outside the U.S. by submitting phony documentation, most commonly a false job letter, in an attempt to overcome the presumption that they are intending immigrants. Applications can be carefully crafted to demonstrate strong ties to the host country, such as employment, money or property.[10]

Training at NFATC provides consular officers with documents in English, but there are very few posts in the world that deal with an entirely English-speaking population. The concept of foreign documentation is briefly covered in anti-fraud training, but it then depends on the individual post whether or not it will be covered once a JO starts working on the visa line. More often than not, fraud training is sacrificed to workload constraints, and visa officers are forced to learn about document fraud trends as they are discovered by more seasoned officers.

On the other hand, documents can become a crutch for linguistically insecure JOs, where they pay no attention to what the applicant may or may not be saying and focus only on the documents in front of them. Regardless of technique, it is an understood norm that first-tour JOs are not expected to immediately grasp interview particulars such as body language. The *Advanced Consular Course* offered to mid-level officers, is when that information is relayed. The advanced class teaches officers how to interpret facial expressions and details how close observance of eye glances, involuntary smiles, and posture is essential in determining the veracity of the information in an interview. Unfortunately, JOs will have at least two years of visa work before they can attend the class, and then it is usually only consular "coned" officers who are invited.

Passports

Passports are the backbone of the visa documentation materials. Without a passport, a foreign national is unable to apply for a visa. In recent years, DOS has called for universal use of machine-readable passports for foreigners; passports that, when scanned in embassies, consulates, and ports of entry, instantly relay the holder's information into provided software. These new passports include many security checks, supposedly preventing counterfeit documentation from entering the system. Training at NFATC teaches new officers to look for fraud indicators (photo substitution, ripped pages, etc.) typical to older passports that may have been tampered with, in order to determine malfeasance. However, training rarely covers identity fraud, which is something much harder to determine. Unfortunately, it has become all too easy to circumvent the bona fide passport system, as was evidenced by 9/11.

The investigation into 9/11 revealed that "two Saudis were carrying passports that might have been provided to them by a family member working in the Saudi passport ministry. The Saudi passport authority was rife with patronage and security weaknesses known by then to the State Department and CIA, but they were not the subject of intelligence analysis, diplomatic or security policy, or countermeasures."[11] While it is unfair to assume that all foreign nationals have nefarious interests such as terrorism as part of their agenda, passport fraud continues to be a problem even four years after September 11.

In many countries throughout Latin America (Mexico, for example), it remains possible to procure a completely valid passport based on fraudulent information. The civil registry in Mexico is rife with fraud, and for a minimal fee, it is possible to purchase a legitimate birth certificate based on a false identity. Cases such as these are recognized by consular officers to be a problem, but are usually seen only with infants who were born to minor daughters in the family and, for cultural reasons, said infants are being claimed by their grandparents as biological children. In most cases, these grandparents receive no more than a slap on the wrist as it is understood by consular officers to be a cultural phenomenon and not alien smuggling or passport fraud. The fraudulent passport, which by law is property of the Mexican passport ministry (the *Secretaria de Relaciones Exteriores*, or SRE), is then returned to the SRE, where the consulate or embassy has no power or influence to instigate an investigation or to file a report against the civil registry official guilty of the fraud. Passport/birth certificate fraud is not a new phenomenon, and is probably a consistent problem in most third-world countries. However, the topic is never addressed during passport training, so officers are unprepared to deal with it when they arrive at post. Domestic antifraud training needs to be augmented to cover passport identity fraud, as good interviewing skills are the only current safeguard against this problem.

Rule 214(b): Guilty Until Proven Innocent?

One particularly difficult aspect of visa work is the finesse involved in refusing a visa. It takes time to learn how to say "no." Training in Virginia ill-prepares new JOs for the future insistence, frustration, and desperation they will encounter in some applicants. A non-immigrant visa is usually refused under Section 214(b) of the *Immigration and Nationality Act* (INA). Section 214(b) states: "Every alien shall be presumed to be an intending immigrant until he establishes to the satisfaction of the consular officer, at the time of application for admission, that he is entitled to a non-immigrant status."[12] To qualify for a visa, an applicant must meet the requirements of Sections 101(a)(15)(B) or (F) of the INA. Failure to do so will result in a refusal of a visa under INA Section 214(b). The most frequent basis for such a refusal concerns the requirement that the prospective visitor or student possess ties to his or her home country that would compel him or her to leave the United States. at the end of a temporary stay. U.S. law places this burden of proof on the visa applicant. Guilty until proven innocent, however, is a very anti-American notion.

Being American citizens, it is countercultural for new visa officers to immediately understand the allure of a document that grants a foreigner access to the United States. The concept of "214(b)" is equally as difficult because it presupposes guilt, or that all non-immigrant visa applicants are intending immigrants until they can prove otherwise. New JOs often find themselves wanting to give their applicants the benefit of the doubt. Although they are trained with 214(b) rhetoric at NFATC, most new officers come to their post unprepared for the difficulty of saying "no." Indeed, some might find it easier to take the path of less resistance and issue visas to borderline cases rather than continuously have to turn people down. If job satisfaction is in question, then lack of personal accountability becomes even more of a liability.

"The Right To Issue"

One of the key problems currently facing visa adjudication is the concept of "consular discretion." Each individual officer has the right to deny or issue a visa based on his or her interpretation of the facts at hand. Of course, it would be career suicide to authorize a visa to a known criminal or terrorist, but hard-line cases are not usually problematic unless specific malfeasance is intended. The problems with individual discretion arise because each officer, no matter how long he or she has been on the job or what background training he or she has, is allowed to form his or her own judgments, with only precursory revision, the minute he or she begins working on the visa line. One of the training SIGs specifies, "Where intentions are clearly honest but resources are limited, you must blend sympathetic understanding with common sense."[13] However, it should be recognized that the common sense being applied by a veteran consular officer in one post and a newly-arrived officer at another post might differ. People bring different perspectives and backgrounds to the visa adjudication process and, in the end, in the absence of any concrete ineligibility, a visa is issued or denied based on whether the officer "believes" that the applicant is bona fide.

Individual interpretations of interview questions can lead to "mirror imaging" on the part of consular officers. This shortcoming is not directly their fault, but an inherent problem of the current system. Officers are asked to make rapid judgments based on brief assessments of complete strangers. Such assessments are often made in languages not native to the officers and based on cultural norms that are completely unfamiliar. Therefore, many officers fall into framing a visa interview within their own cultural values and linguistic norms, and using financial stereotypes. bona fide visa applicants may be refused because the consular officer does not believe veteran blue collar workers have strong ties to their home country due to lack of income, and housewives may be approved because the concept of a mother abandoning her children to live in another country to work as a maid is unthinkable. In the case of the 9/11 hijackers, it was assumed by the adjudicating officers that the men, while single, were wealthy enough to not want to stay in the United States after their studies had been completed, even though their applications demonstrated very few ties to their home countries.

SEVIS

The Student and Exchange Visitor Information System (SEVIS) is a Web-based system created to maintain information on international students and exchange visitors in the United States. SEVIS is administered by the Student and Exchange Visitor Program (SEVP), which is under the jurisdiction of U.S. Immigration and Customs Enforcement (ICE), the largest investigative arm of the Department of Homeland Security (DHS).[14] When a foreign student wants to apply for a visa to study in the United States, the consular officer will use the SEVIS system to determine if the student has been officially acknowledged by the institution. Operational since 2003, SEVIS allows DHS to monitor when persons enter the United States on a student visa but fail to enroll or fail to maintain enrollment in their school or program. As of July 2004, roughly 770,000 students and exchange visitors (F-1, M-1, and J-1 visa categories), along with 100,000 of their dependents, were registered with SEVIS.[15]

SEVIS was created by the Department of Justice (DOJ) in an attempt to restore integrity to the student visitor system after the 9/11 hijackers' abuses of it, and also as a way to mitigate fraud. To register for SEVIS as an institution, ICE investigates the school or program to confirm its working existence and that it is not a front for alien smuggling. Due to the sheer size of the United States, consular officers cannot be expected to know every small private school and program and might be deceived by a clever ploy. It would not be unheard of, for example, for someone to pretend to run a school, create stationery and a Web site, and then have individuals apply for student visas in order to gain legal entry into the United States.

The creation of the SEVIS system is a great step forward for DOJ and DHS and, if monitored properly, will prevent some of the oversights which allowed 9/11 to happen. SEVIS, however, is a tool of DHS—primarily created for domestic use—and has very little to do with DOS. An applicant for a student visa, like any other NIV applicant, must be able to overcome the presumption of 214(b). Consular officers, unfortunately, sometimes use SEVIS as a crutch in determining eligibility. As far as DOS should be concerned, SEVIS is an indicator that the school or program exists, nothing more and nothing less. A survey of "SEVIS-approved" institutions in New York, for example, would show dingy, two-room language schools in the basements of buildings that actively recruit foreigners on the subways. The fact that they are able to register students via SEVIS is part of their marketing. A consular officer should not assume that the official acknowledgment of a student's expected enrollment in a program to learn English for three months means that the applicant is immediately qualified.

DOS should partner with DHS to better train consular officers and educational personnel on the advantages of SEVIS. The system is only as good as its employment, and there is currently some frustration with how it has been working. To begin with, the system is often down—meaning delays for both personnel and visa applicants. Second, the student's SEVIS number (unlike a Social Security number) changes with each application, creating additional confusion in the databases.[16] Also, if school employees become frustrated with SEVIS, then they will be less likely to maintain its integrity and report the inconsistencies of their students.

THE GUEST WORKER PROGRAM

One of the most controversial processes in the non-immigrant visa arena is that of the H2B/H3 "guest worker" category. The H2B (and less-commonly-issued H3) visa is specifically designated for "unskilled labor" recruitment on the part of big industry in the United States. Every industry from agriculture to seasonal tourism utilizes the guest worker program to staff its manual labor-intensive production chains. The majority of these applicants come from Mexico, though other countries participate.

In 2003 alone, 83,158 worker visas were issued for Mexico (including all H- and L-visa categories), but the second largest number (10,069) of worker visas issued was in Jamaica.[17] In fiscal year 2005, Mexican nationals accounted for 108,713 of the H2 visa category. These men and women travel to the United States for various periods of time, up to nine months, and then are expected to return to their home country to await the next contract for their employment. The premise of this visa, unlike other employment visas such as the H1 or the L1, is that the applicant needs to demonstrate adequate ties to his or her home country and a vested interest in returning home after the period of employment ends.

The process is flawed from beginning to end, starting with the paperwork and ending with the fact that, due to a seemingly unending supply of willing workers, companies are very lax in their enforcement of contracted employees remaining on the job or returning to their home countries. While many workers' outbound travel is arranged by the company to bring them directly to their new employment, their return home is not overseen in the same process. Another issue is that even if an applicant does abide by policy and return home each year, for how long can he or she be expected to continuously spend three-fourths of the year living in the United States and not develop substantive ties within a local community? In addition, H2s are allowed to apply with family members, who will also be allowed to travel to the United States on extended temporary status, but who will be unauthorized to work. Having family accompany the workers calls into question not only their motivation to return, but also the reality that increased costs of living might encourage nonauthorized individuals to seek illegal employment.

The process for application begins with the company in the United States, which has the burden of demonstrating that it needs to recruit outside of the domestic employment pool for labor. Once that claim is made, the company must file paperwork indicating the job, number of laborers needed, and all other pertinent details. Petitions can either list the specific names of the applicants they intend to hire or can be "blanket" unnamed petitions for a certain number of workers.

Rather than undertake the cumbersome and linguistically difficult process of screening employees themselves, businesses in the United States contract out the recruitment to firms in foreign countries who are supposed to screen eligible candidates until they meet their quota. These firms find able bodies, assist them in applying for passports and, if approved by the domestic leg of the process, accompany the individuals to their visa appointments and facilitate transport to the United States.

Certifications are made by the Department of Labor and DHS on the basis of documents submitted by the alien. The certifying office has no means of verifying that the alien does, in fact, possess the skills, training, experience, or other qualifications claimed in the documents. Therefore, if a consular officer, based upon the interview or an investigation, has reason to doubt the veracity of these documents, the officer has the responsibility to resolve such doubts.[18] The system assumes that the actual verification of the applicant and his or her intentions will occur during the visa interview, leaving the burden of responsibility on DOS.

DOS has managed to meet demand with guest worker visas, but only just barely. Space and time constraints are a big problem for H2 processing. Finding interviewing officers and visa printing procedures for what can amount to several hundred other individuals, on top of the daily caseload for other categories of visas, is difficult. In fact, until recently, guest worker visa applicants were not interviewed at all, unless the consular database showed prior immigration violations. Visa officers never spoke to these individuals to screen them personally; their passports were dropped off by the recruiters in the morning and picked up in the afternoon. Even now, space and time limitations require officers to interview these applicants in groups of ten or more and basically use their best judgment in determining eligibility. With the right coaching and a little determination, most groups can pass through inspection without too much problem, especially if the interviewing officer is not paying close attention to details.

Naturally, given the volume of H2B/H3 visas, the process is extremely susceptible to fraud. In fact, many recruiters are routinely banned by NIV sections abroad, because they have been found guilty of assisting applicants in obtaining fraudulent identity information, coaching them to pass visa application procedures, privately charging for spaces on the petition, or promoting the employment of persons already known to hold immigration violations. In addition, U.S. companies have been found trying to help valuable employees who they know to be illegal by putting their names on petitions in order to facilitate legal entry and valid immigration status in the United States. But the demand for workers increases every year, as do the voices of small-business owners who claim that the quota is always filled by larger industries who have more money to expedite their plans.

RETURNING WORKER PROGRAM: CHANGE FOR THE BETTER?

In order to respond to DOS' claims of program abuse and also to quiet the quota complaints of U.S. industry, new legislation was introduced.

Unfortunately, it does more for business and less for DOS. The *Save Our Small Businesses and Seasonal Businesses Act of 2005,* part of the Emergency Supplemental Appropriations Package signed into law by President Bush on May 11, 2005, restructures the way non-immigrant workers are counted against the annual numerical cap.[19] The new legislation provides for an exemption for workers who have already been counted toward the H2B cap during any one of the previous three fiscal years.[20] Such workers will be considered "returning workers." A petition for a returning worker must include the returning worker's full name and certification to the DHS that the person is a returning worker. The H2B visa or grant of non-immigrant status for a returning worker will only be approved if DOS confirms that the individual is a returning worker.[21]

In response to allegations of fraud, abuse, and negligence on the part of American industry, the Returning Worker Program has an additional caveat. The legislation imposes a $150 fraud prevention and detection fee on employers filing an H2B petition.[22] This filing fee will go towards the additional staffing, processing, and printing costs that such a numbers-intensive program requires. If a company is accused of fraud or misrepresentation, DHS is authorized to conduct hearings and to fine employers who exhibit a "substantial failure" to meet any conditions of the H2B petition or otherwise provide such status to the H2B employee.[23] Willful misrepresentation of material facts or other crimes are also punishable. However, fines are not to exceed $10,000 and employers, while subjected to denial of H2B petitions and other immigrant petitions filed as additional penalties, will not be penalized for more than five years.[24]

As cynical as it is to point out, the reality of workloads and time is a major factor when pursuing criminality on the part of any federal agency. Many individual cases will be overlooked in the long run, because DHS is not going to take action against a company unless there are many counts of malfeasance against it. It becomes a simple matter of cost-benefit analysis. On the part of big business, a small fine of $10,000 or a momentary freezing of immigration capabilities is not a large incentive to undertake what would amount to a very expensive process of streamlining and reorganization.

TIME VERSUS LOGISTICS

If the problems with the current consular system could be summed up in a single conflict it would be that of time versus logistics. As DOS continues to recommend changes in best practices, it also increases the pressure on posts for rapid turnover of cases to fuel its finances and increases the workload of individual posts.

Information sharing, one of the most important parts of any federal job which deals with security issues, is given minimal attention due to lack of time and resources. The Anti-Fraud Operations SIG clearly states:

> Sharing information about fraud trends and issues is a key component of the battle against fraud. Anti-fraud officers manage the flow of this information through their posts. They are the action officers for cables on fraud trends received from neighboring posts and anti-fraud bulletins sent by CA/FPP (Consular Affairs/Fraud Prevention Programs), and responsible for dissemination information to the consular staff. Some posts conduct regular meetings on fraud concerns, chaired by these anti-fraud officers; others discuss incidences of fraud at consular staff meetings.[25]

Despite the policy direction articulated above, when workload is high, DOS is not always willing to pay overtime for staff meetings. Other programs suffer as well. The drafting of fraud cables for example, mandated by Washington on a quarterly basis, is not necessarily enforced by specific post management. Networking between consulates and embassies is also something which happens less often, usually due to lack of time or the inherent power struggle between the embassies and consular posts.

RECOMMENDATIONS

The current consular system has many shortcomings. Given the present methodology and technology available, the men and women of the Foreign Service have done a remarkable job at keeping the system afloat. However, the new security environment demands that the State Department look inward before it expands upon its policies. The successful confluence of continued growth and security management will become a logistical impossibility if certain practical measures are not taken. As is the case with all federal agencies, time and money are serious constraints to internal reorganization. At some point in the near future, DOS will need to decide if it is willing to compromise quantity for quality. In other words, DOS should scale back on visa operations, allow for more interview time, stop trying to meet same-day demand with tourist visa appointments, and create more training programs for consular-specific positions (and for the individuals managing those positions).. However, many small changes can be made, at no considerable expense, which would vastly improve operations and streamline training.

Training on the Job

When a new officer arrives at post, learning the new job is only part of the acclimation process. The officer has entered a new country, joined a new extended family abroad, moved his or her life's belongings and family to a new home, and grappled with myriad other minutiae which can take months to sort out. General administrative procedure grants any officer two days of leave to sort out his or her household upon arrival, but job acclimation time (to meet colleagues, learn post-specific standard operating procedures, practice interviewing, and participate in fraud and security training) can vary from three days to two weeks, depending on workload. After this training is completed, officers are expected to begin interviewing applicants and to polish interviewing techniques as they go.

Standard professional rhetoric states that a person needs about six months to become fully proficient in a job; however, most jobs are not categorized as "the first line of defense" for U.S. national security. Plainly stated, any first-time visa officer is spending his or her first six months at post training with *real* interviews and *real* visas. This is a security risk which should no longer be overlooked. The acclimation and training time should be extended at all posts and become more standardized and uniformly implemented. If training sessions are to be given by a seasoned peer, the trainers should be vetted through some sort of Internet or written course provided by DOS in order to ensure quality controls.

Language Training on the Job

Foreign language training is an important part of a consular officer's abilities to do his or her job proficiently. However, we are doing a disservice to our FSOs by training them in the United States. Basic language training by standardized methods is an essential component to learning any language, but regional linguistic nuances and idiomatic expressions cannot be taught in a classroom in Virginia. Visa interviewing in a foreign language requires an individual's ability to comprehend slang and local terminology for jobs, neighborhoods, and industry, as well as the ability to converse with an applicant in order to determine adjudication. As individual officers must rely on their own discretion, an inability to understand local terminology hinders accuracy. Nonetheless, current procedures only allow officers those first few acclimation days to learn the regional jargon, and the rest they must acquire for themselves as they go.

In Latin America, especially, linguistics become extremely important because although all applicants speak Spanish (or Portuguese, in the case of Brazil), Peruvian Spanish is very different from Mexican Spanish. In addition, Spanish spoken in Mexico City (for example) has very different intonation than the Spanish spoken in Monterrey or other parts of the country. Foreseeable are cases where foreign nationals from other countries in Latin America manage to acquire Mexican passports and present themselves as Mexicans for interview. If a JO is not well-versed in the nuances of his or her particular region, this fraud could easily go undetected as the officer struggles through basic interview questions without the ability to distinguish subtle linguistic inconsistencies.

It would be more efficient and cost-effective to shorten language training at NFATC to three or four months and then allow for new officers to continue their language training in-country. In addition, NFATC does not provide area studies for all regions and most of their post-specific backgrounders are extremely out of date. Post-provided or sponsored language training would not only allow for greater interviewing accuracy, but also provide time for the new officer to become acclimated with the city, the office environment, and the post-specific visa trends and procedures.

Fraud Training

Post-specific fraud training is a mandatory part of job acclimation. However, this training is only as good as the personnel assigned to the Fraud Prevention Unit, if any. Some workloads at smaller posts are so high that fraud training is haphazard at best, and they staff their fraud offices only half or a quarter of the time. Although regulations require fraud management and training sessions at the consular post, there is no uniformity in compliance. DOS should ensure that fraud training does not become an activity that only takes place "time and space permitting."

CONCLUSIONS

In an unclassified cable drafted by the JO consular team in Guadalajara, Mexico, a critique of Congen consular training was sent to DOS and included recommendations very similar to those in this chapter. The cable was titled "Congen Training and the Realities of Mass NIV Adjudication."[26] The cable outlined the inability of NFATC to prepare JOs for workload, linguistic inexperience, large volumes of fraudulent documents, rapid-paced interviewing, and the frustrations of mass adjudications.[27] In response to this cable, the embassy in Mexico City sent its own judgment to DOS. The embassy stated that it faced the same working situation as the consulate in Guadalajara but that it did not find training at NFATC to be lacking in anyway. Specifically, it said:

> The general training at Congen leaves the Junior Officer with a solid understanding of the application of the *Immigration and Nationality Act* to the adjudication of visas. This 'general' knowledge can always be adapted to the peculiarities of the 'specific' post or region. Congen students are designated for a wide variety of posts, each with its own intangible characteristics that can only be learned through on-the-job observation and experience.[28]

The embassy did not mention in its cable that it is one of the few posts in Mexico to have implemented a mandatory two-week JO on-the-job training program or that it houses the largest NIV staff and fraud prevention program of any of the posts in-country. If there was a response back from DOS to either of these posts, it has not been made publicly available.

The new security environment facing the United States today is creating a unique dilemma. How does the United States deal with the demands of an open economy and still protect itself and the integrity of the visa process? General training cannot be expected to be all things to all people. That much is certain. However, it is unclear how DOS plans to continue promoting security policy when the most basic training gaps, although easily remedied, have not been addressed. Although DOS has raised the bar for its technology and hired thousands of additional personnel since 2001, these same problems will persist. Time, funding, logistics, and training continue to be unknown quantities, yet the demand for visas (from both the domestic and international community) appears to remain constant.

Moreover, experts in terrorism and security policy are beginning to look at the disenfranchised and disillusioned minority populations within countries as sources of eventual threats to Western interests. If second-generation immigrants who are citizens by birth of countries sympathetic to Western causes are posing a threat to security, then the visa process becomes even more important. It is one thing to have screening measures in place to deal with nations that challenge the security interests of the United States; these measures are obvious and will be undertaken with care by any consular officer. However, if growing unrest among minority nationals of "friendly" countries begins to become a threat to U.S security, DOS will have to rely heavily on the competency levels of its consular personnel.

Like the case of the 9/11 hijackers, men and women who wish to cause America future harm will pose as non-immigrant visa applicants, but this time around they will not be on any watch list or from countries having sponsored terrorism in the past. In fact, there will probably be no distinguishing indicators of terrorist intentions. An ideal challenger to these individuals is a savvy interviewer who is well versed in the local language, familiar with the culture and politics of the region, and kept current on trends in fake documentation, identity fraud, and misrepresentation. The first line of defense in the new global security environment is the consular officer, but he or she is only as effective as the resources and training that has been provided. Greater attention to the issues raised in this chapter would certainly improve our ability to secure the homeland from the foreign terrorist threat.

NOTES

1. "See you in the USA" Ejournal, www.usinfo.state.gov.
2. Ibid.

3. Ibid.

4. http://www.careers.state.gov.

5. Ibid.

6. Ibid.

7. Hercules Haralambides and Maria Londonoken, "Supply Chain Bottlenecks: Border Crossing Inefficiencies Between Mexico and the United States." *International Journal of Transport Economics*, XXXI, No. 2 (June 2004).

8. www.travel.state.gov.

9. National Foreign Affairs Training Center, "Nonimmigrant Visa Interviewing," SIG (1998), 2.

10. National Foreign Affairs Training Center, "Consular Fraud Operations," SIG (1998), 13.

11. National Commission on Terrorist Attacks, *9/11 and Terrorist Travel: A Staff Report of the National Commission on Terrorist Attacks Upon the United States* (Franklin, TN: Hillsboro Press, 2004).

12. *Immigration and Naturalization Act* (INA).

13. National Foreign Affairs Training Center, "Visa Indelibility," SIG (1998), 51.

14. http://www.ice.gov/graphics/sevis/.

15. http://www.ice.gov/graphics/news/newsreleases/articles/082704sevisNR.htm.

16. http://www.aacrao.org/pro_development/surveys/SEVIS_Report_final.pdf, p. 1.

17. www.travel.state.gov.

18. Foreign Affairs Manual, chap. 9, "Visas."

19. http://www.usimmigrationlawblog.com/h2b-visa-21-save-our-small-and-seasonal-businesses-act-of-2005h2b-visa-relief.html.

20. Ibid.

21. Ibid.

22. Ibid.

23. Ibid.

24. Ibid.

25. National Foreign Affairs Training Center, "Consular Fraud Operations," SIG (1998), 6.

26. National Foreign Affairs Training Center, "Nonimmigrant Visa Interviewing," SIG (1998), 25.

27. Ibid.

28. Ibid., 29.

PART II

MARITIME AND PORT SECURITY

CHAPTER 12

AMERICA'S MARITIME HOMELAND SECURITY CHALLENGE: PORTS, WATERWAYS, AND COASTAL BORDERS

Joe DiRenzo III and Chris Doane

The United States remains a maritime nation. While aviation has become the dominant mode for domestic and international passenger travel, over 90 percent of the raw materials, parts, and products imported and exported by this nation still move by ship. Internally, a significant percentage of this cargo moves along our more than 26,000 miles of navigable inland rivers and waterways. In addition to economic dependence, the country's over 95,000 miles of coastline accounts for the vast majority of our nation's border. Clearly, the security of our maritime transportation system (MTS) and maritime borders is critical to this nation's economic health and security. One only needs to recall the West Coast labor dispute that closed 29 ports in the fall of 2002 and cost the national economy over $2 billion per day to understand the reality of the nation's maritime dependence.

The U.S. maritime domain encompasses all U.S. ports, inland waterways, harbors, navigable waters, Great Lakes, territorial seas, contiguous waters, customs waters, coastal seas, littoral (shoreline) areas, the U.S. Exclusive Economic Zone (covering nearly 3.4 million square miles), and oceanic regions of U.S. national interest, as well as the sea-lanes to the United States. Within this domain there are over 360 ports, 238 locks at 192 locations, over 3,700 marine terminals, and recreational marinas beyond count. Through 1,400 designated intermodal connections, the MTS connects with over 174,000 miles of rail connecting all 48 contiguous states, as well as Canada and Mexico, over 45,000 miles of interstate highway (supported by over 115,000 miles of other roadways), and over 460,000 miles of pipeline.

The sheer "volume" of vessels, port calls, and cargo transferred to support this nation's economic engine through international trade is impressive. Each year more than 7,500 commercial vessels, sailing under a variety of flags, make over 51,000 port calls within the United States. These vessels unload over nine million 40x8x8-foot marine containers alone onto trucks, barges and rail cars for further transportation to their points of destination. This supports a system of commerce where corporations, both large and small, maintain minimum inventories, relying on "just in time" delivery of goods and materials to sustain operations.

Combining this economic dependence, huge user base, and vast amount of maritime infrastructure makes the U.S. maritime domain a very attractive target with significant vulnerabilities due to its vastness and potentially high consequences to our academy should an attack occur by those who wish this nation ill. Make no mistake that terrorist organizations understand the importance of the MTS and have a demonstrated capability to conduct maritime attacks. The 2001 suicide attack on the *USS Cole* in Yemen resulting in the death of 17 U.S. sailors, the damage inflicted on the French tanker *Limburgh* on October 6, 2002, by another explosive-laden boat, and the 2004 attacks on Iraqi oil platforms provide ample evidence of the terrorist ability to use maritime vectors for attack and their awareness of the value of maritime infrastructure.

The maritime vulnerability is not solely economic; the extensive maritime borders create a significant security concern. To appreciate the difficulty of securing our maritime borders from terrorist attack and infiltration, one need look no further than the war on drugs. For over two decades the U.S. Coast Guard (USCG) and U.S. Customs Service, along with a myriad of other federal, state, and local law enforcement agencies, have struggled to stop the maritime flow of narcotics into this nation from a relatively small number of source nations. Despite heroic efforts and some significant victories in terms of record-breaking seizures, the flow of drugs has been slowed but not stopped.

The problem is simple—our nation's coastlines are too vast to seal and the volume of maritime traffic is too great and too time-sensitive to allow for the inspection of every vessel. Just as the real hope in the drug war is driving down the demand through education, the real hope in the war on terrorism is diminishing the desire and/or will of those who would destroy us by showing the more moderate amongst them that we are not their enemies. In the meantime, securing our maritime domain in order to reduce its vulnerability to illicit activities remains a stopgap measure accomplished through risk management.

In maritime homeland security, risk is viewed as a combination of threat, vulnerability, and consequence. If written in a formula, the equation would be Risk = Threat × Vulnerability × Consequence. In this regard, it is the role of counterterrorist organizations to seek out and remove terrorists before they can attack. On the other hand, security organizations focus on reducing vulnerabilities and consequences. For decades, the lead federal organization for port security—now maritime homeland security—has been the U.S. Coast Guard. Other principal federal organizations include Customs and Border Patrol (CBP), Immigration and Customs Enforcement (ICE), the Transportation Security Agency (TSA) with the Department of Homeland Security (DHS), and the Maritime Administration (MARAD) in the Department of Transportation. Details of each organization will be provided in the following discussion.

This chapter will examine America's maritime homeland security campaign in three phases: (1) historical efforts before 9/11, (2) current efforts following 9/11, and (3) future challenges in view of the asymmetric threat to the maritime domain. The first part of this discussion will review how the United States has sought to secure its maritime domain in the past. This is followed by an exploration of how the United States has responded nationally and as a member of the global maritime community that has come to the realization that terrorism knows no boundary, no respect for human life, and poses a threat to all nations, the world's maritime transportation system, and the world's economic health. Finally, the chapter concludes with a look at what more needs to be done in terms of leveraging technology, employing limited assets, and adjusting cultural views to address the terrorist threat in the maritime.

MARITIME SECURITY PRE-9/11

Security of our ports, waterways, and coastal regions has been a focus of federal agencies since the founding of the country, when the Secretary of the Treasury Alexander Hamilton commissioned the Revenue Marine Cutter Service (the forerunner of today's Coast Guard) to combat smuggling of goods into this nation. Modern day port security, the centerpiece of maritime security, began in 1917 following the July 29, 1916, German sabotage of munitions stored at a marine terminal on Black Tom Island near Jersey City, NJ. In response to the sabotage, Congress passed the *Espionage Act* assigning responsibility for the security of our ports to the Coast Guard. The *Espionage Act of 1917* granted the Coast Guard authority to regulate the anchorage and movement of any vessel in U.S. territorial waters, including the placement of guards on or taking full possession of such vessels. The Coast Guard designated their Captains of the Port with the responsibility to ensure the requirements from the new law were properly enforced.[1] Throughout World War I, Coast Guard personnel patrolled the waterways and waterfronts, ensuring the security of the ports.

Port security efforts waned following the war in concert with the decreased threat. The onset of World War II reinvigorated the Coast Guard's port security operations even as the service was being transferred to the War Department under the Navy. During World War II the number of Coast Guard personnel on active duty grew to 241,093, with 22 percent (or 53,040)[2] specifically assigned to port security duties, a significant difference from the 39,000 active duty men and women currently serving in the Coast Guard worldwide.

Following the end of World War II and the reduction in force, the Coast Guard again returned to a more traditional mission mix for a brief period. With the United States entry into the Korean conflict, Congress again looked at the ports as being a potential critical vulnerability and responded by reinforcing the authorities under the *Espionage Act*. Retitled as the *Magnuson Act*, the Coast Guard's authorities were extended to include protection of vessels, harbors, ports, and waterfront facilities in the United States. The *Magnuson Act* included the authority for the Captains of the Port to establish and enforce security zones to protect sensitive areas or vessels from sabotage and to: "inspect and search any vessel, waterfront facility, security zone, or person, article or thing thereon or therein, place guards, and remove unauthorized persons, articles, and things therefrom."

After the Korean War and throughout the Cold War, emphasis on port security remained primarily a mission for the Coast Guard Reserve in support of military outloads (military outloads are activities in which everything from support equipment to ammunition is loaded onto vessels for deployment elsewhere in support of national objectives). To further strengthen the Coast Guard's responsibilities and authorities for the safety and security of the ports, Congress passed the *Ports and Waterways Safety Act* in 1972. This act authorized the Coast Guard to: "carry out or require measures, including inspections, port and harbor patrols, the establishment of security and safety zones, and the development of contingency plans and procedures, to prevent or respond to acts of terrorism." To better meet the safety and security needs for movements of military cargo through selected ports, the Coast Guard partnered with the Maritime Administration to form Port Readiness Committees in these ports, consisting of federal, state, and local stakeholders to create plans for conducting military outloads and to enhance coordination of these evolutions.

As the 1990s were ending, increases in terrorist attacks worldwide were causing security agencies such as the Coast Guard to review their security roles and processes. The terrorist attack on the *USS Cole* in October 2000 alerted maritime agencies to the potential threat of maritime attacks. Following the attack on the *USS Cole,* the Navy decided to enhance its force protection posture at home as well as abroad and turned to the Coast

Guard, due to its port security responsibilities, for assistance in protecting navy ships in U.S. ports. When the Navy approached the Coast Guard for assistance in domestic force protection, the Coast Guard no longer had active-duty assets assigned to port security operations. In the spring of 2001, the two services entered into discussions on how to best meet the Navy's needs. These discussions resulted in a joint concept of operations for protecting high-value naval assets and a proposed regulation for a permanent Naval Vessel Protection Zone around naval vessels in U.S. waters. The authority for the Naval Vessel Protection Zone was based on a law, 14 USC 91, passed by Congress in 1941, that provided the Coast Guard, and Navy commanders under certain circumstances, the authority to control vessel traffic to ensure the safety and security of naval vessels.

Beginning in the late 1970s and early 1980s, the Coast Guard entered into two new maritime initiatives with homeland security implications, drug and illegal alien immigration interdiction. During this period, the Coast Guard and the U.S. Customs Service began independent and joint operations to interdict drug smugglers at sea. At nearly the same time, the Coast Guard, supported by the Immigration and Naturalization Service, began maritime operations interdicting illegal migrants attempting to reach the United States.

To accomplish these law enforcement missions, Congress had equipped the Coast Guard with a variety of legal authorities. Under 14 USC 1, passed in 1915, the Coast Guard was designated at all times to be an armed service. 14 USC 89 made every Coast Guard petty officer, warrant officer and commissioned officer a law enforcement officer with extensive authorities and jurisdiction to enforce federal law in the maritime. 14 USC 141 authorized the Coast Guard to use its unique abilities to assist other federal law enforcement agencies. And 19 USC 1401 made all Coast Guard law enforcement officers customs officers as well, authorized to conduct border searches of vessels entering the United States.

In addition to these law enforcement activities, the Coast Guard was assigned another responsibility that would become important to maritime homeland security—marine environmental response. Pursuant to the *Clean Water Act* as modified by the *Oil Pollution Act of 1990,* the Coast Guard was assigned the responsibility for coordinating the response to maritime oil spills and hazardous material (HAZMAT) releases. To meet this responsibility, the Captains of the Port were predesignated Federal On-Scene Coordinators (FOSCs) to coordinate and/or direct the response to maritime pollution incidents. To accomplish this responsibility, the Captains of the Port formed Area Committees of local federal, state, and local agency representatives as well as representatives from industry and nongovernment organizations who had an interest, responsibility, or legal authority related to maritime pollution. These committees were formed to develop and exercise response plans and organizations for oil spills and HAZMAT incidents. The response organization the Coast Guard settled on was the National Interagency Incident Management System Incident Command System or NIIMS ICS that had been developed and refined by the National Fire Service for combating wildfires. Using ICS allowed for the creation of a unified command consisting of key members of the Area Committee to coordinate the efforts of all responders to a pollution incident.

By the summer of 2001, the United States had laid the legal foundation dating back to World War I for securing its ports and waterways and had empowered the Coast Guard as the lead agency for maritime security. The Coast Guard had over 80 years of experience in conducting port security and safety operations, adjusting levels of effort to the levels of perceived threat. In addition, the Coast Guard, through its law enforcement and marine environmental response roles, had developed expertise in maritime interdiction, interagency operations, and unified command. Although the Coast Guard had relegated its port security mission to a reserve function primarily in support of military outloads, the Coast Guard and the Navy had initiated port security operations focused on the security of naval vessels and installations in response to the attack on the *USS Cole*. All in all, with its long history of port security operations, extensive legal authorities (see Table 12.1), and solid relationships with other federal, state, local, and private sector stakeholders in the ports, the Coast Guard, although minimally resourced, was otherwise well positioned to provide a maritime security response to the attacks on September 11, 2001.

MARITIME SECURITY POST-9/11

On 9/11, as the attacks were still occurring, port security once again became a primary mission of the Coast Guard. In the port of New York

Table 12.1   U.S. Coast Guard Security Authorities

Year	Code	Description
1915	14 USC 1	Armed Service
1917/50	50 USC 191	*Espionage Act/Magnuson Act*
1930	19 USC 1401	Officer of the Customs
1941	14 USC 91	Safety of Naval Vessels
1949	14 USC 89	Law Enforcement (LE) Authority
1949	14 USC 141	Assistance to Other LE Agencies
1972/86	33 USC 1221/6	*Ports and Waterways Safety Act*
1990	33 USC 2701	*Oil Pollution Act*

and throughout the country, Captains of the Port used their legal authorities to either close or tightly control activities in their ports to ensure the legitimacy of the vessels operating therein and to establish mandatory security measures to protect critical waterfront infrastructure and population centers. This was a significant challenge for a nationwide service that had been "right-sized" to a level smaller than the New York City Police Department and had just recently acknowledged that its operational forces were less than 90 percent of what was needed to meet its pre-9/11 primary missions of search and rescue and law enforcement. Achieving success demanded that the Coast Guard partner with other federal agencies, state and local law enforcement, and industry to build a domestic security coalition to leverage every member's strengths and capabilities.

Following the 9/11 attacks and the Coast Guard's initial response, three strategies became clear to Coast Guard planners: that the strategic goal for countering maritime terrorism should "push our borders out" by identifying and defeating the threat as far from U.S. shores as possible; that a "layered defense"—using increased security measures at various stages of the maritime transportation system to increase the probability of detection while minimizing the impact on legitimate maritime commerce—would be necessary; and, that risked-based decision making would be required to determine how to best employ scarce resources across the spectrum of Coast Guard missions. The concept of minimizing the impact on maritime commerce both defines the need for maritime security given this nation's economic dependence on maritime trade, and creates the complexity that makes securing the maritime a most challenging endeavor.

Within the maritime domain, there are numerous asymmetric attack options available to terrorists. They may choose to use maritime conveyances to smuggle in weapons or operators; they may use explosive-laden small boats to attack critical shipping; they may attack vessels carrying dangerous cargo while transiting through population centers, creating an improvised weapon of mass destruction; they might use a maritime approach to attack critical waterfront facilities; and the list goes on and on. The asymmetric/covert nature of these attacks makes them extremely difficult to predict or detect given the volume of maritime activity and the expanse of waterways and coastal borders. The difficulty is increased exponentially by the need to preserve civil liberties and to avoid disruptions to the flow of maritime commerce that would spell disaster for our economy.

Securing a target-rich maritime domain, highly sensitive to disruption, and open to a wide range of potential methods of exploitation and attack by a covert enemy, is like looking for a needle in a stack of needles, creating a challenge worthy of King Solomon. It is not possible to search every vessel and boat plying our waters or to inspect every container or other cargo entering our nation; the number of personnel and assets that would be required to accomplish this task without significantly disrupting the flow of commerce would be astronomical, well beyond the financial resources of this nation. Therefore, the only practical solution is to reduce the risk of maritime terrorism to an "acceptable" level.

Three significant actions that provided a tremendous boost to the Coast Guard's ability to secure the maritime were the passage of the *Homeland Security Act of 2002*, the passage of the *Maritime Transportation Security Act of 2002*, and the adoption of the *International Ship and Port Facility Security Code.* In addition to creating the Department of Homeland Security and moving the Coast Guard into the new department, the *Homeland Security Act* helped to better define the Coast Guard's missions. Specifically, while ensuring that all of the Coast Guard's traditional missions continued, the act identified ports, waterways and coastal security (PWCS), drug interdiction, migrant interdiction, defense readiness and law enforcement as Coast Guard homeland security missions.

The *Maritime Transportation Security Act of 2002* provided the Coast Guard with important new authorities to mitigate maritime risk. First of all, the act strengthened the Coast Guard's authorities over waterfront facilities and vessels engaged in international trade. Under Coast Guard oversight, owners and operators of these facilities and vessels had to conduct vulnerability assessments and then develop and implement security plans to reduce their vulnerabilities. The scope of this undertaking was significant, involving over 9,600 domestic vessels and 3,100 facilities.

Coast Guard Captains of the Port were designated as the Federal Maritime Security Coordinators under the *Maritime Transportation Security Act.* In this capacity, they were required to develop Area Maritime Security Committees to assess the vulnerability of their respective ports and develop an Area Maritime Security Plan to mitigate these vulnerabilities. These committees are made up of security stakeholders from other federal, state, and local government agencies as well as the private sector. Within the security plan they agree on how they will work together to mitigate vulnerabilities and jointly respond to an incident to ensure unity of effort. The committees also provide a conduit for sharing sensitive threat information as the members are screened and designated as eligible to receive security-sensitive information. This sharing of threat information allows all stakeholders in the port to make best use of their security assets to minimize their vulnerabilities.

The *Maritime Transportation Security Act* also required the Coast Guard to assess port security efforts in other nations with whom the United States conducted maritime trade. This led the Coast Guard to develop an International Port Security Program consisting of Liaison Officers and

Visit Teams. Liaison Officers are assigned between eight to ten countries and are responsible for developing working relationships with the government and industry members involved in maritime security within these nations in order to sustain a dialogue on port security issues and concerns. The Visit Teams cooperatively visit U.S. trading partners to assess the effectiveness of port security measures and to share best practices with a goal of progressive improvement in maritime security. In return, participating nations send teams to the United States to visit our ports and see how we are instituting security. The result is an ongoing dialogue on maritime security and a sharing of best security practices.

This international effort has been significantly aided by the adoption of the *International Ship and Port Facility Security Code* by the International Maritime Organization. This code mirrors the *Maritime Transportation Security Act* by requiring vessels and facilities engaged in international trade to develop and implement security plans. Countries were required to certify their ports as secure and to certify that their ships engaged in international trade had effective security plans by issuing them an International Ship Security Certificate. Ships lacking such a certificate may be denied entry into another nation or subjected to other controlling actions. U.S. Coast Guard Commandant Admiral Tom Collins summed up the importance of this international effort during a Senate hearing: "A cooperative international approach involving partnerships of nation, navies, coast guards, law enforcement agencies, and commercial shipping interests is essential—with all parties acting collaboratively to confront broadly defined threats to our common and interdependent maritime security."

With these new authorities and roles added to its already extensive suite of authorities, the Coast Guard set out to develop a risk-based maritime security strategy. The first step in developing this strategic plan was establishing strategic goals. The Coast Guard, working from the *National Security Strategy,* published its *Maritime Strategy for Homeland Security* laying forth five strategic objectives:

- Prevent terrorist attacks within, and terrorist exploitation of, the U.S. maritime domain.
- Reduce America's vulnerability to terrorism within the U.S. maritime domain.
- Protect U.S. population centers, critical infrastructure, maritime borders, ports, coastal approaches, and the boundaries and seams between them.
- Protect the U.S. maritime transportation system while preserving the freedom of the U.S. maritime domain for legitimate pursuits.
- Minimize the damage and recover from attacks that may occur within the U.S. maritime domain as either the lead federal agency or a supporting agency.

To achieve these objectives the Coast Guard introduced the concept of layered defense, establishing multiple layers of security along the pathways of the maritime transportation system to increase the probability of deterring, detecting, and defeating terrorist threats. No single security layer is perceived to be 100 percent effective in detecting terrorist activities, but combined, all of the layers achieve an acceptable level of effectiveness. This realization that countering the maritime terrorist threat required looking beyond the traditional limits of the port quickly led to the use of the term maritime homeland security, of which port security was a subset incorporating the inner layer of this multilayer strategy.

Key to this strategy of a layered defense is the concept of "maritime domain awareness." Maritime domain awareness can be described as a comprehensive knowledge of the maritime domain combined with a real-time picture of maritime activities that provides maritime security forces with a common operating picture and allows them to readily discern abnormal or suspicious activities that warrant further investigation. Achieving maritime domain awareness requires the development of accurate intelligence and a comprehensive understanding of the maritime transportation system in order to accurately target vessels, cargos, crews, and passengers of interest. This effort extends well beyond U.S. traditional maritime boundaries to include international partnerships. Success in developing maritime domain awareness requires both international and interagency partnering at unprecedented levels of cooperation.

With strategic objectives and a strategic concept for a layered defense, the use of risk-based decision making is required for implementation. Risk, from the Coast Guard's view, is equal to consequence times vulnerability times threat. Since 9/11 the Coast Guard has used risk-based decision making to make resource decisions between missions, considering the relative consequence associated with saving lives at sea, combating the flow of illegal drugs and protecting against terrorism, and within the PWCS mission, prioritizing security activities in view of the terrorist threat based on potential consequences and vulnerability. This risk-based approach to maritime terrorism also provides a means to perceive antiterrorism efforts within three sub-areas: attacking the terrorist threat, reducing vulnerabilities, and minimizing consequences.

With the added authorities and security tools provided by the *Homeland Security Act, Maritime Transportation Security Act,* and the *International Ship and Port Facility Security Code* and its strategic maritime security goals, the Coast Guard was able to better implement its layered defense strategy. This strategy incorporates three general zones, domestic, border/coastal, and international, broken down into six "layers" as follows.

Domestic Zone

Waterways

These are waters within the U.S. baseline (generally the low water mark along the coast as marked on U.S. nautical charts), including navigable rivers and canals. Also included are waterfront facilities on land.

Ports

This "layer" is a special case as it is normally also contained within the U.S. baseline, but refers to a harbor town or city or an area where there are facilities for berthing vessels or taking on or discharging cargo. Ports represent areas that require increased security to ensure there is no interruption or damage to the MTS, of which the ports are such a vital part.

Maritime security operations within the domestic zone include the conduct of waterborne and waterfront patrols, boardings, escorts of high-risk vessels, and point defense of high-risk facilities. Point defense is defined in Joint Pub 1-02 as "the defense or protection of special vital elements and installations; e.g., command and control facilities, air bases."

Border/Coastal Zone

Coastal Approaches

This layer corresponds with the waters from the U.S. baseline seaward to 24 nautical miles (NM). It includes the U.S. territorial sea (from the baseline seaward to 12 NM) and the contiguous zone (from 12 NM to 24 NM from the baseline). The United States exercises sovereignty within its territorial sea and sovereign rights (the control necessary to prevent infringement of its customs, fiscal, sanitation, or immigration laws and regulations) within its contiguous zone.

Maritime Approaches

The maritime approaches extend from the coastal approaches seaward to the high seas 200 NM from the baseline and contain the U.S. Exclusive Economic Zone (EEZ). Jurisdiction in this region largely depends upon vessel registry.

Maritime security operations within the border/coastal zone include surveillance and boardings.

International Zone

Oceanic

The oceanic layer extends from the limit of the maritime approaches to the outermost limit of foreign territorial waters. Jurisdiction is generally dependent upon vessel registry.

Foreign

This layer consists of foreign territory, ports of departure, and foreign territorial waters.

Maritime security operations within the international zone include International Maritime Organization initiatives, flag state inspections, attachés/liaison officers, and cooperative flag state bilateral agreements which can contribute significantly to maritime security and impact ongoing security audits and assessments.

These zones provide the framework for maritime security operations in a post 9/11 environment. The emphasis has shifted to interoperability, unity of effort, and common practices which combine to address the maritime threat in ways unprecedented in the world's history using the previously described layered, international, multiagency approach, coupled with a detailed risk-based approach. Intelligence sharing, for example, is one of greatest "success stories" in the post 9/11 environment.

While the Coast Guard, with its long history of port security operations and extensive authorities, was quickly recognized as the lead federal agency for maritime homeland security, it is not the only federal agency with a significant role in maritime homeland security. Other agencies such as the Department of Defense, U.S. Customs Service, the Maritime Administration, and the new Transportation Security Administration have all been involved in strengthening our maritime security. Of these other federal agencies, the U.S. Customs Service, in its new role as the U.S. Customs and Border Protection within the Department of Homeland Security, and the Department of Defense have been the two most active agencies in addition to the Coast Guard.

Customs—formally, the U.S. Customs and Border Protection (CBP) agency—has a number of ongoing initiatives. One of CBP's most publicized initiatives is the Trade Partnership Against Terrorism (C-TPAT). C-TPAT is a voluntary program whose participants—including importers, brokers, manufacturers, and warehouses—implement required security protocols and submit to validation visits by CBP agents and industry representatives. The program rewards participants by placing their shipments on the "fast track" which means fewer delays for inspections, etc. as the goods move from point of origin to final destination.

To complement the C-TPAT program, CBP introduced the Container Security Initiative (CSI) in January 2002. Teams of CBP personnel work with host nation authorities to prescreen maritime shipping containers judged to pose a risk in their ports of origin before they are shipped to the United States. The program began by focusing on the largest container source ports for the United States and had expanded to 44 ports by the spring of 2006.

CBP collects the information it receives from the C-TPAT and CSI programs at its National Targeting Center (NTC). The NTC uses this information to identify cargo that requires screening upon arrival in the United States. It also shares the cargo information with other agencies like the Coast Guard to aid in their risk assessments and to ensure security operations are coordinated to avoid duplicity of effort.

Confronting the threat of maritime terrorism has also involved the military in a number of areas. One specific effort that is receiving global notice is the Proliferation Security Initiative or PSI. This effort has brought together a number of nations in an international effort to prevent the international flow of weapons of mass destruction (WMD), and their delivery systems and related materials on the ground, in the air and at sea. PSI is consistent with UN Security Council Resolution 1540 that calls upon states to take cooperative actions in accordance with their national legal authorities to prevent the illicit trafficking of WMD.

PSI is not an organization with members, but an initiative endorsed by like-minded nations to "pool" their legal authorities, intelligence information, and interdiction capabilities to thwart the proliferation of WMD. For the United States this means employment of USCG and U.S. Navy assets to interdict suspect WMD shipments in coordination with appropriate PSI partners as fitting to the situation and location. The PSI concept was recently tested in an exercise named "Chokepoint '04."

Chokepoint '04 involved venues including the Mediterranean Sea, North Sea, Baltic Sea, Atlantic Ocean, Pacific Ocean, and the Caribbean Sea. Participants included Australia, Canada, Denmark, France, Germany, Italy, Japan, the Netherlands, Singapore, Spain, the United Kingdom and the United States and the exercise was observed by Argentina, Chile, Liberia, Mexico, Norway, Panama, and Sweden. It required participating countries to work together to refine intelligence information regarding an illicit WMD shipment, to identify suspect vessels, to winnow the list of suspects down to a primary vessel, and then to conduct an at-sea interdiction using a multinational force. By all accounts the exercise was a huge success.

Speaking before the U.S. House of Representatives Subcommittee on Coast Guard and Maritime Transportation, Committee on Transportation and Infrastructure, on June 15, 2005, Rear Admiral R. Dennis Sirois, Chief of Coast Guard Operations (G-O) provided a good overview of PSI: "The President's Proliferation Security Initiative (PSI) encourages all nations to coordinate their efforts to prevent shipments of Weapons of Mass Destruction, delivery systems, and related materials.... The Coast Guard provides negotiators to help craft bilateral PSI agreements, particularly with those nations that have large ship registries. There are currently agreements in Panama, Liberia, the Republic of the Marshall Islands, and Crotia, while negotiations are in progress with Greece, Belize, and Cyprus."[3]

The ever-increasing role of the U.S. Northern Command (NORTH-COM) in U.S. homeland security and defense has also added to the maritime security posture. NORTHCOM has assumed responsibility for the security of all defense assets within its area of responsibility, assets such as Navy bases that are also critical components of the nation's maritime infrastructure. In addition, NORTHCOM is constantly improving its maritime awareness capabilities and its ability to share this information with law enforcement agencies such as the Coast Guard. Finally, NORTHCOM has led or participated in a number of homeland security exercises and events with maritime venues, including the G-8 Summit and the Democratic and Republican Party conventions, further strengthening the Department of Defense's readiness to support federal and state security agencies as the need arises.

CONCLUSION

In sum, maritime security continues to be a long-standing concern of the United States, and has undergone a significant resurgence in the aftermath of 9/11. The U.S. Coast Guard is actively leading a joint effort of federal, state, and local agencies, as well as the private sector, to minimize maritime risk of terrorist attack by reducing maritime vulnerabilities, aggressively seeking to identify terrorists prior to an attack through international cooperation, and by maintaining a readiness to respond and mitigate the consequences of an attack should one occur. While the maritime security of the United States. has been strengthened considerably, the risk of a terrorist attack can never be eliminated. Our maritime domain is too vast and target-rich, and our society is too open to be completely secured. However, by continuing to strengthen the layered defense approach described here, while improving our understanding of maritime risk and enhancing our maritime domain awareness, the risk can be reduced to acceptable levels.

NOTES

1. Gary Felicetti and John Luce, "Posse Comitatus Act: Setting The Record Straight on 124 Years of Mischief and Misunderstanding Before Anymore Damage Is Done," *Military Law Review* (March 2003): 128–141.

2. http://www.grolier.com/wwii/.

3. http://www.house.gov/transportation/cgmt/06-15-05/sirois.pdf.

CHAPTER 13

INTERNATIONAL COOPERATION FOR MARITIME SECURITY

Tracey Gray and Frank Jones

At 3:00 p.m., on October 12, 2000, the tall, slender, photogenic U.S. Secretary of Defense, William S. Cohen, entered the Pentagon's press briefing room and stood still behind the lectern with the official seal of his department. Accompanying him was Admiral Vern Clark, the U.S. Navy's Chief of Naval Operations (CNO). Their faces were pinched, their mood solemn, and Cohen's opening words to the assembled reporters were a noticeably flat "Good afternoon." He then glanced down at the document he was holding and proceeded to read a prepared statement. "At 5:15 this morning, Washington time, a large explosion blew a hole in the hull of the *USS Cole* as she was mooring at Aden, Yemen, to refuel." Cohen continued by stating that the initial reports indicated that several of the guided missile destroyer's crew members were dead, wounded, or missing and that these figures would likely change once more information was learned. He added that the Department of Defense did not know the cause of the blast. However, according to an eyewitness, the explosion occurred when a small boat that was participating in the mooring approached the *USS Cole*. He then remarked, "I want to repeat that we do not yet know the cause of the explosion. If, however, we determine that terrorists attacked our ship and killed our sailors, then we will not rest until we have tracked down those who are responsible for this vicious and cowardly act."[1]

Within a few weeks, U.S. investigators concluded that the explosion that left a 20-foot by 40-foot hole at the waterline on the port side of the ship was the result of a terrorist attack, making it the "most lethal attack against the U.S. military since 1996, when a truck bomb killed

19 American servicemen near Dharan, Saudi Arabia."[2] By January 2001, in separate investigations, the U.S. Navy as well as the Department of Defense (DoD) *USS Cole* Commission concluded that the Navy needed to challenge every assumption about how it conducted naval operations around the world, especially in high-threat environments, "whether the battle is with other military forces or criminal terrorists."[3] Going further, the DoD Commission declared that the incident demonstrated a seam in the fabric of efforts to protect maritime forces and that enhanced U.S. policies and practices for deterring, disrupting, and mitigating terrorist attacks in the maritime domain were needed. Yet, subsequent events would demonstrate military ships were not the only maritime targets terrorists were interested in destroying.[4]

Almost exactly two years later, terrorists in a small boat off the coast of Yemen attacked the merchant vessel *Limburgh,* a French oil tanker. The attack reportedly killed one crew member and spilled 90,000 barrels of oil into the Gulf of Aden. This event had an even more chilling effect on the maritime industry. It was another clear recognition that ships and their cargo can be used as weapons, and terrorists may set their sights on ships of all types. In its 2002 annual report, the International Maritime Bureau said incidents such as what happened to the *Limburgh* are difficult to prevent. "No shipboard response can protect the ship in these circumstances," the report stated. The report may have added that it is difficult to protect against terrorist threats regardless of the circumstances given the large number of ships transiting the oceans of the world and the maritime domain's enormity.[5]

It is easy to underestimate the enormity of the world's oceans; they cover more than two-thirds of the earth's surface. Although geographers have bestowed names on them to distinguish one from another, they are a global commons, or in military parlance, a global battlespace. The oceans are not under any sovereign's rule except for a nation's territorial waters. Nations adjacent to the oceans greatly depend on them as a source of living and nonliving resources as well as a place for livelihood and recreation. Yet, even landlocked states are reliant upon the oceans, as more than 80 percent of the world's trade travels by water. As these two incidents underscore, the maritime domain is also the means by which security threats, such as transnational terrorists, can move anonymously and penetrate a nation's defenses undetected. Additionally, maritime infrastructure and inland transportation systems are targets for dangerous and illicit activities. In short, the maritime domain is an immense and largely unsecured medium for a number of threats.

INTERNATIONAL COORDINATION FOR MARITIME SECURITY BEFORE 9/11

From the end of World War II until the dissolution of the Soviet Union and the demise of the Warsaw Pact, maritime security had two thrusts: national military operations and the development of treaty organizations or alliances. The former, national military operations, was designed to thwart direct attack from adversaries while the latter afforded nations the opportunity to befriend one of the two superpowers, although there were notable exceptions such as India, which was a leading member of a group of nations known as the nonaligned states. Given the friction that the Cold War created in the international system, organizations such as the United Nations were not a useful mechanism for maritime security. For example, the United Nations adopted a convention in 1948 establishing the International Maritime Organization (IMO) and made it operational a decade later. The charter for the organization states succinctly its purpose, which was not security: "From the very beginning, the improvement of maritime safety and the prevention of marine pollution have been IMO's most important objective."[6]

Thus, during this period, maritime security clearly focused on the state actor as the primary threat in the strategic environment. Efforts to promote multilateral cooperation on maritime security issues were based upon regional linkages, such as the treaty organizations mentioned previously. One of the most significant regional agreements that was foundational for regional maritime security cooperation in the West was the North Atlantic Treaty Organization (NATO), aimed at countering the threat of aggression from the Soviet Union and safeguarding the freedom of the North Atlantic Community. The military structure of NATO included a Supreme Allied Commander Atlantic, located in Norfolk, Virginia, who was responsible for meeting the threat posed by the Soviet Navy. As Alliance leaders then understood it, the Soviet Union could use its sea power in two means: first, as support in the Baltic on the right wing of Warsaw Pact forces as they advanced westward across the central European plain and second, to attack the critical Allied transatlantic lifeline with their submarines. Accordingly, NATO's maritime strategy rested on the components of sea control, power projection, and oceanic reinforcement around the rim of Europe. The key to this effort was effective antisubmarine warfare, but NATO Allies also regularly conducted exercises to practice merchant convoy techniques, amphibious assault, and carrier air offensive strikes. If war broke out in Europe, NATO maritime forces had to be prepared to keep the sea-lanes open.[7]

During the 1990s, NATO faced new strategic challenges. Ethnic tensions and violence in some former Soviet-dominated states created economic and political instability that, in turn, prompted the Alliance to embrace major internal reforms as well as new, unconventional missions. Collective defense remained a fundamental principle, but crisis response, conflict prevention, peacekeeping, and humanitarian assistance established more prominent roles in NATO's repertoire of capabilities.[8]

To meet these emerging demands, the Alliance adopted the Combined Joint Task Force (CJTF) concept. Defined as "a multinational, multi-service deployable task force generated and tailored primarily...for military operations not involving the defense of Alliance territory," a CJTF would place at the disposal of its commander an impressive array of Allied forces. These might include ground units up to the size of an army corps, multiple carrier/amphibious task forces, appropriate Special Forces (psychological and/or special warfare units) and the potential air campaign planning capability to conduct 1,000 sorties per day.[9]

Additionally, during this decade, regional cooperation became a focus, designed to promote capable coalitions of willing nations based along either regional or functional affiliations, which were capable of responding to security challenges. This strategic goal was advanced by a substantial number of naval exercises among allies and partners. As an example, the U.S. Navy alone conducts more than 100 exercises per year with nations throughout Asia. These exercises are an essential part of the U.S. security cooperation program, and are imperative to building friendships and maintaining interoperability.[10] Further, the United States has longstanding security treaties with six nations in the Pacific-Indian Ocean region, and military-to-military contacts with more than two dozen others. Forward deployed forces have routinely participated in bilateral and multilateral exercises to act as a facilitator for confidence building measures among our friends and allies. These exercises undertaken by the U.S. Navy Seventh Fleet reassure allies and strategic partners within the theater that U.S. maritime forces are trained, able, and ready to respond to any security scenario. In short, such engagement efforts ensure an opportunity to maintain and achieve peace within the region, and build upon the concepts of collective security.[11]

The U.S. Coast Guard has also been integrally involved in international maritime security cooperation efforts for a number of years. U.S. Coast Guard units regularly interact with other nations in the course of performing their missions. Daily law enforcement actions involve foreign nationals, aircraft, and vessels. The Coast Guard also conducts combined exercises and other cooperative efforts with numerous international counterparts. Frequently, the Coast Guard is requested to assist other nations in enhancing or developing their maritime services. Assistance to other nations is provided in a variety of ways, ranging from complete design of a coast guard service to answering operational questions about coast guard equipment or activities. Technical assistance is provided through expert analysis and counsel, equipment transfers, and training.[12]

Coast Guard liaison officers, advisors, and attaches are assigned to U.S. Embassy staffs and geographic U.S. combatant commanders in many locations. Other Coast Guard officers serve on international narcotics task forces, such as illegal drug interdiction in the Gulf of Mexico, or are part of the U.S. overseas security assistance network. The Coast Guard also participates in personnel exchange programs with other nations, such as the United Kingdom, Canada, and Argentina. Agreements provide for the long-term reciprocal exchange of pilots with the Royal Air Force, the Royal Navy, and the Canadian Forces. The Argentina Coast Guard (*Prefectura Naval*) also has a liaison officer assigned to U.S. Coast Guard Headquarters. In addition to the experience gained, the service derives benefit from the experience provided by officers from other countries. These exchanges offer partner services and the Coast Guard a better understanding of each other's operations and organizations.[13]

THREATS TO MARITIME SECURITY TODAY

Countering terrorism is the primary objective for the United States and many other nations, as the widely dispersed terrorist networks present an immediate danger to national interests at home and overseas. Terrorism experts emphasize that one of the most significant areas of vulnerability for the global economy is the maritime domain. They readily point out the difficulties that exist. These challenges range from tracking suspect vessels over the vast oceans to the existence of a shadowy al Qaeda fleet that may number as many as 300 vessels with the ability to execute operations or collect intelligence.[14] Terrorism experts underscore that evidence already exists to suggest that the maritime domain is one of the most vulnerable areas by citing the aforementioned attacks on the *USS Cole* and the French supertanker *Limburgh*. Other scenarios involving seaports are even more troubling. The reason is that ports are more vulnerable and are an even more enticing target than ships because of their size, the open accessibility by water and land, their metropolitan location, the amount of material being moved through them, and the ready transportation connectivity they offer to locations within the country.[15]

It is conceivable that terrorist organizations could load a vessel with a nuclear device and detonate it in a commercial or naval port. Therefore, a major concern is the likelihood of terrorist groups to use chemical, biological, radiological and nuclear (CBRN) weapons and using the maritime domain as the means for transporting the weapons, components, or material. Approximately seven million ocean containers enter U.S. ports each year.[16] Therefore, a container ship is a perfect means of bringing a weapon of mass destruction to a target. Experience from the "war on drugs" suggests that the methods that would be used to detect such a device are grossly inadequate. Estimates are that the contents of less than 2 percent of all containers are checked for verification..[17] Nonetheless, efforts by the U.S. government have focused largely on port security and container tracking. Measures to enhance port security and the security of the global sea-container shipping system are needed and prudent.

The threat of conflict between nations has not abated in the post-Cold War era. The U.S. intelligence community, as an example, continues to keep watch on a number of nations that are of concern because of military strength, geographic location, or antipathy to U.S. national interests. Thus, the traditional military intelligence disciplines are still required to provide national security policy makers, defense planners, and operational commanders the information they need to conduct their missions successfully. Efforts to furnish adequate warning of attacks and understanding of an adversary's military capability, doctrine, and war plans remain of interest to military intelligence agencies. Rogue nations also pose an immediate and continuing threat to the United States, allies, and friends, particularly as these states are often interested in selling weapons of mass destruction to others, including terrorists.

Just as the world's oceans are avenues for commerce, they are also the means for the import or export of illegal or untaxed commodities. The maritime smuggling of illegal drugs or aliens, the import of untaxed seaborne cargoes, and the maritime export of unauthorized technologies will remain a major threat to security. The permeability of international borders, the connectivity of oceanic transport, and the inability of governments to address effectively these transnational criminal threats continue to lure both individuals and organizations looking for enormous profits.

Illegal international migration, fueled by political instability, tremendous population increases in developing countries, and uneven global economic growth, will also be an important factor affecting maritime security through 2020. In addition, there is the potential for terrorists to take advantage of the human smuggling networks, through maritime means, in attempts to circumvent border security measures.

Piracy, in any of its many modern forms, along with other types of maritime crimes, has flourished with the growth in global trade and exchange of commercial goods, financial instruments, and people. "Not only has piracy never been eradicated, but the number of pirate attacks on ships has also tripled in the past decade—putting piracy at its highest level in modern history. ...The total damage caused by piracy—due to losses of ships and cargo and to rising insurance costs—now amounts to $16 billion per year."[18] Today's pirate is very different from those of yesteryear. Most "piratical" acts occur within territorial seas, not high seas, which presents a problem of legal definition. In fact, "42 percent of pirate attacks took place in 2003" in the Strait of Malacca, the 500-mile corridor separating Indonesia and Malaysia.[19] The pirates are often well-equipped with heavy weapons, high-speed craft, and advanced communications.

SECURING THE MARITIME DOMAIN TODAY

Five years after Defense Secretary Cohen declared from the podium at the Pentagon that the United States would join with its international partners to find and prosecute those that attacked the *USS Cole,* the Secretary of the Department of Homeland Security, Michael Chertoff, asked how we move beyond simply partnering on an occasional, episodic basis to building a true partnership that will operate with a mission-oriented focus.[20] Recognizing the amorphous transnational threat that the United States faces, Secretary Chertoff wants to move toward a world that is banded together by security envelopes, defined as secure environments through which people and cargo can move rapidly, efficiently, and safely without sacrificing security or privacy.

The attacks on the *USS Cole* and the horrific acts of terrorism on September 11, 2001, forced U.S. government policy makers to think and act anew in the maritime domain. While the nation-state threat remains a concern for the United States, it has increased its focus on potential "9/11-like" scenarios in the maritime domain. According to the Central Intelligence Agency, "At no time since the formation of the Western alliance system in 1949 have the shape and nature of international alignments been in such a state of flux."[21]

In order to understand and to act effectively in today's maritime environment, the United States and other nations must consider a number of mechanisms to enhance international cooperation in the maritime domain—strengthening regional cooperative security efforts, expanding U.S.-led mechanisms, promoting regional leadership, and creating hemispheric coalitions. The tools available to employ each mechanism include bilateral and multilateral sharing of information to enhance awareness of events occurring in the maritime domain; the transfer and sharing of technology for this purpose; regional maritime security initiatives that have as their basis law enforcement and military operations; command and control and organizational changes; and the international response to catastrophic events that damage severely global maritime commerce. Before examining the initiatives and programs associated with strengthening security in each area, one must understand the strategic context for the maritime environment.

The Strategic Context

The Bush Administration has set forth a number of strategic documents that clearly articulate the need for enhanced cooperation with international partners. The statements range from the *National Security Strategy* (NSS) to the *National Strategy for Maritime Security.*

The overarching strategic document for U.S. national security is the *National Security Strategy,* published in 2002. When Dr. Condoleezza Rice,

Assistant to the President for National Security Affairs, unveiled the NSS, she insisted that "we will work with coalition partners on every continent, using every tool in our arsenal—from diplomacy and better defenses to law enforcement, intelligence, cutting off terrorist financing, and, if needed, military power."[22] The *Strategy* reinforces her statement by suggesting "Wherever possible, the United States will rely on regional organizations and state powers to meet their obligations to fight terrorism. Where governments find the fight against terrorism beyond their capacities, we will match their willpower and their resources with whatever help we and our allies can provide."[23] Similar statements reinforce this notion in other U.S. strategic documents such as the *National Defense Strategy* that was published in 2005.[24]

More recently, President Bush signed a directive (National Security Presidential Directive-41/Homeland Security Presidential Directive-13) that details his vision for a fully coordinated U.S. government effort to protect national interests in the maritime domain.[25] Specifically, this document provides for new initiatives while integrating them with existing policies and programs to ensure interagency alignment and focus.[26] This directive established a Maritime Security Policy Coordinating Committee to coordinate maritime security efforts across the U.S. government, provided a policy statement on maritime security, and tasked the development of a *National Strategy for Maritime Security* and eight supporting national maritime plans. The maritime focus of the eight plans includes domain awareness, intelligence integration, commerce security, transportation security, and infrastructure recovery, as well as domestic and international outreach. Specifically, the presidential directive requires that the United States enhance its maritime security through each of the following actions:

- Prevent terrorist attacks or criminal acts or hostile acts in, or the unlawful exploitation of, the maritime domain, and reduce the vulnerability of the maritime domain to such acts and exploitation;

- Enhance U.S. national security and homeland security by protecting U.S. population centers, critical infrastructure, borders, harbors, ports, and coastal approaches in the maritime domain;

- Expedite recovery and response from attacks within the maritime domain;

- Maximize awareness of security issues in the maritime domain in order to support U.S. forces and improve United States Government actions in response to identified threats;

- Enhance international relationships and promote the integration of U.S. allies and international and private sector partners into an improved global maritime security framework to advance common security interests in the maritime domain; and

• Ensure seamless, coordinated implementation of authorities and responsibilities relating to the security of the maritime domain by and among Federal departments and agencies.

The directive also requires that the U.S. government has a coordination process for all maritime security initiatives undertaken with foreign governments and international organizations and requires the development of a comprehensive outreach strategy to solicit international support for an improved global maritime security framework.[27]

How is this strategy and discourse translating in practice? How does the United States intend to employ all traditional instruments of national power while not losing sight of the evolving threat? Specifically, has the United States translated each of these policy statements into action?

Translating Policy into Action

Admiral Clark stated at the 2003 International Seapower Symposium "no navy has the capability or the budget to address its military needs without limitation but every navy can benefit from the synergy of combining force structure, technology, intelligence, and situational awareness." Addressing the subject of maritime coalitions against terrorism, the CNO's remarks underscore that all nations must contribute to a collective security because all nations derive an individual benefit.[28] To this end, it is useful to understand how current international cooperation efforts in the maritime domain support the policy actions propounded in the Maritime Security Presidential Directive.

Regional Cooperative Security Efforts

One of the primary tools that the Department of Defense utilizes in cultivating relationships with partners to strengthen maritime security is cooperative security initiatives. The most notable example of this relationship is the Regional Maritime Security Initiative (RMSI) in the United States Pacific Command (USPACOM) area of responsibility. Other commands have similar efforts underway to include Operation Active Endeavor and Operation Sea Cutlass in the United States European Command (USEUCOM) area of responsibility and Operation Enduring Friendship in the United States Southern Command (USSOUTHCOM) area of responsibility.

Announced by Admiral Tom Fargo, USPACOM Commander, in March 2004, RMSI seeks to encourage international actions, using existing international and domestic laws, against threats in territorial waters. Additionally, it is designed to contribute to the security of international seas, gain maritime situational awareness through the sharing of information and intelligence and, ultimately, build responsive decision making authorities, resource cueing, and law enforcement capacities. The final objective is to enhance maritime interdiction capacity to facilitate each nation taking effective action, as it deems appropriate. RMSI demonstrates a clear linkage to the U.S. strategy to prevent attacks, enhance maritime domain awareness, integrate global maritime intelligence, and strengthen relationships with allies and friends. To achieve the desired RMSI goals, USPACOM has developed a partnership of willing nations within its area of responsibility.[29]

One scholar notes that while such regional initiatives address cooperation on the high seas and territorial waters, cooperative efforts must not abandon other critical measures such as port security. Too much focus on seagoing efforts may lead to overlooking other elements in the production-supply chain, failing to account for the high costs associated with such programs, diminishing the need for capacity building in other areas, or neglecting other threats to maritime security such as seafarer certification, the Flags of Convenience system, and other transnational crimes with maritime aspects.[30] Taking heed of this caution, a number of other U.S.-led initiatives have been launched to address it, including the Container Security Initiative (CSI), the Proliferation Security Initiative (PSI), the Megaports Initiative, and the Customs-Trade Partnership Against Terrorism (C-TPAT).

U.S.-Led Mechanisms

The purpose of the CSI is for teams of U.S. Department of Homeland Security's Customs and Border Protection officers to work in concert with their host nation counterparts. Announced by Customs and Border Protection Commissioner Robert Bonner on January 17, 2002, the CSI consists of four core elements:

- Using intelligence and automated information to identify and target containers that pose a risk for terrorism;
- Pre-screening those containers that pose a risk at the port of departure before they arrive at U.S. ports;
- Using detection technology to quickly prescreen containers that pose a risk; and
- Using smarter, tamper-evident containers.[31]

Twenty countries have joined CSI and are at various stages of implementation.

PSI is an effort by the United States to lead the international community to stop the proliferation of weapons of mass destruction (WMD), their delivery systems, and related materials to states and non-state actors of proliferation concern by interdicting WMD-related shipments and shutting down proliferation networks. It responds to the growing challenge posed by these materials through coordination with like-minded states that have a stake in combating WMD proliferation and the willingness to take steps to stop the flow of such items at sea, in the air, or on land. More than 60 nations are currently part of this initiative.[32]

Third, the Megaports Initiative, led by the U.S. Department of Energy, works closely with international partners to equip major foreign seaports with radiation detection equipment that will enhance their capabilities to deter, detect, and interdict illicit trafficking in nuclear and other radioactive material as it moves through the global maritime shipping network. The Megaports Initiative helps reduce the probability that these materials could be used in a weapon of mass destruction or a radiological dispersal device against the United States, its allies, and friends.[33]

The Customs-Trade Partnership Against Terrorism (C-TPAT) is a public-private initiative that teams government with importers, carriers, brokers, and other industry sectors to emphasize a seamless security-conscious environment throughout the entire commercial process, from manufacture through transportation and importation to ultimate distribution. Under the C-TPAT initiative, business participants providing verifiable security information are eligible for special benefits. Begun in November 2001, C-TPAT now has more than 7,000 members and is the largest partnership of its type in U.S. history.[34]

Promoting Regional Leadership

To increase maritime cooperation while not appearing to be heavy-handed, the United States must work with strategic partners and allies in a multinational context. The Chief of Naval Operations correctly stated, "I believe the next step is to join forces and form a worldwide coalition of military and law enforcement organizations to keep our oceans free and safe."[35] This requires incorporating the best practices and lessons learned from cooperative efforts like RMSI, opening a dialogue for international cooperation, and establishing a strategic framework *with* partners rather than *for* partners.

An excellent example where this concept is at work is in South Asia and the Indian Ocean. Shortly after the events of September 11, 2001, the United States sought a strategic partnership with India along with Pakistan. India represents one of the best prospects for enhancing maritime security. Therefore, the United States and other nations not in the region should welcome the opportunity to team with the Indian Navy to optimize regional security.

In a June 2005 speech at the Carnegie Endowment for International Peace in Washington, D.C., Indian Defense Minister Pranab Mukherjee addressed the importance of this issue to his country. As the prime minister remarked, India is both a "continental and maritime nation" with a coastline of 7,500 square kilometers.[36] It is also distinctly situated at the base of the Asian continent and the top of the Indian Ocean. "It is a vantage point," he continued, "in relation to both the West, Central, continental and South-east Asia, and the littoral states of the Indian Ocean from East Africa to Indonesia."[37] Further, because of its peninsular projection, it has a stake in the security and stability of these waters. This stake is enormous. The Persian Gulf, as an example, is an important source of India's, the region's, and East Asia's energy. Therefore, the defense minister specifically underscored that the maritime security environment demands additional attention. Not only is the Indian Ocean from East Africa to Southeast Asia an area busy with ships moving cargo and supporting trade—some 60,000 ships transit through the Straits of Malacca —but it is a locale busy with terrorists as well as criminal enterprises trafficking in drugs, arms and humans, and piracy. It also contains some of the most important ports in the world.[38]

Cooperative naval activity is high as Indonesia, Malaysia, and Singapore increase their number of patrols in the Straits of Malacca, while India and Thailand patrol the northern approaches to the Strait. India has coordinated maritime patrolling with Indonesia, Thailand, and Sri Lanka. The Indian Navy provided security measures for the 2004 African Union Summit in Mozambique and its navy and coast guard have been active in antipiracy efforts, and have partnered with Singaporean, Thai, and Filipino counterparts in these endeavors.[39] India has conducted joint naval exercises in the Indian Ocean with the United States that involved air operations and replenishment at sea, as well as exercises with France, Singapore, Russia, Oman and others.[40] Equally important, having a significant Indian naval presence in the Indian Ocean means that other nations' navies do not have to patrol there. For example, in 2002, the Indian Navy provided escort operations for high value U.S. naval assets passing through the Malaccan Straits, thereby freeing up U.S. Navy ships from escort duty.[41]

While it is difficult to know the extent to which RMSI contributes to greater cooperation among countries in its area of responsibility, the trends are challenging. The aging Indonesian Navy has only 30 percent of its 117 ships seaworthy of protecting its 17,000 islands.[42] The Malaysian Navy finds itself in a similar predicament. While the United States recognizes the negative consequences of sending U.S. ships to patrol the area, enabling other nations through exercise, training, and educational programs allows for enhanced security in the region. A study sponsored by the U.S.-Indonesia Society suggested that the United States allocate $30 million over five years to help the Indonesian Navy improve communications, intelligence, and operations.[43] As the India defense minister remarked, maritime security in this region demands attention.

Creating Hemispheric Coalitions

One strategic framework underway is the Security and Prosperity Partnership of North America (SPP). This trilateral partnership, formed by President Bush, Prime Minister Martin of Canada, and President Fox of Mexico, aims to "develop new avenues of cooperation that will make our open societies safer and more secure, our businesses more competitive, and our economies more resilient."[44] Through the SPP, the United States, Canada, and Mexico seek to develop a common security strategy to further secure North America by focusing on securing North America from external threats, preventing and responding to threats within North America, and streamlining the secure and efficient movement of legitimate and low-risk traffic across our shared borders.[45]

While this strategic partnership applies government-wide, there is tremendous potential that can be achieved in the maritime domain. Advancing this concept through the lens of maritime security allows for enhanced partnership in intelligence and information sharing, compatible screening methods for goods and cargo, and improved transportation and port security. Furthermore, this partnership may allow for the development of regional response procedures for natural disasters or terrorist incidents in the maritime domain and more joint naval exercise and training.

All of these efforts underscore that maritime security is not only a massive undertaking, but that no one nation can undertake it alone. Therefore, the U.S. Navy and U.S. Coast Guard must continue to expand its exercise program with other foreign navies and coast guards. The focus in these exercise programs should not only be the ability to detect, identify, and track vessels, but also, in keeping with the guidance in the DoD's *Strategy for Homeland Defense and Civil Support,* the critical capability to interdict and defeat threats at a distance from the United States and in the maritime approaches to the United States.[46] Exercises with Canada and Mexico are essential as is the maturing of such existing programs as Operation Enduring Friendship in the U.S. Southern Command area of responsibility. Moreover, exercises in the Atlantic and Pacific are important as well, particularly since the naval components of USEUCOM, USPACOM, and USSOUTHCOM may hand off command and control to USNORTHCOM during a national security event. The time to assess the effectiveness of operational protocols and procedures is in an exercise, not during a national emergency.

CONCLUSION

The strategic framework for enhancing international cooperation in the maritime domain is being addressed by a number of efforts as outlined earlier. The central idea advanced is that no single nation has the wherewithal to protect the maritime domain. The maritime nations of the world must work together to overcome the serious challenges posed predominantly by the threat of terrorism.

Over the past several years since the attack on the *USS Cole,* the Department of Defense has made significant progress in addressing the amorphous maritime threat that replaced the threat of the Soviet Union and its satellite states. Overall, security of the maritime domain has become the focus of numerous individual states and international bodies and has evolved to reflect the new strategic environment and transnational terrorist threat. However, much work remains to be done. The United States, as the world's sole superpower, needs to keep an eye on near-term competitors as well as lesser threats to its security and sovereignty such as illegal international migration and piracy. The primary focus must remain on preventing terrorism. Working to achieve this end must move beyond the conceptual to the practical. Thus, advancing a strategic vision and related policies to enhance U.S. maritime security at home and abroad is commendable and necessary as a means of addressing current and future security threats, vulnerabilities, challenges, and opportunities in a systematic way. Once implemented, the United States will have a maritime vision that accounts for the full spectrum of activity from preventing attacks to responding if an attack takes place. Supporting the sequenced plans are crosscutting maritime policies that address maritime domain awareness and enhanced cooperation on shores near and far. However, the United States cannot undertake its maritime security regimen alone. One of the most important tools to strengthen maritime security in the global battlespace is through enhanced international cooperation.

The tools to enhance international cooperation in the maritime domain include strengthening regional cooperative security efforts, expanding U.S.-led mechanisms, promoting regional leadership, and creating hemispheric coalitions. Recognizing that U.S.-led initiatives have proven to be successful with close strategic partners, the United States should seek to increase maritime security by enabling other nations. This can be achieved by sharing expertise, information, and technology. Finding common ground and mutual strategic interests allows for synergy greater than any one nation can achieve, as evinced by the newly agreed to Security and Prosperity Partnership. Let this document be a guide for other regions of the world, with or without the participation of the United States. The transnational terrorist threat in the maritime domain is a global menace and it demands a global response.

ACKNOWLEDGMENTS

The views expressed herein are those of the authors and do not purport to reflect the position of the U.S. Department of Defense.

NOTES

1. U.S. Department of Defense, News Briefing, Thursday, October 12, 2000, 3 p.m. EDT, http://www.defenselink.mil/transcripts/2000/t10122000_t012cole.html.

2. Jeffrey Bartholet, "A World of Trouble: A Sneak Attack," *Newsweek,* October 23, 2000, 27.

3. U.S. Department of Defense, "Navy Announces Results of Its Investigation on USS Cole," News Release, January 19, 2001, http://www.defenselink.mil/releases/2001/b01192001_bt031-01.html.

4. U.S. Department of Defense, *DoD USS Cole Commission Report,* Executive Summary, January 9, 2001, http://www.defenselink.mil/pubs/cole20010109.html.

5. Lorraine Gorski, "Terror on the Seas," *Best's Review* 103 (March 2003): 44.

6. "Introduction to IMO," http://www.imo.org/home.asp.

7. "NATO Striking Fleet Atlantic History," http://www.secondfleet.navy.mil/history/csfl_history.htm.

8. Ibid.

9. Ibid.

10. "Pacific Fleet Exercises," http://www.globalsecurity.org/military/ops/ex-pacfleet.htm.

11. Ibid.

12. U.S. Coast Guard, International Affairs, http://www.uscg.mil/hq/g-ci/affairs/brochure.pdf.

13. Ibid.

14. Maki Becker, "Terror Lurks on High Seas, *New York Daily News,* September 21, 2003, 26.

15. General Accounting Office, "Port Security: Nation Faces Formidable Challenges in Making New Initiatives Successful," GAO-02-9993T (Washington, DC: U.S. General Accounting Office, August 2002), 3.

16. General Accounting Office, "Container Security: Expansion of Key Customs Programs Will Require Greater Attention to Critical Success Factors," GAO-03-770 (Washington, DC: U.S. General Accounting Office, July 2003), 5.

17. Martin van de Voort, Kevin A. O'Brien with Adnan Rahman and Lorenzo Valeri, "Seacurity: Improving the Security of the Global Sea-Container, Shipping System," in *Homeland Security and Terrorism: Readings and Interpretations,* ed. Russell Howard, James Forest, and Joanne Moore (New York: McGraw-Hill, 2005).

18. Gal Luft and Anne Korin, "Terrorism Goes to Sea," *Foreign Affairs* 83 (November/December 2004): 61–62.

19. Ibid., 63.

20. "U.S. Homeland Security Secretary Chertoff Advocates 'Security Envelopes,'" May 23, 2005, http://www.gmfus.org/event/detail.cfm?id=35.

21. National Intelligence Council's "Mapping the Global Future," December 2004, http://www.odci.gov/nic/NIC_globaltrend2020.html.

22. "Dr. Condoleezza Rice Discusses President's National Security Strategy," October 1, 2002, http://www.whitehouse.gov/news/releases/2002/10/20021001-6.html.

23. George W. Bush, *The National Security Strategy of the United States* (Washington, DC, White House, 2002), 7.

24. Donald Rumsfeld, *The National Defense Strategy of the United States* (Washington, DC: U.S. Department of Defense, 2005). Page iv of this *Strategy* indicates: "We will expand the community of nations that share principles and interests with us, and we will help partners increase their capacity to defend themselves and collectively meet challenges to our common interests."

25. *Maritime Security Policy National Security/Homeland Security Presidential Directive,* http://www.dhs.gov/dhspublic/display?theme=67&content=4566.

26. Ibid., 22.

27. Ibid.

28. Admiral Vern Clark, speech at the International Seapower Symposium: Seapower for Peace, Prosperity & Security, October 27, 2003, http://www.nwc.navy.mil/pao/CNO%20remarks.htm.

29. "RMSI: The ideas, the facts, Regional Maritime Security Initiative," http://www.pacom.mil/rmsi (accessed August 11, 2005).

30. Tamara Renee Shie, "Ports in a Storm? The Nexus between Counterterrorism, Counterproliferation, and Maritime Security in Southeast Asia," *Pacific Forum CSIS* (July 2004).

31. "Keeping Cargo Safe: Container Security Initiative," http://www.customs.gov/xp/cgov/border_security/international_activities/csi.

32. "Proliferation Security Initiative," http://www.state.gov/t/isn/c10390.htm.

33. "Megaports Initiative," http://www.nnsa.doe.gov/na-20/sld.shtml.

34. "Partnerships to Secure the Supply Chain: Customs-Trade Partnership Against Terrorism," http://www.customs.gov/xp/cgov/import/commercial_enforcement/ctpat.

35. Admiral Vern Clark, speech at the International Seapower Symposium: Seapower for Peace, Prosperity & Security, October 27, 2003.

36. Pranab Mukherjee, Indian Defence Minister, speech at the Carnegie Endowment for International Peace, Washington, DC, June 27, 2005, http://www.carnegieendowment.org/files/Mukherjee_Speech_06-27-051.pdf.

37. Ibid.

38. Ibid.

39. Ibid.; *Jane's Defense Weekly,* June 4, 2003; Rahul Bedi, "A New Doctrine for the Navy," *Frontline* 21, no. 14 (July 16, 2004).

40. Sumit Ganguly, "The Start of a Beautiful Friendship?: The United States and India," *World Policy Journal* 20 (Spring 2003): 25.

41. Ibid.

42. Gal Luft and Anne Korin, "Terrorism Goes to Sea," *Foreign Affairs* 83 (November/December 2004): 69.

43. "U.S., Indonesia Urged to Boost Maritime Security Work," *Reuters,* June 16, 2005, http://www.defensenews.com/story.php?F=919077&C=asiapac.

44. "Fact Sheet: Security and Prosperity Partnership of North America," March 23, 2005, http://www.whitehouse.gov/news/releases/2005/03/20050323-4.html.

45. Ibid.

46. U.S. Department of Defense, *Strategy for Homeland Defense and Civil Support* (Washington, DC: U.S. Department of Defense, June 2005), 24–7.

CHAPTER 14

HOMELAND SECURITY AND THE UNIQUE CHALLENGES OF ALASKA

Jerry A. Kidrick

Alaska's population is 634,892, spread out over a land area of 586,400 square miles—one-fifth the size of the lower 48 states. It is larger than the next three largest states—Texas, California, and Montana—combined (see Figure 14.1). Size and remoteness make Alaska vulnerable and difficult to defend.

The state's 16 boroughs should not be viewed in the emergency management context as being the equivalent of county governments—in fact, only in four of the boroughs and municipalities will one find government-run emergency services similar to county-style agencies. In the other 12 boroughs, emergency services, if any, are highly decentralized and provided by scattered, independent services. The boroughs cover approximately 38 percent of the land mass and encompass 86 percent of the population; the remaining 14 percent of the population resides in a vast, sparsely inhabited area called the "unorganized borough."

CLIMATE, TERRAIN, AND ECONOMICS

Due the extreme variances that exist with respect to climate, terrain, and economics, the distinct features of six different regions must be considered.

Southeast

Because the Southeast Region is composed of thousands of islands and a rugged strip of mainland bordering British Columbia and the Yukon

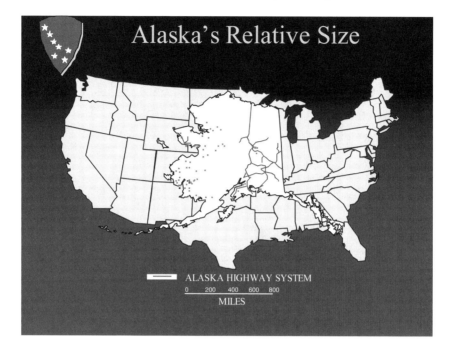

Figure 14.1   Alaska's Relative Size

Territory of Canada; the majority of its communities can only be reached by marine or air travel. With winter-summer averages ranging from +10° F to +70° F, the climate is mild by Alaskan temperature standards. By locale, average annual rainfall varies from 25 to 155 inches. Principal communities include Craig, Haines, Juneau, Ketchikan, Petersburg, Sitka, and Wrangell. Fishing and fish processing, mining, and tourism constitute the major industries. A declining timber industry also exists.

Southcentral

Curving 650 miles north and west from the coastal areas of the Gulf of Alaska to the Alaska Range, this region includes coastal waters rich in sea-life, fertile river valleys, rugged mountain ranges, forests, and glaciers. The Gulf of Alaska moderates coastal temperatures, providing a normal range of zero to 70° F. Anchorage has the most diverse economy in the state, with heavy involvement in government services and the oil industry, and is home to approximately 60 percent of Alaskans. Anchorage is also the state's primary transportation hub. Its airport is one of the state's three international airports, providing the major connections for in-state air travel and air freight service. A major military presence is maintained at both Elmendorf Air Force Base and Fort Richardson within the municipality of Anchorage.

Other key communities include Kenai and Soldotna, areas that serve oil, gas, and petrochemical interests in the Cook Inlet; Seward and Whittier, important ports for the Alaska Railroad; and Valdez, the terminus and port for the Trans-Alaska Pipeline.

Southwest

The Southwest Region includes the Alaska Peninsula, which stretches 550 miles from Cook Inlet to its tip at False Pass, the Kodiak Island Group to the south, and the Aleutian Island Chain which reaches out another 1,100 miles from False Pass toward Asia. Its Aleutian Range forms the spine of an arc of volcanoes, many of which are active. The region's maritime climate is comparatively mild, temperature-wise, but the islands are often fog-shrouded and storm-struck. Kodiak is the region's largest city, home to a U.S. Coast Guard station and rocket launch facility. Currently, a National Missile Defense Radar site is under construction on Adak Island. Commercial shipping, fishing, and fish processing are economic mainstays. Travel is primarily accomplished by boat or aircraft.

Western

Reaching north from the head of Bristol Bay to the Seward Peninsula, the Western Region is remote. It includes Nunivak and St. Lawrence Islands and encompasses the Yukon-Kuskokwim Delta. Winters are characterized by high winds and humidity; in summer, cool, foggy, rainy weather prevails. Bethel, a city of 5,449 people on the north bank of the Kuskokwim River, is a regional hub. Air is the principal mode of travel to and from the region; however, boats, snow machines, and all-terrain vehicles are widely used within.

Interior

Larger than Montana, this region is bordered on the south by the Alaska Range and on the north by the Brooks Range. Between these mountain ranges, the Yukon River and its drainages arc 1,875 miles across the state from the Canadian border to the Bering Sea. Temperatures that can reach 95° F in summer occasionally plunge to -60° F and colder in winter. Fairbanks, Alaska's second largest city, is mostly central to the region. It provides the northern terminus of the railroad where logistical support to the North Slope is moved overland via the Dalton Highway. Fairbanks is also the distribution point for military interests in the Interior, such as Fort Wainwright, Eielson Air Force Base, and the missile defense site at Fort Greely.

Arctic

This barren, treeless region of rolling tundra lies between the Brooks Range and the Arctic Ocean. Summer temperatures average 40° F. Winter temperatures, which average -17° F, frequently yield much lower effective temperatures because of high winds. Winter also means 67 days without daylight; the sun sets on November 18, and does not rise again until January 24. The region is also arid, with annual precipitation averaging less than 5 inches. This region contains the North Slope oil fields and the Red Dog Mine (zinc).

The majority of its sparsely populated coastal plain is inhabited by Alaska natives who live a traditional subsistence lifestyle of hunting and fishing. Barrow, Nome, and Kotzebue are the largest communities. Air is the principal method of travel. Boat use is seasonal, as the Arctic Ocean's shores are ice-locked for 7 to 8 months annually.

GENERAL HAZARDS OF ALASKA

Naturally occurring events have caused nearly two-thirds of Alaska's disaster emergencies. In one sense, Alaska is fortunate that its vast, sparsely populated regions allow events that would be devastating elsewhere to take place with little or no impact on its population. On the other hand, when these remote occurrences threaten or devastate on a widespread basis, then the factors of distance, harsh climate, rugged terrain, and dependence on air travel make relief efforts challenging, with outcomes uncertain at times, and, in all cases, costly.

Attack/Terrorist Attack

Despite the fading threat of global nuclear war once the Cold War ended, Alaska is still home to several large military installations and its geographical location assures its importance to Northern Hemisphere strategies (see Figure 14.2). Alaska produces 20 percent of U.S. domestic crude oil. It is the national leader in zinc and tin production, and has six of the nation's top ten producing ports for commercial fishing interests. Nearly 1.5 million tourists visit Alaska each year via cruise ships, state ferries, and commercial air. These factors provide ample basis to presuppose Alaska's involvement in future conflicts with even limited objectives, or its capacity to present targets for criminal acts of terrorism or sabotage.

High-Capacity Passenger Vessels (Cruise Ships and State Ferries)

Although not a hazard per se, high capacity passenger vessels constitute a unique vulnerability for the state. Two-thirds of Alaska's annual 1.5 million visitors arrive via high-capacity vessels, and almost 80 percent arrive via cruise ships. At any given time during the summer cruise ship

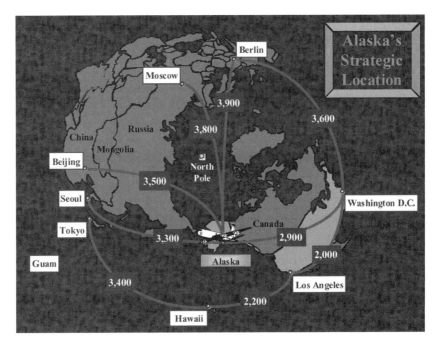

Figure 14.2   Alaska's Strategic Location

season there may be up to 30 large cruise ships off the coast of Alaska, or docked in Alaska's ports, with an average of 2,300 passengers and crew on each (this is in addition to the passengers on the Alaska Marine Highway System, which recorded 2,150 sailings in 2002). Through either accidents or acts of terrorism, these ships have the potential to create disaster emergency situations and introduce large numbers of victims into local communities, which will have varying degrees of ability to cope with these victims.

TERRORISM IN ALASKA

Despite its elevated notoriety, al Qaeda is not the only terrorist organization of concern. There are 74 organized groups (as recognized by the U.S. State Department) throughout the world committed to attacking the United States, and which have the capability to do so. Domestic terrorism, including random acts of violence, has also been a threat, for more than 100 years, and remains so today. In fact, domestic terrorist groups seem to be more focused and more sophisticated than in the past, and, because of the increasing polarization of sides on several "hot button" issues, and what they may view as the successes of international terrorists, domestic terrorists may well be more of a threat now than they have been in the past.

Alaskans are all too familiar with natural disasters—floods, earth-quakes, volcanic eruptions—because they frequently witness them, or are even directly affected by them; they know these kinds of events will occur in the future. The Exxon Valdez oil spill and many lesser, but still noteworthy events, are vivid reminders of the potential for technological disasters. But for many Alaskans it is difficult to envision a terrorist attack in their state. However, Alaska most certainly has its share of potential targets, to include people and national symbols—symbols of government, military power, and financial strength.

On October 4, 2001, an individual shot a hole in the Trans-Alaska Pipeline with a rifle. The resulting oil spill was damaging to the environment and the cleanup was costly. This event demonstrated the difficulties authorities in Alaska face in trying to protect its critical infrastructure from attack and in responding to an incident when one occurs. The September 11, 2001, attack proved that Alaska does not have to be the target of an attack to be affected by one. For example, because Alaskans travel to and from the lower 48 states so frequently, a bioterrorist attack initiated there could have significant impacts here, and vice versa. Ignorance of any specific threat to Alaska and its people does not mean the threat does not exist, or that an attack is not being planned.

Critical Infrastructure Protection

The state of Alaska has consolidated a prioritized list of critical infrastructure and potential targets. Many of Alaska's critical assets and high-visibility potential targets are owned by private sector companies. Under most threat conditions, the state relies on its private sector partners to protect their own facilities from terrorist attacks. Although the state provides assistance in the form of vulnerability assessments and recommendations during the readiness phase, private sector entities must independently increase their security posture in response to increased threat conditions. But when Alaska is at threat level RED (severe), or a credible threat to specific infrastructure sectors or specific facilities exists, the state can and will provide security forces to augment those already in place at the threatened facilities.

The primary organization the state looks to for protection of critical assets, at high-threat levels, is the Alaska State Defense Force (ASDF), which—when directed by the Commissioner of the Department of Military and Veterans Affairs (DMVA)—deploys to conduct critical asset protection in accordance with various operations plans. If physical security requirements exceed ASDF's capabilities, the DMVA Commissioner may deploy the Alaska National Guard.

The Port of Valdez is the terminus of the Alaska Oil Pipeline and is considered part of the critical national infrastructure. The oil supertankers that traverse the Valdez Narrows and load crude oil at one of the four berthing docks are vulnerable to terrorist attack by high-speed pleasure craft carrying high explosives. What is the extent of vulnerability to attack at this economically important oil port? How adequate are existing response plans for dealing with the resultant oil spill? Are adaptable plans and equipment available/accessible to protect public health and safety, quickly restore essential functions and operations, and provide emergency relief if this sort of terrorism occurs? These are questions which this chapter will address, within the larger context of Alaska's homeland security challenges.

THE POSSIBILITY OF A SEABORNE ATTACK USING HIGH-SPEED PLEASURE CRAFT AND HIGH EXPLOSIVES ON A LOADED OIL SUPERTANKER IN OR AROUND THE PORT OF VALDEZ ALASKA

Terrorists have demonstrated that they can and will strike critical targets that have the greatest potential for economic and social impact. The Port of Valdez is just such a target (see Figure 14.3). Most, if not all, oil tanker spill protection measures in the Valdez harbor are designed to counter an "accidental" oil release by a tanker. While oil spill response plans and equipment available in Valdez are vastly improved since the Exxon Valdez oil spill of 1989, they are not sufficient to prevent an

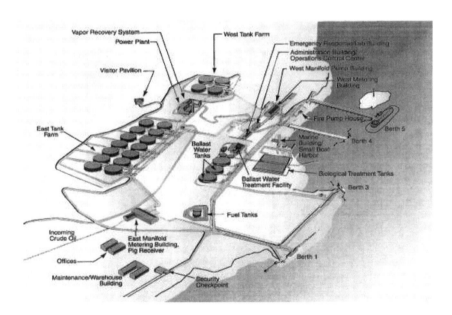

Figure 14.3 Overhead View of the Port of Valdez

environmental catastrophe, which can only be addressed through improved prevention methods. How will current multiagency public/private consequence management planning restore this essential oil port to full operation, if it continues to focus solely on environmental recovery actions, and neglects security procedures and the potential of terrorist attack?

The Port of Valdez

The oil from the Alaska Oil Pipeline accounts for roughly 20 percent of U.S. oil production annually. One-tenth of all oil Americans use daily passes through this pipeline and port. The Valdez terminal oil storage capacity is 9.2 million barrels, and every month, 50 supertankers sail from the Prince William Sound to bring oil to the rest of the United States, and overseas (see Figure 14.4).

The U.S. Department of Homeland Security has determined the Port of Valdez to be high on the list of critical infrastructure targets (with the actual priority classified). During the Christmas holidays in 2003, the Department of Homeland Security, through Northern Command (NORTHCOM) issued a "credible threat" alert for an attack on five locations in the United States, and the Port of Valdez was one of these five targets. In response, state and federal military forces, law enforcement, and state homeland defense personnel established a joint defense capability to "detect, deter, and respond to any attack on the Port of Valdez."[1] No

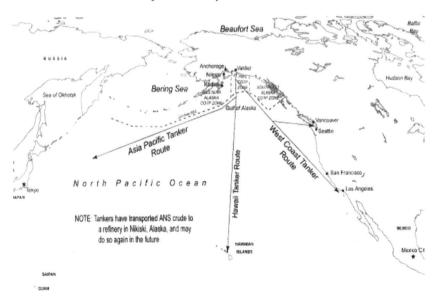

Figure 14.4   Routes to/from Port of Valdez

such attack occurred, and as with all attacks that never happen, it is generally impossible to determine (or can't be revealed) if or at what point the potential attack was deterred by defensive efforts.

For several reasons, the preponderance of terrorist attacks against U.S. citizens has involved the use of bombs. In 1998, a total of 96 of 111 attacks used bombs, and an additional five were fire bombings. The number of attacks rose to 169 in 1999, including 111 bombings and 12 fire bombings.[2] Bombs statistically remain the weapon of choice for terrorists as the technology and materials are readily available, and bombs containing high explosive have a low "difficulty factor" in preparation and prevention of detection. It could be argued that in using aircraft on September 11, 2001, the al Qaeda terrorists used conventional "bombs" by virtue of the explosive nature of an aircraft fully loaded with fuel. A high-speed pleasure craft could easily be the bomb "delivery vehicle" used to cripple a supertanker in the Port of Valdez.

Pleasure Craft in Alaska

Alaska has more coastline than the rest of the United States combined. Fully 80 percent of Alaska is not reachable by the road system.[3] Pleasure craft operations are one of the most underregulated methods of transportation in the country. The nature of the pleasure boat sales/rental/charter industry does not readily lend itself to security procedures because of economics, the volume of marine vehicles, and multiple ports of access. A false sense of security exists because there lacks any historical memory of a tragic incident of national importance involving pleasure boats loaded with explosives within U.S. territorial waters. However, as was demonstrated by the attacks on the *USS Cole* and the French supertanker *Limburgh,* terrorists have already provided a stark illustration of their interest in maritime targets. Pleasure craft operations in Alaska are vulnerable to abuse by terrorists for use as weapons delivery vehicles, and as a consequence, supertankers within the Port of Valdez are also vulnerable.

Vulnerability

America's energy infrastructure as a whole is highly vulnerable to asymmetrical terrorist threats. Further, there is no doubt that al Qaeda is intent on hurting the United States and the "West" economically by interrupting the flow of oil to American, European, and Asiatic markets; al Qaeda leaders have vowed to cut the "economic lifelines" of industrialized societies.

Oil supertankers and pipelines are very vulnerable targets. Tankers are too slow and cumbersome to maneuver away from attackers; they don't have any protection, and they cannot conceal their movements as a defensive measure. Tankers are especially vulnerable when passing through narrow straits or when moored at loading berths.

The geography of the Middle East forces tankers carrying oil to pass through one or more of three narrow straits: the entrances to the Red Sea (Bab-el-Mandeb) and the Persian Gulf (Strait of Hormuz), and the Straits of Malacca between Indonesia and Malaysia.[4] The Valdez Narrows is a no less vulnerable "choke point" and, by restricting its use through a terrorist attack on a tanker, an even more devastating blow could be struck by al Qaeda than if it attacked one of the strategic passages named. In fact, it could be argued that if the Port of Valdez oil movements were interrupted for even a short period (such as by a burning supertanker), U.S. dependence on foreign oil would require use of the National Petroleum Reserves, and its certain impact on the price of oil and the U.S. economy would achieve major al Qaeda psychological and economic goals.

Since the tragic Exxon Valdez accident and its resulting environmental damage, many changes relating to tanker safety in and around Valdez have been made. The U.S. Coast Guard now monitors fully-laden tankers via satellite as they pass through the Valdez Narrows. Two escort vessels (tugs) accompany each tanker while passing through the entire sound. Their role is to assist in the event of power or rudder control loss. Specially trained pilots are aboard for 25 miles as they exit the sound. Legislation was enacted after the Exxon Valdez incident requiring that all tankers in the Prince William Sound be double-hulled by the year 2015 (per the *Oil Pollution Act of 1990*). Contingency plans now address a spill of up to 12.6 million gallons. And finally, "skimming" equipment, containment booms, and stockpiles of chemical dispersant are all available in significant quantities.[5]

These tanker safety procedures are specifically intended to reduce the risk of an accident like the grounding of the Exxon Valdez on Bligh Reef in 1989. What the procedures fail to address is the deterrence or interdiction of a determined attacker. As mentioned, although escorted, the tankers have no defense. The U.S. Coast Guard does not provide an armed sea or air escort through the narrows or in port. Interestingly, a state-of-the-art infrared camera system, touted as a "port security surveillance system" by the U.S. Coast Guard, is only turned on and monitored for limited intervals. According to the Marine Safety Office (MSO) Valdez, "because of warranty issues on the equipment, it is only turned on in bad weather and for short periods." According to the MSO authorities, they recognize that there is "definitely a risk to tankers by fast-moving pleasure craft," and that they would "not be able to stop a boat determined to crash into a loaded tanker in the port."[6]

The attack on the *USS Cole* effectively demonstrated the devastating impact of even a rudimentary attack. In a classic economy-of-force action, terrorists were able to attack and blow a gaping hole in the armor of a U.S.

warship, killing 17 sailors. Despite advances in tanker safety (28 percent of the U.S. tanker fleet is double-hulled),[7] tankers are not designed to withstand an explosive attack of the type that so devastated the *USS Cole*.

Supertanker vulnerability in the Port of Valdez while moored to a loading berth is also an issue, in that some basic protection measures are not in place. Several products are available to protect ships in port. The U.S. Coast Guard in Alameda has placed a floating security barrier around its pier in the Oakland Estuary to protect cutters from potential terrorist attack.[8] These barriers, originally designed as high-endurance breakwaters, are used increasingly in a homeland security role because the hardened floating boom-type barriers can prevent vessels from entering protected zones. Serious consideration should be given to arming tankers during those times when they are most vulnerable. If a "master" pilot is flown aboard a tanker about to transit a critical area, Coast Guard gunners should also be used as part of vulnerability mitigation efforts.

In the past 36 months, terrorists have targeted oil and gas operations with increasing frequency. Their goals in these efforts have included the destabilization of western economies, adverse psychological impact, and discouragement of foreign governments from participation in regional affairs. The targets of those attacks are sometimes pipelines, workers, and the worldwide fleet of oil tankers. Most of these attacks have taken place on Middle Eastern infrastructure targets, more than likely due to proximity, the number of potential targets, and lapses in security practices. The impact of these attacks can and do have far-reaching effects, and are part of an effective asymmetric strategy to strike at the economic lifeblood of developed nations, while at the same time causing environmental damage which affects the global community as a whole.

While the preponderance of the worst attacks have taken place outside U.S. territory, the events of 9/11 demonstrate the will and capacity to strike at the heart of the United States. The oil industry is no less desirable a target in the United States than it is in the Middle East.[9] In fact, given our environmental sensitivities, it could be argued that the result of a terrorist attack on an oil tanker domestically would have more impact on the national will than on the national economy.

The Port of Valdez, Alaska and the oil supertankers that ply the waters of Prince William Sound are a part of the nation's critical infrastructure. As potential terrorist targets, they are vulnerable to attack because of a failure to conduct a target risk assessment. The United States is currently engaged in an asymmetric war with Islamic terrorists who have demonstrated skill, planning, and creativity in attacking the United States. It is therefore not difficult to assert that while many safety procedures are in place to prevent/respond to an accidental oil spill in Alaskan waters, little, if anything, has been done to identify and protect this critical part of the U.S. economy as a possible target.

Many basic measures for tanker protection are not in place, including armed escort or protective barrier emplacement at loading berths. The Marine Safety Office in Valdez acknowledges a vulnerability to fast-moving boats with explosives in the Valdez Narrows and Port, and, due to funding concerns, does not use the installed security cameras to monitor ship traffic. These are fundamental holes in even basic security procedures, and are inexcusable in light of the sensitivity of the target and the ease with which this protection could be provided.

During World War II, protection of the U.S. homeland became an "every person" job. Ports, cities, and production facilities became "hardened targets," using things like "barrage balloons" flown over cities to prevent air attacks. It is well past time to recognize that we are at war with a cunning and crafty enemy, and that our critical infrastructure needs an increased level of protection from deliberate attack. The Port of Valdez is part of this infrastructure.

In oil spills, the best solution is prevention. An attack and its resultant spill in the Valdez harbor would be an environmental and economic disaster, and response teams could not prevent oil from reaching critical habitat from such a close-in event. Despite Consequence Management Plans and equipment in place which are second-to-none in the world, there are limitations to what we can expect of them, and the event for which they are best suited is not necessarily the only probable disaster risk facing this area.

AN AIRBORNE ATTACK ON THE PORT OF VALDEZ ALASKA USING GENERAL AVIATION COMMERCIAL AIRCRAFT (FIXED- OR ROTARY-WING) AND HIGH EXPLOSIVES

As the terminus of the Alaska Oil Pipeline, the U.S. Department of Homeland Security has determined the Port of Valdez to be high on the list of critical infrastructure targets. In addition to a maritime attack, the pipeline, loading docks, storage tanks, and oil tankers are also vulnerable to attack by small general aviation (GA) aircraft (fixed- and rotary-wing) carrying high explosives. Commercial GA operators who fly "flightseeing" aircraft in and around the Prince William Sound and the Port of Valdez were surveyed in 2004 with questions about security infrastructure, current policies, and compliance with regulatory and recommended procedures, to determine the port's vulnerability to attack. The results were not encouraging.

General Aviation in Alaska

Alaska has more aircraft and fewer miles of roads, per capita, than any other state in the Union. Fully 80 percent of Alaska is not reachable by the road system. GA is one of the most underregulated methods of transportation in the country. As this chapter will show, the nature of the "small" air carrier industry does not readily lend itself to intensive security procedures because of economics, remote low-traffic operations, and a false sense of security. This false sense of security is based on a history without a tragic incident of national importance involving GA aircraft. General aviation aircraft in Alaska are vulnerable to abuse, and so is the Port of Valdez.

General Aviation Survey

A survey was developed and delivered to GA commercial aviators that operate aircraft for hire within the reach of the Port of Valdez. Ten respondents completed all or most of the questionnaire. The survey reflected a full spectrum of commercial GA operators. Several operated up to ten aircraft and were based in a major metropolitan area with "full function" airfields, air traffic control towers, security fences, and high air traffic volume. Others were single aircraft operations based at relatively remote "unimproved" airfields with a generally low air movement count.

In the general category of security infrastructure, the survey indicated a variety of shortcomings (see Table 14.1). To begin with, only 10 percent of those surveyed were aware of any security plan, identification verification system, or security training programs in their area.

While a majority (70 percent) knew their local law enforcement point of contact (POC), only 40 percent were aware of any law enforcement patrols of general aviation terminals.

Table 14.1 Survey of Commercial GA Operators

Security Infrastructure Component	Yes (compliance)	No (noncompliance)
Restricted Access	40%	60%
Perimeter Fencing	40%	60%
Law Enforcement POC	70%	30%
Law Enforcement Patrols	40%	60%
Airfield Security Discussion	20%	80%
Awareness of Security Plan	10%	90%
ID Check System	10%	90%
Aircraft Theft Precautions	60%	40%
Security Training Programs	10%	90%
Security Signage	20%	80%

In the general category of flight security (i.e., passenger/cargo screening, hijack prevention, and in-flight emergency procedures), the survey results were even more alarming (see Table 14.2).

Two questions focused on how vulnerable respondents felt they were to having prohibited material like explosives placed onboard their aircraft. While these questions are somewhat subjective, the previous questions in the survey illuminated security shortcomings for respondents and provided a basis for reflection on their relative vulnerability. Most respondents (90 percent) felt they were vulnerable or very vulnerable to having prohibited material brought onboard. Further, 40 percent felt they were vulnerable or very vulnerable to hijack, and another 40 percent felt they were slightly vulnerable (in other words, eight out of ten respondents indicated some level of vulnerability to attack).

The remaining questions in the survey focused on the kinds of changes respondents would like to see in security measures taken to prevent these situations, and their views on additional resources (i.e., funding) needed to implement these measures. While some respondents had no suggestions for improved security, 50 percent felt that additional funding was

Table 14.2 Survey of Commercial GA Operators, Part 2

Flight Security Component	Yes (compliance)	No (noncompliance)
Cargo Screening Devices Used	0%	100%
Hand Screening Passengers	0%	100%
Bags Checked	0%	100%
Detecting Explosives/Prohibited Materials	0%	100%
Passenger ID Check	30%	70%
Aircraft Transponder Capable (Transmit Emergency)	40%	60%
Operate at Altitudes Sufficient for Radar	50%	50%
Capable of Transmitting on Emergency Frequency (Radio Transmission)	80%	20%
Passenger Prohibited from Riding Up-Front (at or near flight controls)	0%	100%
Pilots Trained Against Event of Hijack	30%	70%
Ever Experienced Attempted Takeover	10%	90%
Turned Away Suspicious Passengers	10%	90%
Ever Contacted by TSA Reference Security	10%	90%

needed and had specific recommendations for security measures. The most common specific response was in favor of airfield fencing, followed by signage, and a security guard present at the airfield. Surprisingly, 60 percent indicated that security had not improved at all at their airfield since September 11, 2001. Additionally, while the majority of operators felt vulnerable or very vulnerable to misuse of their aircraft, none recommended purchase of passenger and/or cargo screening equipment, or increase in scrutiny level provided by the Transportation Security Agency (TSA). Given the independent nature of the respondent population, this is somewhat understandable. Nonetheless, when considering the overwhelming level of vulnerability relative to the importance of the possible infrastructure targets available, the reluctance to implement some of these very basic improvements seems hard to understand.

Historically, GA airports and operators have not been subject to federal rules regarding airport security. Prior to Sept. 11, 2001, the federal government's role in airport security focused exclusively on those airports serving scheduled operations. Now, however, the TSA and other responsible agencies must consider the vulnerability of GA operations to misuse by terrorists, especially as vulnerabilities in other areas of aviation are reduced.[10] On August 9, 2004, the TSA issued an alert about the possibility of tourist flightseeing helicopters being used by terrorists in New York.[11] The fact that GA has been identified for possible use by terrorists warrants increased scrutiny across the industry.

General aviation includes a broad range of aircraft and aviation activity. They vary greatly in size, function, and operational characteristics, as indicated by survey respondents. For example, a privately owned airstrip in rural Alaska would not need to implement the same security measures as a large GA airport near a major metropolitan area. The challenge is providing enough security for any one location to prevent misuse by terrorists. In the case of the Port of Valdez and local GA operators, any security awareness would be an improvement over the current status quo.

CONCLUSION

Prevention of an attack anywhere in the United States or on U.S. interests abroad is best done by preemption. The in-depth defense approach recognizes the need to layer defenses to first detect, then deter, an attack. Given the variables that affect the success of the interdiction approach, this author accepts the premise that al Qaeda operatives can reach Alaska and, through GA operations, can reach the Port of Valdez. It follows, then, that the prevention must take place at the operator level by enforcement of sufficient security measures to do the detection and deterrence locally. At present, procedures are not in place to accomplish this task.

The area around the Port of Valdez and terminus of the Alaska Oil Pipeline is what is termed a "target-rich environment." The U-6 DeHavilland Beaver float-equipped aircraft is a common sight at flightseeing operations around Alaska. This aircraft is capable of carrying a useful load (passenger and cargo) of 900 lbs.[12] The aircraft has a dual set of flight controls which is typical and, as the survey indicated, all of the respondents allow passengers to fly up front in the second pilot seat. Other passengers ride behind the pilot. The survey also demonstrated that none of the operators verify passenger cargo/baggage content or screen passengers for prohibited items. Given these lapses in even basic security practices, it is not difficult to build a scenario that places a flightseeing aircraft over the Port of Valdez with 500 lbs. of C-4 or any other high-velocity-type military explosive[13] on board, with the pilot dead or incapacitated, and no defensive measures in place to stop what would be an incident of national importance.

The TSA needs to act now to identify GA vulnerability nationwide and act quickly to close this potentially catastrophic loophole in the public transportation system. As part of our national in-depth defense-, the only way to prevent misuse of GA aircraft is to train and equip GA operators to use current technology and equipment as a deterrent to misuse. Further,- operators must be forced to comply through federal regulations that direct increased security measures as part of our nationwide strategy. Without regulation, compliance will be impossible to enforce.

The Port of Valdez Alaska and terminus of the Alaska Oil Pipeline is a possible al Qaeda target of national significance. Those agencies responsible for transportation security in the United States cannot overlook the significant risk posed to this important part of national infrastructure by the vulnerability of GA aircraft to misuse. GA operators around the port are not required by regulation to screen passengers or cargo, and a survey indicates they do very little voluntarily to enforce even minimal security standards. Large commercial carriers have been subject to federal regulation almost from the beginning of their industry. Passengers and airline employees are used to intense regulation and in general can see the need for the high level of security in place today. GA operators, on the other hand, have been largely unregulated in the area of security procedures.[14] According to a statement by the Airline Owners and Pilots Association, the industry does not see GA misuse as a possible threat to our national infrastructure; and this is supported by the stated position that "the industry has taken voluntary steps to enhance security."[15]

Results of the survey discussed in this chapter indicate just the opposite, including in some cases a strident opposition to changing the status quo. Given the nature of the stated threat by al Qaeda to the United States today and al Qaeda's ability to be "creative" in weapons employment, the status quo is no longer sufficient. Federal regulations, enforcement, and funding to pay for security equipment and training are needed now if al Qaeda or other terrorists are to be stopped from using GA aircraft or high-speed watercraft as a weapon to attack critical Alaska infrastructure.

ACKNOWLEDGMENTS

The views expressed herein are those of the author and do not purport to reflect the position of the Alaska National Guard, the Department of the Army, or the Department of Defense. The author would like to thank SGT Eric M. Hamilton for his assistance with preparing this chapter.

NOTES

1. Deputy Chief of Staff for Operations, *Alaska National Guard AAR Valdez Operation, Christmas 2003,* January 2004.

2. Ibid.

3. State of Alaska Department of Public Policy, *State of Alaska Census Report,* January 2004.

4. Institute for Analysis of Global Security, *Threats to Oil Transport,* December 3, 2004, http://www.iags.org.

5. Alaska Regional Response Team, *Prince William Sound,* November 2, 2004, http://www.akrrt.com (accessed November 2, 2004).

6. Lieutenant Burns, Marine Safety Officer, USCG Valdez, telephone interview, December 6, 2004.

7. Ibid.

8. *Maritime Port Security Glossary,* Whisprwave Innovative Maritime Solutions, December 7, 2004, http://www.whisprwave.com.

9. For more on this topic, please see the chapters in Volume III of this publication by Kevin Freese and Thomas Quiggin.

10. United States Transportation Security Administration, *Security Guidelines for General Aviation Airports,* May 2004, http://www.tsa.gov/interweb/assetlibrary/security_guidelines_for_general_aviation_airports_may_2004_a-001.pdf (accessed April 2, 2006).

11. David Johnston and Eric Lichtblau, "Tourist Copters in New York City a Terror Target," *The New York Times,* August 9, 2004, http://query.nytimes.com (accessed August 12, 2004).

12. Scott McPherson, "Private Planes: Freedom, Security, and Responsibility," *The Freemen: Ideas on Liberty,* 2002, http://www.fee.org/vnews.php?nid=5258 (accessed December 10, 2004).

13. *General Aviation and Homeland Security: A Security Brief by the Aircraft Owners and Pilots Association,* January 23, 2004, http://www.aopa.org/whatsnew/newsitems/2002/020621_homeland_security.html (accessed April 2, 2006).

14. David Hoffman, *The Oklahoma City Bombing and the Politics of Terror,* August 9, 2004, http://www.apfn.org/apfn/hoffman.htm.

15. For more on this topic, please see the chapters in Volume III of this publication by Kevin Freese and Thomas Quiggin.

CHAPTER 15

MARITIME SECURITY AND THE PACIFIC COAST: POST-9/11 CHALLENGES IN TRADE AND TOURISM

Priya Dixit

Maritime security is a topic that covers a wide range of areas and can be used to define different activities. A brief overview of maritime security ranges from safeguarding maritime vessels from piracy to dealing with public health threats aboard cruise ships. Maritime security, as it relates to homeland security, is about protecting the United States and its coastal areas, especially its major ports, from both external and internal threats. In other words, a large part of maritime security deals with incoming vessels and aims to ensure safety of goods and passengers entering and leaving the country. In addition, making sure that no unauthorized entry occurs is also part of U.S. maritime security initiatives. Vessels journeying to and from the United States are of two main kinds: trade-related and tourism-related. These include large ships as well as smaller tour and fishing vessels. In this globalized world, maritime security does not involve only internal security of the United States homeland but is also linked to external foreign policy and international trade issues.

This chapter explores how maritime security of the Pacific coastal areas of the United States has been defined, how plans to ensure the safety and security of the Pacific coasts, especially its major ports, have been formulated and operationalized, and what types of challenges remain since September 11. The Pacific coastal area stretches from California in the south to Washington in the north. It also includes the coastline of Alaska in the far north. The Pacific coastline stretches for approximately 1,300 miles in mainland United States and a further 6,640 miles in Alaska.[1] Compared to the East Coast of the United States, there are fewer states and thus fewer state resources to guard coastal areas in the Pacific. Therefore, when it comes to surveillance, the security personnel of each Pacific state is stretched quite thin. Overall, the challenges of patrolling the Pacific coast are thus greater than such challenges in the eastern United States. There is a large volume of international trade and tourism since the trans-Pacific trade with East Asia, especially China, continues to grow. Also, there are a large number of private ships, yachts, and fishing boats which ply their way around the Pacific coastal areas, making it difficult to keep them all under surveillance. Thus, maritime security of the Pacific coast is important in maintaining overall security of the U.S. homeland.

The first section of this chapter provides a brief history of the maritime security efforts in the Pacific region of the United States. This is followed by a brief analysis of trade and tourism-related activities in three major ports of the U.S. Pacific coast: Seattle, Los Angeles, and Long Beach. With regard to each of these ports, case studies of trade and tourism illustrate their importance to the socioeconomic health of the United States. Obviously, ports are important to U.S. security because there are hundreds of public ports in the United States, through which about 95 percent of U.S. overseas trade passes.[2] The chapter then describes some of the major initiatives that have been operationalized to ensure port security in the post-9/11 era. Threats are not just military-based, since economic risks faced by any disruption in trade and tourism activities in this area can lead to big changes in the U.S. economy, in addition to destructions of lives and livelihoods. The final section looks at the unique challenges facing U.S. Pacific maritime security in terms of new security threats, such as bioterror and geographical challenges, and makes some recommendations for improving maritime security.

MARITIME SECURITY IN THE PACIFIC COAST: MAJOR DOMESTIC ACTORS AND SECURITY INITIATIVES SINCE SEPTEMBER 11

The major issue in Pacific coastal security is how to facilitate trade and tourism while ensuring security. Security challenges are multidimensional since there is a need to facilitate the safety and security of the supply chain as well as of the vessels and passengers, while ensuring related areas such as docks, storage facilities, and cruise terminals, and the personnel working in such areas, are safe. Trade is important for the United States, since imports are about three-fourths higher than exports, in cash terms.[3] But, trading needs have to be balanced with security, especially in the wake of September 11. The *Maritime Transportation Security Act* (MTSA), passed in November 2002, identified U.S. coasts and ports as a key vulnerable site for potential terrorist attacks. It said that ports were often "very open and exposed" and added that they were "susceptible to large scale acts of terrorism that could cause a large loss of life or economic disruption."[4] The Department of Homeland Security, established after September 11 and incorporating the work of many related agencies, has primary responsibility to safeguard the United States. Among its goals are to strengthen border security measures and to make transportation more efficient, both of which are important in maintaining and improving Pacific maritime security.

Important security issues with regard to Pacific waterborne trade and tourism include procedural security (ensuring all the procedures are followed, both within the United States and outside, especially the processing of documents, highlighting if there are any cargo discrepancies, manifest procedures, etc.); conveyance security (ensuring the security of the containers and cargo during the supply chain including seals, inspections, and storage); personnel security (preemployment verifications, background checks, and ensuring the security of people along the supply line, the dock workers, the inspectors, the police and Coast Guard, the people on the ships that transport cargoes, transport workers, etc.); and physical security (fencing, lighting, parking, locking, alarms, video surveillance, etc.).[5] Apart from these, supply line security and constant vigilance to ensure ships and containers are not tampered with during the course of their voyage to the United States are also key. In addition, surveillance of areas around the Pacific coast and Alaska in the north, and also around U.S. territories such as Hawaii and Guam, is important. All of this means there are multiple levels to ensuring security, with different areas of focus needed.

Overall, the major responsibility for maintaining security goes to the U.S. Coast Guard (USCG)[6] and the U.S. Customs and Border Protection (CBP) Agency. The CBP has the primary responsibility for "securing America's borders."[7] After September 11, 2001, a new combined organization of the Border Patrol, the Immigration and Naturalization Services, Agriculture Inspection, and the United States Customs Service became the Customs and Border Protection Agency in the Department of Homeland Security. In the international arena, CBP works closely with the World Customs Organization (WCO) and other international port authorities to make sure global trade is secure from potential attacks. CBP has been working to implement WCO's Framework of Standards to Secure and Facilitate Global Trade. The Pacific coastal ports are important elements in this strategy since a large volume of global trade passes through these ports. CBP has the major task of surveillance of ports. CBP not only inspects cargo but also has overseas surveillance operations, thus keeping various tasks under one main organization. CBP makes sure that entry requirements for imports are complied with and that shipping and cruise companies closely follow entry guidelines. For the purposes of vessels landing at U.S. ports, "entry" means complying with the state and federal regulations of the port of entry and not just physically arriving at the port.

The CBP has begun security-related initiatives for the protection of U.S. borders, especially major entry points such as the Pacific coast ports. For example, the CBP's Container Security Initiative (CSI), started after September 11, 2001, has as its motto, "keeping cargo safe."[8] The CSI focuses on protecting the overall international trading system and does not just concentrate on the U.S. mainland. This is because there has been increasing recognition of the international dimensions of world trade and tourism, especially with ships being from varied nations with crew members of varied nationalities. CSI includes bilateral arrangements under which CBP inspectors work in nearly 20 countries to ensure the security of the cargo and to make sure that containers being transported to the United States are secure. Prescreening of cargo and usage of smarter, tamper-evident containers are part of this initiative. Around 90 percent of the world's cargo is transported by ships so it is important to ensure their safety. For the United States, about half of the incoming trade enters into the country by sea containers.[9] The CSI aims to identify high-risk cargo through prescreening and information sharing. CSI is a reciprocal program, which means other countries can also station their officials at U.S. ports. So far, Canadian and Japanese officials are working with U.S. officials in various U.S. ports.[10] Other CBP initiatives include radiation portal monitors which allow the CBP to screen trucks, ships, etc. for the presence of nuclear and radiological materials without the system itself being dangerous to humans. The $58 million Operation Safe Commerce is another program of the U.S. government meant to increase security in international supply chains. CBP works with foreign governments to obtain intelligence about the risks of shipments, especially to note high-risk shipments, so that such shipments can be tracked and inspected as necessary. CBP's task is immense, as it enforces over 400 regulations from over 40 other U.S. government agencies, in addition to its own laws.[11]

In terms of regulations affecting Pacific maritime security, one of the major post-September 11 developments in the United States was the *Trade Act of 2002*, which says that importers and arriving ships have to transmit information about their cargoes before arrival at a U.S. port. This is the 24-hour advanced manifest regulation. This requires the presentation of cargo information before the vessel is allowed to enter the United States. The advanced manifest regulation is applicable for all modes of transportation in and out of the United States. The time frame for providing the information differs according to type of cargo and the length of the journey. For containerized cargo, it is 24-hours before loading at the foreign port from where the cargo is to be shipped to the United States. Precise descriptions and weight of the cargo are required as well as information about the shipper(s) and country of origin of the goods. This means CBP will be able to analyze information about the cargo before the ship reaches U.S. territory. Lack of all the required information could lead to the ship not being allowed to unload its goods or enter U.S. ports. Other important legislation includes the MTSA, briefly described earlier. The MTSA is in line with international legislation, especially that of the International Maritime Organization (IMO). The IMO implemented new regulations after 9/11 by amending existing and creating new relevant chapters of the International Convention for the Safety of Life at Sea (SOLAS).[12] A new International Ship and Port Facility Security Code (ISPS Code) was implemented and governments (and their port authorities) had to comply with the security requirements of this code. Both the ISPS Code and the MTSA have complementary features, leading to cooperative efforts in ensuring U.S. homeland security.

A major security initiative is the Free and Secure Trade Program (FAST), which is a border initiative among the United States, Mexico, and Canada, which allows importers and traders to participate in a voluntary compliance initiative.[13] If enrolled, FAST companies benefit as FAST shipments are deemed to be low-risk since the security of their supply chains has been previously evaluated and confirmed. Hence, FAST allows for more efficient shipment and movement of goods across the borders. The CBP's Customs Trade Partnership Against Terrorism (C-TPAT) program is yet another major post-September 11 initiative. C-TPAT is a voluntary, incentives-based supply chain security program with about 8,200 members. C-TPAT importers were said to be six times less likely to undergo a security-related cargo search and four times less likely to undergo a trade-related cargo search.[14] From March 25, 2005, importers interested in joining C-TPAT had to follow and meet specific basic security criteria, and currently enrolled companies also had to ensure these criteria were met before continuing on in the program. C-TPAT is part of CBP's goal to improve security along the entire supply line instead of only concentrating on U.S. ports and borders, since importers participating in C-TPAT have to make sure their business partners also comply with C-TPAT security standards. Information sharing is the key goal behind the Automated Information System (AIS). The AIS is also a post-September 11 program which uses satellite tracking to relay information about ships and where they are.[15] This will help in identifying the ships traveling to the U.S., making it easier to contain risks.

With all these initiatives and new regulations, Pacific maritime security has been evolving and changing, especially in the past few years. Ports are key elements in homeland security, especially the busy ports of Long Beach, Los Angeles, and Seattle on the Pacific coast. Ports not only deal with the landing and shipping of goods but also have terminal operations, cruises, cargo packing and trucking, ship repairs, banking services, storage, vessel fueling, forwarding freight, passenger terminals, car parks, shopping centers, hotels, and so on. Therefore, even after the landing of goods and passengers, there is a wide range of areas where security has to be ensured and constant vigilance maintained. Security therefore does not only mean protecting the ports but also ensuring the safety of services in surrounding areas and waterways and also other means of transportation. Trade and tourism operations at the three Pacific coast ports—Long Beach, Los Angeles, and Seattle—illustrate the amount of goods and people passing through ports annually and the economic and social impacts of any potential disruption through a terrorist threat or attack.

TRADE AND TOURISM IN LONG BEACH, LOS ANGELES, AND SEATTLE: THE IMPORTANCE OF PORTS TO MARITIME SECURITY IN THE U.S. PACIFIC COAST

Long Beach and Los Angeles Ports

Both Long Beach and Los Angeles are in the United States' most populous state of California, which means any potential terrorist attack in these ports could cause a great deal of damage, even if occurring within a relatively small area. In trade terms, California is the second largest producer of goods exported from the United States and is the largest recipient of foreign direct investment, all of which combine to make it an attractive place for investors but, at the same time, lead to a high volume of waterborne traffic. The ports are side by side but are operated differently: one by the city of Los Angeles and the other by the city of Long Beach. There are some joint infrastructural and transport facilities, such as the Intermodal Container Transfer Facility (ICTF). The ICTF is located approximately five miles from the ports of Los Angeles and Long Beach and serves both ports. It opened in 1986 and is used by various shipping lines. It moved more than 7 million containers from 1986 to 1999. Its main gates are open 24 hours per day and the facility can handle about 1,800 transactions daily.[16] But, mostly, trading is separate, with the ports of Long Beach and Los Angeles competing for business. In terms of world port rankings, Long Beach and Los Angeles combine to rank as the third busiest, just after Hong Kong and Singapore, in terms of TEU (twenty-foot equivalent units) volume.[17]

The Port of Long Beach

This is the third largest U.S. port for imports, after New York and Los Angeles. The port of Long Beach is the world's 12th busiest container cargo port and second largest container seaport in the United States, after Los Angeles. It supports nearly 30,000 jobs. This represents roughly about one in eight jobs in the city of Long Beach itself.[18] In Southern California overall, 315,000 jobs, or one in 22 jobs, are supported by the port, making its continued and uninterrupted operation essential to the California and U.S. economies. With regard to cargo, the port handled more than 4.6 million TEUs in 2003 with the cargo valued at nearly US$96 billion. This turned out to be, on average, the equivalent of 12,000 TEUs each day, which is a very high rate. The latest figures show an increase, with a total of nearly 5.8 million TEUs being transported through the port in 2004. The cargo value in 2004 was US$100 billion. The port covers 3,240 acres of land with 10 piers and 80 berths. It has a harbor staff of about 350 but many more associated employees. In 2001, the total value of goods imported into the city of Long Beach was about US$2.6 billion and the value of goods imported into Los Angeles County, through the port of Long Beach, was around US$29 billion. In 2003, the total value of the cargo through the port was nearly US$96 billion. Overall, trade has risen sharply, as container throughput has increased by 175 percent since 1990. The top imports are machinery, electrical machinery, vehicles, toys and sports equipment, and furniture and bedding. In 2005, the top five trading partners were China, South Korea, Hong Kong, Japan, and Malaysia, with neighboring Mexico close behind. Overall, trade with East Asia accounts for more than 90 percent of the shipments through the Long Beach port.[19] Therefore, the trans-Pacific route is very important to the continued workings of this port and any terrorist threat or attack that disrupts trade along this route is likely to havevery significant impact since the volumes of trade passing are very high.

The Port of Los Angeles

This is the second largest U.S. port for imports, after New York, and is physically the largest port complex. The port complex covers 7,500 acres, 3,300 acres of water and 4,200 of land. There are 26 cargo terminals with 8 juts for containers.[20] The Harbor Department employs 764 people; the entire port complex employs an additional 16,000 local jobs, 259,000 regional jobs, and more than 1 million jobs throughout the United States. Los Angeles' annual container volume was 7.4 million TEUs in 2004, an increase from 6.7 million TEUs in 2003. With regard to container volume, it is the eighth busiest container port in the world.[21] The cargo value was US$122 billion in 2003, a rise from US$110.3 billion in 2002. Facilities to transport goods from the harbor to the shipment areas include intermodalism, i.e., an integrated system of trains, vehicles, and light rail including doublestack train service which allows containers to be stacked at double the rate they usually are in other ports. There are five intermodal rail yards. This speeds up the transport of goods. The top five imports in 2003 were furniture, apparel, electronic products, toys, and computer equipment. The top trading partners were China, Japan, Taiwan,

Thailand, and South Korea, with 2,813 vessels arriving at the port in 2004 compared to 2,845 in 2003. Around 80 shipping lines call in at the port of Los Angeles, making surveillance, monitoring, and enforcement of security legislation highly complex.

With regard to tourism, there were 803,308 cruise passengers in 2004, a slight decrease from 1.01 million passengers in 2003.[22] More than 15 cruise lines call in at the port. In terms of cruise traffic, the LA port is the busiest in the West Coast and the fourth busiest in the United States. The World Cruise Center, located at the port, is the largest and busiest such facility on the Pacific coast. There are plans to increase this section of the port even further with a 20-acre expansion.

The Los Angeles port suffered a downturn in business in early 2005 with business down nearly 2 percent in 2005, compared to high increases in businesses at other U.S. ports.[23] The reasons for this decrease included a week-long record congestion that occurred in 2004 when the port could not handle a sudden increase in shipments. At one time, 83 ships were waiting to be unloaded at the ports of Los Angeles and Long Beach. Also, once unloading started, it was slower than usual, with each ship taking six to eight days, more than double the usual time.[24] Services remained slow in the first half of 2005.[25] Overall, ports seem unprepared to handle sudden changes in circumstances as is also evidenced by delays and slow-downs resulting from the 2002 West Coast port shutdowns. The 2002 labor dispute shut down all 29 Pacific coast ports for ten days. The recovery time from this shutdown was over a month, as ports had to deal with the backed-up incoming vessels and also with outgoing ships.[26] At that time, nearly 200 large container-carrying ships were stranded at various West Coast ports.[27] While the 2002 shutdown and the 2004 backup of ships in Los Angeles may be unrelated, the effects of both incidences were increased congestion among ships waiting to unload; decreased confidence among investors, producers, and receivers about the ports' abilities to handle rapid changes in circumstances; delays in the just-in-time delivery systems of companies; and increased concern about whether the ports are adequately prepared to continue operations or to deal with the aftermath in case of a security threat or an actual terrorist attack. Also, in both incidences, the economic damage to the ports and to the cities was high.

The Port of Seattle

The port of Seattle is the closest to Asia, compared to any other U.S. port. The number of vessels calling into the port of Seattle decreased from 1,095 during 2000 to 964 during 2001. But, the figure rose to 990 the year after and to 1,094 in 2004. Waterborne cargo volumes, especially international imports, decreased from 1,201,841 TEUs in 2000 to 1,052,789 TEUs in 2001 but have steadily increased to 1,466,251 in 2004. Seattle trades mostly with East Asia. Out of Seattle's top 20 trading partners, only Canada (at no. 13), Russia (at no. 14), and Chile (at no. 20) are not located in the Asia-Oceania region. In percentage terms ranked according to U.S. dollar value, around 93 percent of Seattle's total waterborne trade is done with Asia and another 1.7 percent with Oceania, making it that nearly 95 percent of Seattle's trading is conducted with the Asia-Oceania region. Apparel, vehicle parts, footwear, games, and video games and electrical equipment formed the top five imports through Seattle in 2004.[28] There was an increase of 35 percent in terms of inbound container cargo through Seattle between 2004 and 2005.[29]

In Seattle, tourism is a growing industry as well. An estimated 345,000 passengers passed through the port as part of cruise travel in 2003. The number rose sharply to 563,000 in 2004 and rose further to 686,357 in 2005. An estimated 735,000 passengers are expected to pass through Seattle in 2006. The number of cruise ships passing through the port has also increased steadily with 170 ships passing through in 2005. The number is expected to rise even further in 2006.[30] Almost all cruise lines from Seattle have services from Seattle to Alaska and shorter cruises to other Pacific Northwest areas. This makes transport and movement of people through the Pacific coastal areas easy and also difficult to monitor.

Domestically, similar to Long Beach and Los Angeles, the port of Seattle is part of the city itself, but in the case of Seattle, the docks are only separated from the city by a highway viaduct which was built in the early 1950s. Seattle is also the closest metropolitan city to Pyongyang and the threat of airborne strikes can be said to be higher in Seattle than in other U.S. cities. The cargo terminals for the port are located in an area which also has the Safeco Field, the sports stadium for Seattle's popular baseball and football teams. The same area also has a new cruise terminal and the terminal and offices for the Washington State ferries. This, as well, makes Seattle vulnerable if there were to be a large-scale attack on the port, since associated businesses and venues are all concentrated within a reasonably small area.

MARITIME SECURITY CHALLENGES AND RECOMMENDATIONS FOR THE U.S. PACIFIC COAST

As can be seen from the above examples of the Long Beach, Los Angeles, and Seattle ports, there are major challenges involved in Pacific maritime security due to the high volume of goods and people moving through these ports. This is especially true in the case of tourism and trade since the majority of U.S. trade to and from the Asia-Pacific region is conducted through these ports. Any attack on these ports would not only cause deaths and damages but also greatly impact the U.S. economy and, therefore, the global economy. Even the possibility of such attacks is likely to reduce confidence among the United States' trading partners, leading to loss of much-needed trade revenue and also increasing job-related stress and uncertainty for port employees. With respect to tourism, as can be seen from the high number of cruise ships passing through the ports under discussion, the effect on the travel industry in case of suspected or real insecurity in the ports would be high. The brief shutdown of ports in 2002 showed how the entire trading system can be disrupted. Therefore, even minor delays in the time taken for ships to enter U.S. ports can lead to high losses, damage ports' and companies' reputations overseas, and negatively impact the job market. Some of the other related challenges and recommendations on how to deal with them are briefly outlined in the following:

Geographical vastness: This is a twofold challenge. On the one hand, maritime security efforts in the Pacific have to include Hawaii and Guam as well as survey and patrol the large expanse of the Pacific Ocean trading and shipping routes. On the other hand, the Pacific coastline of the United States stretches for 1300 miles (excluding Alaska) and patrolling this is itself a difficult endeavor.[31] The U.S. Coast Guard, which has the main responsibility for this, is already overstretched and dependent upon an aging fleet of equipment and ships.[32] Also, while the southern parts of the Pacific coastline are fairly smooth and regular, the northern parts, especially in northern California, Oregon, and Washington, are irregular. This means the coastline dips and juts out to form a number of bays, fjords, peninsulas, and islands, many of them in fairly remote areas. This makes it difficult to keep all such areas under surveillance. Also, the irregular coastline and remote areas facilitate the illegal movement of people, since the remote bays and inlets can provide places for hiding. In addition, the Alaskan coastline—in the Pacific and Arctic Oceans—is around 6,640 miles long and most of it is unpopulated, making travel difficult, but also making surveillance nearly impossible. Most of the coastline of Alaska consists of bays, fjords, and mountains, especially in the southern, more accessible areas, making it easy for people to travel undetected.[33]

Recommendations for dealing with geographical challenges include improving surveillance technologies and adding such technologies to various remote parts of the coastline. The U.S. Coast Guard has already taken steps with using radar and remote-controlled underwater vehicles to keep vessels under surveillance.[34] Also, focusing on using and integrating new technologies to survey remote areas would help in reducing long-term costs since such technologies would mean security personnel could concentrate on other, more densely populated areas, where they could reinforce technologies by on-the-ground and on-sea patrols.

Proximity of ports to population centers: This is a major challenge in the case of Seattle and also San Francisco and Los Angeles. In Seattle, the port is closely connected to the city of nearly 4 million people. Seattle is located directly on Eliott Bay in Puget Sound, only around 113 miles south of the Canadian border. This means an attack on the port could lead to high casualties because of its proximity to downtown Seattle. Los Angeles is the busiest port and the largest populated area on the Pacific coast, making it vulnerable to attacks. The densely packed city area, with thousands of people and numerous ships and businesses, could make it easy for terrorists to evade surveillance and blend in with the crowd. Also, any damage would lead to high human and economic costs due to the concentration of people and services. As seen in previously described cases of the 2002 ports shutdown and the 2004 logjam in Los Angeles, even a slight disruption of services of the ports can lead to high losses. In addition to foreign trade and tourism, the ports also have extensive fish-processing facilities and numerous fishing boats make trips up and down the coast. Such boats, usually being small and fast and also, often, not having a permanent base, are extremely difficult to keep under surveillance. The government and the state could combine to assist fishing boat companies and fishing boat owners and operators to report their activities to each other and form information-sharing networks by setting up Internet-based user groups and listservs. This would be very helpful in coordinating data, finding out where different boats are located, and ensuring that any suspicious activities are reported quickly to the authorities concerned.

Linkage of trade and tourism: The close connection between trade and tourism means the possibility of high economic impact and also impact on the future of trading and tourism should any security breach occur. People lose confidence when there is a lack of security in the ports or at the cruise centers. Also, a delay at any of the ports (or all of the ports) can decrease confidence in trading partners—this was seen in the case of Los Angeles, which lost some of its trade based on the 2004 congestion when ships were not unloaded as fast as they should have been, leading to backlog and extended delays. This was due to a lack of infrastructure and personnel to cope with a sudden rise in trade volume.[35] While the Los Angeles port Web site claims that such problems have been dealt with by providing increased numbers of workers and better facilities, trade recovery has been slow. Such shutdowns, for whatever reason, can greatly affect the economic growth of the Pacific coastal region and also affect the U.S. economy and disrupt the livelihoods of millions of people who are dependent on the activities of these ports, either directly or indirectly. Any attack on a port disrupts its operations and potentially destroys infrastructure. IAn attack would affect all the people who are dependent on the smooth running of the ports for their living and could lead to high levels of unemployment or underemployment throughout the United States. Recommendations for preventing damage from port shutdowns or slowdowns include increasing cooperation among the different levels of authority such as the federal government, the state government, the port authorities, and the shipping and tour operators. It must be made clear that everyone benefits from increased security. Also, information sharing is important, especially consolidating different types of information into a central database, if possible, so names of passengers and crew can be checked.

Recent and ongoing changes in regulations: Most of the regulations and compliance requirements described above and most of the agencies themselves have come about since September 11, 2001. This means that there is a short history of knowing how compliance has occurred and determining whether any changes in regulations are necessary. In the case of very recent changes, such as C-TPAT's requirement for companies registering with it to have minimum safety standards, the time and effort needed to comply and to monitor compliance could be high. Also, the increased checking of cargo and screening of crew and passengers adds valuable time to the time cargo spends at sea or at ports and to the time people spend boarding and disembarking cruise ships. Most of the importers and exporters in the United States, as well as companies in other countries which export goods to the United States, are slowly getting used to the new regulations, but this takes time. In terms of travel, increased security is seen in a more thorough approach to checking the luggage and hand-carried goods of cruise passengers. Also, in many cases, only people with cruise tickets are allowed to board the cruise ships. Recommendations for making sure ship operators here in the United States and overseas understand the new legislation and what they have to do to comply with them include having publicity campaigns both in the United States and overseas about the new requirements for entry and also about the documentation (both paper and/or electronic) required before a ship is allowed to sail for and enter the United States. This is a recommendation not only for governments but also for shipowners and operators. Thus, the entire supply chain has to cooperate in ensuring better security. Better understanding of the laws will facilitate quick turnaround of goods since all the needed documents will be ready.

Advanced technologies: These make surveillance and detection easier but also make it easier for potential terrorists to set off remote bombs, etc. As explained above, there are areas where small boats can cross from Canada or Alaska or from Mexico into the United States, and the fact that the patrol of the coasts is done by the relatively small U.S. Coast Guard means that there are areas where incoming vessels may be able to avoid detection. Therefore, development and use of new technologies, such as radiation monitors, aerial surveillance, and other types of water- and land-based surveillance are needed to ensure the Pacific coastal areas remain safe. Technologies include the use of smart containers, which are containers that can share information if their locks are opened in unauthorized areas by unauthorized persons. New improved surveillance and satellite tracking will be important in securing the Pacific coast of the United States. In one Coast Guard initiative explained earlier, remote-controlled underwater marine surveillance vessels are being used to examine the underneath of large vessels to make sure no unauthorized object or person is present. Even if technologies may be expensive in the short term, their investment return will be high in the longer term. It is essential to work in coordination with the private sector for developing newer and better technologies to ensure safety along the global supply and distribution chains.

Private fishing boats and tours: As described above, these are difficult to regulate and to keep under surveillance. However, working with fishermen's groups, fishing boat owners and operators, and local communities is likely to lead to better results in terms of increased surveillance and awareness of threats.

Bioterrorism: The threat from bioterrorism is especially high in waterborne traffic. In cruise ships, as seen in a few cases in the past few years, a virus can spread easily, affecting thousands of passengers and crew. In container cargo, one contaminated container can lead to security risks of high proportions, especially if it is allowed to enter the United States undetected. Hence, it is essential to maintain security along the entire supply chain rather than focusing only on entry points.

CONCLUSION

Thus, demonstrated by the examples provided in this discussion of trade and tourism in the three major West Coast ports, there are multidimensional challenges involved when dealing with security on our nation's Pacific coast. As both trade and tourism involve various other countries, it is difficult to draw boundaries as to where homeland security stops and external security begins. This means it is also difficult, if not impossible, to focus homeland security efforts, especially with respect to Pacific maritime security, only on certain regions. A broad definition and comprehensive enforcement of security, involving security along entire supply chains, and a focus on interagency and international cooperation must be implemented if the United States is to be successful in maintaining Pacific security.

One recent measure to ensure maritime security involves simulated emergency scenarios for preparing against potential terrorist acts. For example, on September 25, 2005, in Seattle, the Marine Terrorism Response Exercise involved four simulated emergency scenarios for preparation in case of terrorist attacks. Two were "on paper only" scenarios but the other two were full-scale simulations. Funded by a $2 million grant from the Department of Homeland Security, a wide range of agencies worked together to conduct it. The focus was therefore on coordinated efforts to maintain security, and this focus has to continue, since U.S. security is linked to global security, especially in the case of Pacific maritime security where a lot of goods and services are involved.

Overall, recommendations for the U.S. government, state governments, port authorities, and the private sector are to increase and strengthen ties among each other for information sharing, technology development, and dissemination and publicity of new initiatives and regulations. International cooperation is also key since maritime security of the Pacific coastal areas involves—as described throughout this chapter—not just local but global trading and tourism connections and globally-based actors such as transnational shipping companies and cruise lines. Therefore, it is important for the United States to cooperate with transnational corporations (such as shipping and cruise companies), other governments, private sector organizations, and local communities. In addition to technology dissemination and sharing of information, coordination and cooperation with other partners, both local and transnational, will help in sharing the expenses of new technology development and of implementing changes in regulations.

Such an emphasis on coordinated efforts to ensure security has extended to external cooperation, and some initiatives are already under way. Since 2003, Seattle has been part of the Asia Pacific Economic Cooperation (APEC) Secure Trade in the APEC Region (STAR) program. There have been cooperation efforts and bilateral agreements on security enhancement, especially container security, with Thailand, Singapore, and Hong Kong. As part of these bilateral agreements, U.S.-bound cargo at foreign ports in these countries will be catalogued and inspected to make sure the cargo is secure. This will also facilitate the tracking of cargo during the ship's voyage to the United States. The Port of Seattle is the first port in the United States to enter into formal agreements with these countries to ensure container safety.[36]

Overall, homeland security is a contentious issue, especially in the case of maritime security, since maritime security is more closely bound up with external security than are other types of security. For instance, as seen above, high levels of trade are ongoing between the United States and other countries, and securing this trading system means making sure the shipments are safe at the port from which they originate as well as at various ports in-between. Just focusing on the Pacific coast and on the ports on the United States mainland is not enough. Similarly, cruise companies are often based outside the United States, hire their employees outside the United States, and call at ports in many different countries.

However, it is important to balance surveillance and the need to have up-to-date records of vessels, goods, and passengers with concern about the civil rights of people. Indiscriminate surveillance or inspections based on country of origin, the location of ports where the cruise ship or container vessel has called, or on the nationalities of the people working on the ships would lead to negative perceptions of the United States overseas. This would affect trading and tourism in the United States as well as potential cooperation efforts with trading partners. Right now, trade with Asia is growing rapidly. For instance, shipboard container traffic out of China is growing at an annual rate of 15 percent.[37] Along with increased trade comes the need for increased but nonintrusive security measures. Thus, there has to be a balance between securing the coasts, patrolling the seas, and ensuring trading partners and visitors are treated with consideration. Increased cooperation with local and overseas partners (along the lines of the CSI initiative and Seattle's links with Southeast Asian countries) and better interagency coordination are key to achieving a safer, more secure United States.

NOTES

1. "United States Geography," *MSN Encarta Encyclopedia,* http://encarta.msn.com/encyclopedia_1741500822_20/United_States_(Geography).html (accessed September 20, 2005).

2. "Establishment of U.S. Antiterrorism Maritime Transportation System," *The American Journal of International Law,* 98, no. 3 (July 2004): 588.

3. Economist Intelligence Unit, "Country Report for the United States," September 2005, http://www.eiu.com.

4. "Establishment of U.S. Antiterrorism Maritime Transportation System," 588.

5. "C-TPAT Frequently Asked Questions," http://cbp.gov/xp/cgov/import/commercial_enforcement/ctpat/ctpat_faq.xml (accessed September 20, 2005).

6. For more on the role of the U.S. Coast Guard, please see the chapter in this volume by Joe DiRenzo and Chris Doane.

7. U.S. Customs and Border Protection Web site, http://www.cbp.gov (accessed October 3, 2005).

8. Container Security Initiative (CSI) Web site, http://www.cbp.gov/xp/cgov/border_security/international_activities/csi (accessed October 3, 2005).

9. "Downloadable CSI Fact Sheet," July 2005, http://www.cbp.gov/xp/cgov/border_security/international_activities/csi/ (accessed October 3, 2005).

10. For more on international cooperation for maritime security, please see the chapter in this volume by Tracey Gray and Frank Jones .

11. U.S. Customs and Border Protection Web site, http://www.cbp.gov (accessed October 3, 2005).

12. The International Maritime Organization (IMO) adopted a series of measures in December 2002 to strengthen maritime security worldwide in the post-9/11 era. As part of these measures, the IMO amended and added to the chapters of the International Convention for the Safety of Life and Sea (SOLAS). The most wide-ranging of these changes was the implementation of a new International Ship and Port Facility Security Code (ISPS Code). The new global security regime went into force in July 2004. Part A of the ISPS Code contains mandatory security-related requirements for governments, port authorities, and shipping companies,

and Part B, a nonmandatory section, consists of guidelines on how to meet these requirements as efficiently as possible. Further information is available at the IMO Web site, http://www.imo.org/About/mainframe.asp?topic_id=583&doc_id=2689.

13. "FAST Reference Guide," March 2005, http://www.cbp.gov/linkhandler/cgov/import/commercial_enforcement/ctpat/fast/fast_ref_guide.ctt/fast_ref_guide.pdf (accessed October 3, 2005).

14. "C-TPAT Frequently Asked Questions," http://cbp.gov/xp/cgov/import/commercial_enforcement/ctpat/ctpat_faq.xml (accessed September 20, 2005).

15. Ted McKenna, "Armed and Ready," *JED, the Journal of Electronic Defense* (August 2003): 47.

16. Port of Los Angeles Web site, www.portoflosangeles.org. Statistics available at "Port at a Glance," http://www.portoflosangeles.org/factsfigures_Portataglance.htm and also at "Annual Statistics," http://www.portoflosangeles.org/factsfigures_Annual.htm (accessed October 2, 2005).

17. "World Port Rankings for 2003, by Container Traffic"; available at the American Association of Port Authorities Web site, http://www.aapa-ports.org/pdf/WORLD_PORT_RANKINGS_2003.xls (accessed October 2, 2005).

18. Port of Long Beach Web site, http://www.polb.com/. Specific data are available at "Overview," http://www.polb.com/html/1_about/overview.html; "Yearly TEUs" (for annual trade figures), http://www.polb.com/html/1_about/ps_teusAnnual.html; and "Port Statistics Index" (for information about related statistics),http://www.polb.com/html/1_about/portStatsMain.html (accessed October 3, 2005).

19. Ibid.

20. Port of Los Angeles Web site, www.portoflosangeles.org. Statistics available at "Port at a Glance," http://www.portoflosangeles.org/factsfigures_Portataglance.htm and also at "Annual Statistics," http://www.portoflosangeles.org/factsfigures_Annual.htm (accessed October 2, 2005).

21. Ibid.

22. Ibid.

23. Ronald D. White, "Image Woes Shrink Traffic at Port; Business is Down 2% at the L.A. Facility, Partly Because of Memories of Congestion Last Year,"*Los Angeles Times,* August 28, 2005, C1.

24. Doug Bartholomew, "Cargo Crunch!," *Industry Week* (March 2005): 43.

25. Ibid., 44.

26. "West Coast Port Congestion Easing," *CNN,* http://archives.cnn.com/2002/US/West/11/11/port.cargo.ap/ (accessed October 3, 2005).

27. Doug Bartholomew, "Cargo Crunch!," 44.

28. Port of Seattle Web site; seaport information available at www.portofseattle.org/seaport; statistics available at www.portofseattle.org/seaport/statistics/ (accessed March 12, 2006). Please see http://www.portseattle.org/seaport/statistics/cruisepassengers.shtml for details on cruise passenger figures and http://www.portseattle.org/seaport/statistics/vesselcalls.shtml#type for the types of ships entering the port.

29. Ronald D. White, "Image Woes Shrink Traffic at Port; Business is Down 2% at the L.A. Facility, Partly Because of Memories of Congestion Last Year,"*Los Angeles Times,* August 28, 2005, C1.

30. Port of Seattle Web site; seaport information available at www.portofseattle.org/seaport; statistics available at www.portofseattle.org/seaport/statistics/ (accessed March 12, 2006). Please see http://www.portseattle.org/seaport/statistics/cruisepassengers.shtml for details on cruise passenger figures and http://www.portseattle.org/seaport/statistics/vesselcalls.shtml#type for the types of ships entering the port.

31. "United States Geography," *MSN Encarta Encyclopedia,* http://encarta.msn.com/encyclopedia_1741500822_20/United_States_(Geography).html (accessed September 20, 2005).

32. Mimi Hall, "Coast Guard Plagued by Breakdowns," *USA Today,* July 6, 2005.

33. For more on the unique challenges of homeland security in Alaska, please see the chapter in this volume by Jerry Kidrick.

34. Ted McKenna, "Armed and Ready," 49.

35. Ronald D. White, "Image Woes Shrink Traffic at Port; Business is Down 2% at the L.A. Facility, Partly Because of Memories of Congestion Last Year,"*Los Angeles Times,* August 28, 2005, C1.

36. Port of Seattle Web site, http://www.portofseattle.org/seaport/.

37. Chris Kraul and Deborah Schoch, "Major Port Proposed for Baja Region; Shippers Want to Build in Mexico Because of Logjams at the Complex in L.A. and Long Beach," *Los Angeles Times,* April 9, 2005, A1.

APPENDIX A

U.S. STRATEGIC POLICIES OF HOMELAND, BORDER, AND PORT SECURITY

While the attacks of September 11, 2001, brought the issue of homeland security to the attention of the entire nation, Congress had already chartered several commissions to examine terrorist threats and the government's response to such threats.[1] Examples include the President's Commission on Aviation Security and Terrorism, which issued its final report in May 1990, the Bremer Commission (the National Commission on Terrorism, chaired by Ambassador Paul Bremer), which issued its report in June 2000, and the Hart-Rudman Commission (the U.S. Commission on National Security/21st Century, chaired by Senators Gary Hart and Warren B. Rudman), which issued its final report in March 2001. The recommendations of these commissions were the subject of extensive policy debate in Washington, D.C., but it can be argued that they received far less public attention than their post-9/11 siblings, like the Gilmore Commission (the Advisory Panel to Assess Domestic Response Capabilities for Terrorism Involving Weapons of Mass Destruction, chaired by Governor James S. Gilmore III), which issued its final report in December 2003, and the 9/11 Commission (the National Commission on Terrorist Attacks Upon the United States, chaired by Governor Thomas H. Kean), which issued its final report in July 2004.[2]

These commissions, in turn, have influenced a flurry of Congressional legislation and national strategic documents which help frame our understanding of the homeland security environment and our efforts to improve it. For example, Congress passed the *Airport and Transportation Security Act of 2001*, the *Homeland Security Act of 2002*, the *Uniting and Strengthening America by Providing Appropriate Tools Required to Intercept and Obstruct Terrorism Act* (better known by its acronym, the *USA PATRIOT Act*), the *Maritime Security Act of 2002*, and the *Enhanced Border Security*

Act of 2002, among many others. These kinds of homeland security legisla-tion provide a legal framework within which the U.S. government can work to combat terrorism, among other threats to homeland security. The works of the Congressional commissions have also informed several important strategic documents which articulate how the nation will go about the daunting task of improving homeland security.

To begin with, the overarching strategic document for U.S. national security is the *National Security Strategy of the United States* (NSS), pub-lished by the White House in 2002. The NSS identifies the national secur-ity goals of the United States, describes the foreign policy and military capabilities necessary to achieve those goals, evaluates the current status of these capabilities, and explains how national power will be structured to utilize these capabilities. It devotes a chapter to combating terrorism that focuses on the disruption and destruction of terrorist organizations, the winning of the "war of ideas," the strengthening of homeland security, and the fostering of cooperation with allies and international organiza-tions to combat terrorism.[3] Strategic documents like this are important in that they frame our understanding of and response to the "big picture" of threats to our nation's security. In 2004, the U.S. Government Account-ability Office (GAO) published a report which identifies the main ele-ments of a strategy that make it useful for homeland security efforts at the federal, state and local level (see Table A.1).

Our national effort to improve homeland security since 9/11 is driven by the overall *National Security Strategy* that includes many of the ele-ments identified in the GAO report. For example, it defines a clear purpose (securing the nation), defines key terms, identifies roles and responsibilities, and articulates an envisioned "end-state." Four major action steps are also identified in the NSS:

1. Strengthen alliances to defeat global terrorism and work to prevent attacks against us;
2. Prevent our enemies from threatening us with weapons of mass destruction;
3. Ignite a new era of global growth through free markets and free trade; and
4. Transform America's national security institutions to meet the challenges and opportunities of the twenty-first century.[4]

However, given the enormous complexity of securing a nation as large (in both territory and population) as the United States, there is a consider-able need for more details on how to address specific aspects of homeland security. Thus, the White House has also issued several new strategic documents that relate to specific aspects of homeland security and com-bating terrorism. These include the *National Strategy for Homeland Security* (NSHS), the *National Strategy for Maritime Security,* the *National Strategy for*

Table A.1   Desirable Characteristics for a National Strategy

A national strategy should address . . .	For example, it should include . . .
why the strategy was produced, the scope of its coverage, and the process by which it was developed;	• A statement of broad or narrow purpose, as appropriate. • How it compares and contrasts with other national strategies. • What major functions, mission areas, or activities it covers. • Principles or theories that guided its development. • Impetus for strategy, e.g., statutory requirement or event. • Process to produce strategy, e.g., interagency task force; state, local, or private input. • Definition of key terms.
the particular national problems and threats the strategy is directed towards;	• Discussion or definition of problems, their causes, and operating environment. • Risk assessment, including an analysis of threats and vulnerabilities. • Quality of data available, e.g., constraints, deficiencies, and "unknowns."
what the strategy is trying to achieve, steps to achieve those results, as well as the priorities, milestones, and performance measures to gauge results;	• Overall results desired, i.e., "end-state." • Hierarchy of strategic goals and subordinate objectives. • Specific activities to achieve results. • Priorities, milestones, and outcome-related performance measures. • Specific performance measures. • Process for monitoring and reporting on progress. • Limitations on progress indicators.
what the strategy will cost, the sources and types of resources and investments needed, and where resources and investments should be targeted by balancing risk reductions and costs;	• Resources and investments associated with the strategy. • Types of resources required, such as budgetary, human capital, information technology, research and development, contracts. • Sources of resources, e.g., federal, state, local, and private. • Economic principles, such as balancing benefits and costs. • Resource allocation mechanisms, such as grants, in-kind services, loans, or user fees. • "Tools of government," e.g., mandates or incentives to spur action. • Importance of fiscal discipline. • Linkage to other resource documents, e.g., federal budget. • Risk management principles.

who will be implementing the strategy, what their roles will be compared to others, and mechanisms for them to coordinate their efforts; and	• Roles and responsibilities of specific federal agencies, departments, or offices. • Roles and responsibilities of state, local, private, and international sectors. • Lead, support, and partner roles and responsibilities. • Accountability and oversight framework. • Potential changes to current organizational structure. • Specific processes for coordination and collaboration. • How conflicts will be resolved.
how a national strategy relates to other strategies' goals, objectives and activities—and to subordinate levels of government and their plans to implement the strategy.	• Integration with other national strategies (horizontal). • Integration with relevant documents from implementing organizations (vertical). • Details on specific federal, state, local, or private strategies and plans. • Implementation guidance. • Details on subordinate strategies and plans for implementation, e.g., human capital, and enterprise architecture.

Source: Government Accounting Office (GAO-04-408T), 2004.

the Physical Protection of Critical Infrastructure and Key Assets, the *National Strategy to Secure Cyberspace,* the *National Strategy for Combating Terrorism,* and the *National Strategy to Combat Weapons of Mass Destruction.* In addition, the Administration published the *2002 National Money Laundering Strategy,* which was updated from pre-September 11 versions to specifically include terrorism. Table A.2 provides a brief description for each of these strategies.[5]

These strategies are national in scope, cutting across levels of government and sectors and involving a large number of organizations and entities (i.e., the federal, state, local, and private sectors). In addition, national strategies frequently have international components, and they may be part of a structure of overlapping or supporting national strategies. Furthermore, the federal government does not control many of the sectors, organizations, entities, and resources involved in implementing the national strategies.[6] On the more detailed level of implementation, however, the national homeland security effort is best understood by the U.S. federal agency-specific strategic plans like the *National Border Patrol Strategy* and the Coast Guard's *Maritime Strategy for Homeland Security,* as well as state and local strategic plans for improving security and responding to emergencies.

Together, these national strategies and agency-specific plans frame our understanding of homeland security. The remaining pages of this

Table A.2   Specific National Strategies in Support of Homeland Security

Strategy	Description of the Strategy
National Strategy for Homeland Security Issued by the President, July 2002	The *Homeland Security* strategy addresses the threat of terrorism in the United States by organizing the domestic efforts of federal, state, local, and private organizations. It aligns and focuses homeland security functions into six critical mission areas, set forth as (1) intelligence and warning, (2) border and transportation security, (3) domestic counterterrorism, (4) protecting critical infrastructure and key assets, (5) defending against catastrophic threats, and (6) emergency preparedness and response. Additionally, it describes four foundations that cut across all the mission areas, across all levels of government, and across all sectors of society as being (1) law, (2) science and technology, (3) information sharing and systems, and (4) international cooperation. It also addresses the costs of homeland security and future priorities.
National Strategy for Combating Terrorism Issued by the President, February 2003	The *Combating Terrorism* strategy elaborates on the terrorism aspects of the *National Security* strategy by expounding on the need to destroy terrorist organizations, win the "war of ideas," and strengthen security at home and abroad. Unlike the *Homeland Security* strategy that focuses on preventing terrorist attacks within the United States, the *Combating Terrorism* strategy focuses on identifying and defusing threats before they reach the borders of the United States. In that sense, although it has defensive elements, this strategy is an offensive strategy to complement the defensive *Homeland Security* strategy.
National Strategy to Combat Weapons of Mass Destruction Issued by the President, December 2002	The *Weapons of Mass Destruction* strategy presents a national strategy to combat weapons of mass destruction (WMD) through three major efforts: (1) nonproliferation, (2) counterproliferation, and (3) consequence management in WMD incidents. The plan addresses the production and proliferation of WMD among nations, as well as the potential threat of terrorists using WMD agents.

National Strategy for the Physical Protection of Critical Infrastructures and Key Assets Issued by the President, February 2003

The *Physical Infrastructure* strategy provides a statement of national policy to remain committed to protecting critical infrastructures and key assets from terrorist attacks and is based on eight guiding principles, including establishing responsibility and accountability, encouraging and facilitating partnering among all levels of government and between government and industry, and encouraging market solutions wherever possible and government intervention when needed. The strategy also establishes three strategic objectives. The first is to identify and assure the protection of the most critical assets, systems, and functions, in terms of national level public health and safety, governance, and economic and national security and public confidence. The second is to ensure protection of infrastructures and assets facing specific, imminent threats. The third is to pursue collaborative measures and initiatives to ensure the protection of other potential targets that may become attractive over time.

National Strategy to Secure Cyberspace Issued by the President, February 2003

The *Secure Cyberspace* strategy is intended to provide an initial framework for both organizing and prioritizing efforts to protect our nation's cyberspace. Also, it is to provide direction to federal departments and agencies that have roles in cyberspace security and to identify steps that state and local governments, private companies and organizations, and individual Americans can take to improve the nation's collective cybersecurity. The strategy is organized according to five national priorities, with major actions and initiatives identified for each. These priorities are: (1) a National Cyberspace Security Response System, (2) a National Cyberspace Security Threat and Vulnerability Reduction Program, (3) a National Cyberspace Security Awareness and Training Program, (4) Securing Governments' Cyberspace, and (5) National Security and International Cyberspace Security Cooperation. In describing the threats to, and vulnerabilities of, our nation's cyberspace, the strategy highlights the potential for damage to U.S. information systems from attacks by terrorist organizations.

| 2002 *National Money Laundering Strategy* Issued by the Secretary of the Treasury and the Attorney General, July 2002 | The *Money Laundering* strategy is intended to support planning for the efforts of law enforcement agencies, regulatory officials, the private sector, and overseas entities to combat the laundering of money generated from criminal activities. Although the 2002 strategy still addresses general criminal financial activity, that plan outlines a major governmentwide strategy to combat terrorist financing. The strategy discusses the need to adapt traditional methods of combating money laundering to unconventional tools used by terrorist organizations to finance their operations. |

Source: Government Accounting Office (GAO-04-408T), 2004.

appendix contain the Executive Summary of the *National Strategy for Homeland Security,* while Appendices B, C, and D review the strategic policy documents that pertain to the two specific areas of concern for this volume: border security and maritime/port security.

THE NATIONAL STRATEGY FOR HOMELAND SECURITY
EXECUTIVE SUMMARY

July 16, 2002

This document is the first *National Strategy for Homeland Security.* The purpose of the *Strategy* is to mobilize and organize our Nation to secure the U.S. homeland from terrorist attacks. This is an exceedingly complex mission that requires coordinated and focused effort from our entire society—the federal government, state and local governments, the private sector, and the American people.[7]

People and organizations all across the United States have taken many steps to improve our security since the September 11 attacks, but a great deal of work remains. The *National Strategy for Homeland Security* will help to prepare our Nation for the work ahead in several ways. It provides direction to the federal government departments and agencies that have a role in homeland security. It suggests steps that state and local governments, private companies and organizations, and individual Americans can take to improve our security and offers incentives for them to do so. It recommends certain actions to the Congress. In this way, the *Strategy* provides a framework for the contributions that we all can make to secure our homeland.

The *National Strategy for Homeland Security* is the beginning of what will be a long struggle to protect our Nation from terrorism. It establishes a foundation upon which to organize our efforts and provides initial guidance to prioritize the work ahead. The *Strategy* will be adjusted and amended over time. We must be prepared to adapt as our enemies in the war on terrorism alter their means of attack.

STRATEGIC OBJECTIVES

The strategic objectives of homeland security in order of priority are to:

- Prevent terrorist attacks within the United States;
- Reduce America's vulnerability to terrorism; and
- Minimize the damage and recover from attacks that do occur.

THREAT AND VULNERABILITY

Unless we act to prevent it, a new wave of terrorism, potentially involving the world's most destructive weapons, looms in America's future. It is a challenge as formidable as any ever faced by our Nation. But we are not daunted. We possess the determination and the resources to defeat our enemies and secure our homeland against the threats they pose.

One fact dominates all homeland security threat assessments: terrorists are strategic actors. They choose their targets deliberately based on the weaknesses they observe in our defenses and our preparedness. We must defend ourselves against a wide range of means and methods of attack. Our enemies are working to obtain chemical, biological, radiological, and nuclear weapons for the purpose of wreaking unprecedented damage on America. Terrorists continue to employ conventional means of attack, while at the same time gaining expertise in less traditional means, such as cyber attacks. Our society presents an almost infinite array of potential targets that can be attacked through a variety of methods.

Our enemies seek to remain invisible, lurking in the shadows. We are actively engaged in uncovering them. Al-Qaeda remains America's most immediate and serious threat despite our success in disrupting its network in Afghanistan and elsewhere. Other international terrorist organizations, as well as domestic terrorist groups, possess the will and capability to attack the United States.

ORGANIZING FOR A SECURE HOMELAND

In response to the homeland security challenge facing us, the President has proposed, and the Congress is presently considering, the most extensive reorganization of the federal government in the past fifty years. The establishment of a new Department of Homeland Security would ensure greater accountability over critical homeland security missions and unity of purpose among the agencies responsible for them.[8]

American democracy is rooted in the precepts of federalism—a system of government in which our state governments share power with federal institutions. Our structure of overlapping federal, state, and local governance—our country has more than 87,000 different jurisdictions—provides unique opportunity and challenges for our homeland security efforts. The opportunity comes from the expertise and commitment of local agencies and organizations involved in homeland security. The challenge is to develop interconnected and complementary systems that are reinforcing rather than duplicative and that ensure essential requirements are met. A national strategy requires a national effort.

State and local governments have critical roles to play in homeland security. Indeed, the closest relationship the average citizen has with government is at the local level. State and local levels of government have primary responsibility for funding, preparing, and operating the emergency services that would respond in the event of a terrorist attack. Local units are the first to respond, and the last to leave the scene. All disasters are ultimately local events.

The private sector—the Nation's principal provider of goods and services and owner of 85% of our infrastructure—is a key homeland security partner. It has a wealth of information that is important to the task of protecting the United States from terrorism. Its creative genius will develop the information systems, vaccines, detection devices, and other technologies and innovations that will secure our homeland.

An informed and proactive citizenry is an invaluable asset for our country in times of war and peace. Volunteers enhance community coordination and action, whether at the national or local level. This coordination will prove critical as we work to build the communication and delivery systems indispensable to our national effort to detect, prevent, and, if need be, respond to terrorist attack.

CRITICAL MISSION AREAS

The *National Strategy for Homeland Security* aligns and focuses homeland security functions into six critical mission areas: intelligence and warning, border and transportation security, domestic counterterrorism, protecting critical infrastructure, defending against catastrophic terrorism, and emergency preparedness and response. The first three mission areas focus primarily on preventing terrorist attacks; the next two on reducing our Nation's vulnerabilities; and the final one on minimizing the damage and recovering from attacks that do occur. The *Strategy* provides a framework to align the resources of the federal budget directly to the task of securing the homeland.

Intelligence and Warning

Terrorism depends on surprise. With it, a terrorist attack has the potential to do massive damage to an unwitting and unprepared target. Without it, the terrorists stand a good chance of being preempted by authorities, and even if they are not, the damage that results from their attacks is likely to be less severe. The United States will take every necessary action to avoid being surprised by another terrorist attack. We must have an intelligence and warning system that can detect terrorist activity before it manifests itself in an attack so that proper preemptive, preventive, and protective action can be taken.

The *National Strategy for Homeland Security* identifies five major initiatives in this area:

- Enhance the analytic capabilities of the FBI;
- Build new capabilities through the Information Analysis and Infrastructure Protection Division of the proposed Department of Homeland Security;
- Implement the Homeland Security Advisory System;
- Utilize dual-use analysis to prevent attacks; and
- Employ "red team" techniques.

Border and Transportation Security

America historically has relied heavily on two vast oceans and two friendly neighbors for border security, and on the private sector for most forms of domestic transportation security. The increasing mobility and destructive potential of modern terrorism has required the United States to rethink and renovate fundamentally its systems for border and transportation security. Indeed, we must now begin to conceive of border security and transportation security as fully integrated requirements because our domestic transportation systems are inextricably intertwined with the global transport infrastructure. Virtually every community in America is connected to the global transportation network by the seaports, airports, highways, pipelines, railroads, and waterways that move people and goods into, within, and out of the Nation. We must therefore promote the efficient and reliable flow of people, goods, and services across borders, while preventing terrorists from using transportation conveyances or systems to deliver implements of destruction.

The *National Strategy for Homeland Security* identifies six major initiatives in this area:

- Ensure accountability in border and transportation security;

- Create "smart borders";
- Increase the security of international shipping containers;
- Implement the Aviation and Transportation Security Act of 2001;
- Recapitalize the U.S. Coast Guard; and
- Reform immigration services.

The President proposed to Congress that the principal border and transportation security agencies—the Immigration and Naturalization Service, the U.S. Customs Service, the U.S. Coast Guard, the Animal and Plant Health Inspection Service, and the Transportation Security Agency—be transferred to the new Department of Homeland Security. This organizational reform will greatly assist in the implementation of all the above initiatives.

Domestic Counterterrorism

The attacks of September 11 and the catastrophic loss of life and property that resulted have redefined the mission of federal, state, and local law enforcement authorities. While law enforcement agencies will continue to investigate and prosecute criminal activity, they should now assign priority to preventing and interdicting terrorist activity within the United States. The Nation's state and local law enforcement officers will be critical in this effort. Our Nation will use all legal means—both traditional and nontraditional—to identify, halt, and, where appropriate, prosecute terrorists in the United States. We will pursue not only the individuals directly involved in terrorist activity but also their sources of support: the people and organizations that knowingly fund the terrorists and those that provide them with logistical assistance.

Effectively reorienting law enforcement organizations to focus on counterterrorism objectives requires decisive action in a number of areas. The *National Strategy for Homeland Security* identifies six major initiatives in this area:

- Improve intergovernmental law enforcement coordination;
- Facilitate apprehension of potential terrorists;
- Continue ongoing investigations and prosecutions;
- Complete FBI restructuring to emphasize prevention of terrorist attacks;
- Target and attack terrorist financing; and
- Track foreign terrorists and bring them to justice.

Protecting Critical Infrastructure and Key Assets

Our society and modern way of life are dependent on networks of infrastructure—both physical networks such as our energy and transportation systems and virtual networks such as the Internet. If terrorists attack one or more pieces of our critical infrastructure, they may disrupt entire systems and cause significant damage to the Nation. We must therefore improve protection of the individual pieces and interconnecting systems that make up our critical infrastructure. Protecting America's critical infrastructure and key assets will not only make us more secure from terrorist attack, but will also reduce our vulnerability to natural disasters, organized crime, and computer hackers.

America's critical infrastructure encompasses a large number of sectors. The U.S. government will seek to deny terrorists the opportunity to inflict lasting harm to our Nation by protecting the assets, systems, and functions vital to our national security, governance, public health and safety, economy, and national morale.

The *National Strategy for Homeland Security* identifies eight major initiatives in this area:

- Unify America's infrastructure protection effort in the Department of Homeland Security;
- Build and maintain a complete and accurate assessment of America's critical infrastructure and key assets;
- Enable effective partnership with state and local governments and the private sector;
- Develop a national infrastructure protection plan;
- Secure cyberspace;
- Harness the best analytic and modeling tools to develop effective protective solutions;
- Guard America's critical infrastructure and key assets against "inside" threats; and
- Partner with the international community to protect our transnational infrastructure.

Defending against Catastrophic Threats

The expertise, technology, and material needed to build the most deadly weapons known to mankind—including chemical, biological, radiological, and nuclear weapons—are spreading inexorably. If our enemies acquire these weapons, they are likely to try to use them. The consequences of such an attack could be far more devastating than those we suffered on September 11—a chemical, biological, radiological, or nuclear terrorist attack in the United States could cause large numbers of casualties, mass psychological disruption, contamination and significant economic damage, and could overwhelm local medical capabilities.

Currently, chemical, biological, radiological, and nuclear detection capabilities are modest and response capabilities are dispersed throughout the country at every level of government. While current arrangements have proven adequate for a variety of natural disasters and even the September 11 attacks, the threat of terrorist attacks using chemical, biological, radiological, and nuclear weapons requires new approaches, a focused strategy, and a new organization. The *National Strategy for Homeland Security* identifies six major initiatives in this area:

- Prevent terrorist use of nuclear weapons through better sensors and procedures;
- Detect chemical and biological materials and attacks;
- Improve chemical sensors and decontamination techniques;
- Develop broad spectrum vaccines, antimicrobials, and antidotes;
- Harness the scientific knowledge and tools to counter terrorism; and
- Implement the Select Agent Program.

Emergency Preparedness and Response

We must prepare to minimize the damage and recover from any future terrorist attacks that may occur despite our best efforts at prevention. An effective response to a major terrorist incident—as well as a natural disaster—depends on being prepared. Therefore, we need a comprehensive national system to bring together and coordinate all necessary response assets quickly and effectively. We must plan, equip, train, and exercise many different response units to mobilize without warning for any emergency.

Many pieces of this national emergency response system are already in place. America's first line of defense in the aftermath of any terrorist attack is its first responder community—police officers, firefighters, emergency medical providers, public works personnel, and emergency management officials. Nearly three million state and local first responders regularly put their lives on the line to save the lives of others and make our country safer.

Yet multiple plans currently govern the federal government's support of first responders during an incident of national significance. These plans and the government's overarching policy for counterterrorism are based on an artificial and unnecessary distinction between "crisis management" and "consequence management." Under the President's proposal, the Department of Homeland Security will consolidate federal response plans and build a national system for incident management in cooperation with state and local government. Our federal, state, and local governments would ensure that all response personnel and organizations are properly equipped, trained, and exercised to respond to all terrorist threats and attacks in the United States. Our emergency preparedness and response efforts would also engage the private sector and the American people.

The *National Strategy for Homeland Security* identifies twelve major initiatives in this area:

- Integrate separate federal response plans into a single all-discipline incident management plan;
- Create a national incident management system;
- Improve tactical counterterrorist capabilities;
- Enable seamless communication among all responders;
- Prepare health care providers for catastrophic terrorism;
- Augment America's pharmaceutical and vaccine stockpiles;
- Prepare for chemical, biological, radiological, and nuclear decontamination;
- Plan for military support to civil authorities;
- Build the Citizen Corps;
- Implement the First Responder Initiative of the Fiscal Year 2003 Budget;
- Build a national training and evaluation system; and
- Enhance the victim support system.

THE FOUNDATIONS OF HOMELAND SECURITY

The *National Strategy for Homeland Security* also describes four foundations—unique American strengths that cut across all of the mission areas, across all levels of government, and across all sectors of our society. These foundations—law, science and technology, information sharing and systems, and international cooperation—provide a useful framework for evaluating our homeland security investments across the federal government.

Law

Throughout our Nation's history, we have used laws to promote and safeguard our security and our liberty. The law will both provide mechanisms for the government to act and will define the appropriate limits of action.

The *National Strategy for Homeland Security* outlines legislative actions that would help enable our country to fight the war on terrorism more effectively. New federal laws should not preempt state law unnecessarily or overly federalize the war on terrorism. We should guard scrupulously against incursions on our freedoms.

The *Strategy* identifies twelve major initiatives in this area:

Federal level

- Enable critical infrastructure information sharing;

- Streamline information sharing among intelligence and law enforcement agencies;
- Expand existing extradition authorities;
- Review authority for military assistance in domestic security;
- Revive the President's reorganization authority; and
- Provide substantial management flexibility for the Department of Homeland Security.

State level

- Coordinate suggested minimum standards for state driver's licenses;
- Enhance market capacity for terrorism insurance;
- Train for prevention of cyber attacks;
- Suppress money laundering;
- Ensure continuity of the judiciary; and
- Review quarantine authorities.

Science and Technology

The Nation's advantage in science and technology is a key to securing the homeland. New technologies for analysis, information sharing, detection of attacks, and countering chemical, biological, radiological, and nuclear weapons will help prevent and minimize the damage from future terrorist attacks. Just as science has helped us defeat past enemies overseas, so too will it help us defeat the efforts of terrorists to attack our homeland and disrupt our way of life.

The federal government is launching a systematic national effort to harness science and technology in support of homeland security. We will build a national research and development enterprise for homeland security sufficient to mitigate the risk posed by modern terrorism. The federal government will consolidate most federally funded homeland security research and development under the Department of Homeland Security to ensure strategic direction and avoid duplicative efforts. We will create and implement a long-term research and development plan that includes investment in revolutionary capabilities with high payoff potential. The federal government will also seek to harness the energy and ingenuity of the private sector to develop and produce the devices and systems needed for homeland security.

The *National Strategy for Homeland Security* identifies eleven major initiatives in this area:

- Develop chemical, biological, radiological, and nuclear countermeasures;
- Develop systems for detecting hostile intent;
- Apply biometric technology to identification devices;

- Improve the technical capabilities of first responders;
- Coordinate research and development of the homeland security apparatus;
- Establish a national laboratory for homeland security;
- Solicit independent and private analysis for science and technology research;
- Establish a mechanism for rapidly producing prototypes;
- Conduct demonstrations and pilot deployments;
- Set standards for homeland security technology; and
- Establish a system for high-risk, high-payoff homeland security research.

Information Sharing and Systems

Information systems contribute to every aspect of homeland security. Although American information technology is the most advanced in the world, our country's information systems have not adequately supported the homeland security mission. Databases used for federal law enforcement, immigration, intelligence, public health surveillance, and emergency management have not been connected in ways that allow us to comprehend where information gaps or redundancies exist. In addition, there are deficiencies in the communications systems used by states and municipalities throughout the country; most state and local first responders do not use compatible communications equipment. To secure the homeland better, we must link the vast amounts of knowledge residing within each government agency while ensuring adequate privacy.

The *National Strategy for Homeland Security* identifies five major initiatives in this area:

- Integrate information sharing across the federal government;
- Integrate information sharing across state and local governments, private industry, and citizens;
- Adopt common "meta-data" standards for electronic information relevant to homeland security;
- Improve public safety emergency communications; and
- Ensure reliable public health information.

International Cooperation

In a world where the terrorist threat pays no respect to traditional boundaries, our strategy for homeland security cannot stop at our borders. America must pursue a sustained, steadfast, and systematic international agenda to counter the global terrorist threat and improve our homeland security. Our international anti-terrorism campaign has made significant progress since September 11. The full scope of these activities will be further described in the forthcoming *National Security Strategy of the United States* and the *National Strategy for Combating Terrorism*.

The *National Strategy for Homeland Security* identifies nine major initiatives in this area:

- Create "smart borders";
- Combat fraudulent travel documents;
- Increase the security of international shipping containers;
- Intensify international law enforcement cooperation;
- Help foreign nations fight terrorism;
- Expand protection of transnational critical infrastructure;
- Amplify international cooperation on homeland security science and technology;
- Improve cooperation in response to attacks; and
- Review obligations to international treaties and law.

COSTS OF HOMELAND SECURITY

The national effort to enhance homeland security will yield tremendous benefits and entail substantial financial and other costs. Benefits include reductions in the risk of attack and their potential consequences. Costs include not only the resources we commit to homeland security but also the delays to commerce and travel. The United States spends roughly $100 billion per year on homeland security. This figure includes federal, state, and local law enforcement and emergency services, but excludes most funding for the armed forces.

The responsibility of providing homeland security is shared between federal, state and local governments, and the private sector. In many cases, sufficient incentives exist in the private market to supply protection. Government should fund only those homeland security activities that are not supplied, or are inadequately supplied, in the market. Cost sharing between different levels of government should reflect the principles of federalism. Many homeland security activities, such as intelligence gathering and border security, are properly accomplished at the federal level. In other circumstances, such as with first responder capabilities, it is more appropriate for state and local governments to handle these responsibilities.

CONCLUSION: PRIORITIES FOR THE FUTURE

The *National Strategy for Homeland Security* sets a broad and complex agenda for the United States. The *Strategy* has defined many different goals that need to be met, programs that need to be implemented, and responsibilities that need to be fulfilled. But creating a strategy is, in many respects, about setting priorities—about recognizing that some actions are more critical or more urgent than others.

The President's Fiscal Year 2003 Budget proposal, released in February 2002, identified four priority areas for additional resources and attention in the upcoming year:

- Support first responders;
- Defend against bioterrorism;
- Secure America's borders; and
- Use 21st-century technology to secure the homeland.

Work has already begun on the President's Fiscal Year 2004 Budget. Assuming the Congress passes legislation to implement the President's proposal to create the Department of Homeland Security, the Fiscal Year 2004 Budget will fully reflect the reformed organization of the executive branch for homeland security. That budget will have an integrated and simplified structure based on the six critical mission areas defined by the *Strategy*. Furthermore, at the time the *National Strategy for Homeland Security* was published, it was expected that the Fiscal Year 2004 Budget would attach priority to the following specific items for substantial support:

- Enhance the analytic capabilities of the FBI;
- Build new capabilities through the Information Analysis and Infrastructure Protection Division of the proposed Department of Homeland Security;
- Create "smart borders";
- Improve the security of international shipping containers;
- Recapitalize the U.S. Coast Guard;
- Prevent terrorist use of nuclear weapons through better sensors and procedures;
- Develop broad spectrum vaccines, antimicrobials, and antidotes; and
- Integrate information sharing across the federal government.

In the intervening months, the executive branch will prepare detailed implementation plans for these and many other initiatives contained within the *National Strategy for Homeland Security*. These plans will ensure that the taxpayers' money is spent only in a manner that achieves specific objectives with clear performance-based measures of effectiveness.

Source: The complete text of this document is available online at http://www.whitehouse.gov/homeland/book/.

NOTES

1. Normal J. Rabkin (Managing Director, Homeland Security and Justice Issues), "Homeland Security: Observations on the National Strategies Related to

Terrorism," Testimony Before the Subcommittee on National Security, Emerging Threats, and International Relations, Committee on Government Reform, House of Representatives (GAO Report 04-1075T), September 22, 2004.

2. These strategic documents and commission reports are all available online at http://www.teachingterror.net. For a detailed analysis of the recommendations from these and other commissions, please see John Parachini, Lynn David and Timothy Liston, *Homeland Security: A Compendium of Public and Private Organizations' Policy Recommendations* (Santa Monica, CA: RAND, 2003), http://www.rand.org/pubs/white_papers/WP127/WP127.pdf.

3. "Combating Terrorism: Evaluation of Selected Characteristics in National Strategies Related to Terrorism" (GAO-04-408T). Statement of Randall A. Yim, GAO Managing Director of Homeland Security and Justice Issues, prepared for the Subcommittee on National Security, Emerging Threats, and International Relations, Committee on Government Reform, House of Representatives, February 3, 2004.

4. *National Security Strategy,* 1–2.

5. These descriptions appear in "Combating Terrorism: Evaluation of Selected Characteristics in National Strategies Related to Terrorism" (GAO-04-408T). Statement of Randall A. Yim, GAO Managing Director of Homeland Security and Justice Issues, prepared for the Subcommittee on National Security, Emerging Threats, and International Relations, Committee on Government Reform, House of Representatives, February 3, 2004. However, the *National Strategy for Maritime Security* was issued in 2005, after this report was prepared.

6. "Combating Terrorism: Evaluation of Selected Characteristics in National Strategies Related to Terrorism" (GAO-04-408T). Statement of Randall A. Yim, GAO Managing Director of Homeland Security and Justice Issues, prepared for the Subcommittee on National Security, Emerging Threats, and International Relations, Committee on Government Reform, House of Representatives, February 3, 2004.

7. The *National Strategy for Homeland Security* (NSHS) defines "State" to mean "any state of the United States, the District of Columbia, Puerto Rico, the Virgin Islands, Guam, American Samoa, the Canal Zone, the Commonwealth of the Northern Mariana Islands, or the trust territory of the Pacific Islands." The *Strategy* defines "local government" as "any county, city, village, town, district, or other political subdivision of any state, any Native American tribe or authorized tribal organization, or Alaska native village or organization, and includes any rural community or unincorporated town or village or any other public entity for which an application for assistance is made by a state or political subdivision thereof." Please note: In the NSHS, this is provided as footnote 1.

8. The distribution of the *National Strategy for Homeland Security* coincides with Congress' consideration of the President's proposal to establish a Department of Homeland Security. The *Strategy* refers to a "Department of Homeland Security" only to provide the strategic vision for the proposed Department and not to assume any one part of the President's proposal will or will not be signed into law. Please note: In the NSHS, this is provided as footnote 2.

APPENDIX B

SELECT POLICY STATEMENTS AND INITIATIVES ON BORDER SECURITY

HOMELAND SECURITY PRESIDENTIAL DIRECTIVE-2 (HSPD-2)

Combating Terrorism Through Immigration Policies

The White House, October 29, 2001

The United States has a long and valued tradition of welcoming immigrants and visitors. But the attacks of September 11, 2001, showed that some come to the United States to commit terrorist acts, to raise funds for illegal terrorist activities, or to provide other support for terrorist operations, here and abroad. It is the policy of the United States to work aggressively to prevent aliens who engage in or support terrorist activity from entering the United States and to detain, prosecute, or deport any such aliens who are within the United States.

1. FOREIGN TERRORIST TRACKING TASK FORCE

By November 1, 2001, the Attorney General shall create the Foreign Terrorist Tracking Task Force (Task Force), with assistance from the Secretary of State, the Director of Central Intelligence and other officers of the government, as appropriate. The Task Force shall ensure that, to the maximum extent permitted by law, Federal agencies coordinate programs to accomplish the following: 1) deny entry into the United States of aliens associated with, suspected of being engaged in, or supporting terrorist activity; and 2) locate, detain, prosecute, or deport any such aliens already present in the United States.

The Attorney General shall appoint a senior official as the full-time Director of the Task Force. The Director shall report to the Deputy Attorney General, serve as a Senior Advisor to the Assistant to the President for Homeland Security, and maintain direct liaison with the

Commissioner of the Immigration and Naturalization Service (INS) on issues related to immigration and the foreign terrorist presence in the United States. The Director shall also consult with the Assistant Secretary of State for Consular Affairs on issues related to visa matters.

The Task Force shall be staffed by expert personnel from the Department of State, the INS, the Federal Bureau of Investiga-tion, the Secret Service, the Customs Service, the Intelligence Community, military support components, and other Federal agencies as appropriate to accomplish the Task Force's mission.

The Attorney General and the Director of Central Intelligence shall ensure, to the maximum extent permitted by law, that the Task Force has access to all available information necessary to perform its mission, and they shall request information from State and local governments, where appropriate.

With the concurrence of the Attorney General and the Director of Central Intelligence, foreign liaison officers from cooperating countries shall be invited to serve as liaisons to the Task Force, where appropriate, to expedite investigation and data sharing.

Other Federal entities, such as the Migrant Smuggling and Trafficking in Persons Coordination Center and the Foreign Leads Development Activity, shall provide the Task Force with any relevant information they possess concerning aliens suspected of engaging in or supporting terrorist activity.

2. ENHANCED INS AND CUSTOMS ENFORCEMENT CAPABILITY

The Attorney General and the Secretary of the Treasury, assisted by the Director of Central Intelligence, shall immediately develop and implement multi-year plans to enhance the investigative and intelligence analysis capabilities of the INS and the Customs Service. The goal of this enhancement is to increase significantly efforts to identify, locate, detain, prosecute or deport aliens associated with, suspected of being engaged in, or supporting terrorist activity within the United States.

The new multi-year plans should significantly increase the number of Customs and INS special agents assigned to Joint Terrorism Task Forces, as deemed appropriate by the Attorney General and the Secretary of the Treasury. These officers shall constitute new positions over and above the existing on-duty special agent forces of the two agencies.

3. ABUSE OF INTERNATIONAL STUDENT STATUS

The United States benefits greatly from international students who study in our country. The United States Government shall continue to foster and support international students.

The Government shall implement measures to end the abuse of student visas and prohibit certain international students from receiving education and training in sensitive areas, including areas of study with direct application to the development and use of weapons of mass destruction. The Government shall also prohibit the education and training of foreign nationals who would use such training to harm the United States or its Allies.

The Secretary of State and the Attorney General, working in conjunction with the Secretary of Education, the Director of the Office of Science and Technology Policy, the Secretary of Defense, the Secretary of Energy, and any other departments or entities they deem necessary, shall develop a program to accomplish this goal. The program shall identify sensitive courses of study, and shall include measures whereby the Department of State, the Department of Justice, and United States academic institutions, working together, can identify problematic applicants for student visas and deny their applications. The program shall provide for tracking the status of a foreign student who receives a visa (to include the proposed major course of study, the status of the individual as a full-time student, the classes in which the student enrolls, and the source of the funds supporting the student's education).

The program shall develop guidelines that may include control mechanisms, such as limited duration student immigration status, and may implement strict criteria for renewing such student immigration status. The program shall include guidelines for exempting students from countries or groups of countries from this set of requirements.

In developing this new program of control, the Secretary of State, the Attorney General, and the Secretary of Education shall consult with the academic community and other interested parties. This new program shall be presented through the Homeland Security Council to the President within 60 days.

The INS, in consultation with the Department of Education, shall conduct periodic reviews of all institutions certified to receive nonimmigrant students and exchange visitor program students. These reviews shall include checks for compliance with record keeping and reporting requirements. Failure of institutions to comply may result in the termination of the institution's approval to receive such students.

4. NORTH AMERICAN COMPLEMENTARY IMMIGRATION POLICIES

The Secretary of State, in coordination with the Secretary of the Treasury and the Attorney General, shall promptly initiate negotiations with Canada and Mexico to assure maximum possible compatibility of immigration, customs, and visa policies. The goal of the negotiations shall be to provide all involved countries the highest possible level of assurance that only individuals seeking entry for legitimate purposes enter any of the countries, while at the same time minimizing border restrictions that hinder legitimate trans-border commerce.

As part of this effort, the Secretaries of State and the Treasury and the Attorney General shall seek to substantially increase sharing of immigration and customs information. They shall also seek to establish a shared immigration and customs control data-base with both countries. The Secretary of State, the Secretary of the Treasury, and the Attorney General shall explore existing mechanisms to accomplish this goal and, to the maximum extent possible, develop new methods to achieve optimal effectiveness and relative transparency. To the extent statutory provisions prevent such information sharing, the Attorney General and the Secretaries of State and the Treasury shall submit to the Director of the Office of Management and Budget proposed remedial legislation.

5. USE OF ADVANCED TECHNOLOGIES FOR DATA SHARING AND ENFORCEMENT EFFORTS

The Director of the OSTP, in conjunction with the Attorney General and the Director of Central Intelligence, shall make recommendations about the use of advanced technology to help enforce United States immigration laws, to implement United States immigration programs, to facilitate the rapid identification of aliens who are suspected of engaging in or supporting terrorist activity, to deny them access to the United States, and to recommend ways in which existing government databases can be best utilized to maximize the ability of the government to detect, identify, locate, and apprehend potential terrorists in the United States. Databases from all appropriate Federal agencies, state and local governments, and commercial databases should be included in this review. The utility of advanced data mining software should also be addressed. To the extent that there may be legal barriers to such data sharing, the Director of the OSTP shall submit to the Director of the Office of Management and Budget proposed legislative remedies. The study also should make recommendations, propose timelines, and project budgetary requirements.

The Director of the OSTP shall make these recommendations to the President through the Homeland Security Council within 60 days.

6. BUDGETARY SUPPORT

The Office of Management and Budget shall work closely with the Attorney General, the Secretaries of State and of the Treasury, the Assistant to the President for Homeland Security, and all other appropriate agencies to review the budgetary support and identify changes in legislation necessary for the implementation of this directive and recommend appropriate support for a multi-year program to provide the United States a robust capability to prevent aliens who engage in or support terrorist activity from entering or remaining in the United States or the smuggling of implements of terrorism into the United States. The Director of the Office of Management and Budget shall make an interim report through the Homeland Security Council to the President on the recommended program within 30 days, and shall make a final report through the Homeland Security Council to the President on the recommended program within 60 days.

GEORGE W. BUSH

Source: HSPD-2 is available online at http://www.whitehouse.gov/news/releases/2001/10/20011030-2.html.

HOMELAND SECURITY PRESIDENTIAL DIRECTIVE-6 (HSPD-6)

Integration and Use of Screening Information to Protect against Terrorism

The White House, September 16, 2003

To protect against terrorism it is the policy of the United States to (1) develop, integrate, and maintain thorough, accurate, and current information about individuals known or appropriately suspected to be or have been engaged in conduct constituting, in preparation for, in aid of, or related to terrorism (Terrorist Information); and (2) use that information as appropriate and to the full extent permitted by law to support (a) Federal, State, local, territorial, tribal, foreign-government, and private-sector screening processes, and (b) diplomatic, military, intelligence, law enforcement, immigration, visa, and protective processes.

This directive shall be implemented in a manner consistent with the provisions of the Constitution and applicable laws, including those protecting the rights of all Americans.

To further strengthen the ability of the United States Government to protect the people, property, and territory of the United States against acts of terrorism, and to the full extent permitted by law and consistent with the policy set forth above:

(1) The Attorney General shall establish an organization to consolidate the Government's approach to terrorism screening and provide for the appropriate and lawful use of Terrorist Information in screening processes.

(2) The heads of executive departments and agencies shall, to the extent permitted by law, provide to the Terrorist Threat Integration Center (TTIC) on an ongoing basis all appropriate Terrorist Information in their possession, custody, or control. The Attorney General, in coordination with the Secretary of State, the Secretary of Homeland Security, and the Director of Central Intelligence shall implement appropriate procedures and safeguards with respect to all such information about United States persons. The TTIC will provide the organization referenced in paragraph (1) with access to all appropriate information or intelligence in the TTIC's custody, possession, or control that the organization requires to perform its functions.

(3) The heads of executive departments and agencies shall conduct screening using such information at all appropriate opportunities, and shall report to the Attorney General not later than 90 days from the date of this directive, as to the opportunities at which such screening shall and shall not be conducted.

(4) The Secretary of Homeland Security shall develop guidelines to govern the use of such information to support State, local, territorial, and tribal screening processes, and private sector screening processes that have a substantial bearing on homeland security.

(5) The Secretary of State shall develop a proposal for my approval for enhancing cooperation with certain foreign governments, beginning with those countries for which the United States has waived visa requirements, to establish appropriate access to terrorism screening information of the participating governments.

This directive does not alter existing authorities or responsibilities of department and agency heads to carry out operational activities or provide or receive information. This directive is intended only to improve the internal management of the executive branch and is not intended to, and does not, create any right or benefit enforceable at law or in equity by any party against the United States, its departments, agencies, entities, officers, employees or agents, or any other person.

The Attorney General, in consultation with the Secretary of State, the Secretary of Homeland Security, and the Director of Central Intelligence, shall report to me through the Assistant to the President for Homeland Security not later than October 31, 2003, on progress made to implement this directive and shall thereafter report to me on such progress or any recommended changes from time to time as appropriate.

GEORGE W. BUSH

Source: HSPD-6 is available online at http://www.whitehouse.gov/news/releases/2003/ 09/20030916-5.html.

EXECUTIVE ORDER 13323

Assignment of Functions Relating to Arrivals in and Departures from the United States

The White House, December 30, 2003

By the authority vested in me as President by the Constitution and the laws of the United States of America, including section 215 of the Immigration and Nationality Act (INA), as amended (8 U.S.C. 1185), and section 301 of title 3, United States Code, and to strengthen the national security of the United States through procedures and systems to manage and control the arrival and departure of persons from the United States, it is hereby ordered as follows:

Section 1. Functions of the Secretary of Homeland Security. The Secretary of Homeland Security is assigned the functions of the President under section 215(a) of the INA with respect to persons other than citizens of the United States. In exercising these functions, the Secretary of Homeland Security shall not issue, amend, or revoke any rules, regulations, or orders without first obtaining the concurrence of the Secretary of State.

Section 2. Functions of the Secretary of State. The Secretary of State is assigned the functions of the President under section 215(a) and (b) of the INA with respect to citizens of the United States, including those functions concerning United States passports. In addition, the Secretary may amend or revoke part 46 of title 22, Code of Federal Regulations, which concern persons other than citizens of the United States. In exercising these functions, the Secretary of State shall not issue, amend, or revoke any rules, regulations, or orders without first consulting with the Secretary of Homeland Security.

Section 3. Judicial Review. This order is not intended to, and does not, create any right or benefit, substantive or procedural, enforceable at law or in equity by a party against the United States, its departments, agencies, entities, officers, employees or agents, or any other person.

[signed:] George W. Bush
THE WHITE HOUSE,
December 30, 2003

Source: Executive Order 13323 is available online at http://www.fas.org/irp/offdocs/eo/eo-13323.htm.

HOMELAND SECURITY PRESIDENTIAL DIRECTIVE-11 (HSPD-11)

Comprehensive Terrorist-Related Screening Procedures

The White House, August 27, 2004

(1) In order more effectively to detect and interdict individuals known or reasonably suspected to be or have been engaged in conduct constituting, in preparation for, in aid of, or related to terrorism ("suspected terrorists") and terrorist activities, it is the policy of the United States to:

(a) enhance terrorist-related screening (as defined below) through comprehensive, coordinated procedures that detect, identify, track, and interdict people, cargo, conveyances, and other entities and objects that pose a threat to homeland security, and to do so in a manner that safeguards legal rights, including freedoms, civil liberties, and information privacy guaranteed by Federal law, and builds upon existing risk assess-ment capabilities while facilitating the efficient movement of people, cargo, conveyances, and other potentially affected activities in commerce; and

(b) implement a coordinated and comprehensive approach to terrorist-related screening – in immigration, law enforcement, intelligence, counterintelligence, and protection of the border, transportation systems, and critical infrastructure – that supports homeland security, at home and abroad.

(2) This directive builds upon HSPD-6, "Integration and Use of Screening Information to Protect Against Terrorism." The Terrorist Screening Center (TSC), which was established and is administered by the Attorney General pursuant to HSPD-6, enables Government officials to check individuals against a consolidated Terrorist Screening Center Database. Other screening activities underway within the Terrorist Threat Integration Center (TTIC) and the Department of Homeland Security further strengthen the ability of the United States Government to protect the people, property, and territory of the United States against acts of terrorism.

(3) In this directive, the term "terrorist-related screening" means the collection, analysis, dissemination, and use of information related to people, cargo, conveyances, and other entities and objects that pose a threat to homeland security. Terrorist-related screening also includes risk assessment, inspection, and credentialing.

(4) Not later than 75 days after the date of this directive, the Secretary of Homeland Security, in coordination with the Attorney General, the Secretaries of State, Defense, Transportation, Energy, Health and Human Services, Commerce, and Agriculture, the Directors of Central Intelligence and the Office of Management and Budget, and the heads of other appropriate Federal departments and agencies, shall submit to me, through the Assistant to the President for Homeland Security, a report setting forth plans

and progress in the implementation of this directive, including as further described in sections 5 and 6 of this directive.

(5) The report shall outline a strategy to enhance the effectiveness of terrorist-related screening activities, in accordance with the policy set forth in section 1 of this directive, by developing comprehensive, coordinated, systematic terrorist-related screening procedures and capabilities that also take into account the need to:

(a) maintain no less than current levels of security created by existing screening and protective measures;

(b) encourage innovations that exceed established standards;

(c) ensure sufficient flexibility to respond rapidly to changing threats and priorities;

(d) permit flexibility to incorporate advancements into screening applications and technology rapidly;

(e) incorporate security features, including unpredictability, that resist circumvention to the greatest extent possible;

(f) build upon existing systems and best practices and, where appropriate, integrate, consolidate, or eliminate duplicative systems used for terrorist-related screening;

(g) facilitate legitimate trade and travel, both domestically and internationally;

(h) limit delays caused by screening procedures that adversely impact foreign relations, or economic, commercial, or scientific interests of the United States; and

(i) enhance information flow between various screening programs.

(6) The report shall also include the following:

(a) the purposes for which individuals will undergo terrorist-related screening;

(b) a description of the screening opportunities to which terrorist-related screening will be applied;

(c) the information individuals must present, including, as appropriate, the type of biometric identifier or other form of identification or identifying information to be presented, at particular screening opportunities;

(d) mechanisms to protect data, including during transfer of information;

(e) mechanisms to address data inaccuracies, including names inaccurately contained in the terrorist screening data consolidated pursuant to HSPD-6;

(f) the procedures and frequency for screening people, cargo, and conveyances;

(g) protocols to support consistent risk assessment and inspection procedures;

(h) the skills and training required for the screeners at screening opportunities;

(i) the hierarchy of consequences that should occur if a risk indicator is generated as a result of a screening opportunity;

(j) mechanisms for sharing information among screeners and all relevant Government agencies, including results of screening and new information acquired regarding suspected terrorists between screening opportunities;

(k) recommended research and development on technologies designed to enhance screening effectiveness and further protect privacy interests; and

(l) a plan for incorporating known traveler programs into the screening procedures, where appropriate.

(7) Not later than 90 days after the date of this directive, the Secretary of Homeland Security, in coordination with the heads of the Federal departments and agencies listed in section 4 of this directive, shall also provide to me, through the Assistant to the President for Homeland Security and the Director of the Office of Management and Budget, a prioritized investment and imple-menta-tion plan for a systematic approach to terrorist-related screening that optimizes detection and interdiction of suspected terrorists and terrorist activities. The plan shall describe the scope, governance, principles, outcomes, milestones, training objectives, metrics, costs, and schedule of activities to implement the policy set forth in section 1 of this directive. The Secretary of Homeland Security shall further provide a report on the status of the implementation of the plan to me through the Assistant to the President for Homeland Security 6 months after the date of this directive and shall thereafter report to me on such progress or any recommended changes from time to time as appropriate.

(8) In order to ensure comprehensive and coordinated terrorist-related screening procedures, the implementation of this directive shall be consistent with Government-wide efforts to improve information sharing. Additionally, the reports and plan required under sections 4 and 7 of this directive shall inform development of Government-wide information sharing improvements.

(9) This directive does not alter existing authorities or responsibilities of department and agency heads including to carry out operational activities or provide or receive information. This directive is intended only to improve the internal management of the executive branch of the Federal Government, and it is not intended to, and does not, create any right or benefit enforceable at law or in equity by any party against the United States, its departments, agencies, entities, officers, employees, or agents, or any other person.

GEORGE W. BUSH

Source: HSPD-11 is available online at http://www.whitehouse.gov/news/releases/2004/08/20040827-7.html.

ENHANCED BORDER SECURITY AND VISA ENTRY REFORM ACT OF 2002

(Public Law No: 107-173)[1]

Title: To enhance the border security of the United States, and for other purposes.
Sponsor: Rep Sensenbrenner, F. James, Jr. [WI-9] (introduced 12/19/2001)

Congressional Research Service Summary[2]

Title I: Funding

- Directs the Attorney General, during each of FY 2003 through 2006, to increase the number of Immigration and Naturalization Service (INS) investigators and inspectors by at least 200 full-time employees over the number authorized by the USA PATRIOT ACT.

- Authorizes appropriations for INS, Border Patrol, and consular personnel, training, facilities, and security-related technology, effective October 1, 2002. Provides for machine-readable visa fees.

Title II: Interagency Information Sharing

- Directs U.S. law enforcement and intelligence entities to share alien admissibility- and deportation-related information with INS and the Department of State until implementation of the information sharing plan provided for by this title.

- Amends the USA PATRIOT ACT to eliminate an Office of Homeland Security alien screening report requirement.

- Directs the President to: (1) report respecting admission- and deportation-related law enforcement and intelligence information needed by INS and the Department of State; and (2) develop a related information-sharing plan within 15 months of enactment of the USA PATRIOT ACT. Requires such plan to provide source and privacy protections. Provides criminal penalties for information misuse.

- Amends the USA PATRIOT ACT to advance the deadline from: (1) two years to one year for development and certification of a technology standard to certify the identity of alien applicants for admission; and (2) 18 months to six months for a related report.

(Sec. 202) Directs: (1) INS to fully integrate its databases and data systems; and (2) the President to develop and implement an interoperable law enforcement and intelligence data system (Chimera system) (with name-matching and linguistic capacity, including at least four priority languages) for visa, admissibility, or deportation determination purposes, which shall include the INS integrated system. Also directs the Central

Intelligence Agency to issue certain reports and guidelines required under the Intelligence Authorization Act for Fiscal Year 1998. And it authorizes appropriations for name search, linguistic, and reporting activities.

(Sec. 203) Directs the President to establish the Commission on Interoperable Data Sharing, which shall: (1) monitor information misuse protections under the alien screening plan; (2) provide oversight of the interoperable data sharing system; and (3) report annually to Congress. Authorizes appropriations.

(Sec. 204) Authorizes the Attorney General, respecting the Chimera system, to hire necessary scientific, technical, engineering, and other personnel. Directs the Attorney General to report to the appropriate congressional committees concerning intended uses of authority and Government organization and employee-related provisions being waived.

Title III: Visa Issuance

• Amends the Immigration and Nationality Act (Act) to direct the Secretary of State (Secretary), upon issuance of an alien visa, to provide INS with an electronic version of the alien's visa file prior to the alien's U.S. entry.

(Sec. 302) Sets forth technology standard and interoperability requirements (including October 26, 2004 implementation deadlines) respecting development and implementation of the integrated entry and exit data system and related tamper-resistant, machine-readable documents containing biometric identifiers. Requires a visa waiver country, in order to maintain program participation, to certify by October 26, 2004, that it has a program to issue to its nationals qualifying machine-readable passports that are tamper-proof and contain biometric identifiers. Authorizes appropriations.

(Sec. 304) Directs the Secretary to: (1) establish a Terrorist Lookout Committee at each U.S. mission, and report to the appropriate congressional committees respecting such Committees; (2) provide consular staff with visa screening training; and (3) provide for the use of terrorist-related intelligence in such activities' performance. Authorizes appropriations.

(Sec. 306) Prohibits the admission of an alien from a country designated to be a state sponsor of international terrorism (as defined by this Act) unless the Secretary has determined that such individual does not pose a risk or security threat to the United States.

(Sec. 307) Conditions participation in the visa waiver program upon a country's timely reporting to the United States of its stolen blank passports. Reduces from five years to two years the required periodic evaluation of the program's effects on U.S. security and immigration interests. It also requires INS to perform a check of lookout databases prior to permitting an alien's U.S. admission.

(Sec. 308) Directs: (1) the Secretary and the Attorney General, as appropriate, within 72 hours of notification of a lost or stolen U.S. or foreign passport, to enter such passport's identification number into the interoperable data system; (2) the Attorney General to enter into the system such information on passports lost or stolen prior to the system's implementation; and (3) the Attorney General to enter such information into the interim system prior to the interoperable system's implementation.

(Sec. 309) Directs the Attorney General to ensure that refugees and asylees are issued work authorizations, which shall contain fingerprint and photo identification.

Title IV: Inspection and Admission of Aliens

- Directs the President to study the feasibility of establishing a North American National Security Program (United States, Canada, Mexico), including consideration of alien preclearance and preinspection. Authorizes appropriations.

(Sec. 402) Amends the Act to: (1) require commercial aircraft or vessels arriving at, or departing from, the United States to provide United States border officers (as defined by this Act) with specified passenger, other occupant, and crew manifest information; (2) prohibit carrier entry until such information has been provided; (3) provide monetary and non-entry penalties for noncompliance; (4) require electronic manifest transmission by January 1, 2003; (4) provide the Attorney General with waiver authority; and (5) direct the President to conduct a feasibility study and report to Congress regarding such provisions' extension to commercial land carriers.

(Sec. 403) Directs INS to adequately staff ports of entry.

(Sec. 404) Authorizes United States border inspections agencies, including INS, to conduct joint United States-Canada inspection projects to provide for alternative inspection services and harmonized inspection criteria. Directs the Attorney General and the Secretary of the Treasury to report annually to Congress.

Title V: Foreign Students and Exchange Visitors

- Amends the Illegal Immigration Reform and Immigrant Responsibility Act of 1996 to direct the Attorney General to develop an electronic means of verifying and monitoring the foreign student and exchange visitor information program, including aspects of: (1) documentation and visa issuance; (2) U.S. admission; (3) institution notification; (4) documentation transmittal; and (5) registration and enrollment.

- Requires an institution to notify INS of the failure of a foreign student or exchange visitor to enroll within 30 days of the registration deadline.

- Increases student data collection requirements. Specifies information required for foreign student visa applications.

- Sets forth transitional foreign student monitoring requirements, including: (1) restrictions on visa issuance; (2) INS notification of visa issuance; (3) institution notification of U.S. entry; and (4) INS notification (by the institution) of failure to enroll. Directs the Attorney General to provide the Secretary with a list of institutions approved to accept foreign students or exchange visitors. Authorizes appropriations.

(Sec. 502) Provides for INS and Department of State biennial review of institutions authorized to enroll or sponsor foreign students and exchange visitors. Provides that an institution's failure to comply with recordkeeping and reporting requirements shall result in termination or at least a one year suspension of its approval to receive such students or exchange visitors.

Title VI: Miscellaneous Provisions

- Amends the Illegal Immigration Reform and Immigrant Responsibility Act of 1996 to extend the deadline for presentation of biometric border crossing identification cards.

(Sec. 602) Directs: (1) the Comptroller General to determine the feasibility of requiring each nonimmigrant alien to report annually to INS respecting his or her address and employer's address; and (2) the Secretary and INS to study alternative approaches to for encouraging or requiring Mexico, Canada, and visa waiver countries to develop an intergovernmental network of interoperable international electronic data systems.

(Sec. 604) States that this Act shall not be construed to impose requirements that are inconsistent with the North American Free Trade Agreement, or to require additional documents for certain nonimmigrant emergency or in-transit liens for whom documentary requirements are waived.

(Sec. 605) Directs the Attorney General to report annually respecting aliens who fail to appear at removal proceedings after release on their own recognizance.

(Sec. 606) Directs the Department of State to retain every nonimmigrant visa application in judicially and administratively admissible form for a period of seven years from the date of application.

Source: The full text of this bill, as well as this summary, are available online at http:// thomas.loc.gov.

NATIONAL BORDER PATROL STRATEGY
EXECUTIVE SUMMARY

**Office of Border Patrol U.S. Customs and Border Control,
Department of Homeland Security**

September, 2004

In the wake of the terrorist attacks of September 11, 2001, the Border Patrol has experienced a tremendous change in its mission. With the formation of a new parent agency, U.S. Customs and Border Protection (CBP), the Border Patrol has as its priority mission preventing terrorists and terrorist weapons from entering the United States. The Border Patrol will continue to advance its traditional mission by preventing illegal aliens, smugglers, narcotics, and other contraband from entering the United States as these measures directly impact the safety and security of the United States.

To carry out its missions, the Border Patrol has a clear strategic goal: to establish and maintain operational control of the border of the United States. All of our efforts must be focused on this goal.

The Border Patrol's strategy consists of five main objectives:

* Establish substantial probability of apprehending terrorists and their weapons as they attempt to enter illegally between the ports of entry;
* Deter illegal entries through improved enforcement;
* Detect, apprehend, and deter smugglers of humans, drugs, and other contraband;
* Leverage "Smart Border" technology to multiply the effect of enforcement personnel; and
* Reduce crime in border communities and consequently improve quality of life and economic vitality of targeted areas.

To carry out these objectives, the Border Patrol will employ a highly centralized and strengthened organizational model with a direct chain of command from the Commissioner of CBP to the Chief of the Border Patrol to field locations. National guidance for planning and implementation will ensure that resources are focused in the highest risk areas and that the foundation for operational control over our Nation's border is established and maintained. Operational control is defined as the ability to detect, respond, and interdict border penetrations in areas deemed as high priority for threat potential or other national security objectives. Operational control may be limited to specific smuggling corridors or other geographically defined locations. This centralized structure will ensure accountability for the implementation and success of this Strategy.

This National Strategy will build on the successes of the previous 1994 "prevention through deterrence" Strategy. The Border Patrol will continue to acquire and deploy the proper balance of personnel, equipment, technology, and border infrastructure to achieve incremental and focused operational control of our Nation's borders. The Border Patrol will also strengthen and enhance its ability to rapidly deploy, both on a temporary and permanent basis, a highly motivated, well trained workforce of agents to respond to potential terrorist and other national security threats. This response capability will include specialized teams within the Border Patrol who will provide a flexible and rapid response to potential terrorist incidents and other threats, both domestic and foreign.

Critical to the National Border Patrol Strategy will be the use of tactical, operational, and strategic intelligence to assess risk, target enforcement efforts, and drive operations. Intelligence collection and sharing efforts will be strengthened within the Department of Homeland Security and with outside agencies (federal, state, local). As part of its intelligence efforts, CBP Border Patrol will develop and deploy the next generation of border surveillance and sensoring platforms. These systems will maximize the Border Patrol's ability to detect, respond, and interdict cross-border intrusions and will increase the certainty of apprehension – especially in cases with a potential nexus to terrorism or which represent a threat to U.S. national security.

This Strategy provides the framework for the Border Patrol, as part of CBP, to plan and carry out its missions within the Department of Homeland Security. It provides the necessary goal, objectives, strategies, and measures for Border Patrol planning and operations and will be used as the basis for management decisions and resource deployment.

The National Border Patrol's Strategy directly supports CBP's 2006-2010 Strategic Plan. This strategy specifically addresses three of CBP's strategic goals, including:

- *Preventing Terrorism*—Detect and prevent terrorists and terrorist weapons, including weapons of mass effect, from entering the United States.

- *Strengthening Our Control of the United States Borders*—Strengthen national security between the ports of entry to prevent the illegal entry of terrorists, terrorist weapons, contraband, and illegal aliens into the United States.

- *Protecting America and its Citizens*—Contribute to a safer America by prohibiting the introduction of illicit contraband, including illegal drugs, and other harmful materials and organisms, into the United States.

Actions taken under this Strategy also complement work being done at the ports of entry by CBP officers and agricultural specialists, and draw on the support of many individuals throughout CBP, including intelligence analysts, information technology specialists, finance and logistics officers, and those with expertise in training and communication. Finally, this Strategy directly supports the strategic goals of the Department of Homeland Security to increase awareness, prevention, and protection against terrorism.

THE THREAT AND ENVIRONMENT

The priority mission of CBP is to prevent terrorists and terrorist weapons from entering the United States. With the establishment of CBP, for the first time in our Nation's history, one agency within the U.S. government has responsibility for the security of our Nation's borders. CBP Border Patrol has primary responsibility for monitoring and responding to illicit border intrusions across thousands of miles of border between U.S. ports of entry.

Prior to the terrorist attacks of 9/11, the primary focus of the Border Patrol was on illegal aliens, alien smuggling, and narcotics interdiction. The Border Patrol arrests over one million illegal aliens annually, and routinely seizes over 1 million pounds of marijuana and 15–20 tons of cocaine every year. After 9/11, it was apparent that smugglers' methods, routes, and modes of transportation are potential vulnerabilities that can be exploited by terrorists and result in terrorist weapons illegally entering the United States. The Border Patrol's expertise in countering this threat is critical to ensuring the security of the United States.

Although the threat and strategic response vary across the Northern, Southern and Coastal Borders, the potential exists for a single individual or small group to cross the border undetected with biological or chemical weapons, weapons of mass effect, or other implements of terrorism. CBP's National Border Patrol Strategy has been developed with measures and initiatives designed to eliminate or mitigate this threat.

The Border Patrol will address a wide variety of threats and vulnerabilities by deploying an appropriate mix of personnel, equipment, technology, and border infrastructure. The differing threat locations outlined below result from the geographical diversity of the border and from other related factors, such as differences in population centers, routes of ingress and egress from the border, economic stability of neighboring countries, and immigration patterns. These differences are wide-ranging and require the Border Patrol to maintain a high degree of flexibility in its approach to the border security mission.

Southern (U.S.–Mexico) Border

The Southern Border with Mexico consists of approximately 2,000 miles of border, some of which is extremely inhospitable and harsh terrain. Hundreds of aliens die each year as a result of failed smuggling efforts while attempting to cross the Southern Border. Within these 2,000 miles of border, there are three primary smuggling corridors: South Texas corridor; West Texas/New Mexico corridor; and California/Arizona corridor. These corridors are largely dictated by transportation routes, geography, and population centers. More than ninety percent of the one million plus annual arrests that the Border Patrol makes occur along the U.S.-Mexico border within these smuggling corridors.

The Border Patrol has experienced success in gaining operational control of the border in some of the highest trafficked areas, such as San Diego, El Paso, and McAllen. However, many other areas along the southwest border are not yet under operational control, and the daily attempts to cross the border by thousands of illegal aliens from countries around the globe continue to present a threat to U.S. national security. Some would classify the majority of these aliens as "economic migrants." However, an ever-present threat exists from the potential for terrorists to employ the same smuggling and transportation networks, infrastructure, drop houses, and other support and then use these masses of illegal aliens as "cover" for a successful cross-border penetration.

The Border Patrol arrests hundreds of aliens each year from "special interest" countries. The State Department has determined that these countries present a potential terrorist threat to U.S. national security. Cross-border illegal penetrations by terrorists and those potentially smuggling terrorist weapons are not mutually exclusive from penetrations by illegal aliens, criminals, and narcotics traffickers.

Past experience has shown that a balanced mix of personnel, technology, and border infrastructure, such as roads, lights, fencing, and facilities, are critical to expanding control over the Southern Border. The Border Patrol will build on the successes won by the deployment of these resources on the Southern Border, and continue to expand state of the art sensoring technologies, intelligence, skills and training, and nationally driven deployment of personnel and material.

Northern (U.S.-Canada) Border

The U.S.-Canada border consists of approximately 4,000 – 5,000 miles of border, some of which is water boundary and includes the Great Lakes area and surrounding waterways. Some of these waterways freeze during the winter and can easily be crossed on foot or by vehicle or snowmobile.

Under this Strategy, the Border Patrol must also address issues inherent in locations along the Northern Border designated as reservation lands for Native American peoples, that allow more limited access on both the U.S. and Canadian sides of the border. Further threats result from the fact that over ninety percent of Canada's population lives within one hundred miles of the U.S.-Canada border. Although the U.S. and Canada enjoy an extremely cooperative relationship, intelligence indicates that some individuals and organizations in Canada who reside near the border represent a potential threat to U.S. national security. The Northern Border also has well-organized smuggling operations, which can potentially support the movement of terrorists and their weapons.

The number of actual illegal border penetrations along the U.S.-Canada border is small in comparison to daily arrests along the U.S.-Mexico border. While resources have been significantly increased since 9/11 from approximately 350 agents to 1,000 agents, the Border Patrol's ability to detect, respond to, and interdict illegal cross-border penetrations along the U.S.-Canada border remains limited. Continued testing, acquisition, and deployment of sensing and monitoring platforms will be key to CBP Border Patrol's ability to effectively address the Northern Border threat situation.

To identify specific Northern Border threats, CBP Border Patrol has strengthened its partnerships with Canadian law enforcement and intelligence officials, and with officials from other federal, state, local, and tribal organizations by leveraging information and increasing communication and cooperation. The Integrated Border Enforcement, Maritime, and Intelligence Teams (IBET/IMET/IBIT) are examples of this effort, which the Border Patrol will continue to strengthen under this Strategy.

Coastal (Caribbean) Borders

In the U.S. Coastal areas, the Border Patrol works with a variety of law enforcement agencies, such as the U.S. Coast Guard, to address the threat of potential mass migrations, maritime smuggling, and crewman control. While the number of illegal entrants migrating through Coastal areas is currently lower than on the land borders, the threat faced by the Border Patrol is increased by local government corruption and inadequate tracking systems which fail to monitor those who transit those countries.

The proximity of these nations to the United States coastline requires that all CBP components remain vigilant and promote a common operational picture. Therefore, investing in air and maritime assets, continuing partnerships with other DHS components, and leveraging available assets operating in this environment are critical to ensuring that CBP has flexible response capabilities to address the threat in Coastal sectors.

Objective 1

Establish substantial probability of apprehending terrorists and their weapons as they attempt to illegally enter the United States between the ports of entry.

National Objectives

This National Strategy identifies the objectives, tools, and initiatives the Border Patrol needs to meet its priority goal: to establish and maintain operational control over our Nation's borders. The objectives outlined below directly support CBP's mission "to control U.S. borders to prevent entry into the United States of terrorists and terrorist weapons." The focus on these strategic Border Patrol objectives is critical and must be at the forefront of planning throughout the CBP organization. Five overarching objectives were developed to guide the Border Patrol in the planning and implementation of this National Strategy. These objectives will serve as the focus for planning and implementation, both nationally and at the sector and station levels.

Continued testing, acquisition, and deployment of technologies and initiatives to identify terrorists and their weapons will be critical. Examples include the Integrated Automated Fingerprint Identification System (IAFIS), and radiation detection and monitoring equipment at Border Patrol checkpoints and other strategic locations. These technologies will be complemented by rapid response teams such as the Border Patrol Tactical Team (BORTAC), the Border Patrol Search, Trauma, and Rescue Team (BORSTAR), Special Response Teams (SRT), and bomb and alien detection canines. The Border Patrol will increase the use of targeting information from the National Targeting Center and other data and intelligence sources to identify potential terrorists. In coordination with CBP's Office of Anti-Terrorism, the Border Patrol will also increase participation in Joint Terrorism Task Force units where operationally feasible. In addition, the Border Patrol will rely on CBP's overseas assets in key locations, such as Canada and Mexico City, for information and operational support.

Objective 2

Deter illegal entries through improved enforcement.

The Border Patrol's 1994 Strategy was based on a philosophy of "prevention through deterrence." This direction has proven effective in key high-traffic corridors along the southwest border, near San Diego, El Paso, McAllen, and most recently, Tucson. The control resulting from this Strategy is even more important in the post–9/11 environment as any illegal entry could be a terrorist. To control the border, the 1994 Strategy relied on the strategic deployment of a mix of personnel, equipment, technology, and border infrastructure, including all-weather roads, lights, and fencing. In addition to deploying these assets along the immediate border, the Border Patrol used checkpoint operations to further control potential routes of egress, and these have been critical to the success of border enforcement operations.

Past success has demonstrated that effective deployment of the proper mix of assets increases the "certainty of apprehension" of those intending to illegally cross our borders. Certainty of apprehension, along with a vigorous prosecution strategy for recidivists and smugglers, has established a deterrent effect in targeted locations. This strategic approach to border control has set the foundation for establishing focused operational control for other areas along our Nation's borders, especially in high-traffic/high-threat areas where illegal border-crossing and smuggling is prevalent.

CBP must continue similar strategies to gain, maintain, and expand operational control to other priority corridors. These priority areas will be defined by threat analysis to guide resource deployment and decision-making. Maintaining and expanding a strong enforcement posture along U.S. borders, including sufficient flexibility to address dynamic enforcement challenges, is critical to bringing operational control to our borders. Coordination with the Office of Field Operations and potential impact on ports of entry will be included in planning and analysis, as will partnership with the Offices of Anti-Terrorism and Intelligence.

Objective 3

Apprehend and deter smugglers of humans, drugs, and other contraband.

The Border Patrol also maintains its traditional mission of preventing the entry and smuggling of illegal aliens, narcotics, and other contraband from entering the United States between official ports of entry. Drug and alien smuggling has become an increasingly sophisticated and complex criminal enterprise. The Border Patrol will continue to deploy its resources in order to meet geographic and threat requirements to detect, interdict, and respond to alien smugglers, smugglers of illicit narcotics, and other contraband. The ability to collect, share, and process intelligence, data, and other information will be important to the detection, identification, and prosecution of criminal aliens, smugglers, and their networks. The Border Patrol and the Office of Information Technology must continue to test, acquire, and deploy technology to assist agents to detect and identify alien smugglers, criminals, and narcotics traffickers. Further partnership with the National Targeting Center, the development and use of tactical and strategic intelligence, and the expansion of IAFIS is also important to this objective.

The Border Patrol, in coordination with Immigration and Customs Enforcement (ICE), will continue to expand its ability to target cross-border smuggling operations, consistent with agreed upon roles and responsibilities. The Border Patrol's continued participation and expansion in task force operations will also be a component of achieving this objective when operationally feasible and necessary.

Objective 4

Leverage "Smart Border" technology to multiply the effect of enforcement personnel.

The Border Patrol currently uses a mix of agents, information, and technology to control the border. The Border Patrol's ability to establish situational awareness, monitor, detect, respond to, and identify potential terrorists, instruments of terrorism, and criminals relies heavily on interdiction and deterrence-based technology.

Having the necessary technology to support the Border Patrol priority and traditional missions cannot be overstated. In the future, there must be continued assessment, development, and deployment of the appropriate mix of personnel, technology, and information to gain, maintain, and expand coverage of the border and ensure that resources are deployed in a cost-effective, efficient fashion.

Technology which enhances operational awareness and effectiveness includes camera systems for day/night/infrared work, biometric systems such as IDENT/IAFIS, processing systems like ENFORCE, sensoring platforms, large-scale gamma X-rays, and aerial platforms, and other systems. Technologies requiring modernization sinclude wireless and tactical communications and computer processing capabilities.

Coordination between Border Patrol and inspectional personnel at the ports of entry ensures the most efficient use of trained personnel and technology. In the future, the Border Patrol will take advantage of the targeting and selectivity tools made available in the Automated Commercial Environment (ACE) and the National Targeting Center. The continued testing, evaluation, acquisition, and deployment of appropriate border enforcement technologies will be pursued vigorously so that the maximum force-multiplier effect is achieved in support of both the priority and traditional missions.

Objective 5

Reduce crime in border communities and consequently improve the quality of life and economic vitality of regions.

Past successes in border enforcement operations have demonstrated that a border under operational control directly correlates to reduced crime associated as high levels of illegal border incursions significantly impact border communities. The overall quality of life of border residents, economic expansion, and environmental protection significantly improves in areas where the Border Patrol's Strategy has been successfully implemented. The Border Patrol will continue to deploy resources and conduct public outreach in areas deemed high-threat or high-priority to improve the overall quality of life, reduce social service costs, and decrease crime in border areas.

By maintaining an active presence in border communities, Border Patrol agents provide a deterrent to active smuggling, partner with local residents to identify illegal activity, and support cooperative local law enforcement efforts in both urban and remote areas of the country. The Border Patrol will also continue to expand and strengthen its current Border Safety Initiative to enhance the safety of migrants and border residents.

TACTICS AND TECHNOLOGY

The following represents the tactical and technological approaches, under the direction of the CBP Commissioner and Chief of the Border Patrol, that the Border Patrol will pursue in addressing this Strategy's objectives: a more flexible, well trained, nationally-directed Border Patrol; specialized teams and rapid-response capabilities; intelligence-driven operations; and infrastructure, facility, and technology support.

Approach 1

A more flexible, well-trained, nationally directed Border Patrol.

The Border Patrol will use a highly centralized organizational model with a direct chain of command from the CBP Commissioner, to the Chief of the Border Patrol, to the Sector Chief Patrol Agents. This national command structure will facilitate national determinations on threat and resource priorities and will allow for the rapid deployment of Border Patrol assets, both on a short-term, temporary basis, as well as on long-term or permanent operations. This nationally directed mobility, with supporting national policies, will allow the Border Patrol to rapidly respond to emerging threats and hot spots along the border in a proactive prevention and response capacity. This type of flexibility is critical to address the present terrorist threat.

Anti-terrorism training is critical to ensuring that Border Patrol agents are fully prepared to address the terrorism threat. In conjunction with the Office of Training and Development, the Border Patrol will continually assess its anti-terrorism training requirements to ensure that agents, supervisors, and managers have the necessary multi-disciplinary training to effectively carry out the Border Patrol's priority anti-terrorism mission. The Office of Training and Development will work with the Border Patrol to ensure this training is developed and delivered in the most effective and operationally efficient manner, using methods such as computer-based modules, mobile training teams, train-the-trainer instruction, class-room and Academy training.

The Border Patrol will continue to deploy assets to interior U.S. locations where there is a direct nexus to border control operations, such as at transportation hubs, airports, and bus stations to confront routes of egress for terrorists, smugglers, and illegal aliens, and to support ICE-led interior efforts when appropriately coordinated and approved at the national level.

Approach 2

Specialized teams and rapid-response capabilities.

CBP will expand the training and response capabilities of the Border Patrol's specialized BORTAC, BORSTAR, and Special Response teams to support domestic and international intelligence-driven and anti-terrorism efforts as well as other special operations. These teams will assist in terrorism prevention through planning, training, and tactical deployment. As a highly mobile, rapid-response tool, they will significantly increase CBP's ability to respond operationally to specific terrorist threats and incidents, as well as to support the traditional Border Patrol mission.

Approach 3

Intelligence-driven operations.

The Border Patrol will expand the use of national security and terrorist-related intelligence and targeting information to improve intelligence-driven operations. This will enable the Border Patrol to deploy its resources effectively to target areas of greatest risk. These operations will be coordinated with the Office of Field Operations to ensure maximum effectiveness at and between the ports of entry. In order to support tactical and strategic operations, the Border Patrol will enhance its own organic intelligence program by coordinating with CBP's Office of Intelligence. In addition, the Border Patrol will leverage the intelligence capabilities of the Offices of Intelligence, Field Operations, and Anti-Terrorism to increase threat assessment, targeting efforts, operational planning, and communication to support its anti-terrorism and traditional missions.

Approach 4

Infrastructure, facility, and technology support.

Integrating increased numbers of agents and new technology into the Border Patrol's enforcement activities has strained resources previously dedicated to infrastructure, facility, and technology support. To ensure the objectives of this Strategy are not negatively impacted by a degradation of its infrastructure, the Border Patrol will continue to assess and address critical needs for this support, which include new construction; the preservation of buildings, technology, vehicles, and fences; and the deployment and maintenance of new technologies, ranging from remote cameras to computer and intelligence systems. This support is critical to ensuring that the investment made in new agents and new technology maintains its effectiveness in the face of shifting patterns of border threat and changing criminal tactics.

STRATEGIES TO ADDRESS AREAS OF THREAT

Southern Border

Strategic Focus:

- Achieve proper balance between personnel, equipment, technology, and border infrastructure;
- Gain, maintain, and expand control of borders based on threat and priority; and
- Enhance rapid response capabilities.

Anti-terrorism concerns result in part from the risk of terrorists becoming lost in the massive flow of illegal immigration along the Southern Border and the potential use of well-established smuggling networks. The strategic approach on the Southern Border is to leverage the success of the 1994 Border Patrol Strategy, which focused on deployment of the proper balance of personnel, equipment, technology, border infrastructure, and the establishment of a "prevention through deterrence" posture. The continued expansion of this Strategy will deter smuggling and illegal entries by reducing smugglers' ability to use existing infrastructure to facilitate their operations.

The Border Patrol will also strengthen and expand partnerships with other law enforcement agencies to increase the overall enforcement density along our country's borders. To carry out this approach on the Southern Border, CBP Border Patrol will:

- Deter or deny access to urban areas, infrastructure, transportation, and routes of egress to smuggling organizations through checkpoints, intelligence-driven special operations, and targeted patrols;
- Expand control through increased and more mobile personnel and improved air and ground support;
- Increase rapid response capabilities;
- Continue and expand the appropriate mix of improved infrastructure and technology;

- Sensing systems, Remote Video Surveillance and Sensing (RVSS) cameras, air support, and Unmanned Aerial Vehicles (UAVs)
- Radiation detection equipment
- Improved communication infrastructure (Land Mobile Radio, cellular coverage, satellite communication capabilities)
- Remote access to national law enforcement databases through the use of mobile computing solutions
- Mobile alien processing capabilities to support field enforcement activities
- Checkpoints and high-intensity enforcement zones
- Roads, lights, fencing, and vehicle barriers

- Expand cooperation with other agencies; and
- Continue deterrence efforts.

The primary challenges will be improved detection and surveillance capabilities to augment and support existing agent resources and to address developing and dynamic threats and vulnerabilities, which will require significant fiscal investment. Other challenges include increasing cooperation with Mexico on policies to improve safety and slow migration.

STRATEGIES TO ADDRESS AREAS OF THREAT

Northern Border

Strategic Focus:

- Balance intelligence use, other agency liaison efforts, technology, and equipment use, and personnel;
- Identify threat areas and resource requirements to mitigate and defeat threats;
- Acquire communications and data infrastructure to support detection and response;
- Expand detection technologies and sensoring platforms; and
- Improve mobility and rapid response capability.

The Northern Border presents unique challenges. The Border Patrol recognizes that the geographic distinctions along the Northern Border yield a much greater vulnerability for terrorist border-crossing attempts. The challenges and expanses along the Northern Border highlight the need for improved detection and response capabilities. Response levels have been strengthened by an increase in agents along the Northern Border since the 9/11 terrorist attacks. These agents will require more detection and communication technologies since the ratio of agent to miles of terrain will remain high. An improved communication and data infrastructure will be required to support sensor detection, identification, and response to terrorists and their weapons. Improved technologies would include sensors and cameras appropriate to the terrain and weather; new platforms such as UAVs, lighter-than-air ships or satellites to improve detection effectiveness, and signal intercept devices. Enhanced response will also be facilitated through the acquisition of additional aviation assets capable of light observation, medium lift, or fixed-wing flight.

The creation of Border Patrol-led joint task forces with state, local, and tribal law enforcement and the expansion of the Canadian IBET initiatives will also support prevention and response efforts.

Intelligence with predictive value will allow the Border Patrol to identify and respond to terrorism threats as a matter of national priority. To carry out this approach on the Northern Border, CBP Border Patrol will:

- Ensure sufficient mobile workforce levels;
- Expand communications and data infrastructure to support sensing and response capability;
- Develop and expand sensing/camera/UAV technology;
- Acquire and use additional air assets;
- Use checkpoints and other deterrents;
- Create BP-led joint task forces with state/local/tribal law enforcement;
- Expand upon existing IBET initiatives; and
- Improve the dissemination of actionable intelligence.

Challenges include obtaining sufficient funding for the technology infrastructure; fielding adequate numbers of sensing systems, platforms, and mobility assets, and improving the transportation and building infrastructure for Border Patrol operations on the Northern Border.

STRATEGIES TO ADDRESS AREAS OF THREAT

Coastal Border

Strategic Focus:

- Enhance and improve cooperative law enforcement efforts;
- Establish and employ a common operational picture; and
- Expand and enhance interagency planning and operations.

The Coastal Border is disparate in terms of threat and response capabilities. In general, there is not daily mass migration, although the threat of migration emergencies from unstable geopolitical situations can be very high. The Coastal Border also has a higher number of law enforcement agencies that actively coordinate daily operations and has more limited platform requirements for detection. In addition, the mode of transportation for enforcement and illegal entry or smuggling is unique to this environment, as are the safety considerations for waterborne enforcement.

The core concepts for the Coastal Border are similar to those for the Southern and Northern Borders—gain, maintain, and expand shallow and deep-water control in the areas of responsibility in support of the priority anti-terrorism mission. A key strategy to accomplishing this mission is partnership and integration with other law enforcement agency efforts. Due to the size of the geographic area that must be policed and the uniqueness of the environment, the attainment of our mission in this area requires clear, coordinated, federal, state, and local law enforcement activities. Interagency planning and operations will be expanded to provide a well-coordinated response to Coastal threats. The Border Patrol will also work with the U.S. Coast Guard and CBP personnel in the ports of entry to detect and apprehend absconding maritime crewmen.

To carry out this approach on the Coastal Border, CBP Border Patrol will:

- Right-size the maritime fleet;
- Prepare for incidence of mass migration; and
- Conduct threat analysis of future Coastal vulnerabilities.

Challenges for CBP in the pursuit of these strategic initiatives include acquisition of funding for Coastal environment sensing systems, platforms, and maritime fleet assets, and increasing cooperation and collaboration with other law enforcement entities.

STRATEGIC OUTCOME MEASURES

CBP views its performance measurement environment as dynamic. Through its Strategic Plan and other planning and budget documents, CBP strives to maintain the purpose of the Government Performance and Results Act; improving program efficiency and effectiveness, which includes maintaining a results-oriented focus that clearly describes program goals and objectives. Developing an integrated planning methodology that is supported by meaningful per formance measures is a key component in demonstrating business results.

It is often difficult to measure quantitatively how well a law enforcement organization is meeting its challenges. CBP is no exception. Measuring program effectiveness in law enforcement is complex. Although traditional workload measures are a valuable indicator of the challenges CBP Border Patrol faces, they do not always reflect the success or failure of the agency's efforts.

The direct impact being made on unlawful activity is often unknown. Because of these and other unknown variables, the traditional economics and methodologies of measuring performance can be particularly challenging.

Although limitations exist, CBP continues to refine its existing measures as well as propose new ones. To mitigate this challenge, CBP has adopted a mix of qualitative and quantitative measures.

Workload statistics augment these measures because CBP views its workload as preventing windows of opportunity for potential smuggling.

Since September 11, 2001, CBP has focused its activities on homeland security and protecting the American public from acts of terrorism. As part of the post-September 11 analysis, CBP determined that its effectiveness to secure the U.S. border should continue to be measured in both qualitative and quantitative terms. As a result, CBP is developing a new list of potential measures which will help gauge success in these areas, as well as the success of other increased enforcement and facilitation efforts.

The new measures under development reflect the new programs and the priority efforts used in combating terrorism outlined in the National Border Patrol Strategy. The following examples show the types of metrics that CBP is considering for use in assessing the agency's effectiveness at combating terrorism between the ports of entry:

- Expand Border Patrol Operational Planning Model to six high-priority and high-threat sectors beyond the original implementation in the Tucson Sector for FY 2005;
- Create a chronology of measurable and anecdotal terrorism-related enforcement successes;
- Increase operational area-specific apprehensions through more targeted enforcement;
- Increase and improve testing, acquisition, and deployment of technologies and initiatives to identify terrorists and their weapons;
- Reduce overall recidivism, based on a strong law enforcement posture;
- Identify and deny smuggling corridors as measured by the number of smuggling route-deflections;
- Increase and improve deployment of Smart Border technology; and
- Improve quality-of-life in Border communities as measured by indicators such as lower crime rates and reduced costs to taxpayers for cross-border activity related burdens.

There is no one way to measure the effectiveness of CBP efforts to combat terrorism. However, the performance metrics currently being considered by CBP will measure how various initiatives will assist in securing the border between the ports of entry and complement other national CBP initiatives.

FACT SHEET

Combating The Threat of Nuclear Smuggling at Home and Abroad

U.S. Customs and Border Protection (CBP.gov)

SUMMARY

The Customs and Border Protection employs a multi-layered approach to protect America from the introduction of nuclear weapons, radiation dispersal bombs (dirty bombs), and other Weapons of Mass Destruction (WMD).

- As a first line of defense, CBP works to prevent adversaries from illegally obtaining sensitive U.S. technology and components that they may need to assemble a WMD.
- Second, CBP trains and equips foreign authorities to interdict smuggled WMD materials at their own borders, before such materials fall into hostile hands or arrive in America.
- Third, CBP has launched major initiatives to prevent the global trading system from being exploited by terrorists to introduce WMD into this country.
- Finally, CBP uses a variety of systems at America's border, the last line of defense, to ensure that nuclear materials and other WMD do not enter this country.

1. KEEPING NUCLEAR COMPONENTS OUT OF THE HANDS OF ADVERSARIES

Project Shield America—U.S. adversaries frequently seek to illegally obtain sensitive technology and equipment from America for use in developing WMD and other weapons systems. For more than 20 years, CBP has served as the lead agency for enforcing U.S. export control laws to prevent such schemes. CBP relies on strategic investigations, intelligence, and outbound exams to prevent these materials from being illegally exported. In Dec. 2001, CBP enhanced its export enforcement through a program called Project Shield America, which seeks to keep sensitive U.S. weapons components out of the hands of terrorists. As part of the program, CBP has identified key U.S. weapons components that may be sought by terrorists. CBP is partnering with U.S. manufacturers of these items to guard against illegal foreign acquisition. Since Dec. 2001, CBP agents have visited nearly 3,000 U.S. firms to solidify this partnership. These visits have also spawned numerous criminal probes. Over the years, CBP strategic investigations have targeted hundreds of illegal weapons export schemes. Some of the most serious:

- *Nuclear Trigger Devices Bound for Israel*—In April 2002, Richard Smyth, a former NATO advisor and president of Milco International, was sentenced for exporting nuclear trigger devices to Israel. Smyth had been charged in 1985 with exporting 800 devices known as krytrons to Israel without obtaining the required export license. Krytrons have civilian and military uses, but are considered ideal for triggering nuclear weapons. Before trial, Smyth fled. After 16 years on the run, Smyth was arrested in Spain in July 2001 and extradited to Los Angeles where he pleaded guilty to two counts in the original 1985 indictment.

- *Nuclear-Grade Zirconium Bound for Iraq*—In June 1995, CBP agents in New York arrested three men on charges of attempting to smuggle seven tons of nuclear-grade zirconium to Iraq. The investigation, in which undercover CBP agents posed as Iraqi military officials, resulted in the seizure of five tons of zirconium in America and another two tons in Cyprus. Zirconium is a material used to cover nuclear fuel in a reactor core. The zirconium in this case had been smuggled from Ukraine, through Germany, to New York and Cyprus, where it awaited export to Iraq.

- *Nuclear Trigger Devices Bound for Iraq*—In March 1990, CBP agents working with British authorities intercepted 40 nuclear trigger devices in London that were destined for Iraq. The 18-month undercover probe by Customs and Border Protection established that the shipment of krytrons, falsely labeled as "air conditioning parts," had been ordered from America by an Iraqi front company in England called Euromac. Several Iraqi agents were arrested in England in connection with the case.

- *Sarin Nerve Gas Bound for Iran*—In May 1989, Juwhan Yun, the president of a New Jersey firm called Komex International, was convicted of conspiring to export 500 units of sarin nerve gas to Iran. The conviction resulted from an undercover CBP investigation in which agents learned that the defendant was working with a London arms broker whose Iranian clients sought sarin gas to be dropped from aircraft in Mark 94 bombs. The London arms broker, Charles Caplan, remains a fugitive.

2. INTERDICTING NUCLEAR MATERIALS OVERSEAS

International Counter-Proliferation Training—Since the early 1990s, Customs and Border Protection has provided non-proliferation training and equipment to nearly 3,000 border guards and CBP officials in 26 nations to counter the spread of WMD and their components. With funding by the U.S. State and Defense Departments, CBP administers this training to nations in Eastern Europe, Central Asia, the Caucuses, the Middle East, and Asia. CBP also maintains permanent advisors in many of these nations to facilitate local training and equipment delivery. The goal is to help these nations interdict WMD materials being smuggled across their borders before they fall into hostile hands or arrive in America.

CBP delivers WMD training to foreign authorities both in-country and in America. One of the most important courses offered is "RADACAD" or Radiation Academy training at the Department of Energy's Pacific Northwest National Laboratory in Washington State. This is the only program in the world where authorities can train with actual nuclear materials in smuggling scenarios. CBP also provides courses ranging from tracker training to detect WMD smuggling between ports of entry to training in advanced undercover operations.

CBP also delivers millions of dollars worth of high-tech and low-tech detection equipment to foreign authorities to meet the counter-proliferation needs of each nation. CBP has delivered roughly 600 personal radiation detectors (or radiation pagers) to foreign authorities, as well as X-ray vans equipped with radiation detectors, and gamma ray inspection systems. CBP has also provided low-tech items, such as fiber-optic scopes, drills, mirrors, and tools used to search vehicles at borders.

Customs and Border Protection WMD counter-proliferation programs have achieved encouraging results. Since 1998, there have been at least eight significant seizures by foreign authorities that have been attributed to Customs and Border Protection training and/or equipment, including the following:

- *Weapons-Grade Uranium Seized in Bulgaria*—In May 1999, Bulgarian customs officials at the Ruse border crossing in Bulgaria discovered 10 grams of highly enriched uranium (U-235) inside a lead "pig" concealed in an air compressor in the trunk of a car. The 35-year-old Turkish driver was transporting his nuclear cargo from Turkey to Moldova. It is believed the smuggler was offering this small shipment of U-235 as a "sample" to buyers in Moldova in advance of a larger shipment of the same materials. The Bulgarian customs officer who found the U-235 had just received counter-proliferation training from Customs and Border Protection. His supervisor had been trained by Customs and Border Protection at RADACAD. The Bulgarian lab director who examined and identified the materials had also received training from CBP and Border Protection.

- *Radioactive Lead Containers Seized in Uzbekistan*—In March 2000, Uzbekistan customs officials at the Gisht Kuprink border crossing discovered 10 highly radioactive lead containers concealed in 23 tons of scrap stainless steel in a truck entering from Kazakhstan. Documents found in the truck indicated that the Iranian driver was planning to deliver his radioactive cargo to Quetta, Pakistan, near the border of Afghanistan. Uzbeki authorities found the radioactive material after their radiation pagers alerted as the truck entered the customs post. The radiation pagers that alerted to the truck had been provided to Uzbeki authorities by Customs and Border Protection in May 1999. The Uzbeki authorities had also been provided with extensive WMD non-proliferation training by Customs and Border Protection.

3. KEEPING NUCLEAR MATERIALS OUT OF THE GLOBAL TRADING SYSTEM

a. Container Security Initiative—In Jan. 2002, U.S. Customs launched the Container Security Initiative (CSI), an initiative to prevent global containerized cargo from being exploited by terrorists to inflict harm on America and other nations. The initiative is designed to enhance security of the sea cargo container – a vital link in global trade. Some 200 million sea cargo containers move annually among the world's top seaports, and nearly 50 percent of the value of all U.S. imports arrive via sea containers.

One of the core elements of CSI involves placing CBP inspectors at major foreign seaports to pre-screen cargo containers before they are shipped to America. Customs and Border Protection is negotiating with foreign authorities in Europe, Asia, and other locations to place CBP inspectors at some of the world's largest seaports. CBP officials, working with their foreign counterparts, would be in a position to detect potential nuclear materials or WMD in U.S.-bound containers at these foreign ports. Since roughly half of all sea containers that enter the United States pass through 10 major seaports around the globe, CBP is initially focusing on these ports as key "chokepoints" in the global trading system.

- *CBP Inspectors Placed at Select Canadian Seaports*—Customs and Border Protection has already put inspectors at three Canadian seaports through an agreement reached with Canadian Customs. In March 2002, teams of CBP inspectors were placed in Montreal, Halifax, and Vancouver to pre-screen cargo that is offloaded at these ports and destined for America. At the same time, Canadian Customs has placed its own inspectors at the U.S. seaports of Newark and Seattle to pre-screen cargo bound for Canada. The agreement with Canada is expected to be the first of many similar agreements around the globe.

As part of the CSI, CBP is also working with foreign nations to establish basic criteria for authorities to use in identifying high-risk containers. CBP is also working on the deployment of detection technology to foreign ports help screen containers. Finally, CBP is researching and testing new technology, such as tamper-proof seals, to make containers themselves more secure against terrorist exploitation.

b. Customs and Border Protection Trade Partnership Against Terrorism—In April 2002, Customs and Border Protection unveiled an industry partnership program that enlists importers, carriers, and manufacturers to secure every aspect of the international supply chain against the terrorist threat–from the foreign loading dock, to the cargo conveyance, to the port of entry in America. Called the CBP Trade Partnership Against Terrorism or CTPAT, the initiative offers those companies that improve the security of their supply chains expedited processing through Customs and Border Protection. The goal is to enhance the security of cargo entering the U.S. while improving the flow of trade. More than 60 companies, including General Motors, Ford Motor Co., Motorola, Inc, and Daimler-Chrysler A.G., have signed up to participate and 100 more firms have applications pending.

Businesses that participate in CTPAT are required to conduct a comprehensive self-assessment of their supply chain security and submit a security questionnaire to CBP. They must also develop and implement a long-term program to enhance their supply chain security and communicate CTPAT guidelines to other companies that they work with in the supply chain. For companies that take these steps, CBP will provide expedited processing of their goods and conveyances at U.S. borders. CBP may offer participants dedicated commercial lanes and reduced inspections.

4. STOPPING NUCLEAR MATERIALS AT U.S. BORDERS

a. Risk Targeting and Intelligence—Contrary to media reports that CBP only pays attention to two percent of sea cargo entering America, CBP actually employs a multi-layered process that scrutinizes virtually all incoming sea cargo and targets those shipments that pose the highest risk. CBP receives electronic information on more than 95 percent of all U.S.-bound sea cargo before it arrives in this country. This data includes manifest information on the type of commodity, the manufacturer, the shipper, the consignee, the country of origin, the routing, and the terms of payment. CBP uses vast computer systems to sort through this data and assign a numeric score to each shipment indicating its level of risk. Special CBP teams called Manifest Review Units also scrutinize manifest and bill of lading data for each incoming shipment. These units have access to a vast array of databases, including intelligence data, to help them conduct analysis. Based upon rules-based criteria and the analysis of the Manifest Review Units, containers that are determined to pose a potential security risk (high-risk containers) are flagged to receive a security inspection upon arrival using detection technology. This entire process takes place before the cargo arrives.

b. Detection Technology—At the nation's ports of entry, CBP employs a wide range of technology to examine incoming shipments that are high-risk. Many of these technological devices are designed specifically to detect nuclear/radioactive materials. For example, CBP currently has more than 4,000 personal radiation pagers deployed around the country. By next January, this number will more than double to 8,500 radiation pagers nationwide. At many ports, CBP is also installing portal radiation detectors, which are fixed devices that can detect various types of radiation. In addition, CBP is deploying isotope identifiers that allow inspectors to determine whether a source of radiation is a possible terrorist threat or a commercial / medical source of radiation. CBP is also exploring the use of crane-mounted radiation detection devices to detect radioactive materials in sea cargo containers.

CBP also maintains an arsenal of non-intrusive technology that allows inspectors to detect hidden compartments and other anomalies in goods and conveyances entering the country. Gamma-ray imaging systems, known as Vehicle And Cargo Inspection Systems (VACIS), are deployed at major ports of entry. CBP also employs hundreds of X-ray systems at ports around the country, some of which are equipped with radiation detection equipment. Other detection technology in use includes density measuring devices, fiber-optic scopes, acoustic inspection systems, and low-tech tools.

c. Physical Inspections—CBP inspectors conducting physical examinations on the front lines form the most important factor in keeping nuclear materials and other contraband from entering America. Using their training, intuition, and experience to detect anomalies and inconsistencies, these officers are the linchpins of the inspection process. In 1999, the training and intuition of a single CBP inspector was the key to preventing an Al Qaeda terrorist from blowing up a major U.S. airport:

- *Millennium Bomber Intercepted*—On Dec. 14, 1999, an Algerian man named Ahmed Ressam arrived at the tiny U.S. Customs port of entry in Port Angeles, Washington, after taking a ferry from Victoria, Canada. Ressam was the last to drive off the ferry in his rental car. A Customs inspector approached the vehicle and began questioning Ressam. With no advanced warning about this individual or detection technology to help her screen his vehicle, the inspector simply relied on her training and intuition to determine that this traveler posed a serious risk. The inspector noted that Ressam had taken an odd travel route and appeared nervous and uncooperative. Suspicions raised, the inspector asked Ressam to step out of the car for a trunk search. After exiting the vehicle, Ressam fled on foot. Customs inspectors chased him down and arrested him. In the trunk of the car, inspectors found nitroglycerine, timing devices, circuit boards, and more than 100 pounds of bomb making materials. Ressam was later convicted of conspiracy to bomb Los Angeles International Airport with these materials. It was later determined that he had been trained by Al Qaeda in Afghanistan to carry out attacks on America.

Since September 11, CBP inspectors at all the nation's ports of entry have been on Alert Level One. Under this level of alert, CBP inspectors conduct dramatically enhanced inspections of cargo and conveyances entering the country. In recent months, Customs and Border Protection has also increased its counter-terrorism training for officers on the front lines. Inspectors are being given specific instruction in identifying WMD materials, their concealment methods, and how to respond to WMD incidents. Some CBP inspectors are also being trained with "live" nuclear materials in smuggling exercises at RADACAD or the Radiation Academy at the Department of Energy's Pacific Northwest National Laboratory. Tabletop and field exercises involving WMD smuggling are also part of the counter-terrorism training for CBP inspectors.

Report suspicious activity to 1-800-BE-ALERT

FREE AND SECURE TRADE (FAST)

Overview

The Free and Secure Trade (FAST) program is a Border Accord Initiative between the United States, Mexico, and Canada designed to ensure security and safety while enhancing the economic prosperity of each country. In developing this program, Mexico, Canada and the United States have agreed to coordinate, to the maximum extent possible, their commercial processes for clearance of commercial shipments at the border. This will promote free and secure trade by using common risk-management principles, supply chain security, industry partnership, and advanced technology to improve the efficiency of screening and clearing commercial traffic at our shared borders.

Eligibility for the FAST program requires participants (carrier, drivers, importers, and southern border manufacturers) to submit an application, agreement, and security profile depending on their role in the Customs and Trade Partnership Against terrorism (C-TPAT) and FAST programs. The FAST program allows known low risk participants to receive expedited border processing. This enables U.S. Customs and Border Protection (CBP) to re-direct security efforts and inspections where they are needed most - on commerce that is high risk, or unknown risk - while ensuring the movement of legitimate, low-risk commerce.

When decisions are made to elevate the national threat level, all CBP personnel must be cognizant of the heightened threat of terrorism as well a mandated increase in examinations of cargo and conveyances. Elevated alert levels should have no adverse impact on FAST processing. While other conveyances and cargo will be subject to a greater degree of inspection, FAST shipments are considered known low risk. As such, their processing should continue under normal guidelines during heightened alert levels.

BENEFITS OF FAST

The FAST program is voluntary. The benefits for those that apply and are accepted into the FAST program include:

- Dedicated lanes (where available) for greater speed and efficiency in the clearance of FAST Trans-border shipments;
- Reduced number of examinations for continued compliance with Customs FASTrequirements as well secondary priority processing;
- A strong and ongoing partnership with the Canadian Partners in Protection (PIP) and Customs (C-TPAT) administrations;
- Enhanced supply chain security and safety while protecting the economic prosperity of the United States, Mexico, and Canada; and,
- For carrier participants, the knowledge that they are transporting shipments for a C-TPAT approved importer, and on the southern border, a C-TPAT manufacturer.

BASIC PARTICIPATION REQUIREMENTS

FAST is a clearance process for known low-risk shipments, thus, any truck using FAST lane processing must be a C-TPAT approved carrier, carrying qualifying goods from a C-TPAT approved importer, and the driver in the possession of a valid FAST Commercial Driver Registration ID Card. Although FAST participation requirements along the northern and southern border are very similar, on the southern border there are two additional requirements. The manufacturer must be an approved C-TPAT participant, and they must also adhere to CBP high security seal requirements.

C-TPAT is a joint government business initiative to build cooperative relationships that strengthen overall supply chain and border security. C-TPAT recognizes that CBP can provide the highest level of security only through close cooperation with the ultimate owners of the supply chain, importers, carriers, brokers, warehouse operators and manufacturers. Through this initiative, CBP asks businesses to ensure the integrity of their security practices and communicate their security guidelines to their business partners within the supply chain.

1. **Importer Registration:** Importers must complete an application for C-TPAT participation with CBP. Importers authorized to use the FAST program for clearance into the United States will have a demonstrated history of complying with all relevant legislative and regulatory requirements, and will have made a commitment to security enhancing business practices as required by C-TPAT.

2. **Carrier Registration:** Carriers must complete the FAST Highway Carrier Application Process requirements that include corporate information, a security profile, and a written Highway Carrier Agreement.

Northern Border: In order to qualify for FAST Highway Carrier membership into the U.S. and Canada, two separate applications must be submitted to each country's respective FAST Processing Centers. Each country will perform an independent risk assessment and each country will issue independent approvals for participation. For the United States, a FAST approved carrier will have met all aspects of C-TPAT through the FAST registration process.

Southern Border: To qualify for the U.S./Mexico border highway carriers agreement, the carrier must have demonstrated a history of complying with all relevant legislative and regulatory requirements set forth by CBP. The applying carrier must have made a commitment to security-enhancing business practices as required by C-TPAT and use drivers that are in possession of a valid FAST commercial driver card when using FAST clearance.

3. **Commercial Driver Application:** Two separate driver application processes exist for FAST, 1) Northern Border and 2) Southern Border. For northern border applicants, drivers must complete a FAST Commercial Driver Application for the United States and Canada. The application will first be risk assessed by a Canadian consortium of the Canada Border Service Agency (CBSA), Citizenship and Immigration Service for Canada (CIC), and Canada's Agence de Revenu (ARC). Upon approval from Canada, CBP will conduct a full U.S. based risk assessment. Applicants identified as low risk will report to an enrollment center where they will be interviewed, have their original identification and citizenship documents reviewed, fingerprinted and have a digital photo taken. Low-risk applicants will then be issued a FAST Commercial Driver Card.

The procedure for the southern border is similar however the FAST driver application is submitted to the Mellon Financial Corporation in Pittsburgh, Pennsylvania prior to being forwarded to the CBP risk assessment center in St Albans, Vermont. Applicants identified as low risk will report to an enrollment center where they will be interviewed, have their original identification and citizenship documents reviewed, fingerprinted and have a digital photo taken. Low-risk applicants will then be issued a FAST – Commercial Driver Card.

FAST PROCESSING AVAILABILITY

The initial phase of FAST processing for U.S. bound commercial shipments began in December 2002 at the port of Detroit, Michigan. Today, CBP has implemented FAST processing at the following northern and southern border crossings:

Northern Border	Southern Border
Alexandria Bay, New York	Brownsville, Texas
Blaine, Washington	Calexico, California
Buffalo, New York	El Paso, Texas
Champlain, New York	Laredo, Texas
Derby Line, Vermont	Nogales, Arizona
Detroit, Michigan	Otay Mesa, California
Houlton, Maine	Pharr, Texas
Pembina, North Dakota	
Port Huron, Michigan	
Portal, North Dakota	
Sweetgrass, Montana	

Future FAST expansion sites will include:

Northern Border	Southern Border
Houlton, Maine	Tecate, California
Calais, Maine	San Luis, Arizona
Massena, New York	Douglas, Arizona
Ogdensburg, New York	Santa Teresa, New Mexico
Sault Ste Marie, Michigan	Eagle Pass, Texas
International Falls, Minnesota	Del Rio, Texas
Oroville, Washington	Rio Grande City, Texas

CBP anticipates to have these indicated FAST expansion sites available for FAST processing by July 1, 2005.

Cargo Release Method(s)

The two cargo release methods for FAST eligible shipments are the Free and Secure Trade system formerly known as the National Customs Automated Prototype (NCAP), additionally the Pre-Arrival Processing System (PAPS) is also recognized as eligible method of cargo release processing for FAST.

1. **FAST:** FAST is the first fully electronic and completely paperless cargo release mechanism put into place by CBP. Paperless processing is achieved through

advanced electronic data transmissions and transponder technology. FAST is highly automated and allows for the expedited release of highly compliant cargo from major importers, reducing congestion at our land borders.

2. **Pre Arrival Processing System (PAPS):** The Pre-Arrival Processing System (PAPS) is a ACS (Automated Commercial System) border cargo release system that utilizes barcode technology to expedite the release of commercial shipments while still processing each shipment through Border Cargo Selectivity (BCS) and the Automated Targeting System (ATS).

Each PAPS shipment requires a unique barcode label, which the carrier attaches to the invoice and the truck manifest while the merchandise is still in Canada or Mexico. The barcode consists of the Standard Carrier Alpha Code (SCAC) and Pro-Bill number or entry number. The licensed U.S. Customs broker in the United States must indicate this sequencing of SCAC code and unique number (Pro Bill, Entry number or unique set of numbers) in the BCS entry in ACS. Upon the truck's arrival at the border, the CBP officer scans the barcode, which automatically retrieves the entry information from ACS. If no examination is required, the CBP officer then releases the truck from primary reducing the carrier's wait time and easing congestion at the U.S. border.

ADDITIONAL INFORMATION

In addition to the FAST information found on this CBP web site, see FAST information on the Canada Border Security Agency web site at www.cbsa-asfc.gc.ca or you contact a representative at any of the designated FAST sites.

US-VISIT FACT SHEET

Department of Homeland Security

August 11, 2005

US-VISIT: GOALS

- Enhance the security of our citizens and visitors
- Facilitate legitimate travel and trade
- Ensure the integrity of our immigration system
- Protect the privacy of our visitors

US-VISIT: AN OVERVIEW

US-VISIT is a top priority for the U.S. Department of Homeland Security because it enhances security for our citizens and visitors while facilitating legitimate travel and trade across our borders. US-VISIT helps to secure our borders, facilitate the entry and exit process, and enhance the integrity of our immigration system while respecting the privacy of our visitors.

US-VISIT is part of a continuum of security measures that begins outside U.S. borders and continues through a visitor's arrival in and departure from the United States. It incorporates eligibility determinations made by the Department of Homeland Security and the Department of State.

US-VISIT currently applies to all visitors (with limited exemptions) entering the United States, regardless of country of origin or whether they are traveling on a visa. Most visitors experience US-VISIT's biometric procedures – digital, inkless fingerscans and digital photograph – upon entry to the United States.

In those cases where a visitor requires a visa, the Department of State collects the visitor's biometric and biographic information, which is then checked against watch lists, thereby improving the Department of State's ability to make a visa determination. When the visitor arrives in the United States, US-VISIT procedures allow the Department of Homeland Security to determine whether the person applying for entry is the same person who was issued the visa by the Department of State, and additional watch list checks improve the Department of Homeland Security's ability to make admissibility decisions.

US-VISIT entry procedures are currently in place at numerous air, sea and land ports with international arrivals. Entry procedures will be deployed to the remaining land border ports of entry by December 31, 2005. Additionally, biometric exit procedures are operating in several airports and seaports.

As it moves toward fulfilling its vision for an automated entry-exit system at the land border ports of entry into the United States, US-VISIT is continuing to improve the border management system through the innovative use of technology. On August 4, 2005, US-VISIT began testing radio frequency identification technology (RFID) at several U.S. land border ports.

HOW US-VISIT WORKS

Pre-Entry:

- Visitors applying for a visa have their information reviewed before they enter the United States. The Department of Homeland Security and the Department of State play essential roles in determining the eligibility of a visitor to receive a visa.

- Visitors from the Visa Waiver Program (VWP) countries must have a machine-readable passport to enter the United States without a visa. Beginning June 26, 2005, transportation carriers will be fined for transporting any VWP traveler to the United States without a machine-readable passport. Similarly, VWP travelers arriving in the United States on that date without a machine-readable passport will not be admitted into the country without a visa.

Entry:

- Many of the entry procedures in place today at airports and seaports remain unchanged and are familiar to international visitors. When a visitor arrives through an airport or seaport, he or she is enrolled in US-VISIT as part of the primary inspection process. At the nation's 50 busiest land ports of entry, those visitors carrying a foreign passport and/or who are required to complete a Form I 94 are enrolled in US-VISIT at the secondary inspection area. (This does not apply to most Canadian citizens or, initially, to Mexican citizens who use their Border Crossing Cards or "laser visas.")
- As Secretary Chertoff announced in mid-July, DHS will strengthen the US-VISIT Program by requiring 10-finger scans for all first-time visitors to the United States. Subsequent entries and exits at air, sea and land border ports will require two-finger scans for verification. The 10-finger scan enhances security and visitor privacy and increases accuracy, making it less likely that visitors will be referred for secondary inspection.
- Visitors will also look into a camera and have a digital picture taken.
- U.S. Customs and Border Protection Officers will review travel documents and ask questions about the visitor's stay in the United States.
- The biometric enhancements to the entry procedures take just seconds.
- Biometric identifiers also protect our visitors by making it virtually impossible for anyone else to claim their identities should their biometrically-enhanced travel documents (such as a visa) be stolen or duplicated.

Status Management:

- Should a visitor seek to adjust status or extend his/her stay, US-VISIT would be updated with any modifications to the individual's status.

Exit:

- US-VISIT is exploring departure confirmation alternatives at airports and seaports. The tests and evaluation will continue in 2005. Ultimately, all visitors will be required to check out before leaving the United States.
- US-VISIT exit procedures are operating at numerous locations around the United States, including Baltimore/Washington International Airport, Chicago O'Hare International Airport, Dallas/Fort Worth International Airport, Denver International Airport, Detroit Metropolitan Wayne County Airport, Fort Lauderdale-Hollywood International Airport, Hartsfield-Jackson Atlanta

International Airport, Long Beach and San Pedro seaports near Los Angeles, Luis Muñoz Marin International Airport in San Juan, Puerto Rico, Miami International Cruise Line Terminal, Newark Liberty International Airport, Philadelphia International Airport, San Francisco International Airport and Seattle-Tacoma International Airport. Visitors leaving from these locations must check out prior to exiting the United States. The exit program will be introduced at additional airports and seaports in the coming months.

- The exit procedures require visitors to check out at an exit station or with a US-VISIT workstation attendant at the departure gate at the port. After evaluating these exit procedures, DHS will select the most effective process to implement at airports and seaports system-wide. Visitors will go through one of the following three processes, depending on location.

  - Under one alternative, visitors departing the United States will check out of the country at exit stations located within the airport or seaport terminal. As with the process the visitors encounter upon entry at airports or seaports, their travel documents will be read, their two index fingers will be scanned at the exit station, a digital picture will be taken, and they will receive a printed receipt that verifies that they have checked out. A workstation attendant will be available to assist with visitors' checkout.

  - The second alternative still uses the exit station but includes an additional step – verification – at the departure gate. Visitors will be required to present the receipt at their departure gate to confirm that they checked out at the exit station. The workstation attendant will scan the receipt and then ask the visitor to place an index finger on the scanning device. Once the person's identity is matched to the receipt, the workstation attendant will hand back the receipt and the visitor will board the airplane.

  - Another alternative under the pilot program is a biometric checkout process with a US-VISIT workstation attendant at visitors' departure gates.

- Currently, visitors who depart from a port where the departure confirmation system is in place must comply. This exit confirmation information will help facilitate the visitor's future visits to the United States.

- US-VISIT compares arrival and departure biographical manifest data provided by the airlines and cruise lines to know when someone entered and exited the country.

AUTOMATED ENTRY-EXIT AT LAND BORDER PORTS

- US-VISIT intends to build upon the technologies and management systems previously employed for entry in order to realize an automated entry-exit process. RFID technology offers a solution for a potentially faster, biometrically-enabled entry-exit operation.

- Using an automatic identifier, RFID technology can detect a visitor at a distance and provide primary inspection with entry information. RFID can also provide a mechanism for an accurate and timely record of exits without requiring visitors to interrupt their travels by stopping or even slowing down to check out.

- RFID technology testing began August 4, 2005, at the Pacific Highway and Peace Arch in Washington state; Alexandria Bay in New York; and the ports of Nogales East and Nogales West in Arizona. The testing is expected to continue through the spring of 2006.
- US-VISIT will assure that our visitors' information is always protected. The RFID technology used by US-VISIT will protect sensitive information because it will read only a unique serial number that links to visitors' information securely stored in a database. It will also be tamper-proof and difficult to counterfeit or surreptitiously read.

RESPECTING PRIVACY AND THE ENVIRONMENT

- The Department of Homeland Security protects the biometric and biographic information provided by visitors and ensures that their privacy interests are not violated. US-VISIT records will be protected in a manner consistent with all applicable privacy laws and regulations. Personal information will be kept secure and confidential and will not be discussed with or disclosed to any person within or outside the US-VISIT Program other than as authorized by law and as required for the performance of official duties. Appropriate security controls will ensure that the data is not used or accessed improperly.
- US-VISIT has published a Privacy Impact Assessment that ensures that personal information is used appropriately, protected from misuse and improper disclosure and destroyed when no longer needed. This will be updated as necessary.
- A US-VISIT privacy officer is available to answer questions or resolve concerns and may be contacted by sending an e-mail to usvisitprivacy@dhs.gov or by writing to the Chief Privacy Officer, Department of Homeland Security, Washington, D.C. 20528, U.S.A., ATTN: US-VISIT Appeal. Information on the US-VISIT privacy program is available at www.dhs.gov/us-visit.
- US-VISIT complies with all environmental laws and regulations.

TIMING AND DELIVERY

- The Department of Homeland Security has met the December 31, 2003, and December 31, 2004, congressional deadlines to deploy an entry-exit program that strengthens security and facilitates travel for legitimate visitors while respecting their privacy and our environment.
- The US-VISIT Program received $340 million for FY 2004 and has been appropriated $340 million for FY 2005.

RELATED INFORMATION

• US-VISIT Begins Testing Radio Frequency Identification Technology to Improve Border Security and Travel, August 8, 2005.

updated August 11, 2005

Source: http://www.dhs.gov/dhspublic/interapp/press_release/press_release_0710.xml.

NOTES

1. http://thomas.loc.gov/cgi-bin/bdquery/z?d107:h.r.03525: (accessed March 14, 2006).

2. This summary provided by the Congressional Research Service (CRS) of the Library of Congress. Whenever new bills and resolutions are introduced in the House or Senate, CRS legislative analysts write an abstract that objectively describes the measure's most significant provisions in approximately 250 words or fewer. When a measure receives action (i.e., it is reported from a committee or passed by the House or Senate), the analysts then write a fuller digest, detailing the measure's effect upon programs and current law. Additional digests are prepared for each major action. A final Public Law summary is prepared upon enactment into law. For more information, see http://thomas.loc.gov/bss/abt_dgst.html.

APPENDIX C

SELECT INTERNATIONAL STRATEGIES TO IMPROVE BORDER SECURITY

BUILDING A SMART BORDER FOR THE 21ST CENTURY ON THE FOUNDATION OF A NORTH AMERICAN ZONE OF CONFIDENCE

The Canada-U.S. Smart Border Declaration

December 12, 2001

The terrorist actions of September 11 were an attack on our common commitment to democracy, the rule of law and a free and open economy. They highlighted a threat to our public and economic security. They require our governments to develop new approaches to meet these challenges. This declaration commits our governments to work together to address these threats to our people, our institutions and our prosperity.

Public security and economic security are mutually reinforcing. By working together to develop a zone of confidence against terrorist activity, we create a unique opportunity to build a smart border for the 21st century; a border that securely facilitates the free flow of people and commerce; a border that reflects the largest trading relationship in the world.

Our countries have a long history of cooperative border management. This tradition facilitated both countries' immediate responses to the attacks of September 11. It is the foundation on which we continue to base our cooperation, recognizing that our current and future prosperity and security depend on a border that operates efficiently and effectively under all circumstances.

ACTION PLAN

The attached *Action Plan for Creating a Secure and Smart Border* includes the measures already identified by our colleagues as well as new initiatives. Four pillars support the action plan:

(1) *The Secure Flow of People*

- We will implement systems to collaborate in identifying security risks while expediting the flow of low risk travellers.
- We will identify security threats before they arrive in North America through collaborative approaches to reviewing crew and passenger manifests, managing refugees, and visa policy coordination.
- We will establish a secure system to allow low risk frequent travellers between our countries to move efficiently across the border.

(2) *The Secure Flow of Goods*

- We will implement a system to collaborate in identifying high risk goods while expediting the flow of low risk goods.
- We will identify security threats arriving from abroad by developing common standards for screening cargo before it arrives in North America, while working to clear goods at the first port of entry.
- We will adopt compatible security standards at production and distribution facilities to minimize security threats. We will expedite the flow of low risk traffic between our countries by establishing compatible commercial processes at the border.
- We will expedite the flow of low risk goods between our countries by establishing secure procedures to clear goods away from the border, including at rail yards and at marine ports.

(3) *Secure Infrastructure*

- We will relieve congestion at key crossing points by investing reciprocally in border infrastructure and identifying technological solutions that will help to speed movement across the border.
- We will identify and minimize threats to our critical infrastructure including the airports, ports, bridges, tunnels, pipelines and powerlines that link our countries.

(4) *Coordination and Information Sharing in the Enforcement of these Objectives*

- We will put the necessary tools and legislative framework in place to ensure that information and intelligence is shared in a timely and coherent way within our respective countries as well as between them.

- We will strengthen coordination between our enforcement agencies for addressing common threats.

NEXT STEPS

- We will meet again early in the new year to review the critical paths that we have asked our officials to develop for realizing each of the objectives set out in the action plan. We will consult regularly to ensure continued progress on this plan to achieve the goals outlined as quickly as possible.
- This joint action plan is an important step. Our governments are committed to building on this plan to continually identify and implement measures that can be taken to secure a smart border.
- These measures are regarded by both governments as matters of the highest priority.

Ottawa, Canada
December 12, 2001

Source: The White House. *United States-Canada Smart Border Declaration: Building a Smart Border for the 21st Century on the Foundation of a North American Zone of Confidence.* Ottawa, Ontario, Canada: The Office of Homeland Security jointly with the Office of the Deputy Prime Minister, December 12, 2001, accessible at http://www.dfait-maeci.gc.ca/anti-terrorism/declaration-en.asp, and associated Action Plan, accessible at http://www.dfait-maeci.gc.ca/anti-terrorism/actionplan-en.asp.

ENHANCE TRANSPORT SECURITY AND CONTROL OF MAN-PORTABLE AIR DEFENCE SYSTEMS (MANPADS)

A G-8 Action Plan

We, the G8 Leaders, are determined to strengthen our joint efforts to curb terrorist threats against mass transportation. We shall continue to implement the Action Plan we agreed at Kananaskis to ensure safe, secure, efficient and reliable transportation world-wide. We have made important progress in implementing the plan and also have taken a number of new measures. The scope of our endeavors in this field covers five areas:

1. Manpads
2. Air transport
3. People
4. Container security
5. Sea transport

1. CONTROL OF MANPADS

1.1. At the Birmingham Summit in 1998, we recognized the threat posed to civil aviation by the criminal use of Man-Portable Air Defense Systems (Manpads) and called for further work to be done to address this problem. At Kananaskis, we agreed to promote transport security in the light of the terrorist attacks of 11 September 2001.

1.2. Today, at Evian, we reiterate our deep concern about the threat posed to civil aviation by Manpads, especially in the hands of terrorists or States that harbor them.

1.3. Manpads are surface-to-air missile systems specially designed to be carried and fired by a single individual. Manpads are portable and easily concealed, yet capable of potentially catastrophic destruction. We are therefore implementing national measures to combat such illegal use of Manpads, and will encourage other States to do so as well.

1.4. Given the increasing number of Manpads in world-wide circulation, we commit ourselves to reducing their proliferation and call upon all countries to strengthen control of their Manpads stockpiles.

1.5. In the framework of the Wassenaar Arrangement, "Elements for the Export Controls of Manpads" were agreed by all 33 participating States in 2000. This was a valuable step forward. We undertake to promote the application of the principles defined in these "Elements" by a larger number of States.

1.6. In addition, we agree to implement the following steps to prevent the acquisition of Manpads by terrorists:

- To provide assistance and technical expertise for the collection, secure stockpile management and destruction of Manpads surplus to national security requirements;
- To adopt strict national export controls on Manpads and their essential components;
- To ensure strong national regulation of production, transfer and brokering;
- To ban transfers of Manpads to non-state end-users; Manpads should only be exported to foreign governments or to agents authorised by a government;
- To exchange information on unco-operative countries and entities;
- To examine the feasibility of development for new Manpads of specific technical performance or launch control features that preclude their unauthorised use;
- To encourage action in the International Civil Aviation Organisation (ICAO) Aviation Security (AVSEC) Working Group on Manpads.

1.7. We agree to exchange information on national measures related to the implementation of these steps by December 2003. We will review progress at our next meeting in 2004.

2. AIR TRANSPORT

2.1. Measures already being implemented:

- Agreement to implement by November 2003 the new international standards for the installation of flight deck doors, as adopted by ICAO;
- Continued support for the implementation of the ICAO Universal Security Audit Program of all ICAO Member States. First audits have been conducted;
- Increased co-operation on aviation security between us, including implementation of this Action Plan, using ICAO and other relevant international organizations. This will strengthen overall standards across the G8.

2.2. Enhance the air security action plan and develop effective aviation security quality control systems worldwide:

- To review security procedures in place to ensure that staff do not pose a threat to aviation, including, in particular, by examining the feasibility and benefits of ensuring that all staff and items carried are screened when they enter critical parts of security-restricted areas of airports;
- To encourage further work within ICAO to review and adopt the measures related to an enhanced threat level for the standard security procedures;
- To encourage each of us to adopt and implement as soon as possible the harmonized and supplementary provisions on flight-deck door locking issued by the ICAO. Each of us intends to apply these requirements both to international and domestic flights;
- To explore experience gained, inter alia, from installation of on-board TV monitoring systems to control the security inside passenger aircraft;
- To co-ordinate aviation security capacity building efforts for non-G8 countries and to lead in donating funds and advisors to ICAO's aviation security audit program (AVSEC).

3. PEOPLE

3.1. We have developed guidelines for the implementation of international standards governing the use of biometrics to verify the identity of travelers and have forwarded them to the ICAO. We endorse the "G8 Roma and Lyon Groups Statement on Biometric Applications for International Travel" and are resolved in our continued support for the ongoing work within ICAO.

3.2. We also agree to develop a secure, verifiable seafarer identity document at the International Labor Organisation (ILO) and are working together towards agreeing on seafarers and port workers security requirements compatible with trade facilitation at the International Maritime Organization (IMO) and the ILO.

3.3. We are working together to accelerate the use of the joint World Customs Organization (WCO) / ICAO / International Air Transport Association (IATA) guidelines as a global standard for advance passenger information, and will work to ensure that other necessary requirements for passenger information are developed to a global standard.

4. CONTAINER SECURITY

4.1. We are working together to reinforce container security arrangements generally and to develop specifically, within the WCO, joint standards and guidelines for electronic transmission of customs data for cargo and a standardised set of data elements to identify high-risk cargo. We are also working together at the same time to combine security needs with trade facilitation.

4.2. Our active support of pilot projects that model an integrated container security regime contributed to the rapid expansion of the Container Security Initiative (CSI), which is now operational in ten major international ports, seven of which are in G8 countries. Our continued support of CSI will encourage rapidly expanding participation by other ports, further enhancing global container security. As international security is only as effective as its weakest link, we support international co-operation in the WCO to ensure a more co-ordinated approach for all ports handling international cargo.

5. SEA TRANSPORT

5.1. At Kananaskis, we agreed to support in the IMO amendments to the International Convention for the Safety of Life at Sea that require mandatory ship security plans, on-board ship security officers, mandatory port facility security plans and port facility security assessments for relevant ports serving ships engaged on international voyages, to be included during the development of an International Ship and Port Facility Security Code by July 2004. 5.2. In December 2002, the IMO adopted these amendments which also provide for the fitting of Automatic Identification Systems on ships by 31 December 2004. We support the implementation of measures in this sphere as agreed at our 2002 Summit.

Source: G-8 Action Plan: Enhance Transport Security and Control of Man Portable Air Defense Systems (MANPADS). Evian, France: The White House, 2003, accessible at: http://www.g8.fr/evian/english/navigation/news/news_update/enhance_transport_security_and_control_of_man-portable_air_defence_systems_-_manpads_-_a_g8_action_plan.html.

G-8 LEADERS AGREE ON SET OF ACTIONS TO ENHANCE TRANSPORT SECURITY

June 26, 2002

Following is the text of a fact sheet on transportation security measures agreed to at the June 26-27 Group-of-Eight Summit in Kananaskis, Alberta:

COOPERATIVE G-8 ACTION ON TRANSPORT SECURITY

The terrorist attacks on September 11, 2001 illustrated the critical yet fragile nature of the international transport system. For the global economy to flourish, this system must continue to provide safe, secure, efficient and reliable services to travellers and customers in all parts of the world. We have therefore agreed on a set of cooperative actions to promote greater security of land, sea and air transport while facilitating the cost-effective and efficient flow of people, cargo, and vehicles for legitimate economic and social purposes. The G8 will:

PEOPLE

Implement as expeditiously as possible a common global standard based on UN EDIFACT for the collection and transmission of advance passenger information (API). Work towards granting reciprocal bilateral access, on a voluntary basis, to departure and transit lounges, including timely implementation of a pilot project. Work towards agreement by October 2002 on minimum standards for issuance of travel and identity documents for adoption at ICAO, and by June 2003 on minimum standards for issuance of seafarers' identity documents for adoption at the ILO. Work towards developing recommendations on minimum standards for the application of biometrics in procedures and documents by the spring of 2003, with a view to forwarding them to standards organizations. Improve procedures and practices for sharing data on lost or stolen passports and denied entries, with a practical exercise by September 2002.

CONTAINER SECURITY

Recognizing the urgency of securing global trade, work expeditiously, in cooperation with relevant international organizations, to develop and implement an improved global container security regime to identify and examine high-risk containers and ensure their in-transit integrity. Develop, in collaboration with interested non-G8 countries, pilot projects that model an integrated container security regime. Implement expeditiously, by 2005 wherever possible, common standards for electronic customs reporting, and work in the WCO to encourage the implementation of the same common standards by non-G8 countries. Begin work expeditiously within the G8 and the WCO to require advance electronic information pertaining to containers, including their location and transit, as early as possible in the trade chain.

AVIATION SECURITY

Accelerate implementation of standards for reinforced flight deck doors for all G8 passenger aircraft, by April 2003 wherever possible. Support in ICAO the rapid implementation of mandatory aviation security audits of all ICAO contracting states. Enhance cooperation, in a spirit of capacity-building assistance, on aviation security with other countries. The G8 will also share their information and assessments about security vulnerabilities. Encourage non-G8 countries to make, as we have done, proportionate contributions to the ICAO AVSEC mechanism, and encourage MDBs to consider requests to assist developing countries in this area.

MARITIME SECURITY

Support, in the IMO, amendment of the International Convention for the Safety of Life at Sea (SOLAS) to accelerate the date of the installation of automatic identification systems (AIS) on certain ships to December 2004. Support, in the IMO, amendment of the International Convention for the Safety of Life at Sea (SOLAS) to require mandatory ship security plans and ship security officers on board ships by July 2004. Support, in the IMO, amendment of the International Convention for the Safety of Life at Sea (SOLAS) to require mandatory port facility security plans and port facility security assessments for relevant ports serving ships engaged on international voyages by July 2004.

LAND TRANSPORTATION

Develop, in the UN and other relevant international organizations, an effective and proportionate security regime for the overland transportation and distribution of hazardous cargoes which present potentially significant security risks, with initial consultations this year.

IMPLEMENTATION

In order to ensure timely implementation of this initiative, we will review progress every six months, providing direction as required to G8 experts. G8 experts will pursue these priorities and will promote policy coherence and coordination in all relevant international organizations

(ICAO, IMO, WCO, ILO), in partnership with industry. – The Government of the Russian Federation supports the proposal concerning installation of AIS on certain ships by December 2004, as well as the proposal concerning availability of port facility security plans and port facility security assessments for relevant ports serving ships engaged on international voyages by July 2004. However, on grounds of technical feasibility of these proposals, the Russian Federation reserves for itself the right to extend the timeframe of their implementation by the year 2006.

06/26 Kananaskis Summit Document: Cooperative G8 Action on Transport Security

Source: G-8 Transportation Security Initiative. Kananaskis, Alberta, Canada: The White House, June 26–27, 2002, accessible at http://www.useu.be/Categories/Transportation/June2602G8TransportSecurity.html.

G-8 SECURE AND FACILITATED INTERNATIONAL TRAVEL INITIATIVE (SAFTI)

The White House, June 9, 2004

Terrorist attacks against the transportation system remain a serious threat to our citizens and to world commerce. We, the G-8 Leaders, are committed to further assuring the safety of the traveling public while working cooperatively to facilitate movement of travelers across our borders.

At Kananaskis in June 2002, we agreed on a set of actions to promote greater security of land, sea, and air transport, including cargo, to ensure safe, secure, efficient and reliable transportation world-wide. At Evian in 2003, we introduced a plan for the control of Man-Portable Air Defense Systems (MANPADS), and established the Counter Terrorism Action Group (CTAG) to assist willing states in building their capacity to counter the terrorist threat.

Today, at Sea Island, we agree on a set of actions that will further enhance the security of the traveling public while improving the efficiency and facilitating the ease of travel. These include actions to implement and expand the scope of the Evian MANPADS plan.

In the Secure and Facilitated International Travel Initiative (SAFTI), G-8 members support raising standards, modernizing procedures, and exchanging information in order to deter threats, reduce costs, and help ensure safe and efficient movement of passengers and cargo, thereby benefiting international commerce while enhancing security.

We recognize the urgency of our need to work together to counter the terrorist threat within a framework that fully respects the sovereign rights of states to control their borders and that is in compliance with domestic laws and international obligations relating to privacy. We reaffirm our commitment to promote and implement relevant international standards in appropriate fora such as ICAO and IMO. In this regard, we agree to the following shared principles, which underlie our initiative:

- Work collaboratively, cooperatively, and reciprocally to protect borders and facilitate trade and travel.

- Facilitate movement of travelers across international borders quickly and easily, while focusing enforcement resources on enhanced security procedures, including risk analysis methods.

- Permit visa-free travel and simplify and expedite visa processing when acceptable to the receiving state.

- Maximize effective information exchange among partner states as a key element of strengthening international border security.

- Work cooperatively to improve screening methods for international travelers, crews, and cargo for known or emerging threats as far in advance as possible.

- Make all possible efforts to ensure that travel documents are secure, resistant to fraud and globally interoperable.

- Ensure effective, coordinated responses to imminent threats.

To demonstrate our resolve to expeditiously address security vulnerabilities and ensure the traveling public that we are taking all appropriate steps to protect their safety, we announce today that we already have completed the following actions from the SAFTI initiative:

- The promotion and implementation of enhanced international standards for the secure issuance of passports;

- The establishment of a 24-hour aviation point of contact network to address imminent threats to airlines; and

- The preparation of an information manual for assessing the vulnerability of G-8 airports to the MANPADS threat.

The agreed SAFTI Action Plan follows and includes 28 individual action items. Where a projected completion date is not specified for an action item still in progress, we commit to achieving measurable progress by December 2004, with a report on such progress by January 2005.

G-8 SECURE AND FACILITATED INTERNATIONAL TRAVEL INITIATIVE (SAFTI)

Action Plan

Document Interoperability through International Standards

1. Expedite cooperative work to develop and export best practices, including methods of risk analysis, to ensure security while facilitating travel across international borders, particularly for frequent travelers, without compromising existing or future security procedures. We will ensure these best practices are fair and objective.

2. Work with ICAO and others to strengthen international standardized practices for passport issuance, and encourage their adoption and implementation by all governments. We will work to effect implementation by the 2005 Summit.

3. Accelerate development of international standards for the interoperability of government-issued smart chip passports and other government-issued identity documents. We will work for implementation by the 2005 Summit.

International Information Exchange

4. Develop mechanisms, where possible, for real-time data exchange with respect to validation of travel documents, visa watchlist information and advanced passenger information, while fully respecting applicable personal data protection rules. Interim progress by December 2004, with a view toward beginning implementation in 2005.

5. Agree to provide effective and timely information exchange on the terrorist watchlist or lookout data of participating countries on a reciprocal basis, using procedures that satisfy security concerns and are consistent with the privacy and other laws of those countries. Status report to be provided by the end of the year; implement by the 2005 Summit.

6. Agree to start providing information by December 2004 to an Interpol database that allows for real-time information sharing on lost and stolen international travel documents.

7. In carrying out the SAFTI initiative, share best practices on effective cooperation between intelligence and law enforcement officials.

MANPADS Threat Reduction

8. Accelerate efforts to destroy excess and/or obsolete MANPADS and provide assistance to do so where needed.

9. Work toward expedited adoption of the updated 2003 Wassenaar "Elements for Export Controls on MANPADS" as an international standard.

10. Further strengthen controls on transfer of MANPADS production technology to deter marketing of MANPADS by countries that do not maintain strong standards of export controls.

11. Establish a best practices document, that can be adopted as an international standard, on optimal methods for securely storing MANPADS.

12. Develop a methodology to be used by G-8 countries in assessing airport vulnerability to the MANPADS threat and effective countermeasures, taking into account the study conducted by ICAO.

13. Improve methods for enhancing MANPADS identification techniques and countermeasures against smuggling.

Capacity Building and Collaboration

14. Collaborate to improve methodologies, techniques and systems to analyze data on passengers, crew and cargo in advance of travel. Provide a status report by December 2004; where improved approaches are agreed, seek to begin to implement them by the 2005 Summit.

15. Develop procedures, working with ICAO, to ensure that all states have proper inspections and enforcement regimes to ensure that airlines and airports are complying with international standards.

16. Establish a Point-of-Contact network for the communication of imminent threats to civilian air transportation and urgent security requests, and guidelines for responding.

17. Accelerate efforts to develop best practices and procedures for air and ground countermeasures, including the training, qualification and use of guards and sky marshals, as appropriate; examine how to work within ICAO and CTAG to share expertise and information with others. Begin implementation of these agreed best practices and procedures by December 2004; finalize in 2005.

18. Examine ways and means to collaborate, on a reciprocal basis, on the forward placement of document advisors, where this will effectively contribute to aviation security and where mutually acceptable and bilateral arrangements are worked out.

19. Develop arrangements to ensure that passengers and their hold and cabin bags, once screened, are protected from unlawful interference, through the deployment of a "layered security" regime comprising background checks on staff; robust physical access controls; and arrangements to limit access to screened passengers and their bags to persons who are subject to an appropriate security system. Seek to finalize plans in 2005 for implementing the regime.

20. Work to develop and promote cost effective, robust flight deck security, first by pressing for full compliance by October 2004 by all States with the requirements of the ICAO Standards for all passenger aircraft of over 45.5 metric tons or more than 60 passenger seats to be fitted with reinforced flight deck doors, and then by examining ways to reinforce flight deck security, including reinforced bulkheads. All such carriers flying within G-8 airspace

should be compliant on flight deck door security by October 2004. Provide progress report on bulkhead security study by 2005 Summit.

21. Identify and adopt best practices within the G-8, and then promote these practices internationally, to ensure that appropriate information regarding passengers in transit is provided to the transit state from the immediately preceding departure state.

22. Study and assess the need for, and the feasibility of, developing guidelines similar to ICAO Standards of Aviation Security for possible application to General Aviation and Corporate/Business Aviation operations in order to enhance security regulations.

23. Endorse and promote mechanisms for frequent consultation with public and private sector transportation security stakeholders.

24. Expand research and development collaboration on biometric technologies, working with ICAO, to develop for practical implementation a next-generation passenger control concept. Show progress by 2005.

25. Examine ways and means to further improve, simplify and expedite visa procedures to enhance security and facilitate legitimate travel when acceptable to the receiving state.

26. Assess and reduce terrorism-related risk in the maritime domain through focused cooperative efforts, beginning with voluntary self audits and the development of a port facilities security auditing methodology and checklist among the G-8 and within the International Maritime Organization, taking into account the concept of the ICAO audit program for aviation security.

27. Endorse increased support for capacity building through CTAG to willing states to improve their travel document approval and issuance systems, and border controls.

28. Undertake, through CTAG, to examine how the G-8 and other states or organizations can assist states in meeting and sustaining these new security requirements.

Source: G-8 Secure and Facilitated International Travel Initiative. Sea Island, GA: The White House, June 9, 2004, accessible at http://www.whitehouse.gov/news/releases/2004/06/20040609-51.html.

APPENDIX D

SELECT POLICY STATEMENTS AND INITIATIVES ON MARITIME AND PORT SECURITY

Over 95 percent of non-North American trade enters the country through America's 361 commercial seaports, which handle over $740 billion and 2 billion tons off domestic and international freight annually. Over 50,000 foreign vessels enter U.S. ports annually.[1] Clearly, the U.S. relies heavily on this flow of international trade, and must prevent it from being disrupted by terrorism. Maritime and port security is thus a vital part of protecting the homeland. While action on this front was limited prior to 9/11, the U.S. has taken several steps forward in recent years. The *Maritime Transportation Security Act of 2002* provided new resources and established regulations for improving what the U.S. Coast Guard refers to as maritime domain awareness. The major provisions of this act are summarized in Figure D.1.

The remaining pages of this Appendix provide summaries and examples of key U.S. strategic documents in support of port and maritime security, beginning with the National Security Presidential Directive-41/ Homeland Security Presidential Directive-13, signed by President Bush on December 21, 2004.

NATIONAL SECURITY PRESIDENTIAL DIRECTIVE-41/HOMELAND SECURITY PRESIDENTIAL DIRECTIVE-13

December 21, 2004

This directive establishes U.S. policy, guidelines, and implementation actions to enhance U.S. national security and homeland security by protecting U.S. maritime interests. It directs the coordination of United States

> **Domestic Facility and Vessel Vulnerability Assessments**. Tasks the Coast Guard with conducting an initial assessment of vessel types and United States facilities to identify risks. These assessments include critical assets and infrastructures, identification of the threats, and weaknesses in physical security, passenger and cargo security, communications systems, transportation infrastructure, and contingency response.
>
> **Maritime Transportation Security Plans**. Requires a National Maritime Transportation Security Plan for deterring and responding to transportation security incidents. These plans "shall provide for efficient, coordinated, and effective action to deter and minimize damage from a transportation security incident."
>
> **Vessel and Facility Security Plans**. Requires an owner or operator of a vessel or facility to prepare and submit a security plan for the vessel or facility, for deterring a transportation security incident. Such plans are to include provisions for
> - Establishing and controlling access to secure areas of the vessel or facility;
> - Procedural security policies;
> - Communications systems; and
> - Training and periodic unannounced drills.
>
> **Transportation Security Cards**. These cards help enforce new access regulations to prevent individuals from entering areas of a vessel or facility designated as a secure area.
>
> **Security Grants**. Establishes a grant program for port authorities, and State and local agencies that contribute to implementing Area Maritime Transportation Security Plans and facility security plans. Included are costs for acquisition, operation, and maintenance of security equipment, security gates and fencing, marine barriers for security zones, lighting systems, remote surveillance, video systems, security vessels, and other infrastructure.
>
> **Foreign port assessment**. Directs the government to assess the effectiveness of the antiterrorism measures at foreign ports from which foreign vessels depart on a voyage to the U.S.; as well as any foreign port believed to pose a security risk to maritime commerce.
>
> **Container Security**. Requires the DHS to maintain a cargo tracking, identification and screening system for shipping containers shipped to and from the United States. Requires the establishment of standards to enhance the physical security of shipping containers, including seals and locks. Contains other important security enhancements for crew identification, Sea marshals, and vessel transponders to track vessels in U.S. waters.

Figure D.1 Major Provisions of *The Maritime Transportation Security Act of 2002*

Source: Frank Hoffman, 2005. *The Maritime Transportation Security Act of 2002* is available online at http://www.uscg.mil/hq/g-m/mp/mtsa.shtml.

Government maritime security programs and initiatives to achieve a comprehensive and cohesive national effort involving appropriate Federal, State, local, and private sector entities. This directive also establishes a Maritime Security Policy Coordinating Committee to coordinate interagency maritime security policy efforts.

As specified herein, the Assistant to the President for National Security Affairs and the Assistant to the President for Homeland Security, in cooperation with appropriate Federal departments and agencies, will jointly coordinate the implementation of the policy set forth in Section II of this directive.

I. BACKGROUND

For the purposes of this directive, "Maritime Domain" means all areas and things of, on, under, relating to, adjacent to, or bordering on a sea, ocean, or other navigable waterway, including all maritime-related activities, infrastructure, people, cargo, and vessels and other conveyances.

Due to its complex nature and immense size, the Maritime Domain is particularly susceptible to exploitation and disruption by individuals, organizations, and States. The Maritime Domain facilitates a unique freedom of movement and flow of goods while allowing people, cargo, and conveyances to transit with anonymity not generally available by movement over land or by air. Individuals and organizations hostile to the United States have demonstrated a continuing desire to exploit such vulnerabilities.

The United States must deploy the full range of its operational assets and capabilities to prevent the Maritime Domain from being used by terrorists, criminals, and hostile States to commit acts of terrorism and criminal or other unlawful or hostile acts against the United States, its people, economy, property, territory, allies, and friends, while recognizing that maritime security policies are most effective when the strategic importance of international trade, economic cooperation, and the free flow of commerce are considered appropriately.

II. POLICY

The security of the Maritime Domain is a global issue. The United States, in cooperation with our allies and friends around the world and our State, local, and private sector partners, will work to ensure that lawful private and public activities in the Maritime Domain are protected against attack and criminal and otherwise unlawful or hostile exploitation. These efforts are critical to global economic stability and growth and are vital to the interests of the United States.

It is the policy of the United States to take all necessary and appropriate actions, consistent with U.S. law, treaties and other international agreements to which the United States is a party, and customary international law as determined for the United States by the President, to enhance the security of and protect U.S. interests in the Maritime Domain, including the following:

- Preventing terrorist attacks or criminal acts or hostile acts in, or the unlawful exploitation of, the Maritime Domain, and reducing the vulnerability of the Maritime Domain to such acts and exploitation;
- Enhancing U.S. national security and homeland security by protecting U.S. population centers, critical infrastructure, borders, harbors, ports, and coastal approaches in the Maritime Domain;
- Expediting recovery and response from attacks within the Maritime Domain;
- Maximizing awareness of security issues in the Maritime Domain in order to support U.S. forces and improve United States Government actions in response to identified threats;

- Enhancing international relationships and promoting the integration of U.S. allies and international and private sector partners into an improved global maritime security framework to advance common security interests in the Maritime Domain; and
- Ensuring seamless, coordinated implementation of authorities and responsibilities relating to the security of the Maritime Domain by and among Federal departments and agencies.

These actions must be undertaken in a manner that facilitates global commerce and preserves the freedom of the seas for legitimate military and commercial navigation and other legitimate activities as well as civil liberties and the rights guaranteed under the Constitution.

III. POLICY COORDINATION

The Maritime Security Policy Coordinating Committee (MSPCC) is hereby established, consistent with NSPD-1 and HSPD-1. The MSPCC, in consultation with the relevant regional and functional policy coordinating committees of the Federal Government, and without exercising operational oversight, shall act as the primary forum for interagency coordination of the implementation of this directive. As part of that effort, the MSPCC shall review existing interagency practices, coordination, and execution of U.S. policies and strategies relating to maritime security, and shall recommend specific improvements to all of them as warranted. The MSPCC shall provide analysis of new U.S. policies, strategies, and initiatives relating to maritime security for consideration by the Deputies and Principals Committees of the NSC and the HSC, and subsequently by the NSC and the HSC, and shall ensure ongoing coordination and implementation of such policies, strategies, and initiatives. The reviews, plans, and recommendations required by this directive (as set forth in Sections IV and V below) shall be completed by the departments and agencies designated herein in coordination with the MSPCC, and shall then be prepared for consideration by and submitted to the Deputies and Principals Committees of the NSC and the HSC, and subsequently to the NSC and the HSC.

The MSPCC shall be co-chaired by an NSC staff representative selected by the Assistant to the President for National Security Affairs and an HSC representative selected by the Assistant to the President for Homeland Security, and shall include the following officers or their designated representatives:

- The Vice President
- The Secretary of State
- The Secretary of the Treasury

- The Secretary of Defense
- The Attorney General
- The Secretary of the Interior
- The Secretary of Commerce
- The Secretary of Transportation
- The Secretary of Energy
- The Secretary of Homeland Security
- Director, Office of Management and Budget
- The United States Trade Representative
- Chairman of the Council on Environmental Quality
- Director of Central Intelligence
- Chairman of the Joint Chiefs of Staff
- Director, Federal Bureau of Investigation
- Director, National Counterterrorism Center

The co-chairs of the MSPCC may invite representatives of other departments and agencies to attend MSPCC meetings as they deem appropriate.

IV. POLICY IMPLEMENTATION

National Strategy for Maritime Security. A coordinated and integrated government-wide effort to enhance the security of the Maritime Domain requires an over-arching strategy. The Secretaries of Defense and Homeland Security shall jointly lead a collaborative interagency effort to draft a recommended National Strategy for Maritime Security, which shall be submitted for my consideration within 180 days after the effective date of this directive. Such a strategy must present an over-arching plan to implement this directive and address all of the components of the Maritime Domain, including domestic, international, public, and private components. It shall further incorporate a global, cross-discipline approach to the Maritime Domain centered on a layered, defense-in-depth framework that may be adjusted based on the threat level. The strategy shall build on current efforts and those initiated by this directive, as well as complement existing strategies, tools, and resources. All relevant Federal departments and agencies shall cooperate with the Secretaries of Defense and Homeland Security in this effort and provide all appropriate assistance.

V. POLICY ACTIONS

In concert with the development of a National Strategy for Maritime Security, the following actions M shall be taken:

Maritime Domain Awareness (MDA). Maritime Domain Awareness is the effective understanding of anything associated with the global Maritime Domain that could impact the security, safety, economy, or environment of the United States. It is critical that the United States develop an enhanced capability to identify threats to the Maritime Domain as early and as distant from our shores as possible by integrating intelligence, surveillance, observation, and navigation systems into a common operating picture accessible throughout the United States Government.

The Secretaries of Defense and Homeland Security have established a Maritime Domain Awareness Senior Steering Group (MDASSG). The MDASSG is co-chaired by representatives of the Secretaries of Defense and Homeland Security and includes representatives from departments and agencies that will participate in the MSPCC.

The MDASSG shall coordinate national efforts to achieve maximum Maritime Domain Awareness. No later than 180 days after the effective date of this directive, the MDASSG will develop and submit to me, through the Secretaries of Defense and Homeland Security, a national plan to improve Maritime Domain Awareness, which shall include near-term and long-term objectives, required program and resource implications, and any recommendations for organizational or policy changes.

Global Maritime Intelligence Integration. A robust and coordinated intelligence effort serves as the foundation for effective security efforts in the Maritime Domain. In support of this effort, I direct the Secretaries of Defense and Homeland Security, with the support of the Director of Central Intelligence, and in coordination with the Director of the National Counterterrorism Center (NCTC) and the Director of the Federal Bureau of Investigation (FBI), to use existing intelligence capabilities to integrate all available intelligence on a global basis regarding the location, identity, and operational capabilities and intentions of potential threats to U.S. interests in the Maritime Domain. The Secretaries of Defense and Homeland Security, with the support of the Director of Central Intelligence, and in coordination with the Director of the NCTC, the Director of the FBI, and other appropriate departments and agencies, shall submit to me for approval, through the Assistants to the President for National Security Affairs and Homeland Security, a plan for global maritime intelligence integration within 180 days after the effective date of this directive. The plan shall include appropriate interagency participation to ensure effective government-wide sharing of information and data critical to intelligence production.

Domestic Outreach. A successful strategy to implement this directive must include coordination with State and local authorities and consultation with appropriate private sector persons and entities. The Secretary of Homeland Security, in coordination with the Attorney General and the Secretaries of the Treasury, Interior, Commerce, and Transportation, shall lead the development of a comprehensive engagement plan that ensures that the interests of State and local governments and the private sector are considered in the Federal Government's implementation of this directive. The plan shall be completed within 180 days after the effective date of this directive and shall take effect upon approval by the Secretary of Homeland Security.

Coordination of International Efforts and International Outreach. Ensuring the security of the Maritime Domain must be a global effort, in which United States Government efforts are developed and furthered with the support of other governments and international organizations resulting in lasting international cooperation. The Secretary of State shall lead the coordination of United States Government initiatives in the implementation of this directive with regard to activities with foreign governments and international organizations. All Federal departments and agencies shall coordinate with the Department of State on policies, programs, and initiatives relating to the implementation of this directive that could affect the conduct of foreign policy. In addition, the Secretary of State, in coordination with the Secretaries of Defense, Commerce, Transportation, and Homeland Security, and the U.S. Trade Representative, and in consultation with appropriate private sector persons and entities, shall develop, within 180 days after the effective date of this directive, a comprehensive plan to solicit international support for an improved global maritime security framework. Such plan shall take effect upon approval by the Secretary of State.

Maritime Threat Response. The Secretaries of Defense and Homeland Security, in consultation with the Attorney General and the Secretaries of State, the Treasury, Commerce, and Transportation, shall develop a comprehensive National Maritime Security Response Plan to ensure seamless United States Government response to maritime threats against the United States. This plan, when approved by me, shall supplement the National Response Plan required by HSPD-5 and complement the critical infrastructure protection plans required by HSPD-7 and the domestic all-hazards preparedness goals and structures required by HSPD-8. The plan, at a minimum, shall reflect lead agency roles and responsibilities, including recommendations regarding changes to existing policy, including those reflected in PDD-39 and PDD-62, in the following areas:

1) maritime security response and counterterrorism operations;

2) maritime interception operations;

3) prevention and detection of, and response to, the mining of U.S. ports;

4) detection, interdiction and disposition of targeted cargo, people, and vessels; and

5) attacks on vessels with U.S. citizens aboard or that affect U.S. interests anywhere in the world.

The plan also shall: 1) include recommended protocols that establish
clear coordination relationships governing protection and defense of the
United States against threats to its interests in the Maritime Domain; and
2) provide recommendations concerning the designation of an interagency planning and command-and-control entity to ensure unity of
command for national execution of maritime security policy. An interim
plan shall be submitted no later than 180 days after the effective date of
this directive, through the Assistants to the President for National Security Affairs and Homeland Security, and shall be finalized after completion
of the National Strategy for Maritime Security.

Maritime Infrastructure Recovery. Rapid recovery from an attack or
similar disruption in the Maritime Domain is critical to the economic
well-being of our Nation. A credible capability for rapid recovery will
not only minimize an incident's economic impact but also serve as a
deterrent. The Secretary of Homeland Security, in coordination with other
appropriate officials, including the Secretaries of Defense, State, the Treasury, the Interior, Commerce, and Transportation, and in consultation with
key industry stakeholders, shall be responsible for the development of
recommended minimum Federal standards, where appropriate, for maritime recovery operations, and shall develop comprehensive national maritime infrastructure recovery standards and a plan, complementary to the
national preparedness goals and standards required by HSPD-8. Such
standards and plan shall be completed no later than 180 days after the
effective date of this directive, shall focus on the restoration of physical
assets and transportation systems, and shall take effect when approved
by the Secretary of Homeland Security. The standards and plan also shall
describe a maritime infrastructure recovery exercise program consistent
with the National Exercise Program administered by the Department of
Homeland Security. The program shall address coordination with State,
local, and private sector partners, and cooperation with foreign governments and international entities as appropriate.

Maritime Transportation System Security. The Secretary of Homeland
Security, in coordination with the Secretaries of Defense, State,
Commerce, and Transportation, and the U.S. Trade Representative, and
in consultation with appropriate industry representatives, shall develop
recommendations for improvements to the national and international
regulatory framework with respect to licensing, carriage, communications, safety equipment, and other critical systems for all private
vessels, including commercial vessels, operating in the Maritime
Domain. The recommendations shall be submitted to me, through
the Assistants to the President for National Security Affairs and

Homeland Security, no later than 180 days after the effective date of this directive.

Maritime Commerce Security. To implement this directive effectively and to enhance economic growth, the United States must promote global supply chain security practices to reduce the risk of terrorists or criminals acting against the United States from within the Maritime Domain. The Secretary of Homeland Security, in coordination with the Secretaries of Defense, State, the Treasury, Commerce, Transportation, and Energy and the U.S. Trade Representative shall lead a collaborative interagency effort, in consultation with appropriate industry representatives, to develop a comprehensive international maritime supply chain security plan no later than 180 days after the effective date of this directive. The plan shall define supply-chain security requirements, include recommendations to further secure commercial operations from point of origin to point of destination, build on available resources, and provide a recommended framework of roles, responsibilities, and implementation actions. The plan shall define measurable national "end state" supply chain security goals and develop contingency plans to continue the flow of commerce in the event of an incident necessitating total or partial closure of U.S. borders to maritime commerce. The plan shall take effect upon approval by the Secretary of Homeland Security.

VI. GENERAL

This directive does not alter existing authorities or responsibilities of the department and agency heads, including their authorities, to carry out operational activities or to provide or receive information. This directive is intended only to improve the internal management of the Executive Branch and is not intended to, and does not; create any right or benefit enforceable at law or in equity by any party against the United States, its departments, agencies, entities, officers, employees, or agents, or any other person. Nothing in this directive impairs or otherwise affects the authority of the Secretary of Defense over the Department of Defense, including the chain of command for military forces from the President and Commander-in-Chief, to the Secretary of Defense, to the commander of military forces, or military command and control procedures.

The Assistants to the President for National Security Affairs and Homeland Security and the Chairman of the Council on Environmental Quality shall coordinate as appropriate the work of the MSPCC under this directive and the work of the Committee on Ocean Policy under the Executive Order of December 17, 2004.

Source: http://fas.org/irp/offdocs/nspd/nspd41.pdf. Also, see the DHS summary of the *Maritime Security Policy National Security/Homeland Security Presidential Directive.* Online at http://www.dhs.gov/dhspublic/display?theme=67&content=4566.

THE NATIONAL STRATEGY FOR MARITIME SECURITY

(A Brief Summary, by James Forest)

The *National Security Presidential Directive-41/Homeland Security Presidential Directive-13* led to the creation of a Maritime Security Policy Coordinating Committee (which coordinates maritime security efforts across the U.S. government)[2] and the creation of a *National Strategy for Maritime Security* (NSMS), released in September 2005.[3] The NSMS is organized into three main sections, identifying primary threats to maritime security, strategic objectives to counter these threats, and actions through which these objectives will be achieved. In the first section, the document identifies five main categories of threats—three of which are actors (nation-states, terrorists, and transnational criminals and pirates) and the remaining two are specific types of damage to global, political, and economic security that these actors could cause. As the strategy explains, "unprecedented advances in telecommunications and dramatic improvements in international commercial logistics have combined to increase both the range and effects of terrorist activities, providing the physical means to transcend even the most secure borders and to move rapidly across great distances....The maritime domain in particular presents not only a medium by which these threats can move, but offers a broad array of potential targets that fit the terrorists' operational objectives of achieving mass casualties and inflicting catastrophic economic harm."[4] Although the strategy articulates specific concerns about nation-states (specifically, providing safe havens for criminals and terrorists, and seeking weapons of mass destruction), it makes clear that "defeating the threat of the widely dispersed terrorist networks that present an immediate danger to U.S. national security interests at home and abroad remains our foremost objective."[5]

In explaining the capabilities of these terrorist networks, the NSMS notes that "Some terrorist groups have used shipping as a means of conveyance for positioning their agents, logistical support, and generating revenue. Terrorists have also taken advantage of criminal smuggling networks to circumvent border security measures."[6] Similar capabilities are ascribed transnational criminal networks, who "are usually well organized and well equipped with advanced communications, weapons, and high-speed craft. The capabilities to board and commandeer large underway vessels—demonstrated in numerous piracy incidents—could also be employed to facilitate terrorist acts."[7] The document then explores in greater detail the kinds of threats our nation faces from terrorist networks, noting that:

> Terrorists can also develop effective attack capabilities relatively quickly using a variety of platforms, including explosives-laden suicide boats and

light aircraft; merchant and cruise ships as kinetic weapons to ram another vessel, warship, port facility, or offshore platform; commercial vessels as launch platforms for missile attacks; underwater swimmers to infiltrate ports; and unmanned underwater explosive delivery vehicles. Mines are also an effective weapon because they are low-cost, readily available, easily deployed, difficult to counter, and require minimal training. Terrorists can also take advantage of a vessel's legitimate cargo, such as chemicals, petroleum, or liquefied natural gas, as the explosive component of an attack. Vessels can be used to transport powerful conventional explosives or WMD for detonation in a port or alongside an offshore facility.[8]

Later in the document, the NSMS notes that the nation's "ports, waterways, and shores of the maritime domain are lined with military facilities, nuclear power plants, locks, oil refineries, levees, passenger terminals, fuel tanks, pipelines, chemical plants, tunnels, cargo terminals, and bridges. Ports in particular have inherent security vulnerabilities: they are sprawling, easily accessible by water and land, close to crowded metropolitan areas, and interwoven with complex transportation networks. Port facilities, along with the ships and barges that transit port waterways, are especially vulnerable to tampering, theft, and unauthorized persons gaining entry to collect information and commit unlawful or hostile acts."[9] Overall, the NSMS reflects an extensive recognition of the nation's maritime security threats and vulnerabilities.

In framing the nation's response to the threat from non-state actors, the NSMS articulates three overarching principles. "First, preserving the freedom of the seas is a top national priority. The right of vessels to travel freely in international waters, engage in innocent and transit passage, and have access to ports is an essential element of national security. The free, continuing, unthreatened intercourse of nations is an essential global freedom and helps ensure the smooth operation of the world's economy. Second, the United States Government must facilitate and defend commerce to ensure this uninterrupted flow of shipping . The United States is a major trading nation, and its economy, environment, and social fabric are inextricably linked with the oceans and their resources. The adoption of a just-in-time delivery approach to shipping by most industries, rather than stockpiling or maintaining operating reserves of energy, raw materials, and key components, means that a disruption or slowing of the flow of almost any item can have widespread implications for the overall market, as well as upon the national economy. Third, the United States Government must facilitate the movement of desirable goods and people across our borders, while screening out dangerous people and material. There need not be an inherent conflict between the demand for security and the need for facilitating the travel and trade essential to continued economic growth. This Strategy redefines our fundamental task as one of good border management rather than one that pits security against economic well-being. Accomplishing that goal is more manageable to the extent that screening can occur before goods and people arrive at our physical borders."[10]

In terms of this latter point, international cooperation is identified later in the document as vital to the success of the National Strategy for Maritime Strategy. Indeed, only 3 percent of the international waterborne trade of the United States is carried on vessels owned, operated, and crewed by U.S. citizens. "Security of the maritime domain can be accomplished only by seamlessly employing all instruments of national power in a fully coordinated manner in concert with other nation-states consistent with international law."[11]

After describing the three overarching principles, the NSMS offers four objectives to "guide the nation's maritime security activities":

- Prevent Terrorist Attacks and Criminal or Hostile Acts,
- Protect Maritime-Related Population Centers and Critical Infrastructures,
- Minimize Damage and Expedite Recovery, and
- Safeguard the Ocean and Its Resources.

Within each objective, specific steps are identified by which these objectives are meant to be achieved. For example, the NSMS describes the need for "monitoring and patrolling maritime borders, maritime approaches, and exclusive economic zones, as well as high seas areas of national interest, and stopping such activities at any stage of development or deployment."[12] Further, the strategy specifically identifies the need "to detect adversaries before they strike; to deny them safe haven in which to operate unobstructed; to block their freedom of movement between locations; to stop them from entering the United States; to identify, disrupt, and dismantle their financial infrastructure; and to take decisive action to eliminate the threat they pose."[13] In order to accomplish these tasks, it is noted, "Forces must be trained, equipped, and prepared to detect, deter, interdict, and defeat terrorists throughout the maritime domain."[14]

In terms of the second objective, protecting maritime-related population centers and critical infrastructures, the strategy states that "the federal government has three primary responsibilities: (1) to produce and distribute timely and accurate threat advisory and alert information and appropriate protective measures to State, local, and tribal governments and the private sector via a dedicated homeland security information network; (2) provide guidance and standards for reducing vulnerabilities; and (3) provide active, layered, and scalable security presence to protect from and deter attacks."[15] The concept of "layered defense" is explored in greater detail in several chapters of this volume. Overall, the recognition of threats to the nation's maritime assets is matched up (to a reasonable degree) with concomitant strategic objectives.

When an attack does occur, the nation must be prepared to minimize damage and expedite recovery. Further, as the NSMS articulates, the same response capability must be enabled for any other so-called "Incident of National Significance." A comprehensive National Incident Management System, governed by the National Response Plan, is meant to ensure that the nation can respond effectively to any emergency—including those involving maritime security.

The third and final principal section of the National Strategy for Maritime Security articulates five strategic actions which are meant to help achieve the objectives outlined above:

- Enhance International Cooperation,
- Maximize Domain Awareness,
- Embed Security into Commercial Practices,
- Deploy Layered Security, and
- Assure Continuity of the Marine Transportation System.

As noted earlier, international cooperation is vital to the success of any national effort to improve maritime security. Indeed, the *National Security Strategy* emphasizes international cooperation throughout all dimensions of our nation's homeland security and counterterrorism efforts: "Wherever possible, the United States will rely on regional organizations and state powers to meet their obligations to fight terrorism. Where governments find the fight against terrorism beyond their capacities, we will match their willpower and their resources with whatever help we and our allies can provide."[16]

NSPD 41/HSPD 13 NATIONAL STRATEGY FOR MARITIME SECURITY SUPPORTING PLANS

The President and the Secretaries of Homeland Security, Defense, and State approved supporting plans in October 2005. A team representing more than 20 government agencies contributed to the development of the strategy and its supporting plans. Working groups for the Maritime Commerce Security, Maritime Transportation Systems Security, and Maritime Infrastructure Recovery plans also sought public and private sector insight to ensure that those plans reflected maritime industry concerns and knowledge.

Although the implementation plans address different aspects of maritime security, they are mutually linked and reinforce each other. Together,

National Strategy for Maritime Security and its supporting plans represent the beginning of a comprehensive national effort to promote global economic stability and protect legitimate activities, while preventing hostile or illegal acts within the maritime domain.

The National Plan to Achieve Maritime Domain Awareness lays the foundation for an effective understanding of anything associated with the maritime domain that could impact the security, safety, economy, or environment of the United States, and for identifying threats as early and as distant from our shores as possible.

The Maritime Transportation System Security Plan responds to the President's call for recommendations to improve the national and international regulatory framework regarding the maritime domain.

The Maritime Commerce Security Plan establishes a comprehensive plan to secure the maritime supply chain.

The Maritime Infrastructure Recovery Plan recommends procedures and standards for the recovery of the maritime infrastructure following attack or similar disruption.

The International Outreach and Coordination Strategy provides a framework to coordinate all maritime security initiatives undertaken with foreign governments and international organizations, and solicits international support for enhanced maritime security.

The Global Maritime Intelligence Integration Plan uses existing capabilities to integrate all available intelligence regarding potential threats to U.S. interests in the maritime domain.

The Maritime Operational Threat Response Plan aims for coordinated U.S. government response to threats against the United States and its interests in the maritime domain by establishing roles and responsibilities that enable the government to respond quickly and decisively.

The Domestic Outreach Plan engages nonfederal input to assist with the development and implementation of maritime security policies resulting from NSPD-41/HSPD-13.

For more on these plans, see the Department of Homeland Security's Maritime Security Web site at http://www.dhs.gov/dhspublic/interapp/editorial/editorial_0608.xml. The *National Strategy for Maritime Security*, is available online at: http://www.whitehouse.gov/homeland/maritime-security.html.

U.S. COAST GUARD MARITIME STRATEGY FOR HOMELAND SECURITY

Executive Summary

December 2002

The U.S. Coast Guard Maritime Homeland Security Strategy links the objectives of the *National Security Strategy* and the *National Strategy for Homeland Security* to the U.S. Maritime Domain and serves as a capstone document for Coast Guard homeland security operations. The strategy articulated in this document describes how Coast Guard forces will achieve the national objectives for homeland security.

The United States National Security Strategy has shifted focus from traditional concepts of deterrence which dominated defense policies during the Cold War to a forward-reaching, pre-emptive strategy against hostile states and terrorist groups. The purpose of the *National Strategy for Homeland Security* is to mobilize and organize our Nation to secure the U.S. homeland from terrorist attacks. It provides direction and a framework for action to the federal government departments and agencies that have a role in homeland security. This *Maritime Strategy* follows the direction of both higher level strategies while acknowledging the uniqueness of the U.S. Maritime Domain, including the complexity associated with shared use of the oceans and waterways, long-standing international respect for freedom of navigation, and the transitional seams among America's air, land, sea, and subsurface borders.

The U.S. Coast Guard, by virtue of its military, maritime, and multimission character, broad statutory authorities, membership in the Intelligence Community, command and control structure, and extensive experience in conducting or coordinating complex operations, has significant and complex roles in government as validated by the 1999 Interagency Task Force on the U.S. Coast Guard Roles and Missions. For homeland security the Coast Guard serves as: (1) the lead federal agency for Maritime Homeland Security when responses require civil authorities; (2) the Federal Maritime Security Coordinator in U.S. ports as designated by the Maritime Transportation Security Act of 2002; (3) a supporting agency to the Federal Emergency Management Agency for declared disasters or emergencies under the Federal Response Plan; (4) a supporting agency to the lead federal agency for specific events under the provisions of the current *U.S. Government Interagency Domestic Terrorism Concept of Operations Plan* and its projected replacement by the *Federal Incident Management Plan;* and (5) as a supporting or supported commander for military operations conducted under Title 10. Planning in support of this *Maritime Strategy* will focus on providing clarity to these distinct roles and developing appropriate doctrine, training, tactics, and procedures to allow effective command and control and the timely shift of operational forces to counter threats or respond to events.

Maritime Homeland Security is one of the highest priority missions of the U.S. Coast Guard. Deriving both from this imperative and from other national level policy documents, seven Guiding Principles serve as the base upon which the *Maritime Strategy for Homeland Security* is built: (1) the Coast Guard is the lead federal agency (LFA) for Maritime Homeland Security; (2) the Department of Defense acts primarily as a supporting agency to the Coast Guard for Maritime Homeland Security; (3) the Department of Defense acts as the LFA for Maritime Homeland Defense, employing traditional military missions, with the Coast Guard acting as a supported or supporting commander; (4) securing the homeland requires the sharing of responsibilities among agencies; (5) securing the homeland also requires unprecedented information sharing by all agencies; (6) maritime security operations will be focused to meet essential threat-based requirements and conducted within the rule of law; and (7) forces for implementing this *Strategy* will be derived by leveraging the Coast Guard's multi-mission assets, by acquiring new resources, and through partnering with both public and private stakeholders.

The fight against terrorism is a relentless struggle that will prove neither easy nor quick to conclude. The challenge is made more difficult because terrorism can be classified as either a criminal act or an act of war. However, since the Coast Guard is simultaneously and at all times both an armed force of the United States (14 U.S.C. 1), and a law enforcement agency (14 U.S.C. 89), its capabilities are extremely relevant, valuable, and needed for Maritime Homeland Security (MHLS) whether the threat is termed a military or terrorist attack. The Coast Guard's strategic objectives for homeland security, as derived from the *National Strategy for Homeland Security*—and in order of priority—are to:

- Prevent terrorist attacks within, and terrorist exploitation of, the U.S. Maritime Domain.
- Reduce America's vulnerability to terrorism within the U.S. Maritime Domain.
- Protect U.S. population centers, critical infrastructure, maritime borders, ports, coastal approaches, and the boundaries and seams between them.
- Protect the U.S. Marine Transportation System while preserving the freedom of the U.S. Maritime Domain for legitimate pursuits.
- Minimize the damage and recover from attacks that may occur within the U.S. Maritime Domain as either the lead federal agency or a supporting agency.

The Coast Guard's homeland security mission is to protect the U.S. Maritime Domain and the U.S. Marine Transportation System and deny their use and exploitation by terrorists as a means for attacks on U.S. territory, population, and critical infrastructure. Additionally, the U.S. Coast Guard (USCG) will prepare for and, in the event of attack, conduct emergency response operations. And, when directed, as the supported or supporting commander, the Coast Guard will conduct military homeland defense operations in its traditional role as a military service.

To achieve its strategic objectives the Coast Guard's *Maritime Strategy* comprises six elements:

- Increase Maritime Domain Awareness
- Conduct Enhanced Maritime Security Operations
- Close Port Security Gaps
- Build Critical Security Capabilities and Competencies
- Leverage Partnerships to Mitigate Security Risks
- Ensure Readiness for Homeland Defense Operations

Homeland security is critical to maintaining our way of life. The USCG *Maritime Strategy* will increase U.S. homeland security with minimum impact on our fundamental liberties or the economic imperative for the efficient and reliable movement of ships, cargoes, and people through our seaports. Based on the information, knowledge, and actionable intelligence that constitute Maritime Domain Awareness (MDA), Coast Guard forces supported by other military and interagency forces where appropriate will conduct maritime security operations in the U.S. Maritime Domain in the ports and waterways against internal threats and on the high seas against external threats. The Coast Guard by leveraging its unique status and capabilities of its forces—as well as working in partnership with other maritime stakeholders—will prevent terrorists from launching attacks against the Nation within the U.S. Maritime Domain. However, the maritime terrorist threat presents a daunting challenge, and adequate measures against it can never be completely guaranteed. With a vast nation to defend, the Coast Guard can neither predict nor prevent every conceivable attack. And in a free and open society, no department of government can completely guarantee our safety against ruthless killers, who move and plot in shadows. Yet America's Coast Guard will take every possible measure to safeguard our country and people.

Source: U.S. Coast Guard, *Maritime Strategy for Homeland Security.* December 2002. http://www.uscg.mil/news/reportsandbudget/Maritime_strategy/USCG_Maritme_Strategy.pdf.

PROLIFERATION SECURITY INITIATIVE

Statement of Interdiction Principles

September 4, 2003

The Proliferation Security Initiative (PSI) is a response to the growing challenge posed by the proliferation of weapons of mass destruction (WMD), their delivery systems, and related materials worldwide. The PSI builds on efforts by the international community to prevent proliferation of such items, including existing treaties and regimes. It is consistent with and a step in the implementation of the United Nations Security Council Presidential Statement of January 1992, which states that the proliferation of all WMD constitutes a threat to international peace and security, and underlines the need for member states of the U.N. to prevent proliferation. The PSI is also consistent with recent statements of the G8 and the European Union, establishing that more coherent and concerted efforts are needed to prevent the proliferation of WMD, their delivery systems, and related materials. PSI participants are deeply concerned about this threat and of the danger that these items could fall into the hands of terrorists, and are committed to working together to stop the flow of these items to and from states and non-state actors of proliferation concern.

The PSI seeks to involve in some capacity all states that have a stake in nonproliferation and the ability and willingness to take steps to stop the flow of such items at sea, in the air, or on land. The PSI also seeks cooperation from any state whose vessels, flags, ports, territorial waters, airspace, or land might be used for proliferation purposes by states and non-state actors of proliferation concern. The increasingly aggressive efforts by proliferators to stand outside or to circumvent existing nonproliferation norms, and to profit from such trade, requires new and stronger actions by the international community. We look forward to working with all concerned states on measures they are able and willing to take in support of the PSI, as outlined in the following set of "Interdiction Principles."

INTERDICTION PRINCIPLES FOR THE PROLIFERATION SECURITY INITIATIVE:

PSI participants are committed to the following interdiction principles to establish a more coordinated and effective basis through which to impede and stop shipments of WMD, delivery systems, and related materials flowing to and from states and non-state actors of proliferation concern, consistent with national legal authorities and relevant international law and frameworks, including the United Nations Security Council.

They call on all states concerned with this threat to international peace and security to join in similarly committing to:

1) Undertake effective measures, either alone or in concert with other states, for interdicting the transfer or transport of WMD, their delivery systems, and related materials to and from states and non-state actors of proliferation concern. "States or non-state actors of proliferation concern" generally refers to those countries or entities that the PSI participants involved establish should be subject to interdiction activities because they are engaged in proliferation through: (1) efforts to develop or acquire chemical, biological, or nuclear weapons and associated delivery systems; or (2) transfers (either selling, receiving, or facilitating) of WMD, their delivery systems, or related materials.

2) Adopt streamlined procedures for rapid exchange of relevant information concerning suspected proliferation activity, protecting the confidential character of classified information provided by other states as part of this initiative, dedicate appropriate resources and efforts to interdiction operations and capabilities, and maximize coordination among participants in interdiction efforts.

3) Review and work to strengthen their relevant national legal authorities where necessary to accomplish these objectives, and work to strengthen when necessary relevant international laws and frameworks in appropriate ways to support these commitments.

4) Take specific actions in support of interdiction efforts regarding cargoes of WMD, their delivery systems, or related materials, to the extent their national legal authorities permit and consistent with their obligations under international law and frameworks, to include:

a) Not to transport or assist in the transport of any such cargoes to or from states or non-state actors of proliferation concern, and not to allow any persons subject to their jurisdiction to do so.

b) At their own initiative, or at the request and good cause shown by another state, to take action to board and search any vessel flying their flag in their internal waters or territorial seas, or areas beyond the territorial seas of any other state, that is reasonably suspected of transporting such cargoes to or from states or non-state actors of proliferation concerns, and to seize such cargoes that are identified.

c) To seriously consider providing consent under the appropriate circumstances to the boarding and searching of its own flag vessels by other states, and to the seizure of such WMD-related cargoes in such vessels that may be identified by such states.

d) To take appropriate actions to (1) stop and/or search in their internal waters, territorial seas, or contiguous zones (when declared) vessels that are reasonably suspected of carrying such cargoes to or from states or non-state actors of proliferation concern and to seize such cargoes that are identified; and (2) enforce conditions on vessels entering or leaving their ports, internal waters, or territorial seas that are reasonably suspected of carrying such cargoes, such as requiring that such vessels be subject to boarding, search, and seizure of such cargoes prior to entry.

e) At their own initiative or upon the request and good cause shown by another state, to (a) require aircraft that are reasonably suspected of carrying such cargoes to or from states or non-state actors of proliferation concern and that are transiting their airspace to land for inspection and seize any such cargoes that are identified; and/or (b) deny aircraft reasonably suspected of carrying such cargoes transit rights through their airspace in advance of such flights.

f) If their ports, airfields, or other facilities are used as transshipment points for shipment of such cargoes to or from states or non-state actors of proliferation concern, to inspect vessels, aircraft, or other modes of transport reasonably suspected of carrying such cargoes, and to seize such cargoes that are identified.

Source: The White House, *Proliferation Security Initiative, Statement of Interdiction Principles.* Press Release, 4 September 2004. Available online at: http://www.whitehouse.gov/news/releases/2003/09/20030904-11.html.

THE PROLIFERATION SECURITY INITIATIVE (PSI) AT A GLANCE

Arms Control Association, June 2004

http://www.armscontrol.org/factsheets/PSI.asp

President George W. Bush announced May 31, 2003 that the United States would lead a new effort, the Proliferation Security Initiative (PSI), to interdict shipments of weapons of mass destruction (WMD) and related goods to terrorists and countries of proliferation concern. The initiative's aim would be "to keep the world's most destructive weapons away from our shores and out of the hands of our common enemies," Bush declared.

Participants: Ten countries originally joined with the United States to shape and promote the initiative. These countries are Australia, France, Germany, Italy, Japan, the Netherlands, Poland, Portugal, Spain, and the United Kingdom. Canada, Norway, Russia, and Singapore have since joined the effort and some 40 additional states have voiced support for the initiative. PSI participants have downplayed the concept of membership in the initiative, explaining in a press statement that PSI is "an activity not an organization."[17] U.S. officials have courted China to join the regime, but so far it has kept its distance, citing concerns about the legality of interdictions.

Mission: The initiative aims to stop shipments of biological, chemical, and nuclear weapons, as well as missiles and goods that could be used to deliver or produce such weapons, to terrorists and countries suspected of trying to acquire WMD. Initiative participants intend to carry out cargo interdictions at sea, in the air, or on land. For some countries this is not a new practice but an enshrinement and expansion of current operations. The United States and other countries have long records of intercepting illegal trade and smuggling activities, including illicit weapons transactions.

Still, the initiative is designed to make it more costly and risky for proliferators to acquire the weapons or materials they seek. By doing so, members hope that other countries will be dissuaded from pursuing weapons in the first place or experience significant delays in their acquisition efforts.

PSI is limited solely to seizing shipments of WMD and dual-use goods-items that have both civilian, peaceful purposes and that can be used to make weapons-to those countries and nonstate actors viewed as threats by PSI participants. Undersecretary of State for Arms Control and International Security John Bolton, a chief architect of PSI, has indicated that participants will not be targeting the trade of countries perceived as U.S. allies or friends, such as India, Israel, and Pakistan-all three of which possess WMD arsenals, including nuclear weapons.

Principles: The 11 original PSI participants released a set of principles September 4, 2003.[18] The principles call on PSI participants, as well as other countries, to not engage in WMD-related trade with countries of proliferation concern and to permit their own vessels and aircraft to be searched if suspected of transporting such goods. The principles further urge that information on suspicious activities be shared quickly to enable possible interdictions and that all vessels "reasonably suspected" of carrying dangerous cargo be inspected when passing through national airports, ports, and other transshipment points.

Legal Authority: The initiative does not empower countries to do anything that they previously could not do. Most importantly, PSI does not grant governments any new legal authority to conduct interdictions in international waters or airspace. Such interdictions may take place, but they must be confined to what is currently permissible under international law. For example, a ship can be stopped in international waters if it is not flying a national flag or properly registered. It cannot be stopped simply because it is suspected of transporting WMD or related goods. PSI is primarily intended to encourage participating countries to take greater advantage of their own existing national laws to intercept threatening trade passing through their territories and where they have jurisdiction to act. In situations where the legal authority to act may be ambiguous, Bolton said participants might go to the UN Security Council for authorization.[19]

PSI participants are working to expand their legal authority to interdict shipments by signing bilateral boarding agreements with select countries to secure expedited processes or pre-approval for stopping and searching their ships at sea. The United States has concluded such agreements with Liberia and Panama, the two countries with the largest fleets of registered ocean-going vessels in the world.

Structure: PSI is an informal arrangement among countries. To date, there is no list of criteria by which interdictions are to be made (except that the cargo is destined for a recipient that might use it to harm the United States or other countries). There is also no secretariat or formal organization that serves as a coordinating body. Instead, participants aim to readily share information among one another as appropriate and to act when necessary to help seize or thwart dangerous trade.

Status: PSI participants have conducted several interdiction exercises agreed to in July 2003. The exercises, including mock ship boardings, are intended to increase the participants' capabilities to cooperate with one another. They are also intended to put a public face on the initiative and act as a deterrent to potential proliferators.

Bolton said in a November 2003 interview[20] that there have been successful interdictions since the initiative's launch. He and other U.S. and foreign government officials indicate that there are no plans to announce when such interdictions occur because of concerns about compromising future PSI activities.

The one successful interdiction that has come to light was an October 2003 operation to seize centrifuge components destined for Libya. U.S. officials credit the interdiction with helping to further convince Libya, which had been conducting secret disarmament negotiations with the United States and United Kingdom for several months, to publicly renounce its WMD ambitions and programs two months later.

CONTAINER SECURITY INITIATIVE—CSI IN BRIEF

U.S. Customs and Border Protection

In post-9/11 America the Container Security Initiative (CSI) is based on an idea that makes sense: extend our zone of security outward so that American borders are the last line of defense, not the first. Through CSI, which was announced by Commissioner of Customs and Border Protection (CBP) Robert C. Bonner in January 2002, maritime containers that pose a risk for terrorism are identified and examined at foreign ports before they are shipped to the United States. In so doing, Commissioner Bonner hopes to prevent terrorist threats from being carried out.

CSI consists of four core elements:

1. Using intelligence and automated information to identify and target containers that pose a risk for terrorism;

2. pre-screening those containers that pose a risk at the port of departure before they arrive at U.S. ports;

3. using detection technology to quickly pre-screen containers that pose a risk; and;

4. using smarter, tamper-evident containers.

Under the CSI program, the screening of containers that pose a risk for terrorism is accomplished by teams of CBP officials deployed to work in concert with their host nation counterparts.

Containerized shipping is a critical component of global trade because about 90 percent of the world's trade is transported in cargo containers. In the United States, almost half of incoming trade (by value) arrives by containers onboard ships. Nearly nine million cargo containers arrive on ships and are offloaded at U.S. seaports each year.

Early on, CSI focused on implementing the program at the top 20 foreign ports which ship approximately two thirds of the volume of containers to the U.S. Governments from these 20 foreign ports have already agreed to implement CSI.

As CSI has evolved, CBP hopes to expand the program to additional ports based on volume, location and strategic concerns. Strong support from countries on the European, Asian and African continents ensure that CSI will continue to expand to ports in those areas.

Also a reciprocal program, CSI offers its participant countries the opportunity to send their customs officers to major U.S. ports to target ocean-going, containerized cargo to be exported to their countries. Likewise, CBP shares information on a bilateral basis with its CSI partners.

As part of reciprocal CSI agreements with Japan and Canada, those countries currently station their customs personnel in U.S. ports as part of the CSI program.

Source: U.S. Customs and Border Protection, "CSI in Brief." Online at http://www.cbp.gov/ xp/cgov/enforcement/international_activities/csi/.

CONTAINER SECURITY INITIATIVE

Fact Sheet

U.S. Customs and Border Protection

November 2005

The Container Security Initiative (CSI) is an initiative that was developed by U.S. Customs, now U.S. Customs and Border Protection (CBP), in the aftermath of the terrorist attacks of September 11. The primary purpose of CSI is to protect the global trading system and the trade lanes between CSI ports and the U.S. Under the CSI program, a team of officers is deployed to work with host nation counterparts to target all containers that pose a potential threat. Announced in January 2002, CSI was first implemented in the ports shipping the greatest volume of containers to the United States. CBP has entered into bilateral discussions with all the foreign governments where these top ports are located and is now expanding to additional ports in strategic locations.

WHAT ARE CSI'S CORE ELEMENTS?

The Container Security Initiative (CSI) is an initiative that was developed by U.S. Customs, now U.S. Customs and Border Protection (CBP), in the aftermath of the terrorist attacks of September 11. The primary purpose of CSI is to protect the global trading system and the trade lanes between CSI ports and the U.S. Under the CSI program, a team of officers is deployed to work with host nation counterparts to target all containers that pose a potential threat. Announced in January 2002, CSI was first implemented in the ports shipping the greatest volume of containers to the United States. CBP has entered into bilateral discussions with all the foreign governments where these top ports are located and is now expanding to additional ports in strategic locations.

CSI is founded on four core elements: 1) using intelligence and automated information to identify and target containers that pose a risk for terrorism; (2) pre-screening those containers that pose a risk at the port of departure before they arrive at U.S. ports; (3) using detection technology to quickly pre-screen containers that pose a risk; and (4) using smarter, tamper-evident containers.

WHY IS CONTAINERIZED SHIPPING A CRITICAL COMPONENT OF GLOBAL TRADE?

About 90 percent of all world cargo moves by container. Almost half of incoming trade (by value) arrives in the United States by sea containers. Nearly 9 million cargo containers arrive and are offloaded at U.S. seaports each year.

HOW MANY CSI PORTS ARE OPERATIONAL?

41 CSI ports are currently operational. They include: Halifax, Montreal, and Vancouver, Canada (03/02); Rotterdam, The Netherlands (09/02/02); Le Havre, France (12/02/02); Marseille, France (01/07/05); Bremerhaven, Germany (02/02/03); Hamburg, Germany (02/09/03); Antwerp, Belgium

(02/23/03); Zeebrugge, Belgium (10/29/04); Singapore (03/10/03); Yoko-hama, Japan (03/24/03); Tokyo, Japan (05/21/04); Hong Kong (05/05/03); Gothenburg, Sweden (05/23/03); Felixstowe, United Kingdom (U.K.) (05/24/03); Liverpool, Thamesport, Tilbury, and Southampton, U.K. (11/01/04); Genoa, Italy (06/16/03); La Spezia, Italy (06/23/03); Livorno, Italy (12/30/04); Naples, Italy (09/30/04); Gioia Tauro, Italy (10/31/04); Pusan, Korea (08/04/03); Durban, South Africa (12/01/03); Port Klang, Malaysia (03/08/04); Tanjung Pelepas, Malaysia (8/16/04); Piraeus, Greece (07/27/04), Algeciras, Spain (07/30/04), Nagoya and Kobe, Japan (08/06/04), Laem Chabang, Thailand (8/13/04), Dubai; United Arab Emirates (UAE) (03/26/05); Shanghai (04/28/05), Shenzhen (06/24/05); Kaohsiung (07/25/05); and Santos, Brazil (09/22/05), Colom-bo, Sri Lanka (09/29/05), and Buenos Aires, Argentina (11/17/05).

IS CSI LIMITING PARTICIPATION TO THE 20 LARGEST PORTS?

No. All 20 of the 20 original ports have committed to joining CSI and are at various stages of implementation. Additional ports will become opera-tional in the near future. These ports are points of passage for approxi-mately two-thirds of containers shipped to the United States.

While the first 20 largest ports were the starting point, CSI is not limit-ing participation to those locations. Sweden, Malaysia, Sri Lanka, and South Africa are examples of countries with ports not included in the top 20 that have signed on to CSI. Sweden, Malaysia, and South Africa are already operational. Discussions are currently being held with addi-tional expansion ports throughout the world.

CSI is expanding to additional ports that ship substantial amounts of cargo to the United States. These ports must have the infrastructure and technology in place to participate in the program.

International organizations like the World Customs Organization and the G8 have supported CSI expansion through their adoption of resolu-tions that support the implementation of the security measures intro-duced by CSI at ports throughout the world.

HOW DOES CSI WORK?

Under the CSI program, a small number of CBP officers are deployed to work with host nation counterparts to target all containers that pose a potential threat for terrorism. Its purpose is to protect containerized ship-ping from exploitation by terrorists.

WHY IS IT NECESSARY TO SEND U.S. OFFICERS TO FOREIGN PORTS TO ENHANCE SECURITY?

Information sharing between the U.S. and other Customs Services will enhance the ability of both services to identify all containers that pose a potential threat. By working together, we can jointly achieve far greater security for maritime shipping that if we work independently.

WHAT BENEFITS ARE THERE FOR ANY FOREIGN PORTS THAT SIGN UP?

CSI is a deterrent to terrorist organizations that may seek to target any foreign port. This initiative provides a significant measure of security for the participating port as well as the United States. CSI will also provide better security for the global trading system as a whole. If terrorists were to carry out an attack on a seaport using a cargo container, the maritime trading system would likely grind to a halt until seaport security is improved. Those seaports participating in the CSI will be able to begin handling containerized cargo far sooner than other ports that haven't taken steps to enhance security. In short, CSI is an insurance policy against the threat of a terrorist attack.

WILL FOCUSING PRIMARILY ON THE WORLD'S LARGEST SEAPORTS PLACE SMALLER SEAPORTS AT AN ECONOMIC DISADVANTAGE?

CSI is not limited to the world's largest seaports. In June 2002, the World Customs Organization unanimously passed a resolution that will enable ports in all 161 of the member nations to begin to develop programs along the CSI model and on April 22, 2004, European Union and the Department of Homeland Security Signed an agreement that calls for the prompt expansion of CSI through the European Community.

WHAT ARE THE ELIGIBILITY REQUIREMENTS FOR THE EXPANSION PHASE OF CSI?

To be eligible for the expansion phase of CSI, candidate nation must commit to the following minimum standards:

1. The Customs Administration must be able to inspect cargo originating, transiting, exiting, or being transshipped through a country. Non-intrusive inspectional (NII) equipment (including gamma or X-ray imaging capabilities) and radiation detection equipment must be available and utilized for conducting such inspections. This equipment is necessary in order to meet the

objective of quickly screening containers without disrupting the flow of legitimate trade.

2. The seaport must have regular, direct, and substantial container traffic to ports in the United States.

3. Commit to establishing a risk management system to identify potentially high-risk containers, and automating that system. This system should include a mechanism for validating threat assessments and targeting decisions and identifying best practices.

4. Commit to sharing critical data, intelligence, and risk management information with the United States Customs and Border Protection in order to do collaborative targeting, and developing an automated mechanism for these exchanges.

5. Conduct a thorough port assessment to ascertain vulnerable links in a port's infrastructure and commit to resolving those vulnerabilities.

6. Commit to maintaining integrity programs to prevent lapses in employee integrity and to identify and combat breaches in integrity.

WILL THE ADDITION OF U.S. OFFICERS CAUSE DELAYS IN THE FLOW OF GOODS THROUGH PORTS THAT PARTICIPATE IN CSI, REDUCING THEIR COMPETITIVENESS?

No. In fact, it should make the movement of low risk cargo containers even more efficient. Cargo typically sits on the pier for several days waiting to be exported. CSI will target containers and screen them before they depart. This way we are using the waiting time at the port of export to do our work, so when the container arrives in the U.S. it can be immediately released. The containers we target are going to be searched. It's a question of where and when, not if.

WHO WILL PAY FOR SCREENING AND, IF NECESSARY, THE UNLOADING OF CONTAINERS?

The host country will determine who pays for the direct cost of screening and unloading containers. In the U.S., however, the importer pays the costs associated with moving, inspecting, and unloading containers.

HOW MANY U.S. OFFICERS WILL BE ASSIGNED TO A PARTICULAR PORT?

The needs of each port will be addressed individually. Typically we would expect to deploy a small number of officers. We'll assess the program and make adjustments as necessary.

DOES A CSI PORT HAVE AN ECONOMIC ADVANTAGE?

One real advantage would be in the event of a terrorist attack using a cargo container. CSI ports would experience the least disruption because they have a security system, CSI, in place. In the event of a terrorist attack, the CSI ports would have a competitive advantage. They would be rewarded for their foresight.

CAN CSI BE CONSIDERED A FORM OF TRADE BARRIER?

No. The ultimate trade barrier would be a terrorist attack that would halt trade. Imagine the ridicule any responsible port or government official will face, if a terrorist attack was to occur and we had done nothing to protect our maritime infrastructure. CSI is merely a program that screens containers before they depart for U.S. ports of entry rather than after they arrive on U.S. shores.

WILL HOST COUNTRIES INCUR ADDITIONAL COSTS FOR PARTICIPATING IN CSI?

We don't believe this initiative will entail substantial new costs to the host nations. CBP will be paying to deploy officers and computers in foreign seaports and many host nations already have screening and detection technology in place. To the extent that additional detector or IT equipment is needed to implement CSI, the investment is well worth it considering that it is insurance—CSI protects the port and the national economy of a CSI host country.

WILL OFFICERS STATIONED IN FOREIGN PORTS BE ARMED? WILL THEY HAVE ARREST POWERS?

Officers at these ports will not be armed nor will they have arrest powers. The officers will be working jointly with the host country authorities to screen U.S.-bound containers. They will operate in accordance with the guidelines of the host country and the terms of the declaration of principles to implement CSI.

WILL CBP OFFICERS STATIONED AT THE FOREIGN PORTS BE SCREENING ALL CARGO OR JUST CARGO BOUND FOR THE UNITED STATES?

CBP officers deployed in foreign countries will be targeting with the host country, only cargo containers destined or transiting through the United States. Only those U.S.-bound containers identified as potential threats will be examined either by NII or physical exams. Host country officials will conduct the examination and CBP officers will observe the security screening.

WILL PRE-SCREENED U.S.-BOUND SEA CARGO GET EXPEDITED PROCESSING THROUGH CBP UPON ARRIVAL TO THE UNITED STATES?

Yes. If a shipment has already been jointly examined by U.S. and the host country's customs officials, that means one less shipment that CBP officers will have to worry about at a U.S. port. It will allow us to focus more of our attention on high-risk shipments that have not been pre-screened. We are in the process of testing technology, such as tamper-evident seals, that we hope to place on containers that have been pre-screened overseas to assist in this process. Naturally, CBP ultimately reserves the right to inspect any cargo container that arrives in the United States, whether it has been pre-screened or not. However, this will only be done if additional information is available or the integrity of a seal is compromised.

WILL CBP PROVIDE X-RAY OR GAMMA RAY DETECTION TECHNOLOGY TO HELP SCAN CONTAINERS?

CSI implementation requires the host country to have NII equipment. Many of the countries already have large container screening machines. In fact, some ports already have extremely sophisticated detection technology in operation.

ARE MODEL LAWS AND REGULATIONS AVAILABLE TO GUIDE THE IMPLEMENTATION OF CSI IN A HOST COUNTRY?

When discussing the implementation of CSI, a nation depends upon its native laws and customs. Our response has been to draft separate and unique declarations with each participating port to accommodate differences. In addition, as CSI is a cooperative effort, CBP is willing to assist foreign governments in reviewing existing laws and crafting new legislation to support implementation if they so desire.

WILL CSI AFFECT THE WAY TRADE IS CONDUCTED, E.G. WILL THERE BE ADDITIONAL PAPERWORK THAT IS NEEDED PRIOR TO EXPORT AND BEFORE IT CLEARS CBP?

Through collaborative targeting and analysis, the trade will become more secure in each commercial port. For exports destined or transiting the U.S., they must be compliant with the U.S. 24-hour rule, which requires 14 data elements to be reported 24 hours prior to loading aboard a vessel destined for the U.S.

WILL IT TAKE MORE TIME TO EXPORT A PRODUCT WITH CSI?

No. The targeting and examination will be accomplished during the lag time between arrival at the foreign port and loading on a ship for departure to an U.S. port.

HOW WILL TRADE BE AFFECTED IF A PORT JOINS/DOES NOT JOIN?

The advantages of inspecting containers at the earliest possible point in the supply chain will be a benefit to a CSI port. The integrity of the shipment will be better ensured by using pre-arrival information and non-intrusive inspection equipment at foreign port locations, thus expediting their clearance upon arrival in the United States.

WILL THE U.S. BE OFFERING RECIPROCITY WITH CSI PARTICIPATING COUNTRIES?

CSI is a reciprocal program. CBP offers CSI-participating countries the opportunity to send their customs officers to major U.S. ports to target cargo that is exported to their country via ocean containers. CBP will also share its information and pre-arrival data on a bilateral basis with its CSI partners. Sharing of information is intended to be a reciprocal process.

Japan and Canada currently station customs personnel in U.S. ports as part of the CSI program.

INTERNATIONAL SHIP AND PORT FACILITY SECURITY CODE

International Maritime Organization[21]

"IMO adopts comprehensive maritime security measures"

Press Release, December 2002

Conference of Contracting Governments to the International Convention for the Safety of Life at Sea, 1974: 9 - 13 December 2002

A new, comprehensive security regime for international shipping is set to enter into force in July 2004 following the adoption by a week-long Diplomatic Conference of a series of measures to strengthen maritime security and prevent and suppress acts of terrorism against shipping. The Conference, held at the London headquarters of the International Maritime Organization (IMO) from 9 to 13 December 2002, was of crucial significance not only to the international maritime community but the world community as a whole, given the pivotal role shipping plays in the conduct of world trade. The measures represent the culmination of just over a year's intense work by IMO's Maritime Safety Committee and its Intersessional Working Group since the terrorist atrocities in the United States in September 2001.

The Conference was attended by 108 Contracting Governments to the 1974 SOLAS Convention, observers from two IMO Member States and observers from the two IMO Associate Members. United Nations specialized agencies, intergovernmental organizations and non-governmental international organizations also sent observers to the Conference. The Conference adopted a number of amendments to the 1974 Safety of Life at Sea Convention (SOLAS), the most far-reaching of which enshrines the new International Ship and Port Facility Security Code (ISPS Code). The Code contains detailed security-related requirements for Governments, port authorities and shipping companies in a mandatory section (Part A), together with a series of guidelines about how to meet these requirements in a second, non-mandatory section (Part B). The Conference also adopted a series of resolutions designed to add weight to the amendments, encourage the application of the measures to ships and port facilities not covered by the Code and pave the way for future work on the subject.

Speaking at the end of the conference, IMO Secretary-General William O'Neil strongly urged all parties concerned to start putting in place all the necessary legislative, administrative and operational provisions needed to give effect to the decisions of the Conference as soon as possible. In a call for continued vigilance, he added, "In the meantime, all involved in the operation of ships and ports should continue to be aware of the potential dangers to shipping through acts of terrorism and the need to be extremely vigilant and alert to any security threat they might encounter in port, at offshore terminals or when underway at sea."

The Conference has been referred to in the United Nations General Assembly. At its current session, the General Assembly adopted a resolution on "Oceans and the law of the sea", which specifically welcomed initiatives at the International Maritime Organization to counter the threat to maritime security from terrorism and encouraged States fully to support this endeavour.

THE INTERNATIONAL SHIP AND PORT FACILITY SECURITY CODE

In essence, the Code takes the approach that ensuring the security of ships and port facilities is basically a risk management activity and that to determine what security measures are appropriate, an assessment of the risks must be made in each particular case.

The purpose of the Code is to provide a standardized, consistent framework for evaluating risk, enabling governments to offset changes in threat with changes in vulnerability for ships and port facilities.

To begin the process, each Contracting Government will conduct port facility security assessments. Security assessments will have three essential components. First, they must identify and evaluate important assets and infrastructures that are critical to the port facility as well as those areas or structures that, if damaged, could cause significant loss of life or damage to the port facility's economy or environment. Then, the assessment must identify the actual threats to those critical assets and infrastructure in order to prioritise security measures. Finally, the assessment must address vulnerability of the port facility by identifying its weaknesses in physical security, structural integrity, protection systems, procedural policies, communications systems, transportation infrastructure, utilities, and other areas within a port facility that may be a likely target. Once this assessment has been completed, Contracting Government can accurately evaluate risk.

This risk management concept will be embodied in the Code through a number of minimum functional security requirements for ships and port facilities. For ships, these requirements will include:

- ship security plans
- ship security officers
- company security officers
- certain onboard equipment

For port facilities, the requirements will include:

- port facility security plans
- port facility security officers
- certain security equipment

In addition the requirements for ships and for port facilities include:

- monitoring and controlling access
- monitoring the activities of people and cargo
- ensuring security communications are readily available

Because each ship (or class of ship) and each port facility present different risks, the method in which they will meet the specific requirements of this Code will be determined and eventually be approved by the Administration or Contracting Government, as the case may be.

In order to communicate the threat at a port facility or for a ship, the Contracting Government will set the appropriate security level. Security levels 1, 2, and 3 correspond to normal, medium, and high threat situations, respectively. The security level creates a link between the ship and the port facility, since it triggers the implementation of appropriate security measures for the ship and for the port facility.

The preamble to the Code states that, as threat increases, the only logical counteraction is to reduce vulnerability. The Code provides several ways to reduce vulnerabilities. Ships will be subject to a system of survey, verification, certification, and control to ensure that their security measures are implemented. This system will be based on a considerably expanded control system as stipulated in the 1974 Convention for Safety of Life at Sea (SOLAS). Port facilities will also be required to report certain security related information to the Contracting Government concerned, which in turn will submit a list of approved port facility security plans, including location and contact details to IMO.

THE COMPANY AND THE SHIP

Under the terms of the Code, shipping companies will be required to designate a Company Security Officer for the Company and a Ship Security Officer for each of its ships. The Company Security Officer's responsibilities include ensuring that a Ship Security Assessment is properly carried out, that Ship Security Plans are prepared and submitted for approval by (or on behalf of) the Administration and thereafter is placed on board each ship.

The Ship Security Plan should indicate the operational and physical security measures the ship itself should take to ensure it always operates at security level 1. The plan should also indicate the additional, or intensified, security measures the ship itself can take to move to and operate at security level 2 when instructed to do so. Furthermore, the plan should indicate the possible preparatory actions the ship could take to allow prompt response to instructions that may be issued to the ship at security level 3.

Ships will have to carry an International Ship Security Certificate indicating that they comply with the requirements of SOLAS chapter XI-2 and part A of the ISPS Code. When a ship is at a port or is proceeding to a port of Contracting Government, the Contracting Government has the right, under the provisions of regulation XI-2/9, to exercise various control and compliance measures with respect to that ship. The ship is subject to port State control inspections but such inspections will not normally extend to examination of the Ship Security Plan itself except in specific circumstances.

The ship may, also, be subject to additional control measures if the Contracting Government exercising the control and compliance measures has reason to believe that the security of the ship has, or the port facilities it has served have, been compromised.

THE PORT FACILITY

Each Contracting Government has to ensure completion of a Port Facility Security Assessment for each port facility within its territory that serves ships engaged on international voyages. The Port Facility Security Assessment is fundamentally a risk analysis of all aspects of a port facility's operation in order to determine which parts of it are more susceptible, and/or more likely, to be the subject of attack. Security risk is seen a function of the threat of an attack coupled with the vulnerability of the target and the consequences of an attack.

On completion of the analysis, it will be possible to produce an overall assessment of the level of risk. The Port Facility Security Assessment will help determine which port facilities are required to appoint a Port Facility Security Officer and prepare a Port Facility Security Plan. This plan should indicate the operational and physical security measures the port facility should take to ensure that it always operates at security level 1. The plan should also indicate the additional, or intensified, security measures the port facility can take to move to and operate at security level 2 when instructed to do so. It should also indicate the possible preparatory actions the port facility could take to allow prompt response to the instructions that may be issued at security level 3.

Ships using port facilities may be subject to port State control inspections and additional control measures. The relevant authorities may request the provision of information regarding the ship, its cargo, passengers and ship's personnel prior to the ship's entry into port. There may be circumstances in which entry into port could be denied.

RESPONSIBILITIES OF CONTRACTING GOVERNMENTS

Contracting Governments have various responsibilities, including setting the applicable security level, approving the Ship Security Plan and relevant amendments to a previously approved plan, verifying the compliance of ships with the provisions of SOLAS chapter XI-2 and part A of the ISPS Code and issuing the International Ship Security Certificate, determining which port facilities located within their territory are required to designate a Port Facility Security Officer, ensuring completion and approval of the Port Facility Security Assessment and the Port Facility Security Plan and any subsequent amendments; and exercising control and compliance measures. It is also responsible for communicating information to the International Maritime Organization and to the shipping and port industries.

Contracting Governments can designate, or establish, Designated Authorities within Government to undertake their security duties and allow Recognised Security Organisations to carry out certain work with respect to port facilities, but the final decision on the acceptance and approval of this work should be given by the Contracting Government or the Designated Authority.

AMENDMENTS TO SOLAS

The Conference adopted a series of Amendments to the 1974 SOLAS Convention, aimed at enhancing maritime security on board ships and at ship/port interface areas. Among other things, these amendments create a new SOLAS chapter dealing specifically with maritime security, which in turn contains the mandatory requirement for ships to comply with the ISPS Code.

Modifications to Chapter V (Safety of Navigation) contain a new timetable for the fitting of Automatic Information Systems (AIS). Ships, other than passenger ships and tankers, of 300 gross tonnage and upwards but less than 50,000 gross tonnage, will be required to fit AIS not later than the first safety equipment survey after 1 July 2004 or by 31 December 2004, whichever occurs earlier. Ships fitted with AIS shall maintain AIS in operation at all times except where international agreements, rules or standards provide for the protection of navigational information."

The existing SOLAS Chapter XI (Special measures to enhance maritime safety) has been re-numbered as Chapter XI-1. Regulation XI-1/3 is modified to require ships' identification numbers to be permanently marked in a visible place either on the ship's hull or superstructure. Passenger ships should carry the marking on a horizontal surface visible from the air. Ships should also be marked with their ID numbers internally.

And a new regulation XI-1/5 requires ships to be issued with a Continuous Synopsis Record (CSR) which is intended to provide an on-board record of the history of the ship. The CSR shall be issued by the Administration and shall contain information such as the name of the ship and of the State whose flag the ship is entitled to fly, the date on which the ship was registered with that State, the ship's identification number, the port at which the ship is registered and the name of the registered owner(s) and their registered address. Any changes shall be recorded in the CSR so as to provide updated and current information together with the history of the changes.

NEW CHAPTER XI-2 (SPECIAL MEASURES TO ENHANCE MARITIME SECURITY)

A brand-new Chapter XI-2 (Special measures to enhance maritime security) is added after the renumbered Chapter XI-1.

This chapter applies to passenger ships and cargo ships of 500 gross tonnage and upwards, including high speed craft, mobile offshore drilling units and port facilities serving such ships engaged on international voyages.

Regulation XI-2/2 of the new chapter enshrines the International Ship and Port Facilities Security Code (ISPS Code). Part A of this Code is mandatory and part B contains guidance as to how best to comply with the mandatory requirements.

The regulation requires Administrations to set security levels and ensure the provision of security level information to ships entitled to fly their flag. Prior to entering a port, or whilst in a port, within the territory of a Contracting Government, a ship shall comply with the requirements for the security level set by that Contracting Government, if that security level is higher than the security level set by the Administration for that ship.

Regulation XI-2/8 confirms the role of the Master in exercising his professional judgement over decisions necessary to maintain the security of the ship. It says he shall not be constrained by the Company, the charterer or any other person in this respect.

Regulation XI-2/6 requires all ships to be provided with a ship security alert system, according to a strict timetable that will see most vessels fitted by 2004 and the remainder by 2006. When activated the ship security alert system shall initiate and transmit a ship-to-shore security alert to a competent authority designated by the Administration, identifying the ship, its location and indicating that the security of the ship is under threat or it has been compromised. The system will not raise any alarm on-board the ship. The ship security alert system shall be capable of being activated from the navigation bridge and in at least one other location.

Regulation XI-2/10 covers requirements for port facilities, providing among other things for Contracting Governments to ensure that port facility security assessments are carried out and that port facility security plans are developed, implemented and reviewed in accordance with the ISPS Code.

Other regulations in this chapter cover the provision of information to IMO and the control of ships in port (including measures such as the delay, detention, restriction of operations including movement within the port, or expulsion of a ship from port).

Conference resolution 1 (Adoption of amendments to the annex to the international convention for the safety of life at sea, 1974, as amended), determines that the amendments shall be deemed to have been accepted on 1 January 2004 (unless, prior to that date, more than one third of the Contracting Governments to the Convention or Contracting Governments the combined merchant fleets of which constitute not less than 50% of the gross tonnage of the world's merchant fleet, have notified their objections to the amendments) and that the amendments would then enter into force on 1 July 2004.

Conference resolution 2 (Adoption of the International Ship and Port Facility Security (ISPS) Code) adopts the International Ship and Port Facility Security (ISPS) Code, and invites Contracting Governments to the Convention to note that the ISPS Code will take effect on 1 July 2004 upon entry into force of the new chapter XI-2 of the Convention.

Conference resolution 3 (Further work by the international maritime organization pertaining to the enhancement of maritime security) invites the International Maritime Organization to develop, as a matter of urgency, training guidance such as model courses for ship security officers, company security officers and port facility security officers; performance standards for ship security alarms; performance standards and guidelines for long-range ship identification and tracking systems; guidelines on control of ships; and guidelines on "Recognized security organizations", and to adopt them in time before the entry into force of the amendments to the Convention adopted by the Conference.

Conference resolution 4 (Future amendments to Chapters XI-1 and XI-2 of the 1974 SOLAS Convention on special measures to enhance maritime safety and security) recommends that future amendments to the provisions of chapters XI-1 and XI-2 of the Convention should be adopted by either the Maritime Safety Committee of the International

Maritime Organization or by a Conference of Contracting Governments to the Convention.

Conference resolution 5 (Promotion of technical co-operation and assistance) strongly urges Contracting Governments to the Convention and Member States of the Organization to provide, in co-operation with the Organization, assistance to those States which have difficulty in meeting the requirements of the adopted amendments; and to use the Integrated Technical Co-operation Programme of the Organization as one of the main instruments to obtain assistance in advancing effective implementation of, and compliance with, the adopted amendments.

It also requests the Secretary-General of the Organization to make adequate provision, within the Integrated Technical Co-operation Programme, to strengthen further the assistance that is already being provided and to ensure that the Organization is able to address the future needs of developing countries for continued education and training and the improvement of their maritime and port security infrastructure and measures; and invites donors, international organizations and the shipping and port industry to contribute financial, human and/or in-kind resources to the Integrated Technical Co-operation Programme of the Organization for its maritime and port security activities.

It also invites the Secretary General to give early consideration to establishing a Maritime Security Trust Fund for the purpose of providing a dedicated source of financial support for maritime security technical-co-operation activities and, in particular, for providing support for national initiatives in developing countries to strengthen their maritime security infrastructure and measures.

Conference resolution 6 (Early implementation of the special measures to enhance maritime security) refers to the difficulties experienced during implementation of the International Safety Management (ISM) Code and draws the attention of Contracting Governments and the industry to the fact that chapter XI-2 of the Convention does not provide for any extension of the implementation dates for the introduction of the special measures concerned to enhance maritime security. It urges Contracting Governments to take, as a matter of high priority, any action needed to finalize as soon as possible any legislative or administrative arrangements, which are required at the national level, to give effect to the requirements of the adopted amendments to the Convention relating to the certification of ships entitled to fly their flag or port facilities situated in their territory. It also recommends that Contracting Governments and Administrations concerned designate dates, in advance of the application date of 1 July 2004 by which requests for certification should be submitted in order to allow for completion of the certification process and for companies and port facilities to rectify any non-compliance. It also recommends that Contracting Governments and the industry should take early appropriate action to ensure that all necessary infrastructure is in place in time for the effective implementation of the adopted measures to enhance maritime security on board ships and ashore.

Conference resolution 7 (Establishment of appropriate measures to enhance the security of ships, port facilities, mobile offshore drilling units on location and fixed and floating platforms not covered by chapter XI-2 of the 1974 SOLAS Convention) invites Contracting Governments to establish, as they might consider necessary, appropriate measures to enhance the security of ships and of port facilities other than those covered by chapter XI-2 of the Convention; it also encourages Contracting Governments to establish and disseminate, in an appropriate manner, information to facilitate contact and liaison between company and ship security officers and the authorities responsible for the security of port facilities not covered by Chapter XI-2, prior to a ship entering, or anchoring off, such a port.

Conference resolution 8 (Enhancement of security in co-operation with the International Labour Organization) invites the ILO to continue the development of a Seafarers' Identity Document as a matter of urgency, which should cover, among other things, a document for professional purposes; a verifiable security document; and a certification information document, and invites IMO and the ILO to establish a joint ILO/IMO Working Group to undertake more detailed work on comprehensive port security requirements.

Conference resolution 9 (Enhancement of security in co-operation with the World Customs Organization) invites the WCO to consider urgently measures to enhance security throughout international closed CTU movements and requests the Secretary-General of IMO to contribute expertise relating to maritime traffic to the discussions at the WCO.

Conference resolution 10 (Early implementation of long-range ships' identification and tracking) recalls that long-range identification and tracking of ships at sea is a measure that fully contributes to the enhancement of the maritime and coastal States security and notes that Inmarsat C polling is currently an appropriate system for long-range identification and tracking of ships. It urges Governments to take, as a matter of high priority, any action needed at national level to give effect to implementing and beginning the long-range identification and tracking of ships and invites Contracting Governments to encourage ships entitled to fly the flag of their State to take the necessary measures so that they are prepared to respond automatically to Inmarsat C polling, or to other available systems. It also requests Governments to consider all aspects related to the introduction of long-range identification and tracking of ships, including its potential for misuse as an aid to ship targeting and the need for confidentiality in respect of the information so gathered.

Conference resolution 11 (Human element-related aspects and shore leave for seafarers) urges Governments to take the human element, the need to afford special protection to seafarers and the critical importance of shore leave into account when implementing the provisions of chapter XI-2 of the Convention and the International Ship and Port Facility (ISPS) Code. It also encourages Governments, Member States of IMO and non-governmental organizations with consultative status at the Organization to report to the Organization any instances where the human element has been adversely impacted by the implementation of the provisions of chapter XI-2 of the Convention or the Code. It also requests the IMO Secretary-General to bring to the attention of the Maritime Safety Committee and the Facilitation Committee of the Organization, any human element related problems, which have been communicated to the Organization as a result of the implementation of chapter XI-2 of the Convention or the Code.

Officers of the Conference
The Conference elected Mr. J. Franson, Head of the delegation of Sweden, President of the Conference.

The following were elected Vice-Presidents of the Conference:

Mr. William J. S. Elliott (Canada)
Mr. Mitsuo Nakamoto (Japan)
H. E. Alma-Rosa Moreno Razo (Mexico)
Professor Marek Szymonski (Poland)
H. E. El Hadj Amadou Niang (Senegal)

The following were also elected:

Committee of the Whole:
Chairman: Mr. J.F. Wall (United Kingdom)
Vice-Chairman: Mr. D. Baird (Australia)
Vice-Chairman: Dr. S. Ilgin (Turkey)

Drafting Committee
Chairman: Mr. N. Charalambous (Cyprus)
Vice-Chairman: Admiral E. Schroth (Peru)
Vice-Chairman: Mr. I. Ponomarev (Russian Federation)

Credentials Committee
Chairman: Mr. Z. Alam (Singapore)

IMO—the International Maritime Organization—is the United Nations Specialized Agency with responsibility for the safety of shipping and the prevention of marine pollution by ships. Web site: www.imo.org.

For further information please contact:
Lee Adamson, Public Information Manager on 020 7587 3153 (ladamson@imo.org) or
Natasha Brown, Information Officer on 020 7587 3274 (nbrown@imo.org).

NOTES

1. George Bush, "Protecting America's Seaports and Securing Cargo Shipments," remarks at the Port of Charleston, South Carolina, February 5, 2004, http://www.whitehouse.gov/news/releases/20040205-4.html.

2. *Maritime Security Policy National Security/Homeland Security Presidential Directive,* http://www.dhs.gov/dhspublic/display?theme=67&content=4566.

3. *The National Strategy for Maritime Security* is available online at http://www.whitehouse.gov/homeland/maritime-security.html.

4. The White House, *The National Strategy for Maritime Security,* September 20, 2005, http://www.whitehouse.gov/homeland/maritime-security.html.

5. The White House, *The National Strategy for Maritime Security,* September 20, 2005, http://www.whitehouse.gov/homeland/maritime-security.html.

6. *National Strategy for Maritime Security.*

7. *National Strategy for Maritime Security.*

8. *National Strategy for Maritime Security.*

9. *National Strategy for Maritime Security.*

10. *National Strategy for Maritime Security.*

11. *National Strategy for Maritime Security.*

12. *National Strategy for Maritime Security.*

13. *National Strategy for Maritime Security.*

14. *National Strategy for Maritime Security.*

15. *National Strategy for Maritime Security.*

16. George W. Bush, *The National Security Strategy of the United States* (Washington, DC, White House, 2002), 7.

17. The British government issued this statement as part of its Chairman's Conclusions following an October 9–10, 2003 meeting of PSI participants in London. Note: This is provided as note 1 in the original document.

18. The interdiction principles can be found on the State Department's Web site at http://www.state.gov/t/np/rls/fs/23764.htm. Note: This is provided as note 2 in the original document.

19. Bolton stated in a November 4, 2003 interview with *Arms Control Today,* "And the 11 PSI countries also talked about circumstances where one could envision a Security Council resolution that might give authority in certain circumstances." Note: This is provided as note 3 in the original document.

20. The full interview is available at http://www.armscontrol.org/aca/mid-month/November/Bolton.asp Note: This is provided as note 4 in the original document.

21. The International Maritime Organization is the United Nations Specialized Agency with responsibility for the safety of shipping and the prevention of marine pollution by ships. For more information, please see the agency's Web site at http://www.imo.org.

SELECT BIBLIOGRAPHY AND RESOURCES FOR FURTHER READING

Ackleson, Jason. "Border Security Technologies: Local and Regional Implications."*Review of Policy Research* 22, no. 2 (2005): 137–155.

Ackleson, Jason. "Directions in Border Security Research." *The Social Science Journal* 40, no. 4 (2003): 1–9.

Adams, Michael. *Fire and Ice: The United States, Canada and the Myth of Converging Values.* Toronto: Penguin, 2003.

Adler, Emanual, and Michael N. Barnett, eds. *Security Communities.* Cambridge and New York: Cambridge University Press, 1998.

Akst, Daniel. "Cheap Eats." *The Wilson Quarterly* 27, no. 3 (2003): 30–41.

Americas Watch. *Brutality Unchecked: Human Rights Abuses Along the U.S. Border with Mexico.* New York: Human Rights Watch (Organization), 1992.

Andreas, Peter. *Border Games: Policing the U.S.- Mexico Divide.* Ithaca, NY: Cornell University Press, 2000.

Ashcroft, John. "Prepared Remarks of Attorney General John Ashcroft Regarding Human Trafficking." U.S. Department of Justice, January 29, 2004. Document accessed on February 25, 2004, at http://www.usdoj.gov.

Bailey, John J., and Roy G. Godson. *Organized Crime and Democratic Governability: Mexico and the U.S.-Mexican Borderlands.* University of Pittsburgh Press, 2000.

Bartholomew, Doug. "Cargo Crunch!" *Industry Week* (March, 2005): 43–49.

Baumgartner, Frank, and Bryan D. Jones. *Agendas and Instability in American Politics.* Chicago: University of Chicago Press, 1993.

Belelieu, Andre. "Canada Alert: The Smart Border Process at Two: Losing Momentum?" *Hemisphere Focus* 11, no. 31. Washington, DC: Center for Strategic and International Studies, December 10, 2003.

Beresford, Annette D. "Homeland Security as an American Ideology: Implications for U.S. Policy and Action." *Journal of Homeland Security and Emergency Management* 1, no. 3 (2004).

Bertram, Eva, Morris Blachman, et al. *Drug War Politics: The Price of Denial.* Berkeley, Los Angeles: University of California Press, 1996.

Betts, Richard. "The Soft Underbelly of American Primacy: Tactical Advantages of Terror." *Political Science Quarterly* 117, no. 1 (2002).

Bissett, James. *Canada's Asylum System: A Threat to American Security?* Washington, DC: Center for Immigration Studies, May 2002.

Brookings Institution. *Protecting the American Homeland: A Preliminary Analysis.* Washington, DC: Brookings Institution Press, 2002. http://www.brookings.edu/press/books/protecting_the_american_homeland.htm.

Bush, President George W. *Remarks by the President in Address to the Nation.* Washington, DC, June 2002. http://www.dhs.gov/dhspublic/ display? theme=44&content=169.

Camarota, Steven A. "The Open Door: How Militant Islamic Terrorists Entered and Remained in the United States, 1993–2001," *Center Paper 21.* Washington, DC: Center for Immigration Studies, 2003.

Camarota, Steven. "Safety in (Lower) Numbers: Immigration & Homeland Security." Washington, DC: Center for Immigration Studies, 2002.

Carter, Jimmy. "This isn't the real America." *Los Angeles Times,* November 14, 2005.

Castañeda, Jorge. "The Forgotten Relationship," *Foreign Affairs* 82, no. 3 (2003): 67–81.

Celia Toro, Maria. *Mexico's "War" on Drugs: Causes and Consequences.* Boulder and London: Lynne Rienner Publishers, 1995.

Cellucci, Paul. *Unquiet Diplomacy.* Toronto: Key Porter Books, 2005.

Center for Strategic and International Studies (CSIS). *Thinking Strategically About 2005, The United States and South America.* Washington DC: CSIS, 1999.

Center for Strategic and International Studies. *Defending America in the 21st Century: New Challenges, New Organizations, and New Policies.* Executive Summary of Four Working Group Reports on Homeland Defense. Washington, DC: CSIS, 2000. http://www.csis.org/homeland/reports/ defendamer21stexecsumm.pdf.

Cerny, Philip G. "Terrorism and the New Security Dilemma." *Naval War College Review* 58, no. 1 (2005): 11–33.

Chang, Howard F. "Migration as International Trade: The Economic Benefits from the Liberalized Movement of Labor." In *Reconsidering Immigration in an Integrating World,* edited by Christopher Rudolph, *UCLA Journal of Int'l Law & Foreign Affairs* 3, no. 2 (1998), special issue.

Cilluffo, Frank J., Sharon L. Cardash, and Gordon N. Lederman. *Combating Chemical, Biological, Radiological, and Nuclear Terrorism: A Comprehensive Strategy.* Washington, DC: Center for Strategic and International Studies, 2001. http:// www.csis.org/pubs/2001_combatingcbrnt.htm.

Civil Rights Division of the United States Department of Justice. "Trafficking in Persons: A Guide for Non-Governmental Organizations." Report accessed on February 25, 2004 at http://www.usdoj.gov.

Cockburn, Andrew. "21st Century Slaves." *National Geographic,* (September 2003): 2–29.

Collins, Joseph J., and Michael Horowitz. *Homeland Defense: A Strategic Approach.* Washington, DC: Center for Strategic and International Studies, December 2000. http://www.csis.org/homeland/reports/ hdstrategicappro.pdf.

Congressional Quarterly Researcher. *Policing the Borders (Volume 12, No. 7).* Washington, DC: Congressional Quarterly, Inc., February 22, 2002.

Congressional Research Service. "Border and Transportation Security: The Complexity of the Challenge." CRS Report #RL32839. http://www. fas.org/sgp/crs/homesec/RL32839.pdf.

Congressional Research Service. "Border Security: Key Agencies and Their Missions." CRS Report #RS21899. Washington, DC: Congressional Research Service, 2005. http://www.fas.org/sgp/crs/row/RL32735.pdf.

Congressional Research Service. "Immigration: Policy Considerations Related to Guest Worker Programs." CRS Report #RS21899. Washington, DC: Congressional Research Service, 2005. http://fpc.state.gov/documents/organization/48603.pdf.

Congressional Research Service. "Mexico-United States Dialogue on Migration and Border Issues, 2001–2005." CRS Report #RL32735. Washington, DC: Congressional Research Service, 2005. http://www.fas.org/sgp/crs/row/RL32735.pdf.

Congressional Research Service, "U.S. International Trade: Data and Forecasts." CRS Report for Congress. Washington, DC: Congressional Research Service, 2005.

Cornelius, Wayne A. "Controlling 'Unwanted' Immigration: Lessons from the United States, 1993–2004." *Journal of Ethnic and Migration Studies* 31, no. 4 (July 2005).

Cornelius, Wayne A. *The Role of Immigrant Labor in the U.S. and Japanese Economies.* La Jolla, CA: Center for U.S.-Mexican Studies, 1998.

Cornelius, Wayne A., Philip L. Martin, and James F. Hollifield, eds. *Controlling Immigration: A Global Perspective.* Stanford, CA: Stanford University Press, 1994.

Cornelius, Wayne A., Takeyuki Tsuda, Philip L. Martin, and James F. Hollifield, eds. *Controlling Immigration: A Global Perspective* 2nd ed. Stanford, CA: Stanford University Press, 2004.

Cornelius, Wayne A., Thomas J. Espenshade, and Idean Salehyan, eds. *The International Migration of the Highly Skilled.* La Jolla, CA: Center for Comparative Immigration Studies, 2001.

Cornelius, Wayne A., Yasuo Kuwahara, et al. *The Role of Immigrant Labor in the U.S. and Japanese Economies: A Comparative Study of San Diego and Hamamatsu, Japan.* San Diego, Center for U.S.-Mexican Studies, University of California San Diego, 1998.

Coryn, John, and Jon Kyle. "Comprehensive Enforcement and Immigration Reform Act—Short Summary." Available at http://www.cornyn.senate.gov/doc_archive/CEIRA%20Short%20Summary.pdf.

Cottam, Martha L., and Otwin Marenin. "International Cooperation in the War on Drugs: Mexico and the United States." *Policing and Society* 9 (1999): 209–40.

D'Amico, Esther. "More Port Choke-Ups Ahead?" *Chemical Week* 167, no. 17 (18 May 2005).

Daalder, Ivo H., and James M. Lindsay. "The Globalization of Politics: American Foreign Policy for a New Century." *The Brookings Review* 21, no. 1 (2003).

Davidow, Jeffrey. *The U.S. and Mexico—The Bear and the Porcupine: Testimony of the U.S. Ambassador to Mexico 1998–2002.* Princeton: Markus Wiener, 2004.

Davis, Radford G. and Danelle Bickett-Weddle. "Agroterrorism Awareness." In *Agroterrorism Awareness Education (Version 1.2).* Ames, Iowa: Iowa State University Center for Food Security and Public Health, 2004.

de Borchgrave, Arnaud, Frank J. Cilluffo, Sharon L. Cardash, and Michèle M. Ledgerwood. *Cyber Threats and Information Security: Meeting the 21st Century Challenge.* Washington, DC: Center for Strategic and International Studies, May 2001. http://www.csis.org/pubs/2001_cyberthreatsandis.htm.

Department of Defense. "DoD USS Cole Commission Report." Executive Summary, January 9, 2001. http://www.defenselink.mil/pubs/cole20010109.html.

Department of Homeland Security, Office of Inspector General. "Implementation of the United States Visitor and Immigrant Status Indicator Technology Program at Land Border Ports of Entry." OIG-05-11, February 2005. www.dhs.gov/interweb/assetlibrary/OIG_05-11_Feb05.pdf.

Derghoukassian, Khatchik. "Human Security: A Brief Report on the State of the Art." The Dante B. Fascell North-South Center, Working Paper Series, November 2001.

Dvorak, Glenda. "Definitions." In *Bioterrorism Awareness Education (Version 1.2).* Ames, Iowa: Iowa State University Center for Food Security and Public Health, 2003.

"Establishment of U.S. Antiterrorism Maritime Transportation System."*The American Journal of International Law* 98, no. 3 (July 2004): 588–590.

Felicetti, Gary, and John Luce. "Posse Comitatus Act: Setting The Record Straight on 124 Years of Mischief and Misunderstanding Before Anymore Damage Is Done." *Military Law Review* (March 2003): 128–141.

Flynn, Stephen. "America the Vulnerable." *Foreign Affairs* 81, no. 1 (2002): 60–75.

Fournier, Louis. *F.L.Q.: The Anatomy of an Underground Movement.* Toronto: NC Press Limited, 1984.

G-8 Action Plan: Enhance Transport Security and Control of Man Portable Air Defense Systems (MANPADS). Evian, France: The White House, 2003. http://www.g8.fr/evian/english/navigation/news/news_update/enhance_transport_security_and_control_of_man-portable_air_defence_systems_-_manpads_-_a_g8_action_plan.html.

G-8 Secure and Facilitated International Travel Initiative. Sea Island, GA: The White House, June 9, 2004. http://www.state.gov/e/eb/rls/fs/33384.htm.

G-8 Transportation Security Initiative. Kananaskis, Alberta, Canada: The White House, June 26–27, 2002. http://www.useu.be/Categories/Transportation/June2602G8TransportSecurity.html.

Gallagher, Stephen. "Canada's Dysfunctional Refugee Determination System." *Public Policy Sources* 78 (December 2003).

Ganguly, Sumit. "The Start of a Beautiful Friendship? The United States and India." *World Policy Journal* 20 (Spring 2003).

García, Jose Z. "Security Regimes on the U.S.-Mexican Border." In *Transnational Crime and Public Security: Challenges to Mexico and the United States,* edited by John Bailey and Jorge Chabat. La Jolla, CA: Center for U.S.-Mexican Studies, 2002.

Gerges, Fawaz A. *The Far Enemy: Why Jihad Went Global.* Cambridge: Cambridge University Press, 2005.

Ghosh, Bimal, ed. *Managing Migration: Time for a New International Regime?* Oxford: Oxford University Press, 2000.

Gilmore Commission Fourth Annual Report, Advisory Panel to Assess Domestic Response Capabilities for Terrorism Involving Weapons of Mass Destruction. *Implementing the National Strategy.* Fourth Annual Report to the President and the Congress. Washington, DC, December 15, 2002.

Gilmore Commission Second Annual Report, Advisory Panel to Assess Domestic Response Capabilities for Terrorism Involving Weapons of Mass Destruction (known as the Gilmore Commission). *Toward a National Strategy for Combating Terrorism.* Second Annual Report to the President and the Congress. Washington, DC, December 15, 2000. http://www.rand.org/nsrd/terrpanel.

Gilmore Commission Third Annual Report, Advisory Panel to Assess Domestic Response Capabilities for Terrorism Involving Weapons of Mass Destruction. *For Ray Downey.* Third Annual Report to the President and the Congress. Washington, DC, December 15, 2001.

Gladwell, Malcolm. *The Tipping Point: How Little Things can Make a big Difference.* Boston: Little Brown, 2002.

González, Guadalupe, and Stephan Haggard. "The United States and Mexico: A Pluralistic Security Community?" In *Security Communities,* edited by Emanual Adler and Michael N. Barnett. Cambridge and New York: Cambridge University Press, 1998.

Gouré, Daniel. *Defense of the U.S. Homeland Against Strategic Attack.* Washington, DC: Center for Strategic and International Studies, December 2000. http://www.csis.org/homeland/reports/defenseofushmld.pdf.

Government Accountability Office (GAO). *Container Security: Expansion of Key Customs Programs Will Require Greater Attention to Critical Success Factors* (GAO-03-770). Washington, DC: U.S. Government Printing Office, July 2003.

Government Accountability Office. *Combating Terrorism: Evaluation of Selected Characteristics in National Strategies Related to Terrorism* (GAO-04-408T). Statement of Randall A. Yim, GAO Managing Director of Homeland Security and Justice Issues, prepared for the Subcommittee on National Security, Emerging Threats, and International Relations, Committee on Government Reform, House of Representatives, February 3, 2004.

Government Accountability Office. *Food Safety: U.S. Needs a Single Agency to Administer a Unified, Risk-Based Inspection System* (GAO/T-RCED-99-256). Washington, DC: U.S. Government Printing Office, 1999.

Government Accountability Office.*Homeland Security: Observations on the National Strategies Related to Terrorism* (GAO-04-1075T). Washington, DC: U.S. Government Printing Office, September 22, 2004.

Government Accountability Office. *Homeland Security: Risks Facing Key Border and Transportation Security Program Need to Be Addressed* (GAO-03-1083). Washington, DC: U.S. Government Printing Office, September 2003.

Government Accountability Office. *Port Security: Nation Faces Formidable Challenges in Making New Initiatives Successful* (GAO-02-9993T). Washington, DC: U.S. Government Printing Office, August 2002.

Grodzins, C. Morton. "The Federal System." *Classic Readings in American Politics,* edited by Pietro S. Nivola and David H. Rosenbloom. New York, St. Martin's Press, 1990, 61–77.

Haggart, Ron, and Aubrey E. Golden, *Rumors of War.* Toronto: New Press, 1971.

Hampson, Fen-Osler, and Maureen Appel Molot, eds. *Canada Among Nations 2000: Vanishing Borders*Toronto: Oxford University Press, 2000.

Haralambides, Hercules, and Maria Londonoken. "Supply Chain Bottlenecks: Border Crossing Inefficiencies Between Mexico and the United States." *International Journal of Transport Economics* 31, no. 2 (June 2004).

Hart, Gary, and Warren B. Rudman, *America: Still Unprepared, Still in Danger.* Council on Foreign Relations Task Force Report, 2002. http://www.cfr.org/content/publications/attachments/Homeland_Security_TF.pdf.

Hattiangadi, Anita U., Aline O. Quester, Gary Lee, Diana S. Lien, Ian MacLeod, David L. Reese, and Robert W. Shuford. *Non-Citizens in Today's Military: Final Report.* Alexandria, VA: Center for Naval Analyses, April 2005.

Heritage Foundation. *Defending the American Homeland: A Report of The Heritage Foundation Homeland Security Task Force.* Washington, D.C.: The Heritage Foundation, January 2002. http://www.heritage.org.

Hillmer, Norman, and Maureen Appel Molot, eds. *Canada Among Nations: A Fading Power.* Toronto: Oxford University Press, 2002.

Hoffman, David. *The Oklahoma City Bombing and the Politics of Terror,* August 9, 2004. http://www.apfn.org/apfn/hoffman.htm.

Hoffman, Frank. "Border Security: Closing the Ingenuity Gap." In *Homeland Security and Terrorism,* edited by Russell Howard, James Forest, and Joanne Moore. New York: McGraw-Hill, 2005.

Hollifield, James F. *Immigrants, Markets and States.* Cambridge, MA: Harvard University Press, 1986.

Hollifield, James F. "Migration, Trade, and the Nation-State: The Myth of Globalization." In *Reconsidering Immigration in an Integrating World,* edited by Christopher Rudolph, *UCLA Journal of Int'l Law & Foreign Affairs* 3, no. 2 (1998), special issue.

"Human Trafficking and Slavery." *CQ Researcher,* March 26, 2004. http://library.cqpress.com (accessed April 6, 2004).

Huntington, Samuel. "The Hispanic Challenge," *Foreign Policy* (March/April 2004).

Huntington, Samuel. *Who Are We? The Challenges to America's National Identity.* New York: Simon and Schuster, 2004.

Ichniowski, Tom. "Ports Seek Out Funds to Carry Out Security Rules," *ENR: Engineering News-Record* 251, no. 2, July 14, 2003.

Immigration Policy Center. *Maintaining a Competitive Edge: The Role of the Foreign-Born & U.S. Immigration Policies in Science and Engineering,* vol. 3, no. 3. Washington, DC: American Immigration Law Foundation, August 2004.

Institute for Analysis of Global Security. *Threats to Oil Transport,* December 3, 2004. http://www.iags.org.

International Maritime Organization. "Maritime Security on the Agenda as USCG Commandant Visits IMO." In *Oil Spill Intelligence Report,* vol. 28, no. 9, February 24, 2005.

Jacobson, David. *Rights Across Borders: Immigration and the Decline of Citizenship.* Baltimore, MD: Johns Hopkins University Press, 1996.

Jannol, Rebecca, Deborah Meyers, and Maia Jachimowicz. "U.S.-Canada-Mexico Fact Sheet on Trade and Migration." Washington, DC: Migration

Policy Institute, 2003. http://www.migrationpolicy.org/pubs/three_us_mexico_canada_trade.pdf.

Jerome, Fred. *The Einstein File.* New York: St. Martin's Press, 2002.

Johnson, Stephen, and Sara J. Fitzgerald. "The United States and Mexico: Partners in Reform." *Backgrounder No. 1715.* Washington, DC: The Heritage Foundation, December 2003.

Joppke, Christian. "Asylum and State Sovereignty: A Comparison of the United States, Germany, and Britain." *Comparative Political Studies* 30, no. 3 (June 1997): 259-298.

Joppke, Christian. *Immigration and the Nation-State.* Oxford: Oxford University Press, 1999.

Kant, Immanuel. *Perpetual Peace and Other Essays,* translated by Ted Humphrey. Indianapolis, IN: Hackett Publishing, 1983.

Kelly, Philip, and Jack Child. "Geopolitics, Integration and Conflict in the Southern Cone and Antarctica." In *Geopolitics of the Southern Cone and Antarctica,* edited by Philip Kelly and Jack Child. Boulder and London: Lynne Rienner Publishers, 1988.

Keohane, Robert. "Realism, Neorealism and the Study of World Politics." In *Neorealism and its Critics,* edited by Robert Keohane. New York: Columbia University Press, 1986.

Kingsbury, Nancy. "Border Security: Challenges in Implementing Border Technology." *GAO Report* 03-546T. Washington, DC: Government Printing Office, 2003.

Koslowski, Rey. "Real Challenges for Virtual Borders: The Implementation of US-VISIT." Migration Policy Institute Report, June 2005. http://www.migrationpolicy.org/pubs/Koslowski_Report.pdf (accessed August 26, 2005).

Krauze, Enrique. *Mexico, Biography of Power: A History of Modern Mexico, 1810-1996,* translated by Hank Heifetz. New York: HarperPerennial, 1997.

Krikorian, Mark, and Steven A. Camarota. "Immigration and Terrorism: What Is To Be Done?" Washington, DC: Center for Immigration Studies, 2001.

Landesman, Peter. "The Girls Next Door." *New York Times Magazine,* January 25, 2004.

Lesser, Ian. "Countering the New Terrorism: Implications for Strategy." In *Countering the New Terrorism,* edited by John Arquila et al. Washington, DC: Rand Corp., 1999.

Luft, Gal, and Anne Korin. "Terrorism Goes to Sea." *Foreign Affairs* 83 (November/December 2004).

Lumpe, Lora. "The U.S. Arms Both Sides of Mexico's Drug War." *Covert Action Quarterly* 61 (1997): 39–46.

Mackinder, Halford. *Democratic Ideals and Reality.* New York: W.W. Norton & Co., 1962.

Malkin, Michelle. *In Defense of Internment: The Case for Racial Profiling in World War II and the War on Terror.* Washington, DC: Regnery Publishing, 2004.

Martin, Philip L. "Trade, Aid, and Migration." *International Migration Review* 26, no. 1 (1992).

Massey, Douglas S., et al. *Worlds in Motion.* Oxford: Clarendon Press, 1998.

McHale, John. "Homeland Security Focus." *Military and Aerospace Electronics,* (June 2005).

McKenna, Ted. "Armed and Ready," *JED, the Journal of Electronic Defense,* (August 2003): 44–50.

Meyers, Deborah Waller. "Does Smarter Lead to Safer? An Assessment of the Border Accords with Canada and Mexico." *Insight* (June 2003).

Meyers, Deborah. "Security at U.S. Borders: A Move Away from Unilateralism?" *Migration Information Source* (August 2003).

Milner, Helen. *Interests, Institutions and Information: Domestic Politics and International Relations.* Princeton, NJ: Princeton University Press, 1997.

Mittelman, James. *The Globalization Syndrome.* Princeton: Princeton University Press, 2000.

Morgenthau, Hans. *Politics Among Nations: The Struggle for Power and Peace.* New York: Alfred Knopf, Inc., 1973.

Moy, G. G. "Food Safety and Globalization of Trade: A Challenge to the Public Health Sector." *World Food Regulation Review* 8, no. 9 (1999).

National Academy of Sciences. *Making the Nation Safer: The Role of Science and Technology in Countering Terrorism.* Washington, DC: National Research Council, October 2002.

National Commission on Terrorism (the Bremer Commission). *Countering the Changing Threat of International Terrorism,* June 7, 2000. http://www.fas.org/irp/threat/commission.html.

National Commission on Terrorist Attacks Upon the United States. *Report of the National Commission on Terrorist Attacks Upon the United States* (the 9/11 Commission Report). Washington, DC: Government Printing Office, 2004. http://www.gpoaccess.gov/911.

National Commission on Terrorist Attacks. *9/11 and Terrorist Travel: A Staff Report of the National Commission on Terrorist Attacks Upon the United States.* Franklin, TN: Hillsboro Press, 2004.

National Strategy for Homeland Security. The White House, July 16, 2002.

National Strategy for Maritime Security. The White House, September 20, 2005. http://www.whitehouse.gov/homeland/maritime-security.html.

Nevins, Joseph. *Operation Gatekeeper: The Rise of the "Illegal Alien" and the Making of the U.S.-Mexico Boundary.* New York: Routledge, 2002.

Newland, Kathleen, and Demetrios G. Papademetriou, "Managing International Migration: Tracking the Emergence of a New International Regime." In *Reconsidering Immigration in an Integrating World,* edited by Christopher Rudolph, *UCLA Journal of Int'l Law & Foreign Affairs* 3, no. 2 (1998), special issue.

Nye, Joseph S., Jr., *Soft Power: The Means to Success in World Politics.* New York: Public Affairs, 2004.

Nye, Joseph S. *The Paradox of American Power: Why the World's Only Superpower Can't Go It Alone.* Oxford: Oxford University Press, 2003.

O'Hair, H. Dan, Robert L. Heath, and Gerald R. Ledlow, eds. *Community Preparedness and Response to Terrorism* (3 volumes). Westport: Praeger, 2005.

O'Rourke, Kevin, and Jeffrey Williamson. *Globalization and History: The Evolution of a Nineteenth Century Atlantic Economy.* Cambridge, MA: MIT Press, 2001.

Office of Policy and Planning. *Estimates of the Unauthorized Immigrant Population Residing in the United States:1990 to 2000*. Washington, DC, U.S. Immigration and Naturalization Service, 2003.

Paarlberg, Robert L. "Knowledge as Power: Science, Military Dominance, and U.S. Security." *International Security* 29, no. 1 (Summer 2004): 122–151.

Paden, John N., and Peter W. Singer. "America Slams the Door (On Its Foot): Washington's Destructive New Visa Policies." *Foreign Affairs* (May/June 2003).

Papademetriou, Demetrious, and Deborah Meyers.*Caught in the Middle: Border Communities in an Era of Globalization*. Washington, DC: Carnegie Endowment for International Peace, 2001.

Parachini, Lynn David, and Timothy Liston. *Homeland Security: A Compendium of Public and Private Organizations' Policy Recommendations*. Santa Monica, CA: RAND Corp, 2003. http://www.rand.org/pubs/white_papers/WP127/WP127.pdf.

Passel, Jeffrey S. *Estimates of the Size and Characteristics of the Undocumented Population*. Washington, DC: Pew Hispanic Center, 2005. http://pewhispanic.org/files/reports/44.pdf.

Pierce, Alan. "Operation Safe Commerce." *Tech Directions* 64, no. 4 (November 2004): 12.

Pillar, Paul. *Terrorism and U.S. Foreign Policy*. Washington, DC: Brookings Institution Press, 2001.

President's Critical Infrastructure Commission Report. The President's Commission on Critical Infrastructure Protection, Critical Infrastructure Assurance Office, *Critical Foundations Protecting America's Infrastructures*. Washington, DC, October 1997. http://www.cshs-us.org/cshs/cshs.nsf/6d0a0b623aab586b85256af500674bbb/e52acb6daaa5d2d785256d340068365b/$FILE/PCCIPreport.pdf.

Richard, Amy O' Neill. *An Intelligence Monograph International Trafficking in Women to the United States: A Contemporary Manifestation of Slavery and Organized Crime*. Washington, DC, DCI Exceptional Intelligence Analyst Program, Center for the Study of Intelligence, 1999.

Roach, Ashley. "Container and Port Security: A Bilateral Perspective."*The International Journal of Marine and Coastal Law* 18, no. 3 (2003): 341–361.

Rudolph, Christopher. "Globalization and Security: Migration and Evolving Conceptions of Security in Statecraft and Scholarship." *Security Studies* 13, no. 1 (Fall 2004).

Rudolph, Christopher. "Security and the Political Economy of International Migration." *American Political Science Review* 97, no. 4 (2003).

Rudolph, Christopher. "Sovereignty and Territorial Borders in a Global Age." *International Studies Review* 7: no. 1 (2005): 1–20.

Russell, Sharon Stanton. "Migrant Remittances and Development." *International Migration* 30, no. 3–4 (1992).

Sachs, Jeffrey D. *The End of Poverty: Economic Possibilities for Our Time*. New York: Penguin Press, 2005.

Schoultz, Lars. *National Security and United States Policy toward Latin America*. Princeton, NJ: Princeton University Press, 1987.

Shanks, Cheryl. *Immigration and the Politics of American Sovereignty, 1890–1990.* Ann Arbor, MI: University of Michigan Press, 2001.

Sherrid, Pamela. "Seeking Safe Harbors." *U.S. News & World Report* 134, no. 4 (April 28, 2003).

Singer, Daniel. "The Level of Analysis Problem in International Relations." In *American Foreign Policy: Theoretical Essays,* edited by John Ikenberry. New York: Harper Collins Publishers, 1989.

Soysal, Yasemin. *The Limits of Citizenship.* Chicago: University of Chicago Press, 1994.

Stein, Arthur A. "Coordination and Collaboration: Regimes in an Anarchic World." In *International Regimes,* edited by Stephen D. Krasner. Ithaca, NY: Cornell University Press, 1983, 115–140.

Strongin, R. J. "How Vulnerable Is the Nation's Food Supply? Linking Food Safety and Food Security." National Health Policy Forum Issue Brief, No. 773, 2002.

The White House. "Fact Sheet: Strengthening Intelligence to Better Protect America," February 14, 2003. http://www.whitehouse.gov/news/releases/2003/02/20030214-1.html.

The White House. "President Releases National Strategy for Homeland Security," July 16, 2002. http://www.whitehouse.gov/news/releases/2002/07/print/20020716-2.html.

The White House. *Annual Report to Congress on Combating Terrorism,* pursuant to Fiscal Year 1998 National Defense Authorization Act (Public Law 105-85), June 24, 2002. http://www.whitehouse.gov/omb/legislative/combating_terrorism06-2002.pdf.

The White House. *Domestic Preparedness Against Weapons of Mass Destruction.* Statement by the President, Washington, DC, May 8, 2001.

The White House. *Executive Order 13323—Assignment of Functions Relating to Arrivals in and Departures From the United States,* December 30, 2003.

The White House. *Executive Order 13228—Establishing Office of Homeland Security,* October 8, 2001.

The White House. *Homeland Security Presidential Directive-1 (HSPD-1)—Organization and Operation of the Homeland Security Council,* October 29, 2001.

The White House. *Homeland Security Presidential Directive-11 (HSPD-11)—Comprehensive Terrorist-Related Screening Procedures,* August 27, 2004.

The White House. *Homeland Security Presidential Directive-6 (HSPD-6)—Integration and Use of Screening Information to Protect against Terrorism,* September 16, 2003.

The White House. *National Strategy for Homeland Security.* Washington, DC, July 2002. http://www.dhs.gov/interweb/assetlibrary/nat_strat_hls.pdf.

Torpey, John. "States and the Regulation of Migration in the Twentieth-Century North Atlantic World." In *The Wall Around the West,* edited by P. Andreas and T. Snyder. Lanham, MD: Rowman & Littlefield, 2000.

Trebilcock, Michael, and Robert Howse. *The Regulation of International Trade.* London: Routledge, 1999.

Tulchin, Joseph S., and Andrew D. Selee, eds. *Mexico's Politics and Society in Transition.* Boulder: Lynne Rienner, 2003.

U.S. Commission on National Security/21st Century (known as the Hart-Rudman Commission). *Road Map for National Security: Imperative for Change,* Phase III

Report, Washington, DC, February 15, 2001.

United Nations. *The United Nations Protocol to Prevent, Suppress and Punish Trafficking in Persons, Especially Women and Children, Supplementing the United Nations Convention Against Transnational Organized Crime.* New York: United Nations, 2000.

United States Agency for International Development. "Trafficking in Persons: USAID's Response." September 2001.

United States Congress. *Public Law 107-296—Homeland Security Act of 2002.* Washington, DC: U.S. Congress, November 25, 2002.

United States Department of State. *Trafficking in Persons Report.* Washington, DC, 2005.

United States Transportation Security Administration. *Security Guidelines for General Aviation Airports.* July 25, 2004. http://www.dhs.gov.

van de Voort, Martin, and Kevin A. O'Brien with Adnan Rahman and Lorenzo Valeri. "Seacurity: Improving the Security of the Global Sea-Container, Shipping System." In *Homeland Security and Terrorism: Readings and Interpretations,* edited by Russell Howard, James Forest, and Joanne Moore. New York: McGraw-Hill, 2005.

Väyrynen, Raimo. "Illegal Immigration, Human Trafficking, and Organized Crime." World Institute for Development Economics Research, Discussion Paper No. 2003/72 (October 2003): 1–25.

Vernez, Georges. "Mexican Labor in California's Economy: From Rapid Growth to Likely Stability." In *The California-Mexico Connection,* edited by Abraham F. Lowenthal and Katrina Burgess. Stanford, Stanford University Press, 1993, 147–164.

Waltz, Kenneth. *Man, the State and War, A Theoretical Analysis.* New York: Columbia University Press, 1959.

Wasem, Ruth Ellen, et al., *Border Security: Inspections Practices, Policies, and Issues.* CRS Report for Congress. Washington, DC: Congressional Research Service, 2004.

Woodward, John D., Jr., *Biometrics: Facing Up to Terrorism.* Santa Monica, CA: RAND Corporation, 2001.

Zolberg, Aristide R. "Changing Sovereignty Games and International Migration." *Indiana Journal of Global Legal Studies* 2, no. 1 (1994).

WEB SITES

Container Security Initiative (CSI): http://www.cbp.gov/xp/cgov/border_security/international_activities/csi.

"C-TPAT Frequently Asked Questions:" http://cbp.gov/xp/cgov/import/commercial_enforcement/ctpat/ctpat_faq.xml.

FAST Reference guide, March 2005: http://www.cbp.gov/linkhandler/cgov/import/commercial_enforcement/ctpat/fast/fast_ref_guide.ctt/fast_ref_guide.pdf.

Frontier—interdisciplinary program for the historical studies of border security, food safety, and trade policy: http://fss.k-state.edu/frontier.

Mexican Embassy, Washington, DC: http://portal.sre.gob.mx/usa

Migration Policy Institute: http://www.migrationpolicy.org.

Minuteman Civil Defense Corps: http://www.minutemanhq.com.

National Transportation Library: http://ntl.bts.gov/faq/sept11.html.

Pew Hispanic Center: http://pewhispanic.org.

Port of Long Beach: http://www.polb.com.

Port of Los Angeles: http://www.portoflosangeles.org.

Port of Montreal: http://www.port-montreal.com/site/index.jsp?lang=en.

Port of Seattle: http://www.portofseattle.org/seaport.

Security and Prosperity Partnership of North America: http://www.spp.gov.

U.S. Coast Guard: http://www.uscg.mil.

U.S. Customs and Border Protection: http://www.cbp.gov

U.S. Department of Homeland Security: http://www.dhs.gov.

U.S. Department of Homeland Security US-VISIT Program: http://www.dhs.gov/dhspublic/display?theme=91.

U.S. Government Biometric Consortium: http://www.biometrics.org.

U.S. Immigration and Customs Enforcement: http://www.ice.gov.

U.S. Northern Command: http://www.northcom.mil.

U.S. Transportation Security Administration: http://www.tsa.gov.

University of San Diego, Trans-Border Institute: http://www.sandiego.edu/tbi.

World Trade Organization: http://www.wto.org.

World Trade Organization Sanitary and Phytosanitary Measures: http://www.wto.org/english/tratop_e/sps_e/sps_e.htm.

INDEX

ABOUT THE EDITOR AND CONTRIBUTORS

JAMES J.F. FOREST, Ph.D., is Director of Terrorism Studies and Assistant Professor of Political Science at the U.S. Military Academy at West Point, where he teaches undergraduate courses on information warfare and terrorism and directs research initiatives for the Combating Terrorism Center. His recent publications include *The Making of a Terrorist: Recruitment, Training and Root Causes* (3 volumes, 2005); *Homeland Security and Terrorism: Readings and Interpretations* (with Russell Howard and Joanne Moore, 2005); *Oil and Terrorism in the New Gulf: Framing U.S. Energy and Security Policies for the Gulf of Guinea* (2006, with Matt Sousa); and a 200-page *Annotated Bibliography of Terrorism and Counterterrorism* (2004), available at the Center's Web site (http://ctc.usma.edu). His research has also appeared in the *Cambridge Review of International Affairs*, the *Journal of Political Science Education*, and the *Encyclopedia of Intelligence and Counterintelligence*. Dr. Forest received his graduate degrees from Stanford University and Boston College and his undergraduate degrees from Georgetown University and De Anza College.

JASON ACKLESON, Ph.D., is Assistant Professor in the Department of Government at New Mexico State University. A native New Mexican, he spent several years in the United Kingdom as a Truman and British Marshall Scholar, where he earned his doctorate in International Relations at the London School of Economics and Political Science. At the LSE he also served as the senior editor of *Millennium: Journal of International Studies*. He is currently conducting research on the Security and Prosperity Partnership of North America, a project funded by a Canadian studies grant. His publications include articles in *Political Geography, Journal of Borderland Studies,* and *The Social Science Journal*.

DANIELLA E. BOVE-LAMONICA is currently a graduate student at the School for International and Public Affairs (SIPA) at Columbia University. Before beginning her graduate studies in 2004, she worked for the Department of State on a three-year diplomatic fellowship at the U.S. Consulate General in Monterrey, Mexico. While in Monterrey she served as a vice-consul in the world's fourth busiest nonimmigrant visa (NIV) section, served as the NIV training officer, and spent one year running the Consulate's Fraud Prevention Unit.

JOE DIRENZO III is the Anti-Terrorism Coordinator for the Coast Guard's Atlantic Area. He is a retired Coast Guard officer, and former cutter Commanding Officer, who has written and lectured extensively on port security. He has also been a visiting fellow at the Joint Forces Staff College. A graduate of both the Naval War College and Marine Corps Command and Staff College, he is currently a doctoral candidate at Northcentral University in Business Philosophy, Homeland Security Specialty.

PRIYA DIXIT is a doctoral student at the School of International Service, American University. She spent the first half of 2005 as a visiting Ph.D. fellow at the School for Postgraduate Interdisciplinary Research on Interculturalism and Transnationality (SPIRIT) in Aalborg, Denmark, researching British government documents dealing with Ireland and Northern Ireland, especially those related to terrorism. Her research examines terrorism in Nepal and Northern Ireland in order to analyze relations of power in the international system.

CHRIS DOANE is the Chief of Response and Port Security for the Coast Guard's Atlantic Area. He is a retired Coast Guard officer with extensive experience in port security and consequence management. He received a master's degree in Ocean Engineering from the University of New Hampshire, and he has written extensively on maritime security topics.

STUART FARSON, Ph.D., has taught political science at Simon Fraser University since 1991. He is the author of numerous articles on security, intelligence, policing, and terrorism and co-editor of two books in the field. In 1989–90 he served as Director of Research for the Special Committee of the House of Commons on the Review of the *Canadian Security Intelligence Service Act* and the *Security Offences Act.* He has testified before numerous parliamentary committees. Most recently, he was an expert witness for the Commission of Inquiry into the Actions of Canadian Officials in Relation to Maher Arar.

TRACEY GRAY is a program analyst focusing on maritime strategy and interagency coordination for the Office of the Assistant Secretary of Defense for Homeland Defense. He served as the Office of the Secretary of Defense representative and a primary author for the *National Strategy for Maritime Security,* which President Bush approved in September 2005.

FRANK JONES, a member of the Senior Executive Service, is Principal Director for Strategy, Plans, and Resources, Office of the Assistant Secretary of Defense for Homeland Defense. He has held a number of senior positions in the Defense Department, and in 2005, he co-chaired the interagency working group that wrote the *National Strategy for Maritime Security,* which President Bush approved in September 2005.

FARID KAHHAT, Ph.D., is Professor and Researcher in the Social Sciences Department of the Catholic University in Lima, Peru. He is a regular columnist on international affairs for mainstream newspapers in Peru (*El Comercio*) and Mexico (*Reforma*), and he is a regular guest of the Spanish speaking network of *CNN.*

JUSTIN KASTNER, Ph.D., is Assistant Professor of Food Safety and Security in the Department of Diagnostic Medicine/Pathobiology at Kansas State University. He conducts scholarly activities related to trade policy, the history of science, economic history, U.S.-Canadian border issues, and the history of trade disputes regarding food safety and animal disease. He also co-coordinates *Frontier*—an interdisciplinary program for the historical studies of border security, food safety, and trade policy (online at http://fss.k-state.edu/frontier).

MATTHEW T. KENNEY, Ph.D., is Assistant Professor of Political Science at Austin Peay State University in Clarksville, Tennessee. His current research focuses on the evolution of John Rawls' theory of justice. He earned his Ph.D. from Tulane University in 2001.

JERRY A. KIDRICK, Lieutenant Colonel, is a career Army officer currently serving as the Plans, Operations, and Training Officer (G-3) for the Alaska Army National Guard. His undergraduate degree is in Education from Central Washington University, and he has recently earned an M.S. in Homeland Security from American Military University, with an emphasis in Emergency Management.

CHRISTOPHER RUDOLPH, Ph.D., is Assistant Professor of International Politics at American University. A specialist in the areas of international migration, security, international law, and international political economy, his work has appeared in the *American Political Science Review, International Organization, Security Studies,* and the *UCLA Journal of International Law & Foreign Affairs.* His new book, *National Security and Immigration,* provides an in-depth analysis of immigration and border policy development in Western Europe and North America since 1945 (forthcoming from Stanford University Press, 2006).

DAVID A. SHIRK, Ph.D. is the Director of the Trans-Border Institute and Assistant Professor in the Political Science Department at the University of San Diego. He coordinates the Project on Reforming the Administration of Justice, a binational research initiative on criminal justice and the rule of law in Mexico and conducts research on Mexican politics, U.S.-Mexican relations, and law enforcement and security along the U.S.-Mexican border. Recent publications include *Slavery Without Borders: Human Trafficking* *in the U.S.-Mexican Context* (2004) and *Mexico's New Politics: The PAN and Democratic Change* (2005). He received his Ph.D. in Political Science at the University of California, San Diego, and he was a predoctoral fellow at the Center for U.S.-Mexican Studies from 1998–99 and 2001–2003.

MARGARET D. STOCK, J.D., is an Associate Professor of Law in the Department of Law at the United States Military Academy at West Point. An expert in immigration and national security law, she was selected by the American Immigration Lawyers Association for its 2005 Advocacy Award.

JOSEPH E. VORBACH III, Ph.D., is a Commander in the U.S. Coast Guard and a member of the Permanent Commissioned Teaching Staff at the U.S. Coast Guard Academy where he serves as an Associate Professor of International Relations, as the Section Chief of the History/Government Section in the Humanities Department, and as the Supervisor of the Coast Guard Office of Strategic Analysis satellite unit at the Coast Guard Academy. He earned his Ph.D. in International Relations from the Fletcher School of Law and Diplomacy in 2001, and his research interests lie in the study of transnational security threats and the future of security studies education. His awards include the Meritorious Service Medal and the 2003 Coast Guard Academy Alumni Achievement Award.